2 WHEELS
2 YEARS &
3 CONTINENTS

RALPH W. GALEN D. D. S.

A BICYCLIST'S DREAM FULFILLED

Ralph W. Galen

FOREWORD BY
SENATOR WILLIAM SALTONSTALL

2 WHEELS, 2 YEARS, AND 3 CONTINENTS

Copyright © 1997 by Ralph W. Galen, D.D.S.

Maps and drawings copyright © 1997 Chris J. Cronin

Published by:
Spring Garden Publications Co.
P.O. Box 7131-N
Lancaster, Pennsylvania 17604-7131

Printed and bound in the United States of America

ISBN: 0-9612050-7-5

First edition: June, 1997

Dorothy

the love of my life

my spouse—my stoker—my best friend

FOREWORD

When I think of bicycles, I think of Ralph Galen. When I think of Ralph Galen, I can only think of bicycles.

We first met in the 1970s as the Massachusetts Legislature was attempting to enact statutes for the protection of bicyclists, who in some parts of the state were being run off the road by angry motorists. Everyone in the bicycle world said that one should talk to Ralph Galen. This indefatigable dentist gathered groups of cyclists who supported sound legislation and carried the day. Bicycling has been safer in Massachusetts since then—thank goodness.

On the high-wheeled ordinary, on a contemporary ten-speed lightweight, on a tandem fitted for long-range travel, Ralph has covered ground before and since.

Go with this enthusiast on his trips around Boston, trips around Massachusetts, trips in Europe and Africa, a trip across the United States—Ralph has covered it all. This journal of his journeys carried the spirit of the man and the spirit of the two-wheeler—learn and enjoy.

William B. Saltonstall
Massachusetts State Senate
1967-1978

TABLE OF CONTENTS

INTRODUCTION

Two teenage boys, both brothers and patients of mine, were discussing the recent purchase of their ten-speed English-made bicycles. I overheard the conversation. The year was 1965, the beginning of my love affair with the bicycle. Until that time, golf was my avocation.

A Dawes *Double Blue* became my means of transportation to the office and home until my first accident. The brake blocks on the rear wheel loosened without my knowledge. Only the front brakes were operational when I came to a sudden stop on Massachusetts Avenue in Arlington. Following a "header," stitches in my chin, and the loss of a Patek Phillippe watch, I made a decision: bicycling is a healthful sport, but it's far too dangerous! The next day I was back on the bike.

In the era of the Dawes *Double Blue*, the only ten-speed bicycle manufactured in the United States was the Schwinn *Paramount*, a hand-made machine with European components. When we visited the Columbia Bicycle Company in Westfield, Massachusetts, in 1970, I asked the president of the firm, "Why don't you produce a ten-speed bicycle?"

His reply: "When you create the demand, we will make the product." At that time I was president of the League of American Wheelmen and co-founder of the Charles River Wheelmen, our local adult bicycle club. The roster of C.R.W. following its first ride was eight charter members. Today the club enjoys a membership in excess of one thousand.

My two wheels, and membership in L.A.W., introduced me to many places that I probably would not have seen if I was still a golfer. In addition to our weekly club rides, I began traveling by bicycle. Sometimes the *Allegro*, an all Campagnolo-equipped touring bike, was in the trunk of my car or on an airplane. I occasionally joined bicycle tours and at other times organized non-profit L.A.W.-sanctioned tours. We pedaled

England, Scotland, Spain, Portugal, Morocco, and Mexico with tent and sleeping bag.

Dorothy, the love of my life, became my tandem partner—I was the captain and she the stoker. Every vacation of our brief marriage was bicycle-related, taking us to Ireland, England, Scandinavia, France, and even mountainous Switzerland. Using the convenient Swiss rail pass, we did not begin our cycling until we reached Lucerne and Lausanne, where the terrain is moderately level. Illness, unfortunately, "put on the brakes" permanently. Until that time, Dorothy and I were planning our retirement.

The rest is personal history culminating in my retirement from the practice of orthodontics and the planning of the BIG ONE for both of us. Our Globetrotter touring tandem bicycle in the basement was the obvious machine to use on this "2 Wheels, 2 Years, and 3 Continents" adventure. I removed the saddle, handlebars, and pedals from the rear section and over the long rear top tube fastened a custom saddle bag designed to carry both summer and winter clothing. One rear pannier carried books and the other was reserved for cooking utensils. The front handlebar bag stored the tools and camera. I wore a sizeable "fanny pack" around my waist for the safekeeping of my watch, wallet, passport, and snack food. A new North Face tent and Sierra down-filled sleeping bag were attached to the Globetrotter. They were "home" for two years. Except for an airline ticket, I was ready. A one-way ticket brought us to Charles deGaulle Airport and Paris on June 5, 1992. Two years to the day later, my Globetrotter and I were back in Cambridge. We arrived on a Saturday.

My only piece of unfinished business was a ride across America. Pedal for Power, an organized tour conducted by the League of American Bicyclists (the new, "politically correct" name for this 117-year-old organization), provided the opportunity of fulfilling three dreams: biking across the North American continent, raising money for the charity of my choice, and completing a chapter in my life and the last chapter in this book.

I did not suspect that I'd meet a fellow cyclist on the ride across America with qualities so unique and so special that I would use his journal instead of my own for the final chapter. Allan Lowe, a practicing patent attorney in Baltimore, radiates the same joy in "Pedal for Power" that I experienced in 2 Wheels, 2 Years, And 3 Continents. We both hope you will enjoy our story.

My Favorite Camel Story

Chapter 1/2
MY FAVORITE CAMEL STORY

I had left my Globetrotter at the hotel and joined the other tourists as we took the surface taxi to Petra. This ancient city carved from sandstone dates to the second century A.D. It is located on the eastern slopes of Wadi el Araba in Jordan, 90 kilometers south of the Dead Sea. An Edomite stronghold and capitol of the Nabataeans, this archaeologic gem is tucked away in the mountains 35 kilometers from the "Kings Highway," a road so named in Biblical times. The instructions from our driver were: "Be at the Petra main road entrance at 5 PM for your ride back to the hotel."

Numerous Arab men and boys greeted us with their offer to transport us by horseback to the entrance of Petra. My impression was as follows: the Jordanian Arab would ride his horse, leading the tourist on another horse. To my surprise, I rode on horseback, while my native friend walked the distance wearing his traditional flip-flop sandals. "If he can walk the distance going, on my return I, too, can go by foot."

Just before sunset I joined other tourists as we started back toward the main road. The winter sunset, the local people with their animals, and the carved ancient sandstone buildings were being photographed for the last time until the following day. My pannier from the Globetrotter served as an all-purpose carrier: lunch, warm clothing, and, of course, my camera were stowed in the bag.

To my left, I noticed two young Arab men trying without success to put a noose on a camel. We use a bit and a halter when we want to lead or ride a horse. A camel driver will use a noose in the same manner. Unfortunately in this case, the camel, probably a male, was winning the contest. Every time the drivers tried to apply the noose, the camel would roll his eyes, make a strange "gurgling" sound in his throat, and then

13

Without comment, I laid my pannier on the sand and walked over to the camel and the two young men. With my right arm I applied an arm lock on the camel's neck, which I believe is known as a "half Nelson." This maneuver immediately restrained the obstreperous animal, preventing him from throwing his head from side to side. Moments later he was under the control of his masters, with the noose properly attached.

The youngest of the camel drivers looked up at me and in English asked, "At home, you have camel?"

Chapter 1
PARIS-BREST

The flight to Paris was restful and comfortable, affording me an opportunity to sleep, though in the sitting position. My female seat companion was friendly yet not overly talkative. Psyched for the trip, I would have traded sleep for further conversation. We (I use "we" throughout this book to refer to the Globetrotter and myself.) landed at Charles de Gaulle Airport at 8:30 in the morning.

The cardboard bike box was delivered at the carousel. I now had the task of assembling the Globetrotter. Two hours later, after inflating the tires, we were ready to head in the direction of the City of Lights. Fortunately, the Woolite stayed in its container instead of turning my cooking equipment and panniers into soap suds as it had the previous evening at Logan Airport, Boston. A note of caution: always lower your tire pressure when flying at high altitude. Cargo spaces of airplanes are not pressurized and inflated bicycle tires can burst as a consequence. Another caution is the careful rethreading of pedals into their cranks during reassembly so that threads do not become cross-threaded. Stripped threads on a crank require professional assistance and crank replacement. I can say this from personal experience.

The usual method of proceeding to Paris is via shuttle bus and train to station Gare du Nord, where another train can be taken or the bike can be ridden into the center of the city. When Dorothy and I arrived several years ago on our first visit to this wonderful city, we had very little difficulty putting the bicycle on the bus even though the Globetrotter is excessively long. Two people can do it. For one person it is an impossibility. I did not even try nor did I seek out the secondary roads into Paris as I should have. To quote Sinatra, I did it "my way!"

Biking on the high-speed network of roads into Paris is not the best way to begin a two-year tour, nor is it the safest.

I must also confess that this was not the last time I resorted to this sort of strategy. The interesting aspect of my "high-speed chase" is that the police were unconcerned as they passed me.

At the St. Denis exit we followed the signs to Gare du Nord, our destination for that day. This was now familiar territory on secondary city streets. The flashing blue lights were no longer a concern. By mid-afternoon on a cool and misty day the Seine River came into view. *Hôtel de Ville*, the French word for City Hall, provided the name and address of a nearby hostel/hotel. I told them I wanted to be near the Louvre as well as Palais Royale, putting me within walking distance of many museums and galleries. This visit to Paris was to be a cultural one, especially with Janson and Janson's A Basic History of Art on board. Centre International de Paris-Les Halles, a hostel-type of hotel, was not the best choice, but it was adequate. My major problem was carrying all my gear to an upper floor, as well as the safe storage of the Globetrotter. A campground would have been much easier and more convenient. I was learning. One memorable moment occurred as I was carrying my second load up the stairs to the third floor. Had someone planted a bomb in my saddlebag that decided to sound an alarm instead of exploding? The solution was much less dramatic. It was my portable radio turned on quite by accident. I was getting high volume static.

My roommate was a young college student from Los Angeles on tour. He had no choice but to step over the accumulation of my baggage that filled our small room. One hundred francs, or approximately twenty dollars, was the cost of the room. Supper cost eighteen. The exchange rate was favorable, but prices were high in spite of my being able to exchange one dollar for five francs. The best exchange rate that Dorothy and I experienced on our three previous trips to France was six francs for one dollar.

One might wonder about my fascination for France. This was my fourth visit to a country where many find the people rude and disinterested in visitors. "If you can't speak French, do not go to France" is the advice of many.

At the time I suggested to Dorothy that we take the tandem to France, she said no, a point of view that came as a complete surprise. "We don't speak French." By the time she and I arrived at Charles de Gaulle Airport, I had a first-year college understanding of this beautiful language. My tutor Rita advertised on a 3x5 card at the local supermarket bulletin board: "Beginner and Advanced French. Call Rita." I called! Rita and I spent an entire fall and winter studying from the college textbook of her choice. I had my miniature French-English dictionary in the handlebar bag of the Globetrotter, ready for immediate use. The same dictionary is still in my possession. Since that time, Bunker Hill College, a Massachusetts community college, has provided a formal course of study for me in addition to my membership in the unique Boston French Library. Professor Margo Girodet not only teaches French at Bunker Hill, she invited me to visit her and her professor husband at their summer home in the south of France bordering the Pyrenees Mountains.

PBP is the acronym for Paris-Brest-Paris, a time trial event that challenges the strength and skill of the touring cyclist. For years I thought about entering this *randonnée*, the ultimate in bicycle touring. Now I had the opportunity to cycle from Paris to Brest in a leisurely fashion without the pressure of a time trial. Except for the fact that my new North Face tent was anxiously waiting to be used at a campsite instead of being stowed in a hotel room, the Centre International proved adequate.

I discovered an excellent campground located in the Bois de Boulogne, one of Europe's most beautiful parks. The city of Paris in 1853 acquired a huge tract of wasteland and turned it into what is usually referred to as the Bois, or woods.

Longchamps Racecourse, one of the most celebrated and fashionable tracks in the world, is located in this park, as are seven lakes and waterfalls. The only drawback, according to the local people, is the profusion of prostitutes. I can truthfully say that the prostitutes did not bother me nor did I bother them.

The location of the campground could not have been better from a cyclo-tourist's point of view. We were within approximately three km of the famous Arc de Triomphe and Paris' most famous avenue, the Champs-Elysées. Every morning following breakfast, enroute to the museums, etc., we passed hikers, bikers, as well as those on horseback in the park. The Bois de Boulogne is a taste of the country in the city.

My tent was my principal joy, being the perfect size as well as of excellent quality. I had just enough room to stow my gear and myself inside. Getting in and out, however, was difficult for this 68-year-oldster with his share of arthritis. The technique I worked out became my mode of entry for a period of time until my joint problems disappeared. In other words, biking is good for the joints!

The French word *mélange* means mix, a word that is especially appropriate on the roads and highways of France. It refers to the accommodation of all modes of transport by the driving public. Drivers of motor scooters and/or bicycles have the same rights to the road as the automobile and truck except on limited-access highways.

To my amazement, I had less difficulty biking l'Etoile than pedaling through Harvard Square in Cambridge. Hand signals as well as obeying the traffic pattern gave me equal rights and perhaps more courtesy than is given to the driver of an automobile. Was it that I, an older person on an unusual bicycle was in the mix or was it a courtesy to all self-powered persons? I prefer to think it was the latter. Avenue Victor Hugo to the southwest leads to my campsite in the Bois de Boulogne.

Traffic on my first day as a tourist in Paris was snarled due to a parade of rugby players marching up the Champs-Elysées as though the roadway was their own. Celebrants with faces painted and carrying horns were dressed in black and red. Motorists seemed to enjoy the jubilation despite the delay.

My original plan for this first day included a visit to the famous Louvre with its new entrance designed by I.M. Pei, the architect who designed the John Hancock Tower and Kennedy Library in Boston. His controversial structure, the Glass Pyramid of the Louvre, stands in stark contrast to the otherwise traditional French architecture. To my misfortune, a strike closed the entire museum for the day.

The Army Museum, a part of the Royal Hotel of the Invalides, became my second choice. "Mona Lisa, you will have to wait until tomorrow or until the strike is over. You can be certain I will not leave Paris without a thorough examination. We in dentistry suspect that your unusual smile is due to the lack of teeth. Only your dentist need know."

Within the Royal Dome lies Emperor Napoléon's sarcophagus, a marble tomb of massive proportions. Tombs of former governors are also present, but Napoléon is front and center, stealing the show. Dorothy and I visited the Royal Dome on a previous trip. Forty thousand pieces of arms and armor of Europe and the East are on display, with emphasis on those relating to Napoléon. Mona Lisa was my primary interest, but this well documented museum was impressive. The guards, by the way, permitted me to park the Globetrotter in the guard house. What was their reason for refusing me permission to lock it? Perhaps it was a test of their ability or of my faith in them. In any event, I felt secure.

At six o'clock when the museum closed, I followed my line of sight to the Eiffel Tower, an engineering feat as awe-inspiring as the first time when Dorothy and I saw "la Tour Eiffel." Three more hours of daylight provided more than enough time for me to eat supper at a local restaurant and pedal back to my campsite with the evening traffic.

Tour Eiffel, as it is referred to in France, is without a doubt the city's best known landmark, and well it should be! Completed in 1889 for an international exposition, this steel giant is one of the tallest manmade structures in the world. When illuminated after dark, the Tower is a breathtaking sight. A promise to myself was broken. I intended to go to the top before leaving Paris. Tourists were willing to stand in line for hours awaiting entry, but I could not. I had a **mission** that did not allow this luxury.

The previous evening, I was leaving the Museum of the Army in preparation for a return to my campsite. A gentleman in his 40s on roller blades invited me to an outdoor event called "Environment Without Frontiers" located near the train station Gare d'Austerlitz. The French people are very festive during their celebrations.

I awakened at 8:30 in the morning, well rested, but cold. During the night I could not bring myself to crawl out of my sleeping bag and reach for a pair of socks. Breakfast tentside was adequate to keep me going until noon. In the coffee shops of Paris the price of a cup of coffee is two dollars; using my "little furnace," the cost was negligible.

The morning challenge around the Arc de Triomphe was no more difficult than the previous day as I headed for Napoléon's tomb and the Eiffel Tower. This was the summer tourist season with large crowds at the scenic places. I now had the opportunity of working with my new automatic camera with its zoom lens, especially at the Rodin Museum nearby.

Using my Harvard Museum pass, I gained admission to the museum instead of having to wait in the long line. Fortunately, the expiration date on the card was not noticed. This policy of free or reduced admission applies with very few questions asked at all state or national museums. At no time was the expiration date noticed in Europe or the Middle East.

The Rodin sculptures in the Fogg Museum at Harvard are much more impressive to me than most of the artist's sculptures exposed to the elements in Paris. Those at Harvard are beautifully cared for and are under cover. They probably receive daily polishing, or at least give that appearance. Balzac, The Gates of Hell, the Burghers of Calais, and of course the Thinker, were a pleasure to see firsthand. The lovely Rodin buildings and gardens were bequeathed to the city of Paris by the sculptor. In return he was given life tenancy to his property. As one might expect, children were posing in front of the Thinker, head in hand having their pictures taken.

It was now time for me to visit the "Environment Without Frontiers." Thanks to Gerald Pilgrim, my friend on the 'blades the previous evening, I had little difficulty finding the celebration. The crowd was immense, at the center of which was an inflated gas balloon of huge proportions. The "world" was being rolled down Rue St. Germain by people on roller skates, blades, and on foot. Actors on stilts were performing Molière while a Samba band registered top decibels. The dancing public was signing their own petitions to be presented at a later time to the Minister of the Environment. I also signed a petition. Not unlike Falmouth on Cape Cod, in the summer there was very little room for a bicycle, much less a tandem.

The Bell Helmet Company was well represented by a young American woman from Chicago interviewing the celebrants. Although she granted me an interview, it was not entered into the tabulations; I was not French. She remarked that cyclists in France do not wear helmets.

Good news! The strike at the Louvre was history. Weather permitting, I planned at least one more day in Paris before seeking some recreation. I had not visited either of the Disney theme parks in the USA but I was determined to see

EuroDisney. Our direction would be east instead of west toward Brest, but it made very little difference. I did not come to Europe to be in a race. The question of the moment: does Mickey Mouse speak French?

The rain was a good test of my tent. Seam sealant came with the tent but because of its newness I felt that this was not yet necessary. Wrong! The needle from the sewing machine creates minute holes during fabrication, allowing for penetration of moisture. Of course, when a tent becomes worn it is even less impervious to rain. The only damp areas at that time were in the vicinity of the vestibule.

It was not long before I learned that a ground cover is a necessity, especially at campsites that are not grass covered. Stones can easily push up through the tent floor, doing permanent damage. It also helps to prevent ground moisture from percolating up through the floor and into the luggage. Another technique that is useful but not to the pleasure of the campground attendants is the digging of a trench around the sides and highest elevation to divert rainwater away from the tent site. At one time or another, I employed all these measures. A backpacker pitched his unique tent near mine in the vicinity of St. Malo. His tent was no more than sixteen inches high at any point, requiring him to literally "wear" it. He remarked that he spent as much as a week in confinement during a persistent storm.

Early on in the trip I learned not to burn candles for illumination inside the tent. This had nothing to do with safety. I could easily hang a candle a distance from combustible material. Molten wax was the problem. This wax became a persistent nuisance no matter how carefully I tried. In short order, wax splattered onto my pillow, my bags, and my clothing, leaving a residue difficult to remove. Until my awareness of this situation, I enjoyed writing my journal under cover with the sound of the rain on the tent roof.

24

Eight-thirty was late for an early start in the direction of the Louvre. I must have slept well. Though on the cool side, the rain had stopped. Again my Harvard card worked; I was admitted free. The lack of security in the Louvre was a surprise compared to the Fogg Museum at Harvard. Attendants appeared more interested in each other than their assigned work stations required.

At last I was in the presence of the Mona Lisa as well as the Winged Victory of Samothrace. A copy of "Winged Victory" hangs over the stairwell at the Carnegie Museum in Pittsburgh. As a child living in the Pittsburgh area, within visiting distance of the Carnegie Museum, this Grecian sculpture became my personal possession. I was now looking at the originals of both works of art. Though signs indicate that photography is not permitted, tourists were unconcerned. My photographs are carefully preserved in my slide box. Exposure time predetermined by the camera was excellent.

I brought fifteen rolls of 36-exposure color slide film with the expectation of having them developed as they became exposed. Unfortunately, this is not possible abroad. Film manufactured in the USA by Kodak can only be processed in Switzerland or the United States. Fortunately, all my film arrived safely back in Massachusetts where it was processed and awaited my return.

Two mechanical problems having no easy solution arose. The less serious problem concerned my new handlebar-mounted computer. It began to malfunction, resetting itself without being told to do so. My only alternative was to return it to the dealer via the mail with instructions to return it to me general delivery in Marseille, France. As an alternative, I recorded my mileage by hand on a daily basis, using maps and a certain amount of *guesstimation.*

The other mechanical problem proved to be much more serious and of a troublesome nature for many weeks to come.

A noise started out as a clicking sound in the region of the stoker's bottom bracket. Might it be a broken ball bearing in the bottom bracket? Perhaps a pedal in need of lubrication? Under any circumstances, this annoyance required immediate inspection. No matter how much lubrication I used, the clicking sound prevailed. At one point, I stopped to repack the bearings in my pedals, borrowing grease from a petrol station. The noise persisted. Finally in desperation, I drenched the chain, bottom brackets, and freewheel with penetrating oil. At last the noise and click disappeared. Was this a good idea? Of course not! I merely masked the symptoms and paid the price at a later time. I also had to contend with oil being thrown from the chain onto my saddlebags.

Wearing clean clothes while bicycle touring need not be a problem if the cyclotourist is willing to endure a bit of discomfort. My riding buddy from Concord, Massachusetts, taught me his method of traveling without having to carry soiled clothing. On a nightly basis I washed my limited amount of laundry, hanging it either over my tent or on a line supplied by the campground. A few clothespins proved to be helpful. In the morning, even though my clean wash might not be completely dry, I put it on, letting my body heat finish the drying process. The other alternative is to wash clothes in the morning and put them on wet. Athletic socks, however, do not work out well with this method. They will "droop" at the ankles every time. Lightweight cotton cycling socks solved that minor problem. In this way I always felt clean, ready for the day's adventure.

Another cycling technique in the city as well as in the country requires the possession of a lightweight compass. Asking directions often becomes an imposition to the person being asked; the language barrier requires repetition of the question. The ability to read a compass as well as a map can be exceedingly helpful. Often with my map and compass, I will start in the direction of my evening's destination, but without concern for a specific road or route number. I choose country roads where traffic is at a minimum. Sometimes a dead end occurs, requiring backtracking, but for the most part this technique is successful. Following the proper course on the compass will invariably lead me to the main road and my destination on a designated route shown on the map.

In Paris, my compass kept me out of trouble, taking me in the direction of the Musée d'Orsay. That and the Musée de Delacroix were high on my list of places to see. Passing the Arc de Triomphe, I noticed a huge French flag draped over one side of the structure. Had I missed noticing this flag, or was it something recently added? The arrival of Queen Elizabeth of England prompted this demonstration of French pride.

Formerly a railway terminus, the Musée d'Orsay was officially opened in 1986. It was originally built of cast iron and glass for the 1900 International Exposition. Paintings, sculpture, and *objets d'art* from the national collection as well as new acquisitions made this a most worthwhile visit. I was interested in seeing the Impressionist collection and comparing it to the Fogg Museum at Harvard as well as to the Boston Museum of Fine Arts. The variety of art at d'Orsay is outstanding, with a sizeable collection of van Gogh, Delacroix, Ingres, Rodin, Millet, and many others. Paintings by Monet and Manet were either at a different location or on loan in the United States. Dégas and Gauguin were also well represented. Though it was raining outside, my sun was shining inside.

The display of furniture, *art deco*, artifacts, and crafts is so extensive that many hours of enjoyment are available for the person with sufficient time and motivation. I looked for metal bedroom furniture similar to my parents' art deco furniture, but none was on display. Museums seem to move objects in and out of storage for special exhibits to maintain the continued interest of the visitor.

When the rain abated, I went in search of the Delacroix Museum, formerly the home and studio of the artist. A portrait of Delacroix is imprinted on the 100-franc note, giving credence to this artist, even though the museum itself is not highlighted in my travel guide. Delacroix seldom painted for commission, preferring contemporary events as well as portraying his friends. His portrait of Fréderic Chopin (1838) hangs in the Louvre. Invited by the French government to travel to Morocco, Delacroix developed an interest in Arab history of that era. The museum is hidden behind a cathedral and a charming square. The Delacroix paintings are on loan from the Louvre while many of his sketches and watercolors are a part of his permanent collection.

Many of the 2,000 museums in France are located in Paris. Needless to say, it is possible to visit a mere sampling that this beautiful city has to offer. During my "cultural" day I visited the Galeries Nationales du Grand Palais, Musée du Petit Palais, and Musée de Cluny, a medieval museum in a delightful 15th-century abbey. Excavations on the exterior were still actively going on. An original Roman bath has been excavated as well as religious articles. The famous Tapisseries de la Dame à la Licorne (Lady with the Unicorn) are located in an authentic theater setting. They allude to the medieval legend of the unicorn that could only be tamed by a pure woman.

This was to be my last full day in Paris. "Perhaps on another occasion I can visit the other 1,993 museums." EuroDisney was the planned destination of the moment.

In preference to following specific routes through greater Paris, I decided to use landmarks that might be of interest while traveling eastward. Hôtel de Ville, a familiar location, was followed by Place de la Bastille, Place de la Nation, and finally Porte de Vincennes at the very eastern edge of Paris. One-way streets and intense traffic made the route confusing and tedious. Finally, in spite of my promise to be self-reliant, a truck driver was nice enough to draw a map on the ground with a rock. Chateau Vincennes, you have been found!

The woods and Chateau are 14th and 17th century, originally used as a hunting lodge for royalty as well as a military stronghold. In 1814 one of Napoléon's generals, Général Davmesnil, refused to surrender the fort. This was my longest day of cycling with the Globetrotter fully loaded. While in Paris, the Globetrotter served as my taxi rather than as my Volvo lorry. Total distance covered was 79 km, bringing us to Camp Davy Crockett. With a name like Davy Crockett, it obviously was owned by the Disney Corporation. To my surprise, this campground was filled to capacity. A private campground ten kilometers distant was recommended by the management of Disney.

Ten kilometers are of little concern to the motorist, but to a biker having traveled a full day with a heavy load, that extra distance is not welcome. I also preferred to be immersed in the Americana of Mickey Mouse, a rare opportunity in France. A young family with their caravan (trailer) came to the rescue by allowing me to set up my tent on their campsite. Ronny and Analee, with their two young children, drove from their home in Sweden. We talked about a previous trip when Dorothy and I learned that one Swedish mile is actually seven kilometers. Ronny refused to accept money in exchange for tent space. As an alternative, he suggested that I buy a small gift for each of his children from the Theme Park.

EuroDisney was all I expected and perhaps a little bit more. It was very American and very corny. This was the right thing to do even though we were now headed in the wrong direction. The admission price of 225 FF, or about $45, seemed high, especially for a family. The young parking lot attendant at the entrance to the park did not know the policy for parking bicycles. I was his first bicycle customer. We settled on the motorcycle parking fee.

The lines at EuroDisney were not particularly long, giving me the opportunity to ride and see what I wished. My train ride around the Park was quite an exciting experience, the train being a cross between a train and a roller coaster. Both children and adults were delighted. To the tune of "It's a Small World" we were introduced to the Disney cast of characters. While waiting in line to enjoy the presentation of Peter Pan and a full cast of children, I enjoyed reading my paperback edition of <u>Zen and the Art of Motorcycle Maintenance</u>. *Bicycle* could easily have replaced the word *motorcycle* in the title. I was grateful to my friend Pat for recommending it.

The parade down Main Street was another highlight, especially when the balloon lady gave each child a balloon, putting these young people in a festive mood. One day at EuroDisney, though enjoyable, was sufficient, especially since I did not have the pleasure of sharing the day with my grandchildren.

The following morning I left presents on the steps leading to the caravan owned by my hosts. They were still sleeping. A note of appreciation accompanied the Nestlé's candy as well as Mickey and Minnie pins for the children. I was on my way to Versailles.

The day was Saturday, June 13. Dorothy and I previously toured Versailles, the location of the signing of the armistice in World War I as well as the palace of royalty. It being so large, I looked forward to a second visit. In addition, the prospects of another French campground was inviting.

Most of my cycling toward Versailles was on divided highway where it is legal to bike but not enjoyable pedaling. At one point I left the main road, seeking a post office in a small town, but found it necessary to return to the main road. Frequent mailing of maps and brochures to my home, in addition to my usual letter writing, keeps the weight and bulk of paper in my panniers to a minimum.

The campground in Versailles was a welcome sight, as was an Algerian restaurant nearby. Couscous brochette

Merguez, obviously an Algerian meal, was satisfying and tasty. The next day at the entrance to Versailles, my Harvard Museum pass again gave me VIP status, providing immediate entrance to the palace. The line that I avoided appeared endless.

Versailles originally was a hunting lodge built for Louis XIII, but was developed into a palace by Louis XIV between 1661 and 1710. It became the model for the royalty of all of Europe to imitate. This gigantic structure can house a population of 10,000. Forced labor of peasants numbering 36,000 with 6,000 horses built this monumental structure with its magnificent formal gardens. For over one hundred years Versailles was the home of French kings. During the Franco-Prussian War, Versailles was occupied by Germany and used as the German headquarters. On January 18, 1871, the new German Empire was proclaimed in the Hall of Mirrors. This was the same room in which the Treaty of Versailles was signed on June 28, 1919, ending World War I. The favorite resort of Marie Antoinette, the Petit Trianon, was built by Louis XV in 1776. This smaller palace with its English-style gardens is located on the grounds of Versailles.

I visited the Hall of Mirrors, an elaborate chapel where the kings and queens worshipped, as well as the galleries. Scenes of Napoléon at Austerlitz and George Washington at Yorktown are two of the more memorable paintings in the galleries. Instead of waiting for a tour through the Royal Apartments, I chose a train tour through the gardens with a stop at the Petit Trianon with its wonderful portrait of Marie Antoinette. The visiting public with their video cameras were creating their feature films while I painstakingly took an occasional photo. Rather than take several exposures of the same subject, I relied on a single exposure to record my memories.

The following day was the beginning of an adventure into unknown territory. We headed in the direction of the city of Brest located on the northwestern shores of the Atlantic.

Mont Saint-Michel

France

Letting Go!

Chapter 2
LETTING GO

My original idea was the creation of my own Paris-Brest-Paris randonnée, similar to the celebrated time-trial event, except at a leisurely pace. This tour would hardly qualify as a time-trial except that I could say that I had done my own PBP. It made much more sense, however, for me to bike to Brest as the first leg of 2 Wheels, 2 Years, And 3 Continents, omitting a fifth visit to Paris.

The malfunction of the computer as well as bottom bracket noise continued to be an annoyance in spite of all my attempts at repairs. Even with these mechanical difficulties, I felt energized and ready to venture forth into new territory. Would Dorothy still be with me in the stoker's position now that the Globetrotter was in unfamiliar territory?

I was also thinking about Homestead, Florida, the home of the Paul Dudley White Bicycle Club, a perfect place to park my trailer upon my return so I could ride with old friends into the Everglades and at the same time have the solitude necessary for writing. No one knew that Hurricane Hugo would wipe out Homestead to such an extent that homes, trees, and, yes, a bicycle club, would be leveled by this storm.

The day was June 16th, early into the beginning of the growing season. The sunflowers were perhaps twelve inches high at the time I left the campground at Versailles. Endless numbers of fields were home to the sunflowers that upon maturity would provide tons of safflower oil for the homes and restaurants of France. In the same way, grapes growing on the sides of hills were the source of that year's wine crop. Cultivated and wild rose bushes were equally memorable.

My route was due west in the direction of the town of Alençon, with the wind at my back, an unusual phenomenon in the USA, where the prevailing winds blow in an easterly direction. I am sure the wind had something to do with my 82 accumulated kilometers for the day, as well as the training effect on the road. The good feeling in my knees was testimonial to this "on the road conditioning."

I am in now my tent, using the saddlebags as a backrest as I write my journal. It is nine o'clock in the evening, yet the sun is still shining. Everything in the journal will not go directly into the manuscript. Some dreams are too personal to reveal and probably not relevant to anyone except myself.

"Camping Municipal" deserves commentary. These French campgrounds are exceptional in every way. Except for the large cities, they are so abundant that planning ahead is unnecessary. The Bois de Boulogne in Paris with its campground is unusual for a large city. In the center of towns and/or villages, the municipalities have erected signs with the graphic design of a tent, indicating the direction of "camping municipal." Often the campground is located within the center of the town, or on occasion along a river passing through. Grass-covered tent sites with immaculate toilet facilities are the rule rather than the exception. The same is true of hot water; it's always abundant.

The cost of a tent site varies, but as long as it is municipal the cost is minimal. My campsite that particular night cost 12 francs, 60 centimes, or less than three dollars American. Compare that with state campgrounds in Florida costing sixteen or eighteen dollars for a bicycle. Full-service campsites for trailers and RVs are perhaps even more expensive. This French experience is a testimonial to the fact that the French people love to camp. They are also extremely friendly to bicyclists who have learned basic French and are not afraid to use it. Do not believe all those Americans driving Mercedes who report on the rudeness of the French. It is not so!

Returning from the wash house in the dark, my limited night vision spotted a visitor resembling a sponge more than a live creature inside my tent. A small hedgehog smelled my morning croissants and wanted to share them with me. The moment I reached for my camera it vanished. This was not my last lesson relative to keeping my tent zipped shut.

The next morning the wind shifted and the hills became more and more challenging as we approached Alençon shortly after noon. I was beginning to become acquainted with the terrain encountered during the Paris-Brest-Paris event. The weighted Globetrotter tandem, of course, added to the amount of effort required to reach the top of seemingly endless hills. Thank goodness for my "granny" gear.

Shortly after leaving Alençon, I became aware that, in spirit, Dorothy was with me even though she and I had not traveled this particular route together. Mont St. Michel became the flame and I the moth. I was destined to revisit this well-known tourist attraction, the most southern point on our previous tour of Normandy. Rationalizing this magnetism, I mentally toyed with the thought of purchasing some sort of a souvenir.

The city of Avranches near Mont St. Michel, as well as its monument to General George Patton, brought back some favorite memories that the love of my life and I shared. We were now at the highest elevation west of Paris.

A spa, Bagnoles-de-l'Orne would have been an excellent place to stop, with its casinos, horse racing, radioactive spas, and dance halls, except for the fact that the spa was behind me before I knew it. "Cyclists don't turn back, they just spin their wheels." It was at that time I became acquainted with two French sandwiches, the Croque Monsieur and the Croque Madame. Croque Monsieur is a type of cheese sandwich but his wife was a greater surprise: ham, cheese, and a fried egg between the crusts of French bread. Need more be said? A "sandwich Américain" consists of ham, cheese, lettuce, tomato, and mayonnaise, another excellent choice for noontime refreshment.

While camping, a lone motorcyclist expressed an interest in being friendly. An attorney and economist from Belgium, he was test-driving a BMW on loan from the factory, evaluating it for comfort and amenities. Even the windscreen automatically raised or lowered with the push of a button. The estimated cost of this machine is $20,000. Wouldn't it be nice to test ride a bicycle and at the same time travel long distances for the factory?

The rolling hills of Normandy became a welcome sight, with an abundance of dairy cows as we approached the medieval city of Domfront. This was the perfect place for exploration as well as lunch. As I was leaving the store, my ears picked up spoken English. One couple came from Vermont and the other from Yorkshire, England. Our visit was friendly but brief.

Leaving Domfront after lunch, I was again on the road heading west in the direction of Mont St. Michel when I noticed my English-speaking friends preparing to enjoy their lunch on the grass beside the road. "Come and join us for lunch," said Eileen Fisher. Having just eaten, I declined, but did have an opportunity to converse with these lovely people. We exchanged addresses. A photo of this moment of friendship is preserved in my slide box.

On June 23, 1994, following my return to Cambridge, I received a note from Eileen Fisher from Jericho, Vermont: "Dear Ralph, you may not remember us, but we met you in Domfront, France, in '92 (early summer). You were cycling and planning to end with a six-month stay in Israel. We're returning to England in just a few days to visit our friends again. Although we aren't going to France this trip, you came to mind. Wondered if you wrote '2 Wheels, 2 Years, And 3 Continents.'

Keep well, Dick and Eileen Fisher." She waited two years to write this friendly letter.

St. Hilaire became my destination for the day. This lively town has a theater as well as an American-style supermarket. The main feature at the theater was Jacques Grillot singing songs from Jacques Brel. Unfortunately, basic French limited my understanding of the lyrics, yet the acting ability of this performer was memorable.

Municipal camping nearby presented another mechanical problem. This time the Whisperlite stove required care. My original intent was the use of the stove for an occasional cup of coffee. "Most of my meals will be in restaurants."

A single person in a restaurant can be a boring experience as well as a time-consuming one. It can also be expensive. In France, gourmet food can be purchased at reasonable prices, especially in the charcuterie. Warming this food *gastronomique* on a small camp stove is a simple thing to do, yet produces exceptional results. Of course, with a single burner, one course is prepared at a time. With no refrigeration, food is either eaten or disposed of. Even at home, I seldom eat in restaurants by myself, a habit that was easily acquired after finding myself alone. "A restaurant is to be enjoyed with a companion and not with a book or newspaper." Now that a blue flame on the Whisperlite could not be achieved, my pots and pans became permanently blackened with carbon.

The instruction booklet advised the proper care of my stove. A nearby wash house became the place to do the maintenance. Soon the counter of the wash house was a carboned mess that could only be cleaned with liquid fuel from the stove. At long last, a blue flame returned to the burner head. Others complained about their German-made Whisperlite that malfunctions at the least opportune time. When this occurs to others, I share my stove with my fellow campers, and when it happens to me I go looking for a friend. "How could this product become so universal and still be so troublesome? Surely there must be a better lightweight stove."

I even tried to be friendly to this temperamental product by referring to it as my *petit chauffage*, or little furnace. Flattery got me nowhere. Several months later, when I found a butane stove in Eilat, Israel, the Whisperlite went into the nearest dumpster. The newer purchase acquired the term of endearment "petit chauffage," being for more deserving than its predecessor. Unfortunately, I did not know about the butane powered "little furnace" while I was in France.

Another type of care so necessary to successful cyclotouring is foot care, something that most of us ignore until our feet begin to "talk back." Putting my wash on while wet and letting my body heat become the dryer presented no problems except where it concerned socks. I soon learned to wear dry socks and to use the bungee cord holding my sleeping bag to the bike rack as my on-the-road clothes dryer. There was no better alternative.

Mont St. Michel, we have arrived, but the weather did not want to cooperate; it was misty with a threat of heavy rain. Though the campground was within sight of the causeway leading to this tiny island with its mountain in the center, I could faintly see the cathedral at the summit through the mist.

Legend has it that in 708 an abbey was dedicated to St. Michael, a place of pilgrimage. In 1811 the monastery became a prison for the state. Finally in 1863, Napoléon restored the abbey, making it the major attraction it is today. A causeway was constructed in 1879, enabling tourists to visit without concern for the ferocious tides that are said to come in like "galloping horses." Lives have been lost as a consequence of this tidal phenomenon, particularly during spring tides. The street leading to the abbey at the very top of the mountain is lined with closely packed houses. These houses today are souvenir shops and eating establishments. Though a "tourist trap," Mont St. Michel is a fun place to be.

My original thought of buying a memento was quickly dismissed. No souvenir or piece of stenciled clothing held an interest for me. This moment was too important to center on a piece of "junk." Dorothy and I did not buy on our previous visit and it became obvious that nothing would be bought now. I did, however, purchase a beret, but for different reasons. I needed it for warmth, and still enjoy it for that purpose.

A walking tour to the abbey was my first choice even though Dorothy and I took the tour at an earlier time. In spite of the fact that visibility at the summit was very limited, the tour was once again worthwhile. On the descent I noticed a small chapel, hollowed out of solid rock. A sign at the entrance indicated that for five francs a candle could be purchased as a memorial to a loved one. I knew from past experience that my Blessed would want me to remember her in this way, even though I am not particularly religious.

Placing my candle on a stone altar, I moved the other lighted candles slightly to the side. My candle was now centrally located and of course shining brightly, being the newest. This was a very personal and important moment for me!

Little did I know that my souvenir of Mont St. Michel would be in the form of a time-exposure photograph capturing the moment better than any other tangible item. Almost at the same time, the monk in charge prepared for his departure by removing the burned candles and rearranging the ones still lighted. As he reached for my candle, he became alerted to the waving of my index finger. From my body language he knew that this candle was not to be disturbed. Shortly thereafter we both left the chapel and the island. At that moment a very strange and significant thing occurred to me: Dorothy was no longer on the back of the Globetrotter, though she was, of course, with me for life. I LET GO!

COASTAL *Coasting* FRANCE

Chapter 3
COASTAL COASTING

Evening at Mont St. Michel began with "Do you know what time the tide comes in?" My newest acquaintance, Boris, an Israeli immigrant from Latvia, asked the question. He and I spent the evening together absorbing the beauty of this tiny island and the water surrounding it. To me this was one of many *Chance Meetings.*

Boris, a recently retired physicist, was willing to discuss his adopted country as well as my plans to become an Israeli volunteer. His personality and/or experience did not tell me what I wanted to hear, but at least he was frank in his appraisal of my questions. An example of our conversation centered on my desire to write a book about my travel experiences. "Natural talent for writing, if absent, cannot be developed at the age of 68." When I explained that I was considering a course in writing upon my return to the USA he was not particularly enthusiastic or encouraging.

The subject of volunteering was also guarded when he explained that in his opinion a parallel can be drawn between the British who use the Pakistanis or the Americans, the migrant workers from Mexico and South America, and the volunteers in Israel. "Your head will be filled with socialism and communism while at the same time you will be doing what the Israeli citizens prefer not to do. Working in the health field with your background *might* be more satisfactory," said Boris, who originates from Riga, a city devastated by the Nazis prior to World War II. I learned more about Riga while visiting a holocaust museum in Israel, giving me insight into this personality molded from the past.

"Boris, do you think we look alike? We do come from the same part of the world." His answer was succinct and negative in spite of the fact that there is a resemblance between us.

41

The weather that night and the next morning was very discouraging. Between rain squalls, I prepared my breakfast and then paid a visit to the laundromat, a necessary task. At the same time I utilized my time away from the confinement of my tent. A second promise was then broken: I decided to bike in the rain toward the city of St. Malo, with the hope of being lucky instead of smart. The purchase of plastic bags, if necessary to protect my gear, was the answer to this vexing problem. I do not mind getting wet as long as my gear is protected.

The signs to Camping Municipal in St. Malo brought me within sight of a religious festival, the Festival of Sainte Croix, where I enjoyed the food as well as the women behind the concession booth. One woman dressed in traditional Breton costume showed an interest in me, explaining that she visited Virginia Beach, USA. At the same time swing music was broadcast from the loudspeakers.

"Who will dance with me?" I asked. After the expected smiles and blushing, the ladies pointed to the youngest of the costumed volunteers, who was also the prettiest. She and I danced to "Mack the Knife" and other swing tunes. This was my first and last dance until I reached the city of Eilat, Israel, in December. Did she enjoy it as much as I?

Blessing the fleet was another event of the festival that proved fascinating. Our torch-lit procession snaked its way to the docks where the fishing boats were moored and appropriately blessed by the local parish priest. By becoming a part of the celebration, I had a faint sense of belonging, yet I knew that I was a stranger to these people who were showing a special interest in me. Instinctively I knew that the bicycle was my link to these Bretons.

The weather that night was extreme, culminating in a combination of rain and wind so forceful that I thought my tent would collapse. The baggage as well as myself served as ballast, preventing a disaster. In the morning I assessed the damage: dampness penetrated the tent floor for the first time, leaving the end of my sleeping bag wet. Not wanting to leave my tent in the early morning, I decided to sleep in until the rain abated. It was 9:30 AM before I convinced myself that I should get moving in spite of the weather.

Breakfast at a local cafe, the morning newspaper, and a marine museum kept me occupied in St. Malo. The museum is located in a stone tower with a lookout platform at the top. On display is a collection of paintings, model ships, sculpture done by early captains, and maps from the 13th century. Closing of the museum gave me cause to return to the festival where the booth protected the same ladies from the rain. They seemed to like their American friend, suggesting that I kiss each one on the cheek before leaving. The lady who visited Virginia Beach gave me her address, asking that I write to her from home. This lesson in the French language was a good one.

Being the eternal optimist, I waved goodbye and headed in the direction of Brest, St. Brieuc being my next short-range goal. Unfortunately, the drizzle turned into a heavy rain, requiring plastic bags at any cost. Twenty francs got me an assortment of bags from the local people asking twice that amount. They know an American when they see one. A familiar odor that I was unable to identify permeated the air at the city limits of St. Brieuc.

Potatoes in a large pile in the middle of the road prevented the flow of traffic. "Oh, there must have been an accident." I was naive. The sanitation department was busy cleaning up the mess. Entering the rotary, traffic was in gridlock. The cause was not an accident, it was a protest. Farmers were on strike against the government as a protest against the fixed prices for farm products. Had I not taken a chance on the weather, I would not have been aware of this political event.

I arrived in St. Brieuc in a drizzle that again turned to rain. It was now evening, with no signs to Camping Municipal. Alone and depressed, I asked directions from the local gendarmes in the center of the city. They directed me to a closed campground with the advice that I should stay at a hotel because of the weather. "We will gladly store the bicycle in our garage for you," said the officer in charge. I accepted their advice after seeking out the closed campground. Young people vandalized the property, necessitating its closure. Uncut grass, closed toilet facilities, and rain left me no choice. During the unpacking process, I became aware of water damage in spite of the plastic bags. The reality of bicycle touring in all sorts of weather was now a challenge I could not ignore. I was not discouraged to the point of abandoning my trip, but some hard facts had to be faced.

My American Express card was another problem that I could not readily solve, especially with a lack of experience. I needed money to pay my hotel bill as well as an ATM that would accept my card. Using a toll-free number, I spoke to the American Express Company in the USA asking advice. Their reply was as follows: "Certain banks will accept your card at their ATM, but there is no sign indicating a particular designated bank. You will just have to keep trying until you find a willing bank." The uncertainty of this approach further convinced me that my Gold Card was no better than my checkbook outside the continental US. Thank goodness for Mastercard! I quickly learned what would work for me and what would not. Regretfully I did not own both Visa and Mastercard as further protection in case of a lost card.

Janson and Janson, my paperback art history book, was damaged but not beyond repair. In my hotel room I carefully separated the pages that were partially glued to one another so that upon drying I would still have a readable reference book. Today at my side is the same book with its watermarked pages and well worn cover that is one of my treasures, especially with personal notes on the inside cover written by my classmates wishing me well on my journey. Using the book as a reference to the art of the Mediterranean, Egypt, and Middle

44

East, this text was not only necessary, it possesses sentimental value.

The town of Guingamp (pronounced GANG-aw) is a small and quaint town east of Brest. It is also the home of the Chermat family—Michael, Marie, Laetitia, and her younger sister Virginie. Laetitia and her family are a permanent part of my memories.

Seven forty-five PM found me in a combined épicerie/charcuterie in Guingamp buying my supper, to be enjoyed at the local Camping Municipal. The purchase of food was not as important as the couple who owned the store, as well as one of their last customers of the day. Stores close at 8 PM. We visited, talking about my home and trip as well as my gaining information about the location of the local campground 3-1/2 kilometers to the east. My introduction to Breton hospitality had just begun.

I was climbing a moderate grade traveling eastward, passing some local residents working at the bottom of a driveway leading up a hill to their home. They were laying the foundation for a bicycle ramp so they could easily pedal from the road to the house. In French, Michael called to me, asking if I would like a cold drink. My reply, also in French, was "yes." In one way or another he knew English was my native language. We walked the short distance to the house, where I was introduced to Laetitia, his 15-year-old daughter. Laetitia was studying English in school. "Please talk to Laetitia. We want her to practice her language skills." Did they know I wanted to practice my limited French? Conversation came easily as we paused for cold refreshments on a very warm summer evening.

Photos were in order with my new automatic camera. We selected a garden site as the perfect location. They insisted that I pose in both pictures. Father and Mother took turns as photographer. "My parents would like to invite you for supper," said Laetitia in excellent English. In my French with an

American accent I accepted on one condition: "I have just bought my supper. If you will share with me, I will be pleased to share with you." It was agreed. We adjourned to the house and dinner table, Marie being in the kitchen. When Marie opened her package reserved for their supper and my package reserved for mine, they both contained the same prepared food—baked ham. We had each gone to the same store and bought identical food. Was this fate that we should meet? It was fun to think so.

Our dinner was an international one, where I spoke to Laetitia in English and she translated to her parents and younger sister slowly so I could follow the conversation. This system worked well until we got on the subject of Delacroix, whose portrait is on the 100-franc note. Nuance of the language broke down and we had a good laugh over the misinterpretation when I asked Michael if he had a 100-franc note in his wallet. "Are you in need of money, monsieur?" he asked. "No, I only want you to see the portrait of the artist Delacroix."

At the appropriate time, each member of the family except Laetitia rolled out his or her bicycle in preparation for a ride to the campground. Laetitia felt it necessary to spend this time in preparation for a test the next day in school. Needless to say, I was overwhelmed. Once I had selected a good campsite, the Chermat family bid me adieu in the way that only the French can.

I happened to pass the Chermat home the next morning on my way to the main road toward Brest. No one answered the doorbell. I decided to please Laetitia, her family, and her school chums with a note of appreciation for their wonderful hospitality. "Without a doubt she will read the note in her next English class." I headed west with a feeling of joy.

The date is now August 15, 1994. A portion of my letter to the Chermat family with a mention of their reply will show how this chance meeting has proliferated into a lasting friendship:

"Dear Marie, Michael, Laetitia, and Virginie, I am the cyclist who visited you back in 1992. I would have written to you sooner except that I did not have your address nor do I at this time. I will address the letter to Guingamp in hope of it reaching you. If you will reply indicating that you have received this letter, I will send two photographs that were taken in June of 1992."

Two weeks later I received an envelope from the Chermat family with a letter from each of them. Enclosed with the letters is a copy of the French cycling magazine "Le Cycle" printed on the 9th of March, 1992. On page 12 an article and photograph entitled "Ralph Galen, en route pour 2 ans d'aventure" appears in full color. The interview took place in Nuweiba, Egypt, on the shores of the Red Sea. Laetitia, studying sports physiology at a university, saw the article in "Le Cycle" and decided to save it should I decide to write to them. The full circle has now been closed.

My compass was again a helpful companion, taking me in the direction of Brest after several unsuccessful attempts, both on major roads and then those penetrating the countryside with their large and prosperous farms. Distance traveled and distance accomplished were two separate numbers. It was now 8:30 in the evening. In my usual fashion I began to inquire about campgrounds. Retired hockey professional Roy and his wife Sonia Prichard, both from England, were my hosts for the night. The other campers with their "pop top" vehicle remembered me from Mont St. Michel, where we both camped. The theme song of EuroDisney was again coming true: "It's a Small, Small World." The evening news reported that the farmers in protest entered Paris with their farm machinery in an attempt to create chaos for the motorists.

This was my first camping experience on the *ferme* (farm). It was so comfortable and congenial that leaving was difficult. Tenting on grass with the quality of a golf course fairway is a pleasure that is seldom enjoyed, especially where I had the freedom to erect my tent in any of several locations.

In the morning, following a rather late start, I visited a 15th century church that just happened to be there to see religious figures carved from wood and decorated with fresh flowers. The stained glass windows with their messages in French constituted another lesson in the beautiful language I was intent on learning. Returning to the road, I discovered that the farmers' protests were continuing.

A huge wagon filled with artichokes blocked the entrance to Route N-12, the major highway into Brest. It was interesting to note that the farmers did not dump their produce onto the road in protest; artichokes are too valuable to destroy.

Seeking the secondary road into Brest, I asked directions from a moped driver who tried to reply in English. "Speak in French," I asked. To my pleasure, I could understand him. Soon Camping Municipal in Brest came into view. Soup made from fresh fish and carrots as well as fresh bread completed my evening meal. A beer offered by a fellow camper brought us together in conversation until darkness, suggesting that it was now time for sleep. Paris-Brest was achieved.

Oceanopolis, an ultra-modern facility 2 km. from my tent site, was well advertised on billboards as I entered Brest. Computer science and satellite technology is employed in creating this super-aquarium. Abundant TV screens as well as an auditorium provide information in French. A film demonstrates the act of mating in the world of the whale. The female turns on her back to make copulation and procreation possible.

More than one thousand children were visiting Oceanopolis on this day when they and I watched a diver feeding the sharks and other fish, being careful not to be attacked. The children were encouraged to touch the underwater sea life, especially the live coral. Special lighting gave the coral an irridescence and beauty that was particularly attractive to the one thousand and one of us.

I then used my unloaded Globetrotter to visit the commercial fishing industry at Brest and a maritime museum located in the ruins of a Roman fort and chateau. Objects on display are more maritime than military; huge wooden sculptures are symbolic of Breton art and culture, reminding me of the medieval church I visited the previous day. Neptune, the mythical king of the sea with a horse at his feet, was a good subject for a photograph. The local naval academy with its training ships begged to be photographed. These ships were outfitted with sails. My day reserved for visiting was completed with bread, Roquefort cheese, and coffee—a restful and educational day.

From this point on my computer became useless due to its inaccuracies. The function "distance covered" was nonfunctional, necessitating that I log my daily distance manually, at times estimating it from maps and/or road signs. Road signs helped me to update my French by referring to unfamiliar words in the dictionary. The same was true in Israel when I tried to read the Hebrew instead of the English subtitles.

Two 16-year-old campers, Jane Christensen and Ditte Lolk, and I became friends. These young women referred to me as a "funny old man." My reply was "I am an old man having fun." We said our goodbyes as I headed south in the direction of Quimper, a rather large town of 60,000. Quimper is the center of Breton folk art displayed on ceramic dinnerware. Quaint and colorful Breton costumes are painted on these interesting pieces in bright yellow, blue, and red.

It is not at all unusual for travelers and wayfarers to meet casually and then become companions or more. Young couples either traveling alone or with members of their own gender suddenly become a couple, sharing their tent as well as other intimacies. The future of these relationships is grist for the fortune teller's mill. Two young women and one man from the US in a Quimper *créperie* were no exception. The Globetrotter was the magnet that drew us together. Following supper, I pedaled to Camping Municipal. They hiked. Eric from Fairbanks, Alaska, has published his first book. Janine is a nurse from California, and Susie, also from California, became my special friend. Susie traveled extensively in Israel with her Aunt Rita and Uncle Joel. "When you arrive in Tel Aviv, Ralph, call Aunt Rita. You will have much in common with Uncle Joel, a dentist and an orthodontist." Not only have Susie and I become pen pals, but I spent an evening with her aunt and uncle shortly before leaving Israel for South Africa. These Israelis could not have been more hospitable to a friend of their niece. I also recall that Janine, a nurse, carries a water purification kit with her at all times. Though a health provider, I drink the water from its source without concern. Who is right? Should a traveler adjust his or her system to local conditions or guard against intestinal problems by being cautious? In the morning while my young friends were packing, Susie said to me, "Write that book and be certain to say hello to my relatives."

My Harvard museum pass gained me admission into the Quimper Museum displaying Breton costumes, porcelain developed through the centuries, as well as Breton embroidery. Simple tools on exhibit produced craft of extraordinary quality. Perhaps it was here that I came to a realization that should have become obvious at a much earlier date: the art treasures of the world can be seen in most of the major cities, especially where copies are often indistinguishable from the originals. Indigenous art, however, is best seen in the small rural museums and galleries. Quimper Museum was no exception.

My next seventy kilometers of cycling was more lateral than from point A to B. A compass has no way of detecting a dead end, nor did I. Biking in Maine is similar to my experience south of Quimper on the way to Bordeaux. Route 1 will travel north and south, bypassing the small ports along the shore. These ports have a single connection with Route 1; there is no way of going to and from another port except on Route 1. I was following the Sunday recreational cyclists, not knowing exactly where I was going except that my compass indicated that we were heading south. When I finally realized that the Mediterranean was at the end of the road I decided to reverse direction.

Port Aven, an artist colony, soon came into view. It was here that Paul Gaugin did some of his painting. Unfortunately, the museum was closed for the day. The city of Lorient on the coast was completely destroyed by the Allies in World War II. The newly built city lacks the charm that brings tourists to Europe. The same is true of St. Lô, visited by Dorothy and me on our tour of Normandy. Only a central area of original St. Lô is still standing as it did before German occupation.

We were again on the N-112, a highway I did not enjoy nor belong on, heading south toward the cities of Vannes and Nantes. Rennes, a large city due east of Lorient, was a consideration. After consulting my tour guide, Rennes did not seem exciting enough to do the amount of backtracking required. It's the economic and cultural center of Brittany but a relatively modern city, having burned in the year 1770. Severe damage following World War II required further reconstruction. The towns of Nantes and La Rochelle appeared more interesting.

We left N-112, seeking a secondary road as well as a campsite for the night. My map was of little value, requiring the use of my compass and "nose." Meeting Mr. and Mrs. Jean Mary became my good fortune. They offered me directions to a campground some 20 kilometers distant and then suggested their backyard as a campsite. I had pedaled 70 km., it was nearly dusk, and I had no incentive to go farther. By coincidence, the daughter of these two retirees is an oral hygienist. They encouraged me to use their washer-dryer and bathroom, a luxury seldom found on the road. We "broke bread," drank wine, and spent the evening discussing France, the USA, and potatoes on the highway. Mme. Miebeline Mary cheerfully helped me with colloquial French when needed.

In the morning I was invited for breakfast, my introduction to *brioche*, a tasty French bun. One of my favorite photographs is of this loving couple standing in the doorway of their rural home. "When you arrive in Israel, please write to us so that we will know you are safe, having achieved your goal," said M. Mary. Unfortunately, this was not possible: in Nice I lost my address book.

From my home in Cambridge, in 1994, using the address in my journal, I wrote to the Marys telling them of the loss of my address book and the enclosure of a copy of that favorite photo. Yes, I arrived in Israel safely and would enjoy receiving a letter from them. We are now pen pals, in addition to the Chermat family. Again, a circle has been closed!

The port of Vannes, with its huge marina, was a worthwhile visit. Bicycle and pedestrian paths, recreation areas, park benches, a huge aquarium, and the Palais des Automates Vannes were all equally attractive. On display in the aquarium is a fossilized snail dating back millions of years, and its modern-day counterpart, identical in skeletal construction. A separate exhibit demonstrates the intensity of the killing power of an electric eel capable of generating up to 500 volts. Light and sound are produced following the eel's electrical discharge.

Animated dolls at the Palace of the Automates were originally powered by water, then electricity, and finally by computer. This type of entertainment is a favorite of the French. One display, owned by the Calvados Distillery shows a robust man drinking his Calvados, a distilled apple product from the district of Normandy, while another animated doll portrays a dentist extracting teeth. Marie Antoinette with silver thread woven into her gown was very beautiful.

Had I been in a hurry, the sound of rain on the tent might not have been quite so romantic. Using my handlebar bag in its upside-down position provided a writing surface. A roll of plastic trash bags as well as elastics purchased at the local grocery store were acquired in preparation for a wet departure. French elastics are called bracelets, or *caoutchouc*, meaning rubber. My wet clothing, however, was not romantic. I longed for a dry climate.

A sign, Archeologiques, suggested the Chateau-Gaillard. A wealth of original discovery dating back at least 10,000 years is on display there. Instruments of war, memorabilia from Tahiti, Easter Island, New Guinea, and an Egyptian exhibit drew my attention. Two original tapestries from the Hôtel de Ville warranted a photograph. The sculptured gardens being prepared for Vannes' 3,000-year celebration is another favorite color slide.

One hundred fifteen kilometers, my longest distance in a single day thus far, was effortless with the wind at my back. I arrived in Nantes, the home of Jules Verne. In 1598 Henry IV declared the Edict of Nantes, giving freedom of religious belief to all Protestants. Nantes, an inland port, is located at the southern tip of Brittany and at the beginning of the region of the Loire where Dorothy and I visited on our first tandem tour of France. Signs to Cognac and Limoges brought back pleasant memories. Bordeaux was not far off.

Nantes itself was a bit of a disappointment, especially with the Museum of Fine Arts closed in preparation for a new exhibit. The Cathedral of St. Pierre, a huge structure, is the burial place for Richard I and his two daughters. A video shows the destruction of this cathedral on two separate occasions: the first during World War II and the second in 1970 when a fire leveled the structure.

In a nearby public building, the Exposition 1991-92 attracted large groups of school children with their teachers. Each child wore a headset guiding him or her through a detailed explanation of the workings of the French government, particularly the National Assembly. Admission was free. My thoughts went to my home country and the need there for such an instructive display that would move from city to city where large numbers of children as well as adults could learn about the functioning of the USA's government.

Leaving Nantes, I followed the Express in the direction of La Rochelle and an arrow to an abbey/restaurant. I became thoroughly lost. A young person repairing his motorcycle invited me to share a cold drink of *pamplemousse* (grapefruit juice). Eric gave me directions to La Rochelle via secondary roads, exactly what I wanted and needed.

Le Marne, a town of 800, came into view, with signs indicating open-air camping. After three attempts to find a person in charge, I gave up my search. About ready to move on, Pierre appeared on a bicycle. He opened the door to a gymnasium and wash room. As quickly as he appeared, he was on his way; someone had told him of my need.

This site was a bit more rustic than my usual accommodations, but how could I tell Pierre that it was not exactly to my liking? Would I hurt his feelings? Should I stay? Laying my clothes and sleeping bag on the sweet grass in the sun, they soon took on a fresh fragrance. I occupied the entire Camping Municipal, courtesy of Le Marne. Cold showers were not especially uncomfortable during this warm summer's day. Le Marne, France, could have been almost anywhere in the US where the countryside is rural and the sweet grass "sweet." My first impression was that open-air camping comes very close to vagrancy but after a night's rest I ranked Le Marne as one of my better campsites. Hopefully Pierre could read my note of gratitude in American French.

Now that I was on rural roads, cycling again became pure joy. The contrast between the "N" roads and my two-lane connectors was like day and night. A typical European schoolyard was a perfect location for a luncheon stop. The hinges on the entrance gate bore the fleur de lis design and the wall supporting the gate was typically medieval. The signatures in my journal represent some of the children and teachers with whom I came in contact. They were delighted to have me speak to them in English. Who had the most fun?

I had been on the road for one month, observing the growing season in rural France. Cherries were now ripe and the apples were beginning to take on a blush. Sunflowers, originally a foot high, were fully grown. This was my first experience watching the beginning and the end of a growing season from the saddle of a bicycle. Included were the grapes before and after harvest. I was indeed privileged to be a witness to this work of nature.

Yesterday I was conscious of rolling farm country similar to Bucks County near Philadelphia. Today the landscape changed to seascapes not unlike Cape Cod or perhaps Holland. Proliferation of small ponds and many canals with marsh grasses were suggestive of the ocean nearby. Strong headwinds slowed my progress but were not particularly annoying. A sense of Zen was beginning to permeate my subconscious. Call it Zen or mindset, difficult cycling was no longer tedious; it merely took a little longer. Another adjunct was taking on a force without my having given it thought. I began to chant!

This chanting involved numbers and/or words or parts of words. I found myself unconsciously counting in both directions or making up words or phrases that in themselves had very little meaning. Time passed quickly in this way as the hills flattened or the wind became refreshing instead of being a form of personal punishment. Dan Henry, the originator of the arrows that cycling clubs paint on the road to give members directions without their having to refer to maps, came to mind: his poems about the joys of hill climbing were becoming my joy. Perhaps I had been out in the sun too long!

Musée du pays de Retz is one of those museums that I have previously discussed where local industry is on display. At this museum, fishing, oyster harvesting, shipbuilding, and life near the water are the themes. An old bone-shaker is on display at the entrance, much more sophisticated than the one in my modest collection of antique bicycles. A bone-shaker is a velocipede where pedals are attached to the front wheel, similar to those on a child's tricycle. A spoon brake, so named because of its shape, is applied to the rear wheel rim, thus creating stopping friction. The wheels themselves are modified wagon wheels with metal rims. Bone-shakers originated in the mid-1800s.

Prehistoric skulls showed different stages of dental aging that is prevalent today. One skull has a hole in the cranium about the size of a silver dollar, suggesting that this person did not have time to think about his chewing apparatus. One had prominent upper front teeth that could have benefitted from my braces.

Plastic bags about 50 mil in thickness were effective in the rain if I was careful not to tear the plastic. On arrival at Camping Municipal in the evening, my gear was usually dry. Finding campgrounds, however, was not simply the following of "Camping Municipal" arrows. To avoid backtracking, I began looking for a campground before reaching the centre of town where the signs originate. A pedestrian in a small town advised me to turn off the main road at the first *feu rouge* (traffic light) and proceed from there, but without telling me the distance. Against my principles, I had no choice but to again ask directions. This time I stopped at an auto rental agency where I was warmly greeted. A young man said in English, "I will show you!" Soon we were both pedaling toward the goal, Camping Municipal. "Why are you being so nice to me?" I asked Sebastian. "Because I am French!" was his reply.

La Rochelle, my short-term goal, is situated 183 km. north of Bordeaux. This maritime town with a rich history was a worthwhile objective if the 183 km. could not be achieved in a day. Prior to leaving the campground, the attendant and I discussed the weather, a common subject during these rainy days. His reply was, "You can expect a storm." It would have been impossible for him to contemplate the ferocity of the storm that we were about to experience. Fortunately, there was ample warning.

At the first suggestion of rain, I stowed all gear, including the handlebar bag, safely in trash bags. This prevented my use of maps or reference books until the rain subsided. When the storm struck it hit and then hit again, filling the roads with water. Visibility was impaired as I tried to keep erect. Finally I put my glasses on the end of my nose so I could look over the top of them as I stared into the wet haze, a combination of blurred vision and the downpour. By noon the storm abated and the warming sun began to dry my cycling jersey, shorts, and shoes. A nearby park became my dining room and roast chicken the main course. In a bakery three women offered to show me a route to La Rochelle they felt I would enjoy, especially because it follows a canal. The name of the canal? The Holland Canal.

The balance of the day's riding was again wet and windy. At times the wind was partially in my favor yet at other times sudden gusts pushed me toward the steady stream of oncoming traffic heading into this busy resort town. A coastal town, La Rochelle is attractive to English tourists. Fortunately, the campground is located in the Old Port.

Between the 14th and 18th centuries, La Rochelle, a major port of France, carried on an active trade with North America. The old harbor and defenses have preserved much of the character of the Huguenot period. Classic examples are the immense towers dating from 1384 guarding the entrance to the harbor. The chain linking the two towers at night prevented invasion from the sea. One tower is called Tour St. Nicolas and the other is Tour de la Chaine.

Returning to the campground, I became friendly with an Irish couple, the O'Callaghans. They had the foresight to have name stickers printed prior to their planned vacation. The O'Callaghan small gold label is permanently attached to a page of my journal. Another useful idea is a small rubber stamp made with its own built-in ink pad so that names and addresses can be easily exchanged. The ample supply of labels at my home would have added very little to my gross weight of 180 pounds. Why didn't I think of them?

At 6:45 AM, early risers in the campground awakened me to the sound of rain on my tent. There was no point trying to make an early start toward Bordeaux. I was too comfortable with my air mattress and summer down sleeping bag that I no longer zipped closed as it was originally designed. The opened bag serves as a blanket or "throw" instead of being in a capsule that requires constant bodily adjustments during the night. Even though open, a small pocket at the end remains, providing a receptacle for my feet. This minor adjustment enhanced my sleeping comfort throughout the remainder of the trip.

My limited language skills created a small problem during a lunch stop in La Rochelle. I thought I was ordering two items on one platter but found myself with two plates, two separate entrées, and two sets of eating utensils. I ate "the whole thing" during yet another rain squall.

The town of Rochefort was to be my next stopping place. Is this where that wonderful cheese is produced? Cheese does not come from Rochefort, but the museum of fine arts, truly a gem, made my visit enjoyable. Two original paintings by Gericault, an original of Ruben, an excellent Egyptian collection, as well as a collection of shells from all over the world kept me entertained and informed. Specimens from the area of New Guinea are also on display.

I was then advised to visit the Corderie and the grounds of this naval facility where rope was manufactured for use by the French Navy. Though referred to as rope, the naval term is "line." All of the line used by the French Navy was manufactured here. Guides explain the methods of manufacture in French and English.

The road from Rochefort toward Bordeaux passes through the city of Royan on the coast at the mouth of the Gironde, a body of water that snakes northward from southern France, terminating at the Port of Bordeaux. Being an inland port, Bordeaux is protected from the sea. A toll bridge of immense proportions carries traffic to the south toward Royan. Toll for autos is 45 francs, or about US$9. Bicycles are *gratuit* (free). The roadway beyond the bridge is quite flat. With the assistance of the wind, the entrance to Royan was in sight.

Nearing noontime, a shellfish entrepreneur attracted my attention. Oysters *(huîtres)* and mussels are sold in bulk as well as for individual need. The outdoor picnic area was particularly inviting. One dozen oysters, bread, butter, and a pitcher of white wine satisfied my hunger and my sense of the sublime. A light vinegar was poured over the oysters. I have now tasted French fries, as well as oysters, with vinegar. This maritime setting with its small canals and oyster beds added to the ambiance, especially with the sun shining once again. It was enjoyable to sit at the picnic table in the middle of the day and make entries in my journal without giving thought to the "working world." Retirement has its rewards.

At seven that evening I was still following a sign to a form of camping—camping *à la ferme* (on the farm)—without an indication of the distance to the destination. Another rule I violated was that I was not carrying sufficient food to sustain myself for an evening meal and breakfast. Each time that a new sign "Camping à la ferme" appeared, I was drawn farther from the main road, farther from civilization, and farther from a grocery. The indecision, especially at the end of the day, gave me a feeling of anxiety as I climbed another series of hills into back country. The thought went through my mind that the owners of the farm knew they were located in rural France and would not be successful in attracting tourists if they disclosed the actual distance from the main road. My quest was finally rewarded: I arrived at the farm, but where was the campground? Could it be the small picnic table covered with pine needles and the broken-down building nearby? It was!

The farm is, in fact, a vineyard from which champagne is produced. Though the owners have their own label, the actual champagne is produced through a cooperative. One of their labels is now a part of my memorabilia. The farmhouse is one of those large estate-type homes decorated with works of art from a past era, especially a magnificent French grandfather clock, suggesting prior wealth. To help make ends meet today, income is also derived from camping à la ferme.

To my surprise, the little building contains a small kitchen as well as a heated shower with more than enough hot water for my needs. The problem of the moment: what will I prepare in the kitchen without any food? The son of the owner solved this problem when he brought a tray to my campsite with an assortment of fresh and cooked foods. I chose what I wanted, returning the balance to his kitchen. I was grateful for this "care" package. Though the door to my kitchen was absent, it did have an overhead electric bulb supplying enough light so I could write my journal. The total cost came to 45 francs, about $9 American. Could that help support the needs of this farm that produces the label Domain de Bois Joly? It was incomprehensible that the owners of this substantial farm were pleading poverty for themselves and their neighbor.

For the first time the French government is paying the farmers to grow sunflowers. When harvested they will be sold and then sent to the mill for the production of oil used in cooking.

Nearing Bordeaux, I noticed a sign directing me to the Chateau Didone in the village of Semuesac, a very elegant vintner with attached vineyards and restaurant. They also operate a museum of agriculture where old farm and winemaking equipment is on permanent exhibit. Fordson and John Deere mechanized equipment manufactured in the US are comparable to what we see on our local farms in New England.

To be a farmer, a person must also be a mechanic, in order to keep his equipment operable. Is it little wonder that farmers and their sons have lost fingers, hands, arms, and their lives in the pursuit of their labors? Was it not the Fordson tractor that had a propensity of tipping over?

If I were a poet, I would write my very best poetry this particular morning, viewing the magnificence of the French countryside in the mist over my handlebars. The manicured vineyards, endless fields of sunflowers, grazing cattle, and hay neatly rolled into huge bundles create a vista that I want to remember forever. The early morning mist as well as an absence of people is a storybook setting. Is it possible for me to record this in words? At least I can try.

The steps leading to a home became my office and my knees a desk. The sound of a compressor in the distance was reminiscent of my days in the dental office, as well as of the presence of humanity. Medieval architecture of the homes gave no evidence of modern improvements inside. In addition to the dishwasher and washer-dryer, I tried to visualize the paintings, clocks, and furniture of an earlier era, items of enormous value if sold. Tile roofs of varying shades of brown, collecting moss, added greatly to the scene, a source of inspiration to the painter as well as the poet. Re-entering reality, I knew that the "Grande Route" to Bordeaux was but a moment away.

Chateau Perenne, hosted by Mme. Roumegous Maryse, was another enjoyable experience, especially with this lovely lady as my guide. Her husband is the director of the chateau.

After tasting a dry Bordeaux wine, I purchased a bottle with plans to enjoy it later that evening with my supper. It was Mme. Roumegous Maryse who told me about the medieval town of Blaye as well as the scheduled arrival of the Tour de France in Bordeaux. My concern centered around my ability to experience both sights within a limited amount of time. Was it possible to do both? I decided to try. Unfortunately, I missed the Tour by a mere fifteen minutes.

I must say that the visit to Blaye was very worthwhile; by chance I had the opportunity to meet the mayor, a young man showing some dignitaries his historic city. This fascinating medieval city contains a citadel, theater, and hospital beneath ground level as well as an excellent view of the Gironde. Mme. Roumegous Maryse gave me good advice. I then decided to seek the Tour de France in earnest in Bordeaux.

The main highway, the Express, was closed to traffic, providing safe passage for the cyclists. All that remained upon my arrival in downtown Bordeaux was the Tour de France vans and personnel hawking pins, caps, and jerseys to the remaining spectators.

Had I not seen Blaye, I would have been in Bordeaux with time to spare. Win some, lose some! Unlike Paris, Bordeaux does not offer a campground such as the Bois, nor was I able to conveniently find an ATM that would readily accept my credit cards. It was all a frustration, especially after missing the event of the year, the Tour. It was even too late in the afternoon to visit the *Syndicat d'Initiative*, the local tourist bureau. Memories of Blaye and the mad dash into Bordeaux, however, sustained me. Eventually I found an ATM that accepted my Mastercard. I felt free to leave the city in search of my night's accommodation now that I had money in my pocket. Ten miles out of the city in a westerly direction there was no hope for a campground. At least I found a supermarket that supplied food for both supper and breakfast.

French hospitality again came to my rescue. All that was necessary was a knock on a door, or perhaps a knock on the right door. The Garat family with their dog Diva were my hosts for the night. Diva enjoyed the comfort of my tent following dinner. The Garats were gracious with their offer of the use of their facilities as well as coffee in the morning. By the time I was ready to leave we were good friends. Christophe, my host, had his camera, and I, of course, mine. He gave me his card with a promise to one day visit me in the Boston area.

In a pedestrian mall in Bordeaux, two women were taking a survey. They directed me to the town of Merignac where I was assured I would find a campground. At the Hôtel de Ville in Merignac a security guard directed me to a small house at its entrance. We would call it a carriage house; they refer to it as a *petite maison*, or little house. Thinking this petite maison a public building, a part of the Hôtel de Ville, I entered without knocking. This was my mistake of the day, even greater than missing the Tour de France. The gentleman of the house escorted me to the front door in as forceful a manner as he was capable in spite of the fact that he was partially handicapped. I then of course realized my error.

Fortunately, I knew how to apologize in French and at the same time explain to the owner that I needed a campground. He then realized my confusion and became more friendly, offering advice that eventually took me to the home of the Garat family. I had every intention of returning to the petite maison so I could knock on the door, showing the owner that I really did have better manners than he observed the previous night. The expression "ugly American" is one that most of us want to correct, not augment, by our personal actions. The owner was gracious when I knocked at his door the following day. Hopefully, he understood the purpose of my return visit.

I was back in the city of Bordeaux, anxious to visit St. André Cathedral and the Museum of Fine Arts. St. André is comparable to Notre Dame in Paris: the nave was built in the

12th century. The Museum, located behind the town hall, contains a remarkable collection of paintings representing such masters as Titian, Van Dyck, Rubens, Delacroix, Renoir, Rodin, and others. Out of character, Olga Lisant by Pablo Picasso, a black and white study, is also represented. A female nude in a wheat field by Millet did not particularly hold my interest except in a negative manner.

Arcachon on the coast became my goal for the night, a distance of about 55 km. At the approximate halfway point, though 9:30 at night, I was still enjoying daylight cycling. Hot tea and a recent purchase of fresh baked goods kept me going into the darkness. The generator and lighting system installed by Mike at Ace Wheelworks in Somerville, Massachusetts, supplied ample light for night riding and illumination of road signs. By 11:30 I inquired about accommodations at the local police station in Arcachon. The director of Camping Municipal opened the gate for me as a special consideration. Night riding was not exactly my first choice, yet it was my only choice. A hot shower made it all worthwhile.

This campground, within view of the Atlantic, was worthy of a day's rest. especially after the 55-kilometer ride the previous night. I also knew that this was to be my final view of the west coast of France as I considered my next short-range goal, a visit to the summer home of Professor Margo Girodet and her professor husband Paul.

Chapter 4
THE WIND AT MY BACK (SOME OF THE TIME)

Arcachon on the Gulf of Gascogne was not easy to leave, even though the prices here were somewhat higher than in other places. This includes the cost of the campground. Arcachon is attractive and well populated with tourists.

In spite of the fact that I had considerable distance to travel to Rivesaltes, the summer home of the Girodets, it was time to start making contact with these very busy people. The town of Rivesaltes is in a wine region bordering on the Pyrenees Mountains near Spain. The largest nearby city is Perpignan, located southeast of Bordeaux and Arcachon.

Mont-de-Marsan is the first inhabited area through the extremely flat and dry Gironde-Landes, a huge green area on the map. After a day's rest in Arcachon, where I did more walking than riding, I decided to follow my map in the direction of Mont-de-Marsan.

There was little reason to get an early start; I could hear the rain on the surface of my tent. When the sun came out, we humans began to leave our manmade shelters, pursuing our individual desires.

The flat terrain surrounding Gironde-Landes reminds me of the area east of the city of Denver. The roads have no reason to be other than straight. Similar to Denver, an irrigation ditch follows the course of the road. Though sparsely populated, ample vegetation began to give the terrain a Cape Cod appearance with pine growth on either side of the road. With the wind at my back, I sailed along effortlessly. My friend Myles from Pawtucket, Rhode Island, would surely be singing loudly if he were on this adventure. I recall Myles singing in Scotland as we biked the moors. Except for sheep and an occasional human, we were alone with our environment. I was now alone!

The Musée du Petrole, financed by the Esso Corporation, was a "chance meeting" along the road. Narrated by a guide, the entire process of oil extraction from the earth and its processing is explained in French. Except for being anxious to cycle, this lesson in French was a good one. A sign nearby indicating camping encouraged my decision-making process to not try for Mont-de-Marsan until the following day. I had the campground to myself, except for a young family about 100 yards away. The toilet facilities were unusually good and the shower perfect. My clothes were washed for the next day and I had time to do some rearrangement of my gear.

July 14, four days hence, I had hopes of being in the city of Toulouse. Bastille Day in Boston is a special day, particularly at the French Library. I tried to envision this celebration in France, especially in a large city. At that time I did not suspect that a portion of my trip to Toulouse would be by train with a disabled Globetrotter.

I also had plans to visit Montauban, the home of the artist Ingres, the medieval fortress of Carcassone, as well as an extensive museum dedicated to Toulouse Lautrec in Albi. Musée Goya in the city of Castres was also on my list. It was indeed my good fortune to find so many points of interest that would eventually lead me to Rivesaltes.

Mont-de-Marsan is a special sort of town, particularly during the fluorishing Saturday market. Here lived the well-known sculptor Charles Despiau. His works are permanently on display throughout the town. At the *Syndicat d'Initiative,* I was directed to the Museum of Charles Despiau and Robert Wolerick. This magnificent museum is located in a medieval fortress given by the city in memory of these artists. Four floors of permanent sculpture and ceramics created by Despiau and Wolerick are artistically displayed. Thank you, Mont-de-Marsan. My photographs of the outdoor sculptures will surely be a permanent memory, especially those taken from the bridge connecting one portion of the town to the other. The sun, the

THE WIND AT MY BACK

fresh garden produce at the market, and the sculptures created a special morning for me.

The landscape became hilly once again. Corn was beginning to form its tassles, sunflowers were less abundant, and the vineyards were beginning to reappear. Using my compass instead of a map for general direction, I found myself on a secondary road heading east. A sign "Notre Dame des Cyclistes" unexpectedly came into view, as did a large group of people enjoying what appeared to be a festival. I left the secondary road and followed a driveway to the church and pavilion a few hundred yards to my left. The celebrants, a group of elderly cyclists, came out to greet me as though they were waiting for the Globetrotter and the American traveler. Most of the "ancient" cyclists spoke only French, except for some visitors from Québec fluent in English as well. Wine and glasses appeared a moment later, adding to the festivity of the special Saturday afternoon. Had I not been following my nose and compass, I would surely have missed this "chance meeting." Notre Dame des Cyclistes may be the only house of workship anywhere dedicated solely to cyclists. Strangely, there is no mention of this medieval church in my tour book. "May I see the interior of the church?" I asked. If the interior was as interesting as its medieval exterior, I was surely in for a treat.

The foyer of the church is a bicycle museum with an abundance of antique bicycles and bicycle memorabilia. The guest book next to a bone-shaker was offered to me by one of the members. We then went into the chapel. Hanging on the walls on either side of the pews are jerseys of past Tour de France champions. A jersey belonging to Greg Lemond, among other recent champions, is on permanent display. This opportunity to visit with French cyclists under such unusual circumstances was surely going to be a highlight of my two-year trip.

Shortly thereafter, the party began to disband. We said farewell in both French and English as the "ancients" went on their way. I headed for a campground in the town of Eauze that provided a swimming pool and recreation area. Children and their parents were obviously enjoying their weekend of camping.

Even though the campground was full, I had no difficulty in being assigned a site. As usual, I requested a grassy spot without electricity near the wash house. The convenience of the wash house is always appreciated, as well as being near the path used by other campers. This is one method of becoming acquainted without being too aggressive. I was soon in conversation with those walking past my tent.

Dutch people traveling beyond Holland take advantage of the camping facilities in the country they are visiting. Hans and Claire from Holland were pulling a trailer behind their tandem. They seemed unconcerned that they were carrying an excess of gear. Their oversized tent, heavy pots and pans, and two-burner gas stove made my load seem almost insignificant. Hans, a school headmaster, and Claire, a teacher, biked from their hometown in central Holland, the home of Vincent van Gogh. Dorothy and I visited the van Gogh Museum in Amsterdam but did not know about his birthplace. The art director of a public school system in the Boston area, Dorothy fulfilled a life's dream when we toured Belgium and Holland on the Globetrotter.

What happened to the English cyclist in the town of St. Justin who had a sign hanging from the top tube of his bicycle? It read "10,000 Miles on a Bicycle." At a glance he appeared to be approximately my age. He entered a small grocery and I followed. For unknown reasons, we did not meet. I inquired about this person at Notre Dame des Cyclistes but he was unknown there, too. This mystery may never be solved.

My next door tent neighbor, Clair, pointed to the sky as I was preparing to leave the campground. Forever the optimist, I dismissed the thought of rain as I prepared to continue my journey. Less than one-half hour later I was in someone's backyard putting my possessions into plastic trash bags. For the next four to four and a half hours the rain was torrential. At times on the downhill runs my vision was severely impaired, especially without the aid of glasses. The glasses were on my nose but I was looking over them in an effort to see.

We were no longer in flat country, reminding me of going "across the grain" in Connecticut or Pennsylvania. No sooner were we at the bottom of a steep hill than there was a new one to climb. It may be the lack of traction on the road, or state of invigoration, or both, that makes hill climbing in the rain easier than on dry pavement.

The small medieval town of Condom was the perfect location for lunch during a break in the weather. Farmers were selling paté de foie gras and vegetables from their own farms and gardens. Foie gras, the liver of the goose, is one of the great French delicacies that originates north of Condom in the region of the Dordogne. The price was right and I was hungry. Fresh bread came from the boulangerie.

I arrived in the rain at the entrance to Lectoure. At the bottom of the hill a sign simply stated "No Trucks." A chateau is poised at the summit in a shroud of rain and mist. Determined, I decided to challenge the hill even if there was no admittance once I arrived there. To put it in relative terms, Lectoure is a Mont St. Michel on land instead of being surrounded by water. I felt compelled to experience Lectoure.

The chateau at one time was converted into a hospital and then into a home for patients suffering from Alzheimer's disease. Soaking wet from the rain, I decided to park the Globetrotter in the courtyard and seek a towel in the dry interior. This brought me face to face with the patients as I toweled myself dry, thanks to the generosity of the nursing staff. Even though the patients were probably oblivious to my presence, I stayed long enough to visit with each of them. We each shook hands as I prepared to leave. From the courtyard I could see some of the less handicapped patients and members of the nursing staff waving from the windows. I felt fulfilled!

I recall a morning on the road in need of a toilet. I stopped at a tavern with the hope of also getting warm. The harsh weather was taking its toll. The local brandy Armagnac was to be the answer to this problem. The difference between V.S.O.P. and Armagnac is that the former is distilled twice, while Armagnac is distilled once. Hennesy comes from the Cognac region and Armagnac from the Gascogne. The bartender wanted an American dollar and I wanted the brandy. We struck a deal whereby he got the dollar of lesser value and I the brandy.

The rain finally abated but I had a strong wind to combat. Was it the wind that caused the bike to go out of control? For the first time, I felt unsafe on the Globetrotter. Perhaps the plastic bags protecting my gear from the rain and wind that put the bike out of balance, or was there something else happening that presently was unexplained? Camping Municipal at St. Clar gave me an opportunity to investigate the problem in the morning before going farther. The obvious problem was without a solution.

My newest acquaintance, René Lebret, 71 years of age, was anxious to practice his English. We worked on his English and then on my French, particularly French expressions. In English we might say "Great!", or in Hebrew "Yoffee!" The equivalent in French is "Chapeau!" meaning, literally, hat, but figuratively something else. I learned at an adult education course that in the USA we say that something is "not kosher," but in France the equivalent is that it is "not catholic." Oh,well!

Before leaving St. Clar, I did as much bicycle maintenance as I knew with the hope that the problem of control would be solved. Might the plastic bags have given the tandem a "sail" effect? René, his wife, and I, said our farewells with the suggestion that we meet again either in France or America. I was heading toward Toulouse, the largest city in the region, where I could hopefully get some repairs. It was obvious I needed professional assistance.

The amount of effort needed to keep the machine on the road was out of proportion to the condition of the road. With more and more effort I covered less and less distance. I chose secondary roads when possible so I would not be in conflict with cars. Prevention of a collision required my full concentration and strength. For the first time, I became aware that motorists were fearful that I might veer into them. They used their horns to caution me.

At one point, fatigue set in to such an extent that I had no choice: I lay on the grass beside the road in an effort to recover enough strength to proceed. Sleep was instant. A good Samaritan, a woman, awakened me with a question in French: "Etes-vous malade, monsieur?"

"Non, Madame, seulement fatigué," I replied.

The small town of Mauvezin on the map was a possibility for professional bicycle repair. Mauvezin was not too far distant. With luck and renewed strength I had hope of getting there under my own power.

In Mauvezin the problem was diagnosed but not cured. The bicycle shop owner, using a small pen light, examined the headset, the area where the front fork is welded to a vertical tube. Internally this tube is a part of the steering mechanism. He explained that the weld between these two different parts was partially separated, permitting the fork to overextend. It was the overextension that caused the difficulty in steering. "You must take the tandem to Toulouse where there are professional framemakers. I cannot do this type of work," he explained.

I thought I had two choices, but in actuality only one: the train. My initial thought centered on my being able to pedal either the 42 km to Toulouse or the 12 km to the nearest train. By the time we arrived at the station there was no choice. The bicycle was totally inoperable, especially with its heavy load. It became obvious that the excess weight of my baggage placed a heavier demand on the front fork.

The other consideration was the possibility of a complete fracture of the two parts, dropping me without warning on the pavement. I felt grateful that we arrived at the station without mishap. Forcefully pushing the Globetrotter the final few feet, we reached the platform. One and one-half hours later we were aboard a train destined for Toulouse, the right place to be for bicycle repairs as well as the celebration of Bastille Day.

A 10 PM arrival in Toulouse made decisions relative to camping a bit more difficult. Camping Municipal, the only campground in the city, is six kilometers from the center of town. I chose to walk the distance with the Globetrotter. In the direction of the campground we came upon a restaurant catering to the working person. The waitress seated me at the same table with three other men. An open bottle of red wine was constantly filled as we poured from the same bottle. Beef brochette, French fries, an appetizer of eggs with mayonnaise, chocolate ice cream, and coffee made the next six kilometers a bit more tolerable. It was now past midnight and I had not yet found the campground.

A cluster of caravans seemed a suitable site for the night until I was seen by a group of children. I was unwelcome. They pointed into the darkness as my proper direction. When I asked to speak to their parents for permission for one night's camping they were unresponsive.

Campground #2 was open but appeared unwholesome, especially with a chorus of howling dogs. If fresh water was available, I had little chance of finding it in the darkness. Had I not been exhausted pushing and pulling the bike for at least six kilometers, I probably would have continued my quest in preference to this gypsy enclave. This was my first and last contact with gypsies in France. I erected my tent, safely stowed my gear inside, and padlocked the Globetrotter to a tree. Once inside the tent I felt secure. The mentality of the camper!

Morning brought the reality of the situation into focus. These gypsies were free camping without the benefit of proper sanitation. In the middle of a muddy area a water pipe was open. This was their source of potable water. Perhaps they had toilets within their caravans, there being no evidence of public toilet facilities. A gypsy woman who was trying to sell me her towel for an outrageous price said that the toilet facilities at a nearby swimming pool were free for the asking. This of course proved to be misinformation. At least I rested comfortably and was not robbed. Was Camping Municipal far away?

Fortunately, we were within sight of a full-service camp, a campground that became my home for several days. Not only did I have access to a store, but bus service into Toulouse was within walking distance. My only problem was transporting the Globetrotter six kilometers to a bike shop.

The date was now Monday, July 14, Bastille Day, in celebration of the French Revolution. Stores were closed in recognition of the holiday, one that I was anxious to celebrate. I spent a portion of my morning getting the gypsy out of my system by showering, clothes washing, and, of course, tooth brushing, all of which were put on hold due to the absence of toilet facilities. I was now free to explore Toulouse for the price of a bus ticket.

The bus stopped at Capital Square, the center of the city just opposite the opera house where people were entering. I followed the crowd. An operetta, "Le Rève of Vienne," was being performed in honor of Bastille Day. Admission was free.

One of the last vacant seats became mine. I was in peanut heaven.

This operetta, written by a foremost producer, Frances Lopez, was enthusiastically enjoyed by the audience. Although much of the dialogue passed me by, the dancing spoke a universal language for the appreciation of all. Had I a companion to share this experience, it would have been even more pleasurable.

Now that I was in the center city where the more sophisticated bike shops are located, I decided to find one on this holiday so that the following day I would know where to go. People on the street were helpful: one young person offered to walk with me so I'd be certain to find it as well as my return to the bus stop in Capital Square. He also suggested that I'd be permitted to put the bike on the bus when I was ready to take it to the shop.

Once my gear was removed from the Globetrotter, the steering felt a bit more manageable. I then decided to try biking instead of trying to put the bike on the bus. Six kilometers did not seem so far on this clear morning after eating a wholesome breakfast. I maneuvered the bike with care toward Roland Marc, concessionaire Gitane. Though the labels were "Globetrotter," I knew by the design that the machine was a Gitane. My greatest concern was the possibility of a complete fracture of the fork. Was it worth the risk? Probably not. Was I willing to take that risk? Probably! By the time we arrived at the bicycle shop, further steering was impossible.

Roland Marc promised the completed repair in five days. He also said he would look into the bottom bracket noise that was still a constant nuisance. I was then given a bicycle on loan so I could do some sightseeing and have transportation to and from the campground. My impression was that I would be supplied with a new fork—further misinformation.

The day I picked up the Globetrotter, I discovered the fork was repaired, not replaced. Had I been able to look into the future, I would not have left Toulouse without a replacement part. My fork problems had just begun. Another disappointment: Roland Marc was too busy to look into the bottom bracket noise. At least I was able to proceed toward Rivesaltes and my rendezvous with the Professors Girodet.

My enforced stay in Toulouse gave me an opportunity to thoroughly visit the fourth largest city in France. The purchase of a museum pass gave me access to six museums within the city: the Natural History Museum, Georges Labit Museum, Paul Dupuy Museum, Réfectoire des Jacobins, and Galerie du Chateau d'Eau.

The Natural History Museum is one of the ten most important museums in France. It is huge, reminiscent of the Peabody Museum, a part of Harvard University. The section of prehistoric man was especially interesting. Orthodontists usually consider themselves as amateur anthropologists, having studied the relationship between the teeth and bones of mammals during the development of the animal kingdom, as part of their graduate school studies. On display was a human skull separated at all of its sutures, an incredible achievement. The similarity of the bones of all mammals proves the validity beyond any doubt of the theory of evolution, at least for this primate.

I could not help dwelling on the duplication of effort by the museums of the world as they independently collect similar materials, as well as the possibility of their destruction during acts of war. We seem to exist in a delicate balance between survival and extinction, especially when one considers the effect of natural disasters such as floods and earthquakes.

West of the Place de la Capitole in the center of Toulouse, in the Gothic church of the Jacobins dating to 1225, rest the remains of St. Thomas Aquinas. St. Thomas was an innovative teacher recognized during his lifetime for his intellectual, educational, and religious accomplishments.

The last tourist attraction before leaving Toulouse came as a surprise, and I must say a pleasant one. It was the Museum of the Capital, with a magnificent hall. The ceiling is painted in the same manner as the Sistine Chapel at the Vatican. On the walls are a series of murals depicting man's love of the different ages, as well as an impressionist's interpretation of the seasons of the year.

An inter-racial wedding within the Capitol attracted my attention. A Chinese bride was being married to an obviously well-known local citizen in what appeared to be a rather public ceremony. As expected, they both spoke excellent French.

Dinard, the canard (duck) must have known I was preparing to leave my campsite. Animals and children have a sense of knowing when it is time to find a new friend. Fortunately, I was able to get Dinard's photograph beside my tent. Perhaps another reason was that I no longer had the soft centers of French bread to feed him. In any event, I was now prepared to head for the city of Montauban north of Toulouse, the location of the Ingres Museum. Montauban was not in the direction of the Girodets, but this museum was of special cultural importance to me.

Consulting my compass rather than a map, half of our day's journey was on back roads. Nearing noontime, we intersected the main road to the city. This was not an express highway, but it did carry far more traffic than I experienced in the morning. I felt grateful for the gentle quiet of the morning, especially on the recently repaired Globetrotter.

Peaches, apricots, and nectarines were now in season as I snacked my way from Toulouse to Montauban. Farmers were selling their freshly picked produce along the road, offering them by the crate. When I came alongside a fruit stand and asked to buy two nectarines, they laughed. No matter how little or how much I bought, the price was always the same: two francs.

No doubt the intense summer heat as well as my "great expectation" left me somewhat disappointed in Montauban and the Ingres Museum. "Odalisque", a very sensuous painting of a Turkish harem slave girl hanging in the Louvre, was my concept of Ingres' style and subject. Actually, much of his work on display is of a religious nature. The definition of "Odalisque" is "Oriental Venus." A copy, or perhaps a similar painting to the one in the Louvre, is in the Fogg Museum at Harvard.

When I asked a banker for directions to the museum, he immediately corrected my pronunciation. Ingres is pronounced something like the word "angry" with the "y" replaced by an "e". The museum and its contents, a very large restored building, are owned by the city of Montauban. In addition to paintings, an archæological collection of the artist is on display, as well as works of other painters and sculptors. The well-known portrait of Jean-Auguste-Dominique Ingres by Cambon, in which Ingres is wearing his medal presented by the State, is hanging in the museum. The one by Louis Bertin can be seen in the Louvre.

I had pedaled 40 km from Toulouse to Montauban in the early morning, arriving at noontime when the sun was at its zenith. The temperature inside the museum was somewhat cooler than outside, and especially comfortable as I sat on an upholstered couch before a very large painting. Fatigue set in without prior warning! I nodded off to sleep.

Standing before me, the directress and staff informed me that sleeping is not permitted. I should have been embarrassed, having been admitted free with my Harvard ID, but this was indeed a refreshing interlude that added to the day's pleasures.

The city of Albi, the home of the works of Toulouse Lautrec, was more than an afternoon's run. Until the approach to Gaillac, south and east of Montauban, the riding was rather level, yet the heat of the sun extreme. I ate well during the day but felt the need for a snack at 9 PM. This snack became my most expensive meal: a total of 94 francs.

Although the feeling for Montauban was less than expected, my excitement for Albi grew as a I approached the city. The day was exceptional, the town impressive, and La Cathédrale La Basilique Ste.-Cécile, an enormous and impressive Gothic structure, the center of focus of Albi. Building of the church was begun in 1282 and completed in 1480. A Mass was being concluded as I entered. Following the final blessing, the priest baptized two babies at the same time.

The Toulouse Lautrec Museum, installed in the old Episcopal Palace, contains an extensive collection of the artist. Lautrec did not find it necessary to sell his major works for his sustenance. More than 600 pieces of original art are on exhibit. Also represented are the works of Carot, Dégas, Dufy, Utrillo, Rodin, Maillol, and Matisse. Humor and lightheartedness of Lautrec is ever-present. On display is the walking stick used by the artist, with its flask contained within. When he was taken to the hospital, his walking stick went with him.

Most museums post signs indicating that photographs are not permitted, but are lenient when it comes to enforcement. Photos were forbidden at the Lautrec museum. Reluctantly I left with postcards but no slides. Had there been color slides for sale, I gladly would have purchased a set. I set off reluctantly toward Castres, keeping in mind that I had a telephone appointment with the Girodets at seven in the evening. Though expensive, I used my AT&T calling card, which meant that an operator in the US placed my call in France. This way I was able to use a public phone without having to put coins in the box.

Castres, home of the Goya Museum, lies 56 km south of Albi, toward Rivesaltes. The Bishop's Palace with beautifully landscaped gardens by Le Notre is now the site of the Goya Museum with an outstanding collection of the artist's paintings and drawings. His self-portrait is reminiscent of El Greco, with long fingers and a long neck. Castres is a lovely medieval city with its cathedral and hôtel de ville. The *Syndicat d'Initiative* and the *Opéra* are in the same building as the Hôtel de Ville.

From Castres to Carcassonne, a distance of 47 km, the cycling was very strenuous. We arrived at 10:30 in the evening, fighting a wind that destroyed my "wind" theory that the prevailing winds blow in an easterly direction. This wind was so powerful that I was in my lowest gear, designed for hill climbing, with very little progress—a time to reflect on the book <u>Zen and the Art of Motorcycle Maintenance</u>. Halfway to Carcassonne I took a nap on the grass to regain my strength, with the knowledge that we would be biking in the dark.

Carcassonne is recognized as the finest example of medieval fortification in Europe. The *Cité* atop a hill and its fortifications were thought to be impregnable. The misfortune is the plethora of roadside advertisements for miles before reaching the city. To be frank, the signs were disgusting even though they did give evidence of civilization as I pedaled in the dark.

A three-star campground with a pool, store, and restaurant three kilometers from the center of the city was a welcome sight. I arrived well after closing hours. A convenience with a bicycle that automobiles do not have is access through the pedestrian entrance. At times the entrance is too tight to bring in my "Volvo" without unloading some or all of the gear, but entry is always possible.

Christophe Baudran, an 18-year-old from Toulouse, speaks excellent English. He and I became instant friends.

Christope spends his non-school time in the medieval city with
his guitar and charcoal sketching materials earning money by
sketching willing tourists. His sister drives him to and from
Carcassonne, the Cité. Paper-clipped to my journal is a letter
from Christophe dated June 23, 1994:

> Hello, how do you do? Remember, I'm the young
> little French that you've met in Carcassonne city
> two years ago, in the camping site. I saw you with
> your tandem too much heavy for my little arms.
> And so we talked about your fantastic trip, and you
> said to me: I'll come back in two years....Time has
> passed, I didn't forget you: sixty years old, whites
> hair, smiling....I met many other people traveling
> by bike, or just walking, but I've never seen such a
> man like you! Tremendous! How did you find Is-
> rael? Did you speak with God? (signed) Christophe

The photo I took of Christophe sketching a young female tourist with his other sketches around him is one of my
favorites. He has a print of this slide along with my letter. We
are now pen pals.

Narbonne to the east, a coastal town on the Mediterranean, had a special quality, especially for Americans. This is
the location of the Olympic track tream training center. A Welcome Pavilion in the center of the city, where English is the
spoken language, brought me to the reality that Barcelona, site
of the Olympic Games, was not far off. It was also an opportunity to visit with people from my own country. The changing
countryside from flat to the foothills of the Pyrenees is another
indication that Spain was near.

In the Archæological Museum in Narbonne, antiquity
discovered in this region dates back 40,000 years. Romans,
Greeks, and Etruscans once lived here, depositing their art and
possessions for future generations to find. The art of making
glass, a Roman skill, was explained in detail. This reminded
me of one of my patients early in my practice.

Peter, the son of a Harvard professor, withdrew two objects from his dungarees. "Did I want to see a couple of Roman tear bottles?" he asked. These authentic objects were then stuffed back into his jeans. Did Peter know the value of this antiquity? Did his parents know they were in his pants pockets along with the other paraphernalia that mothers find in the automatic washer following the rinse cycle?

Narbonne, once the principal French port on the Mediterranean, now lies 16 km inland, due to the silting of the harbor. Marseille presently occupies this position of supremacy. The Hôtel de Ville, the former Archbishop's Palace, and the Museum are the principal attractions in the center of the city, in addition to the Olympic Welcome Pavilion.

The campground was not located in Narbonne, but in Narbonne-Plage some distance away on the Mediterranean. It was late in the evening when I arrived at this recreation area packed with vacationing French people as well as those interested in the Olympics. It became obvious that I would have to make the climb back up to Narbonne the next day if I wished to proceed; Narbonne-Plage was a dead end. The only grassy spot available was located behind a caravan away from the high-density camping near the beach. Here the local people with their families displayed friendship that at times is more welcome than improved facilities. I was impressed with the young children walking past my tent with their friends. "Bon appétit" was their greeting to me as I prepared and ate my supper. Their parents sent over dessert and beer with their children. In addition to the beer, Stephen's mother sent a folding chair so I could write my journal in comfort. We exchanged names and addresses with the hope of meeting in the future. Rivesaltes and the Girodets, a distance of 61 km, was my goal for the next day.

Rivesaltes has nothing to do with salt or river. It refers to the banks upon which the town was built, its name being derived from Latin. Rivesaltes is famous for its excellent wine. The town is more Spanish than French in architecture, being built around a plaza. The one- and two-story buildings are of brick construction, with the plaza well planted with trees. A public telephone was within view.

"Where are you?" asked Paul when I called. I described the various stores and buildings I could see from the booth. "You are about 200 feet from our home," he said. "I will come to greet you." I visualized their summer home on a plot of ground where I could erect my tent as I had done at the homes of other French people. Instead, they live in a townhouse within a few feet of the center of town. Fortunately, I was able to bring the Globetrotter indoors, affording convenience as well as security. My reunion with these hospitable people was especially enjoyable so many miles from Bedford, Massachusetts (their home). Margo, my professor, said to her husband, "Have you noticed how well my pupil speaks French?" If only she were truthful, I would have been ecstatic. Margo installed me in the third-floor bedroom with all the comforts of my own home. An open skylight provided fresh air on this warm summer night. The bed and pillow stood in stark contrast to my camping equipment.

We enjoyed an excellent meal and conversation concerning this part of southern France. "You are so close to the Spanish town of Figueras, the home of the Salvador Dali Museum, Ralph. You should include it in your travels," said Margo. She knew I was trying to see as much art as possible. "Of course, if you go to Figueras, you may as well bike to Barcelona to see the Picasso Museum." I thought she might then suggest a detour to Antarctica to see the penguins. We then retired for the night.

As soon as I was satisfied that my hosts were asleep, I returned to the ground floor and my Globetrotter. I quietly removed my sleeping bag and air mattress. Inflating the mattress, I placed it on the tile floor with the sleeping bag. Emotionally, I was comfortably back in my own tent.

I remarked to Paul Girodet the morning of my departure as he was dressing to go hiking in the mountains, "Paul, your legs look like telephone poles."

"Did you ever look at your own?" he remarked. It was obvious that we both enjoyed the outdoors. Paul emigrated to the United States in 1954, where he taught both French and economics on the university level. In his youth he served as a part of the French resistance in which he and his fellow patriots risked their lives to help the Jews escape from France into Spain by killing the attack dogs placed in the mountains by the Nazis. I was thinking that as a civilian he probably did more for the war effort than I in the US Navy. Margo was his French student. She now teaches both Spanish and French at the high school and college level.

Chugging along on a three-speed girl's bike, a fully dressed man approximately my age, with trouser clips on his cuffs, came into view as I headed for the Spanish border. This cyclist gave the appearance of being a commuter who perhaps was on the way to his office, excpet that he had a pack on his rear rack. We were soon within speaking distance. "Are you going to work?" I asked.

"No, I am going to the Olympics!" This cyclist started in Germany, his home, and was headed for Barcelona. I wondered if he polished his black street shoes on a nightly basis. We would have made an unusual team except for the fact that his three-speed bike was slower than the Globetrotter. I waved goodbye.

My concerns about the Pyrenees were unfounded. The road was well graded and in excellent condition. Fresh peaches sold at roadside stands were tasty but not as good as in Narbonne. Perhaps the dryness of this part of France deprived the fruit of some of its flavor. This was the arid region of Languedoc, bordering Spain.

Chapter 5
SPAIN

At the Spanish border, I reached for my passport and then quietly put it away. Customs waved us through. We carefully wove a pattern around the huge camions waiting for clearance. The mountains began to disappear and the rolling hills, mostly downhill, assisted us effortlessly toward Figueras. My bike cap and sunglasses provided limited protection from the sun; it was hot!

A restaurant in Figueras serves what is commonly called *tapas*. A variety of small portions that collectively make up an entire meal are selected from the menu. In this manner patrons enjoy many different flavors in small portions.

Margo was correct in suggesting a visit to the unusual, surrealist Dali Museum. A quotation of Salvador Dali perhaps will help explain the difference between this museum and others: "The museum should not be considered as a museum. It is a gigantic surrealist object. Everything in it is coherent. There is nothing which escapes the net of my understanding." The Dali Theater-Museum occupies the building of the former Municipal Theater. The private collection of Dali in the Hall of the Masterpieces contains works of seven of his most admired artists, one of whom is El Greco, as well as some of his own paintings. His soft self-portrait with fried bacon is but one of the many surrealist objects that may cause the uninformed to pause in wonder, yet with the knowledge that in the mind and eye of the artist everything on exhibit has meaning. A 1941 Cadillac sedan in the Theater Garden with the torsos of three plaster figures can only be appreciated if seen. One a female nude, another the driver, and a third an old man, are central figures in the Garden.

The Spanish town of Gerona is approximately one-third of the distance from Figueras to Barcelona. Gerona was the only logical stopping place that might have camping facilities. The extremely flat road with the wind at my back made cycling in this hot and arid region an easy yet uninteresting experience. Long steep downgrades that went on and on began to occur. The contrast between France and arid Spain was dramatic.

In all the areas of France I have visited, the roads and towns are in pristine condition. In Spain, the general appearance is the reverse. Roadside debris as well as a disagreeable odor in many places attest to a lack of pride of the Spanish people. This condition prevails to such an extent for the full distance to Barcelona as well as the Costa Brava that I felt uncomfortable swimming in the Mediterranean. My daughter Amy, on her honeymoon, had the same experience: she and Mark left Spain in disgust as they returned to France.

Two young French touring cyclists decided to camp in Gerona even though posted signs prohibit free camping. They decided to wait for darkness to hide from the authorities. A fountain served their need for water. We exchanged names and addresses. To my good fortune, a new campground four kilometers south of Gerona was posted. Touring maps did not identify this new facility, owned and operated by Juan and Maria. A young English couple and I were the only occupants. Kelly, Dean, and I became instant friends.

Juan and Maria were more interested in being our hosts than in earning money from their new enterprise. They and their extended family were enjoying a meal of roast pork and wine. We were invited to join them and at the same time watch the lighting of the Olympic flame signifying the start of the Games. The following day, at the same dining room table, we watched the final stage of the Tour de France. A Spaniard won the race, and this family was jubilant!

We felt indebted to these very hospitable people, intent on making our stay as enjoyable as possible. The only request that Juan made was that we sign a petition as visiting tourists to attest to the need for the separation of Catalan and Spain. Catalan, including Barcelona, its capital, is exerting every influence possible short of out-and-out conflict to obtain their independence. The presence of Spanish soldiers at bridges and intersections attests to this burning issue. We willingly signed the petition.

My camp friends Kelly and Dean were getting along on a close budget. When Juan brought a loaf of bread to my tent, I graciously refused but suggested that my friends might enjoy it. They accepted Juan's generosity without hesitation. At one point when I was getting ready to leave, I said to Kelly, "I will really miss you young folks."

Her reply: "You will meet many more friends as you continue your adventure!" Kelly, from London, in her early twenties, earned a university degree but has not put it to use. Except for odd jobs, she permits herself the freedom to wander with her friend Dean, a school dropout. They both appear content to "hang out" as long as their money or the ability to earn some continues. Dean, an obviously bright person, has worked in bars and pubs. Though he considers himself an expert on beers, he claims to be interested in becoming a pastry chef. To my way of thinking, it is Kelly who is the giving half of this couple while Dean is the receiver. I wonder where they are at this time. Are they productive or still seeking? Is Kelly still carrying Dean on her shoulders?

Juan and Maria would not accept any payment for my campsite unless I joined them and their family for supper. Goat, eggplant, tomatoes, and cooked pimientos were the main course, with an ample amount of bread. The beverage *cave* tastes identical to champagne, but unless a wine comes from the area known as Champagne it may not bear that name.

The long dirt road at the campground leads to the main paved highway and a crazy descent to the resort city of Lloret de Mar on the Mediterranean. This cool evening ride brought me to within 75 km of Barcelona and a comfortable campground. It was here that I made the decision to enter notes in my journal in the evening but not in the morning due to the heat. Perspiration dripping from my hand onto the paper made morning writing a near impossibility. At that particular moment I was sitting beneath a tree that is not common to New England. A leaf dropped onto my journal and literally exploded, depositing seeds on the paper. Propagation does seem to have an explosive nature.

The management at El Masnow Campground, 15 km from Barcelona and the only one in the region, informed me that they had full occupancy. The nearby Olympics were keeping them well supplied with tourists. When I explained that I could put my small tent anywhere and that I needed no electricity, they directed me to a large tree with two tents and two bicycles parked nearby. Paul, age 72, biked from Denmark, and Joe, age 52, from Holland. We became known as the "three old men." Paul, as slim as a 25-year-old, claimed to have lost his stomach while cycling the distance with his enormous tent and a complete kitchen. His equipment reminded me of my Dutch tandem friends in France. Joe, a sports physiologist, purchased his tickets for the Games in Holland and was intent on seeing as many contests as possible. He explained that I would not find great difficulty in buying tickets at the Olympic site. I told Joe that I did not come for the Games specifically but was interested in the atmosphere of the Olympics. Barcelona as a city and the Picasso Museum in particular were my principal reasons for detouring into Spain. Both he and Paul tried to discourage me from biking into Barcelona. Traffic as well as the air pollution concerned them both.

I usually take the advice of those more experienced then myself, but this time I wanted to do it my way. Buses are useful for transportation but not for touring an area. Prepared for the worst, I decided to pedal into Barcelona. The worst was an understatement as we traveled along the Costa Brava with the intensity of traffic comparable to the West Side Highway in New York City. Accompanying road noise and pollution convinced me that I either had to find a better route into the city or I would take Paul and Joe's advice the following day.

At El Masnow campground, Paul was the more creative when it came to the preparation of food. He explained to me that he did not like *conservas*, his expression for canned foods. I then understood the reason for his complete kitchen. His supper that evening consisted of mashed potatoes, zucchini, two hamburgers, and bread. In addition to my "conservas," Joe and I shared a packet of olives purchased the previous day. When the Whisperlite one-burner stove failed, Paul loaned me his butane powered stove of French origin. I knew that eventually I too would own one of these lightweight and predictable necessities.

El Masnow, a family-owned enterprise, was not only convenient but it has two other assets that deserve mention: it is safe! I was warned about the prevalence of theft in and around Barcelona. The other asset is their swimming pool, especially during the heat of the day. This was my introduction to topless bathing, an added bonus. I tried not to stare at the young women sunning themselves. They were enjoying the freedom of the Mediterranean not usually found in North America. I am reminded of the expression "you can look but don't touch!"

A caravan across the road from us was stopped by the police and fined on the spot. The fine was 120,000 pesetas in cash. The driver was told by the police that if he wanted to protest the charge, his car and caravan would be impounded. Getting the equipment back would be *his* problem! Not having enough money on his person, the driver explained to the police that he would have to go to the bank. One motorcycle in the lead and one behind, they escorted him to *el banco*.

The opening of the Olympic Games as seen on color TV at the home of Juan and Maria was, of course, broadcast in

Spanish. The Olympic Torch was carried by a famous Spanish basketball player. An archer then shot his ignited arrow in a perfect arc, igniting the Olympic cauldron, starting the Games.

It was difficult getting oriented, as the Olympics were spread throughout the city. At one point I stopped for a bracing cup of Spanish coffee. The 400-meter women's freestyle was being televised. The United States won the event.

Once at España Square in Barcelona, I forgot about the pollution and trash in the streets. The capitol known as the Palace, with its ascending steps and fountains, is monumental. Escalators take visitors part way to the Palace, followed by ascending stairways. Attached to the Palace is the magnificent National Museum of Art of Cataluña. Its spacious galleries are extremely well lighted. Works of art are organized according to their time in history. A video accompanied by the spoken word in Catalonian attests to the fact that the people of this region speak a form of French in preference to Spanish. My lunch at España Square consisted of a sausage sandwich, beer, a bottle of water, and a bag of M&Ms. M&Ms were an official sponsor of the Olympics. The cost: $8.00.

Located off Cataläna Square, the Picasso Museum is on a narrow street in a building that appears to be medieval with ancient beginnings. Looking through the glass-covered floor, a Roman wine cellar can be seen. Earthen vessels implanted in the ground are arranged in a regular geometric pattern. Picasso began his career with a formal art education. He was a conventional classical artist until his transition to his "Blue Period" when he moved to France. While in France he developed his "cubism," ultimately becoming an artist of abstraction. The tour of the museum is that of several different persons instead of the artist that we know. Pablo Picasso lived from 1881 to 1973. Photography is forbidden in the Museum.

Camping Masnow was easy to locate on my return without having to ride on the highly congested roads encountered that morning. A view of the Mediterranean as well as my compass aided me in finding less traveled roads until I came to the Olympic Village. This huge development was difficult to circumvent. I was satisfied that I did not take the advice of Paul and Joe. Before leaving for the campground, I found a note attached to the Globetrotter, locked in a secure location in España Square. Except for the "Jaws of Life," the Citadel lock defies being opened. Even a cutting torch will not penetrate its special composition. The two young French cyclists who preferred to free camp in Gerona saw the Globetrotter. They left a note of greetings.

It was hard to leave my two friends Paul and Joe, but I had a mission to continue in the direction of the Middle East and not to vacation at the Costa Brava, even though poolside was attractive. The town of Bañoles, the site of the rowing contests, offered an alternate route back to France so I would not be plowing the same ground. My map indicated that a campground was located near the lake, suggesting that the return to France might be an interesting experience.

The campground at Bañoles was congested beyond belief. I was given permission to camp if I could find a location. My first choice was near the wash house on a small piece of lawn not occupied by others. A campground employee discouraged the idea, explaining that in the morning when the sprinklers go on I would not appreciate my selection. I then knew why this grassy spot was not overfilled with humanity. There literally was not a piece of earth available large enough to erect a small tent. In desperation, I rolled out my ground cloth, placed my sleeping bag on it, and spent a hot night with the mosquitoes and bugs *sans* tent. In spite of the inconvenience, it was enjoyable being near the lake and the atmosphere of the Olympics. I shall refrain from a description of the preparation of my meal in the dark. Burned spaghetti is not exactly a gourmet's delight. In the middle of the night, when all others had retired, I showered, washed my clothes, and went to sleep.

A rowing event was being held at the time of our departure from Bañoles. Security at that time was uncompromising, especially around the Olympic Village. Some of the security may have been due to the strong secessionist movement within Calataña. This area in the vicinity of Barcelona was the last portion of Spain to surrender to Franco in 1939 during the Spanish Civil War.

My last town in Spain was La Junquera, on the border of France north of Figueras and the Dali Museum, the final opportunity to spend my remaining Spanish currency or convert it into French francs. Joyfully, I returned to my favorite country, France.

Atelier Renoir • France

Chapter 6
BACK TO FRANCE

The city of Perpignan lies at the foot of the Pyrenees near the Spanish frontier, some 10 km from the Mediterranean, near Rivesaltes, the summer home of the Girodets. Casa Pairal, a museum of Catalonian folk art and traditions, was a worthwhile experience, as well the Citadel, built in the 17th and 18th centuries. There is an excellent view of the city from the outer wall of the Citadel.

Markets in Perpignan have an excellent way of speeding up the cashier line not seen in Spain. The customer takes his purchases of fruit and vegetables to a weighing station where he places items in individual plastic bags and weighs them separately. A sticker is then generated on which the price is noted. The customer applies the sticker to the designated bag to be presented to the cashier. Throughout the rest of France the other customers and I enjoyed this convenience.

I had hope of again seeing the Girodets in Rivesaltes, but unfortunately at that time they were in Marseille. A neighbor took the small gift I purchased with a promise to give it to my hosts. Without further delay I consulted my map: Béziers, Montpellier, Nîmes, Arles, and Marseille were now within reach.

My compass brought me to small villages, winding narrow roads, and vineyards rather than the monotony of Route N-11. André, a young German cyclist, was on his way to Barcelona and the Olympics. Though André was a fraction of my age, I felt an immediate bonding. He could have been the perfect traveling companion, reminding me of Joe Lohn. Joe and I met in California in 1971. Unfortunately, André was traveling south and I was going north. In Narbonne, André and I lunched at McDonald's. Our thick chocolate shakes were reminiscent of the US.

Béziers, north of Perpignan, was originally a Roman military colony finely situated atop a hill. Today the economy of Béziers is centered around the wine and brandy industry. The former cathedral of St. Nazaire is located on higher ground with massive towers and a large rose window on the west wall. St. Jacques, an excellent museum, exhibits wine producing equipment of a former era with a huge hand-operated wine press. An unusual collection of circus objects are unique to this museum: coin-operated machines, curved mirrors, pictures of freaks of nature such as Siamese twins, giants, and dwarfs. The directions on one machine stated "Put in one dime." It was obviously made in the US.

The Casino, a chain of supermarkets and cafeterias in France, is hard to beat for variety of food and competitive prices. My supper at a cost of 47 francs consisted of fresh salad with hard-boiled eggs, French fries, watermelon, goat cheese, bread, and Orangina, a tasty soft drink that is also sold in the US. French-speaking children studying English greeted me at the entrance to Camping Municipal; they were anxious to speak English with an American. I was equally anxious for their friendship. In the morning I looked for my friends with my camera, but they were elsewhere. I then headed north toward Montpellier. An interesting thing happened to me enroute that I fondly classify as misinformation:

> A large sign with the picture of a mammoth was worth pursuing. It merely stated "Mammoth." Thinking this was the announcement of a museum featuring prehistoric animals, I followed the sign to additional signs with the same picture. Finally we arrived at the Mammoth supermarket. Surprise! Even though the Mammoth was a disappointment, following my nose instead of a fixed itinerary suited my temperament perfectly. I still had time to bike to Montpellier before dark.

Finely decorated noble mansions and merchants' homes bear witness to the former wealth of Montpellier. Unfortunately, the Fabre Museum in Montpellier is closed on Mondays. This museum houses Italian and Dutch masters as well as the works of modern French painters. The Pavilion du Musée Fabre with an exhibit of the impressionist Fréderic Bazille and the works of Monet, Renoir, and Sisley was scheduled to be open the next day. This exhibit was announced on a banner spanning the main street, a common occurrence in both France and Italy. On my Globetrotter I would merely look up at the banner in any one of the many cities I encountered to see what event of the day or week was being featured.

Bazille was a promising young impressionist born into wealth. Extremely talented, he enjoyed friendship and guidance from Monet, Renoir, and Manet. Unfortunately, Bazille's genius was terminated at an early age in 1870 during the Franco-Prussian War. He enlisted as an officer in the French army and died of wounds in battle. On display at the exhibit was "La Scène d'été" borrowed from the Fogg Museum at Harvard. I felt as though I was back in Cambridge. Bazille is not mentioned in my book A History of Art, but that, of course, does not mean his work is not significant. My paperback textbook is designed for interest, not completeness. Montpellier and the Bazille exhibit became one of my favorite visits.

Leaving Montpellier, the N-9 was not a good choice of road. I was back on a limited-access road with Nîmes as my destination. Fences lined both sides of the road, another indication that I did not belong there. Fortunately, the police were not aware of my indiscretion. As I pedaled along, I reminded myself of my little friend Jeremie whom I met the previous night in the campground. Jeremie was trying to teach me the French words "le fou du roi," or in English, the king's bishop. In desperation, he went to his tent to find the black king and the king's bishop from his chess set. This 8-year-old was probably still asleep in his tent when I left the campground.

Fruits and vegetables were now in full season and readily available from vendors along the secondary roads.

Melons about the size of a softball taste like honeydew melons. They are sweet and very solid, with the seeds confined to the center. Dark green stripes trace their exterior from pole to pole. Both red and green apples were more firm and tasty than our Macs, and the grapes were in the process of maturing. A blue color was beginning to show on the well-formed surface of this luscious fruit.

The city of Nîmes is north and west of Montpellier. It is the French city richest in Roman remains, located between Montpellier to the west and Avignon to the east. My first pleasant surprise was the arena called the *Arènes,* a Roman amphitheater in the center of the city that is so well preserved it is still used for theatrical productions. I enjoyed climbing to the top of the Arènes and photographing the original construction as well as the tile rooftops of the city. One hundred twenty-four exits permit the spectators to leave this building within minutes. In the summer, a huge air cushion supported by non-Roman structures permits theatrical productions and bullfights to be held during inclement weather. Northwest of the Arènes is a well preserved Roman temple, the *Maison Carrée,* built during the reign of Augustus (20-12 B.C.). During the Middle Ages, Maison Carrée was occupied by a monastery, but it now houses the Museum of Antiquities where Roman statues, bronzes, mosaics, and reliefs are exhibited.

An English cycling couple noticed that my Globetrotter had fallen over. Not only did they put it back on its wheels, they entered the museum to give me the news. Fortunately, there was no visible damage. They are both schoolteachers and members of the Cyclists Touring Club of Britain (CTC). Rather than bike the full distance, they prefer to use a car to drive between cities and utilize their bikes for local touring.

The Fine Arts Museum at Nîmes offered a special exhibit of the artist Henri Matisse (1869-1954). His passion was the human form, especially that of the female. Matisse conveys his concept using a very minimum of lines. I must confess to being unable to appreciate the style of this famous painter.

Before leaving Nîmes, I visited what is known as the most beautiful promenade in Europe. The *Jardin de la Fontaine* is built around the Roman baths. Canals, grottos, bridges, and baroque statues are the main points of interest. Had the Globetrotter not been unprotected, I would have climbed to the *Tour Magne,* a Roman monument dating from 15 B.C. This would have afforded me an excellent view of the town and surrounding area.

My compass this time was a hindrance rather than a help as I headed toward *Pont du Gard,* a three-tiered aqueduct built about 19 B.C. during the reign of the Roman emperor Agrippa. This aqueduct is the main source of water for the city of Nîmes, carrying a daily flow of approximately 440,000 gallons. Instead, I ended in the foothills of Nîmes, a suburban area where many of the roads dead-ended. Walking to the top of a mountain, a sign to Uzès and Pont du Gard, confirmed the direction to Avignon. A sign to a discothèque and restaurant was also encouraging, especially when I learned that this was my last opportunity to eat on this mountain road.

Arrival at Camping Municipal in Uzès, my destination for the night, was after dark. The lighting system that Michael at Ace Wheelworks installed served me well until I came to a stop. That is one of the problems with generator-driven lights. The other is, of course, the friction created between the generator and the rear wheel, placing an added burden on the biker and requiring a lower gear.

Visibility at the campground, fortunately, was no problem. My campsite neighbors' son held a flashlight for me so I could erect my tent. When I settled in for the night I did not know that the source of the bottom bracket noise that plagued me for most of the trip had surfaced. In the morning, reality prevented an early departure. Diagnosis of the problem was now simple, though the solution a bit more complex. The problem was definitely not the bottom bracket.

Unlike a single bike, a tandem has two driving chains. This enables the riders to transfer energy to the rear wheel. I was unaware that upon arrival at the campground the previous night the chain connecting the front and rear pedals had fallen off. Had this occurred while riding in the dark I would have been walking instead of pedaling. The cause became obvious: several bolts connecting the chainwheels loosened and fell to the ground, leaving one chainwheel in a "floppy" condition. This was the source of my perennial bottom bracket noise. Finally, when these loose connecting bolts disappeared, the situation became critical. The chain fell to the ground. To my good fortune, three of the connecting bolts, though loose, were still in place. My next-door neighbors again came to the rescue.

Using his heavy-duty pair of pliers and my screwdriver, we tightened the remaining bolts. I could at least pedal to the nearest bike shop in the nearby city of Avignon. We both knew this was an emergency repair. New connecting bolts were a necessity. This congenial Frenchman insisted that I take his pliers with me just in case. The only way I could convince him that I did not want to take his tool was to tell him that it was too large and too heavy for me to carry. He and I met again later that afternoon at Pont du Gard, a very beautiful piece of Roman architecture. Fortunately, the connector bolts were still doing their job.

Beautiful valleys and superb views preceded the bridge. As usual, the surface of the road could not be improved upon. Even the wind was at my back as I arrived at this tourist attraction. Beneath the bridge, swimmers and boaters were enjoying the refreshing waters on this extremely hot summer day. For reasons unknown, the Globetrotter went out of control, taking me with it. With all the weight on board, once off balance there was no direction but down.

The only reason for the fall that took a little skin with it was that I was not paying attention. A young tourist came to my rescue, helping me upright the Globetrotter. We visited for a few minutes. His sister had recently graduated from Harvard University in international business relations. I then felt able to continue to Avignon with its one- and two-mile climbs and subsequent invigorating descents.

On one particularly challenging climb that seemed to go on forever, I shifted into my lowest gear, put my head down, and decided to try for the summit without dismounting. Was it a Zen state that overcame my consciousness or was I merely being influenced by the novel <u>Zen and the Art of Motorcycle Maintenance</u>? In any event, the mountain gradually disappeared. Just prior to the summit the task at hand became easier due to the lessening of the grade. I was now at the summit and back to normal. Even with my heavy load, the climb was not excessively difficult. This climb brought back a memory dating back to 1969.

I pedaled out to Marion, Indiana, to attend my first L.A.W. convention and was now ready to challenge the Allegheny Mountains east of Pittsburgh on my return. This was Route 30, affectionately called the Lincoln Highway. Most of the high-speed traffic utilized the Pennsylvania Turnpike, leaving these beautiful mountains for the enjoyment of the tourists and local traffic. Laurel Mountain was my first major climb out of Pittsburgh.

I did not know about the Zen state at that time but I did know that I wanted to climb Laurel Mountain without dismounting. The combined weight of bicycle and gear was 75 pounds. Though a hot summer day, the shade of the trees made the climb less arduous than it might have been. Finally, after considerable time and effort, the grade at the summit began to decrease, making the final thrust easier. I was now over the top but had no one with whom to share this experience. An unsuspecting

103

pedestrian was walking along the side of the road
as I approached him. "Hello," I said. "Do you know
what I just did? I climbed Laurel Mountain without dismounting." He must have though that I had
lost my Zen.

Crossing the Rhône River into Avignon, I had the
choice of five different campgrounds, one of which was Camping Municipal. Bicycle repair, not sightseeing, was my first
priority. To my good fortune, I found a bike shop that stocked
the needed parts but was refused my use of the necessary tools
to effect a repair. Had the mechanic the time to do the repair, I
would have willingly engaged his services. Unfortunately, he
was booked well in advance. Another shop, the local Peugeot
dealer, was recommended. At least I now had the needed parts.

The owner of the Peugeot shop, a lovely woman, explained that her mechanic was on vacation and there was no
one available to help me. If I chose to do my own repair, she
welcomed my use of his tools. How could I have been so fortunate? Then again, my entire trip was one of *quintessence*. I
went to work! Madame called me from the front showroom
with a request: would I please inflate the tires of a moped owned
by an elderly gentleman? I now felt as though I was completely
accepted and trusted. It was a good feeling! Another memory
from the past came to mind.

Leon and I decided to bicycle to the Kiwanis
International convention in New York City. I was
president of the Cambridge Kiwanis Club and he
was my convention chairman. This was the golden
anniversary of Kiwanis International and our first
long bicycle trip. We planned to bring attention to
our club during this especially important year. He
and I each wore high visibility jackets with a large
Kiwanis emblem sewn on the back.

These were extremely hot days in July and the
cycling through Connecticut was especially diffi-

cult, particularly on roads that were under repair. The dust and heat became overpowering as we passed a package store. One cold beer and relaxation in the shade temporarily postponed our thoughts of the planned entrance at Madison Square Garden. When we offered to pay for our purchase, the owner gave us an alternative: "Put these purchases in this man's car and the beer is free!" We, who probably looked more like bums than dentists, did as he requested. It was then that we learned not to drink beer while bicycling, especially on hot days. Our knees did not want to push on for the next two hours. Half a bottle had settled into each knee.

The Globetrotter was again in good working condition, thanks to the generosity of the Peugeot shop owner who accepted no money for the use of her tools. I gave her my name and address in America with the offer that she visit me when I returned from my tour. We said goodbye in the French manner—a kiss on both cheeks. I felt that I could now visit Avignon with the peace of mind that the annoying bottom bracket noise was but a memory. I was again ready for the road.

The entire town of Avignon is surrounded by a wall 4.8 kilometers long with eight gates and 39 towers. These walls were first built in 1350 and 1368. One of the largest medieval fortresses in the world, the Palace of the Popes is a major attraction in Avignon, with its magnificent example of Gothic architecture. St. Catherine is the dominant theme of the art of the Palace of the Popes; she is known as St. Catherine of Sienne, where she is depicted as a teacher of Jesus.

The Bridge of Avignon, the *Pont St. Benezet,* is perhaps the best known bridge in all of France. Extending into the Rhône River, only four of its original 22 arches remain. An old French nursery rhyme keeps the memory of the Bridge alive. It was built in the 12th century.

Now that it was the cooler portion of the day, I decided to head for the city of Arles, following the Rhône toward Marseille. Marseille was especially important to me, as this was to be my first mail pickup since June 4, my departure date from Boston. My Belgian friends Nicolas Wallons and Guillaume D'hundt were also traveling by bicycle; I met them the previous evening. Someone tried, unsuccessfully, to steal Nicolas' bike at his tent site.

> A woman selling flowers in Barcelona, Spain, approached a particular female tourist. "Buy a flower for only one peseta, Señora." The tourist just came back from the bank with 20,000 pesetas in her purse, the equivalent of about $200. She opened her purse to give the flower lady one peseta and returned to her campground where she discovered 18,000 pesetas missing, the victim of a slight-of-hand maneuver.

> Another story, whether true or not, concerns the gypsies who ride the Metro in Paris victimizing the passengers. A gypsy woman carrying a baby will toss the baby toward a tourist. He or she will instinctively reach out to catch the baby to save it from a fall. During the commotion the tourist's pockets are picked clean.

The city of Arles was an absolute zoo of people and cars. Add to that a miserable campground, and I was not very impressed with Arles even though my tour guidebook gave it considerable coverage. Preservation of Roman and medieval antiquity as well as being the home of Vincent van Gogh during the years 1888 and 1889 gives Arles considerable significance. Its magnificent Roman amphitheater dating to the second century became a fortress during the Middle Ages. Perhaps my problem centered around the masses of people not experienced before. It was now the height of tourist season.

The Saturday open-air street fair was wonderful. Food, clothing, flowers and garden supplies, works of art, crafts, and people covered an enormous area. Fruit was now in season, and I sampled everything in sight. The local ripe pears resembled the picture on the wooden crates depicting the perfect pear with its "blush" rendered to entice the buyer. I kept eating fruit and pizza until there was absolutely no further room.

On a previous bicycle tour in the vicinity of Seville, Spain, pears of this quality could be seen from the road but could not be picked by tourists. A high wall surrounded the entire orchard. "If I cannot pick one, perhaps I can buy one." I rested the bike against a tree at the entrance to a rather large home and began to walk up the driveway. Either the barking dogs or the man sitting on the porch with a gun across his lap, or both, discouraged my appetite for pears.

Arles, a city that I looked forward to seeing, was not hard for me to leave, except for the traffic that was so intense that I had difficulty keeping my heavily weighted Globetrotter under control. Fortunately, my next stop, the town of Salon, 51 km from Marseille, was a gem not soon to be forgotten. Salon is the home of the French astrologer and physican Nostradamus (1503-1556) as well as the Museum of the Empire. The tourist population was apparently in Arles, leaving Salon a quiet and picturesque "old city" with friendly people. Camping Nostradamus, located on Rue Nostradamus, added to the significance of this man, who wrote his book <u>Centuries</u> in verse with prophesies that are vague and open to interpretation. Some believe that he predicted World War II. The Nazis issued their own version of Nostradamus' prophesies to convince the German people and their European enemies of the ultimate German victory. Born in southern France, Nostradamus became a professor at the University of Montpellier, court physician to King Charles of France, and advisor to Catherine de Médicis, wife of King Henry II of France.

The Museum of the Empire, a military museum, houses an enormous collection of military hardware, particularly memorabilia concerning Napoléon. His personal belongings as well as his bedroom taken from the Isle of Elba, where he was exiled, have been moved to this repository. A huge portrait of Napoléon dressed as a Roman emperor with a laurel wreath about his head hangs on a wall. The museum itself is a huge chateau located on the top of a hill in the Old City of Salon.

As I was leaving the museum, a couple was being married; the groom was in the military. A small convertible with the top lowered transported a gallows with the groom hung in effigy. His bride, looking on, was smiling a "knowing" smile.

When I started my journey, Marseille seemed light years away. Now Aix-en-Provence, and then Marseille, were within a two-day ride. The spring corn, merely a few inches above the ground near Paris, was now in season. I looked forward to including corn as a part of my tent-side menu. The closer I came to the coast, the steeper became the climbs, with an increase in the intensity of the wind. Finding my way into Marseille became a frustrating challenge.

A cyclist returning from his day in the Alps gave me detailed information concerning the best route into the city, as well as directions to a campground in the mountains. I carefully wrote this information as he dictated. He described a campground north of Marseille, explaining that there were no places to camp in the city. All of this became part of my repertoire of misinformation. At the same time the darkening sky suggested inclement weather ahead. I forged on.

After several attempts to follow the cyclist's directions, I resorted to my road map showing a direct route via the major highway N-113. Ever climbing, the headwinds finally brought me to a complete stop, followed by considerable walking until the summit. Two tunnels on the descent caused increased anxiety but there was no alternative. N-113 was decidedly no place for a bicycle! Someone or something must have been looking over my shoulder as I arrived safely in the Old Port of Marseille.

The information that there were no campgrounds in Marseille was accurate but availability of this type of facility in the mountains proved to be erroneous. I headed for the town of Rove, following the coastline. An impending storm gave me cause to search out emergency camping sites in case of rain. We climbed further into recreational areas. A posted sign told the complete story: no camping. Then the rain struck with a fury almost beyond description.

The rain hit with such speed and intensity that I had no opportunity to seek shelter. The most I was able to do was locate my plastic trash bags and try to hold them in such a way that they might protect my possessions. The sudden onset prevented any possibility of placing the luggage in the plastic bags. I was totally at the mercy of the storm. The thunder and lightning gave me cause to reflect on a similar storm one Sunday as I was jogging a distance from my home. The lightning literally followed me as I propelled my rain-soaked body down the middle of the road to avoid the trees. The flashes of lightning and crashing sounds of thunder predicted my sudden demise.

This storm was similar except that I was at the bend of a mountain road trying to keep my gear safe from the rain. A torrent of water was now cascading down the road, giving motorists cause for alarm. My only thought during this entire event was to rationalize: "If the storm started, ultimately it will stop." Finally, this is what happened. The rain stopped, the sun came out, and I began to assess the damages. It was obvious that my gear was soaked. Disposing of the wet plastic bags at the side of the road, I began my trek up the mountain and around the bend toward the vacation village of Rove. To my utter dismay, I was staring into a tunnel. Had I known of this tunnel I would have been spared the discomfort as well as the damage from the cold wetness that penetrated my body as well as my canvas bags. Fortunately, the large saddlebag supported by the rear top tube of the bike has a built-in double protective liner. I knew this would be of some help, as well as a hotel where I could not only get warm but dry my possessions.

A nearby restaurant confirmed the misinformation about campgrounds: there are none. A family-owned and operated establishment, I was well fed and taken care of. They telephoned a hotel in Rove to secure a reservation regardless of the time of my arrival. One of the members of this family was preparing to fly to Boston to compete in the Boston Marathon. The entire conversation was held in French.

Hotel Dumond situated on top of a mountain became my refuge. The management permitted me the use of their drying room where they hang linen to air dry. I was given enough space to lay out my clothing and paraphernalia. All books and papers stayed in my room so that I might once again separate the pages lest they permanently cement themselves together. The History of Art gained additional character but was still in usable condition.

The intense storm the previous day brought exceptional weather the next: mine to visit Marseille and the post office. Clear mountain air and the cordial atmosphere of the hotel management enervated me. We headed down the mountain toward Marseille, passing through the infamous tunnel and my bend in the road. Two of the plastic bags remained as a grim reminder of one of the worst storms in my memory. The main post office of the city became my first short-term goal. All my other activities centered around the old port where the tourists gather.

The postmaster searched his file for my name and mail. A folder bearing my name was on file but it was empty. All of my mail was returned. He explained that after holding mail for two weeks it is returned to the sender. I obviously exceeded the limit. This meant that in addition to a lack of contact with those at home, I'd be biking without a computer. Daily logging of estimated mileage remained my only alternative.

The Museum of History of Marseille and the *Petit Train* kept me busy for most of the afternoon. The history of Marseille predates the Romans, the port having been built by the Greeks. Prehistoric man, of course, predated them all. Greek and Roman artifacts, a preserved Greek fish net that was weighted with lead, and the remains of a wrecked ship from the third century were of special interest.

Our *petit train* toured the old city with a stop at the top of the mountain where the religious site Notre Dame de la Garde is located. The 20 percent grades are similar to those in San Francisco. Our train was challenged. This was the perfect location for picture-taking. The harbor with all of its pleasure boats and the blue Mediterranean were truly memorable. It was now time in the remaining daylight to bike back up the mountain to my hotel. Fortunately, I did not have to be concerned about additional storms, for the skies were depleted from the previous day.

My original plan was to bike to Aix-en-Provence and then on to Marseille, but it was more logical to do it in reverse, especially as I was again on top of the mountain. It also set me up for St. Tropez, a must on this or any other trip.

The refresher course in conversational French offered at Brookline High School, within biking distance of my home, was conducted by Walter Gee. Walter gave us advice, particularly as it concerns gypsies. "All you need to say is 'Allez-vous en,' or as we might say in English, 'Go!' They will leave you alone," said Walter.

Before leaving a Marseille museum I used their facilities. Upon exiting the building, a bearded person dressed in a toga-like costume rushed up to me from the bench he was occupying. Remembering the advice of my teacher, I said in a loud and stern voice, "Allez-vous en!" He immediately retreated as I expected. From a distance, however, in body sign language he indicated to me that I forgot to zip up my fly.

The 48-km ride to Aix-en-Provence was rather hilly, a sign of things to come. A fruit store caught my attention before our arrival at the tourism office. Lunch consisted of pears, plums, peaches, and fresh grapes. An Irish couple, Philip and Meg, arrived at the tourism office at about the same time as I. We became friends, particularly because Philip is a dental technician. I felt compelled to tell them of an experience Dorothy and I had when we toured Ireland:

> We were pedaling our tandem along rural roads, passing groups of children walking in the opposite direction. "Good morning, Patrick," I would say in a friendly voice. I could imagine the child saying to his friends, "How did he know me name?" Farther down the road I would say "Hello, Sean" or "Hello, Mary" with the same friendly tone to my voice. "How did he know me name?"

Philip and Meg had a detailed map of the area, indicating hills and mountains between Aix-en-Provence and St. Tropez. They also reported what I already knew: the city of Nice is situated in the Alps.

A minor yet important repair to one of my panniers became necessary due to the opening of an important seam. Was it time to begin looking for new equipment or repair the old? Should I try the repair myself or look for a shoemaker? Using the overhand casting method, I was able to draw the separated parts into proximity with needle and thread but with the knowledge that this repair was temporary due to the stress on the material. Krazy Glue made the repair permanent by spreading the glue over the surface of the repair and letting it air dry. My repair was still as good as the original seam the day I replaced the bag.

Aix-en-Provence is known as the city of fountains. The middle one, the *Fontaine Chaude,* on the main street, draws its water from the local thermal springs. These springs have been visited for reasons of health as well as recreation since Roman times. In addition to many attractions, the museums of the artists Cézanne and Granat are located in this city, the old capital of Provence.

Granat, the son of a wealthy family, was financed by his father as he pursued his career in art. Following several failures in his formative years, his father stopped his allowance. Granat by this time was well acquainted with Renoir, Monet, and van Gogh. As a matter of fact, Monet bought a painting from Granat. His father's death ended Granat's financial problems, inheriting his father's wealth. His love of Rome took him to Italy where he did most of his work.

Looking for Cézanne's studio, I became acquainted with the hills of Aix-en-Provence. This time my compass was of no help, as I retraced my steps. Finally I found the atelier exactly where my map indicated its location. This one-room studio heated with a small stove gives the appearance that the artist had just gone out for a walk and would return shortly. Approximately twelve works of his art are exhibited, one of which is that of Madame Cézanne. In another painting he is paying homage to the artist Eugene Delacroix.

Adjoining the Cathedral is the former Archbishop's Palace that houses the Museum of Tapestries, with 17th and 18th century Beauvais tapestries depicting the life of Don Quixote and his servant. The Palace was used to entertain visiting clergy, with the tapestries for decoration.

My early departure from Aix-en-Provence was uneventful except that quite by accident I discovered a secondary road to Nice. I could now avoid biking on the expressway, a welcome relief. The road was superb, the weather ideal, the wind at my back, and no hills to climb. This was a day to remember! In the vicinity of the town of Brignoles, a touring bike ridden by a young American came alongside. He introduced himself as Greg Pilarowski. Greg was studying at a university in Sweden with plans to return to Ohio State for the completion of his fourth year. Prior to his return home he was in the process of biking from England to Israel, a journey not too different than my own except that his was to be completed in 50 days.

Before long we were joined by two more cyclists. These young people came from Sweden, with one week remaining before returning to their native country. Greg was an experienced cyclist and one who knew the technique of group cycling. The two Swedish students, however, were inexperienced, making my work that much more hazardous. The heavy Globetrotter was vulnerable under less than ideal conditions. I decided to head in the direction of St. Tropez instead of being involved in an unexpected crash with my new friends. I bid the three cyclists adieu and headed toward the mountains and the coast.

At a nearby restaurant, a waiter advised the mountain route to St. Tropez. I headed toward the French Alps. Initially the climb was gentle, with grapes growing on either side of the road. Picked directly from the vine, these luscious blue grapes were intended either for the artist's camera or my taste buds. Heading into the mountains with their innumerable switchbacks, I was able to pedal without dismounting for the first 10 km. Walking then became a necessary alternative.

We reached the summit by about 7 PM, with ample daylight remaining for a safe descent. Cork trees were the dominant tree during this entire experience. I saw cork trees being harvested in Portugal but did not expect the same vegetation in the French Alps. In my mind I began composing a letter to John Vanderpoel, my bike buddy from Concord, Massachusetts: "Dear John, Before you hang up your wheel for the last time, come to France and do what I have just done: climb the Alps on the way to St. Tropez. You will not regret it! Your cycling buddy, Ralph."

Mr. and Mrs. Valles from Grenoble were vacationing in the Alps with their Citröen. Carefully trekking down the mountain, I met these people heading uphill. We both stopped to visit, exchange addresses, and of course picture taking ensued. Using my self-timer, I was in the photo of my first but not last climb in the Alps.

Precipitous views and an absence of guard rails increased the need for extreme caution, but it was all well worthwhile. A small village in the valley was built on the side of the mountain. Camping Municipal was situated on a steep incline, requiring both pedaling and walking. By the light of a full moon I erected my tent before seeking what hopefully would be a hot shower. Wrong again! My clothes, my teeth, and myself felt the energy of fresh cold mountain water, making my Sierra sleeping bag even more desirable. Sleep came easily.

Should I leave my tent erected in Camping Municipal in the village of Collobrières and bike to St. Tropez as a commuter, or leave this little bit of heaven that I had just discovered and take my gear with me? The decision was easily made when I inquired about the route to St. Tropez. I had one more mountain to climb leading to the village of Grimaud. Commuting over a mountain pass was not exactly the most desirable approach, especially on a bicycle.

The second mountain was fortunately of lesser magnitude than the one to Collobrières. Save for rest stops, I was able to pedal the entire distance to the summit in anticipation of the usual frenetic descent. Instead, we gently coasted to the valley below, enjoying the vistas as well as the Côte d'Azur in the distance. Finally the prosperous medieval town of Grimaud came into view. Artists and their studios account for this appearance of prosperity. Michael Sauval, an artist, and his wife were especially friendly. They gave me one of their signed cards as a souvenir. Madame Sauval was intent on correcting my French. I photographed them both as they leaned out of a flower-decorated window.

The Museum of Grimaud is located in a medieval ruins next to a restaurant. These ruins were discovered at the time the restaurant was being built. It has on exhibit tools indigenous to Grimaud, folk costumes, and large Grecian urns. A special exhibit by the artist Josette Del Vaux was also of interest to me, especially with the artist present. Josette let me photograph her with her art. She also gave me her signed card. I was now ready for St. Tropez and Tahiti Beach, or should I say "more than ready?"

St. Tropez, with a population of 6,000, was once a quiet fishing village. Since the Second World War it has become a favorite haunt of artists, with an increase in tourism. Some say it has lost some of its charm, but not for this cyclo-tourist. I found the main street and adjoining port with its many pleasure boats a place of remarkable beauty as well as cleanliness. Even the people were especially friendly.

An exhibit of the native son Paul Signac was located in the Museum of the Annonciade near the water's edge in a large white building surrounded by manicured gardens. Signac discovered the "little fishing village" in 1892, settled there, and brought many of his artist friends with him. One of my favorite paintings is a portrait of the artist at the tiller of a boat. Signac is in sailing attire.

Tahiti Beach is a public beach known for its granular sand and topless bathing. It's located about 10 km from town. Admission is free, as are the bath facilities. Offshore a pleasure craft of huge proportions was laying at anchor. The vessel looked large enough to be commercial, but was privately owned. Was I disappointed in the topless bathers? Not at all!

Back at the campground in Grimaud something occurred that will forever remain unexplained. I returned to my tent after enjoying the warmth, beauty, and waters of Tahiti Beach. In true form the desire for sleep became overpowering. "Monsieur, would you like to have some *bouillabaisse*?" Did I dream this or did it really happen? "No, thank you," I said in my twilight tone. Later, upon awakening I tried to discover the difference between reality and fantasy but, as I say, this is still a mystery. A part of reality, however, was a warm shower and lunch of goat cheese, peach compote, and a carafe of rosé wine. I thought of that television ad concerning Jamaica: "Life is good."

In Camping Municipal Grimaud, I did not have the convenience of being near the wash house, but did enjoy the fresh scent of mint growing nearby. This was far better than the stale odor of a damp sleeping bag. Lavender also grows naturally alongside the road as well as in the fields, imparting a pleasant scent to the air. Côte d'Azur in the direction of Monaco was in full view.

The waiter gave me good advice. The Alps, the cork trees, and small villages of Collobrières and Grimaud added to my memories. Unfortunately, I missed a wine festival in Collobrières, when the town fountain flows with wine instead of water. At least I had the wind at my back, gentle roads to travel, and a memory of the Alps to sustain me. Blue sky, the azure blue water of the Mediterranean, and a continuous shoreline were mine to enjoy. On the hills to my left, prosperous homes and hotels take advantage of their remarkable location, with steep and winding roads accessing their front entrances. Wind surfers, pleasure boats, palm, and date trees followed the undulating road within visual grasp of this "easy rider."

The pedestrian has the right-of-way! Automobiles stop when a pedestrian enters the crosswalk, a courtesy often given to those on bicycles. Even pedestrians are respectful of cyclists, giving them the right of way. They understand that a fully loaded bicycle is difficult to stop. I learned by experience that when a motorist has the right of way he takes it with a vengeance, stopping for no one. He is law-abiding but very aggressive when it is his turn in this multi-mix coexistence of man and machine.

117

The townspeople of Fréjus were almost nonexistent. Where were the people? In a short time I was east of the center near the old city with its cathedral, the 5th, 6th, and 7th century Groupe Episcopal de Fréjus, and coliseum known as the Arènes. The beach within walking distance of Fréjus was the reason for the absence of the population. In the cathedral, the Roman sculpture L'Hermes de Fréjus carved of stone has two faces looking in opposite directions. At the Arènes people were waiting in line to attend the *corrida*, or bullfight. The bull is not killed in the French corrida as it is in Mexico and Spain. Quiet enthusiasm appeared to be the mood of the people as they were entertained with Spanish music.

It was now suppertime. I decided on a picnic alongside the road facing the Mediterranean. By now the hills were beginning to return, requiring constant shifting as I looked for a campground or a place to sleep under the stars.

On a high bluff overlooking the city of Cannes and its beach, I met three young people camping with their VW camper-van: Thom, Eric, and Laititia. They agreed to allow me to lock the Globetrotter to their van in preparation for a night on the rocks overlooking the beach. My only problem was a need for personal hygiene.

"I'll be back after I find a place to brush my teeth. Please save the broth until my return." I then headed toward Cannes and a nearby restaurant where I asked permission to use their facilities. In my usual fashion I made a purchase and a request at the same time. If the request was refused I would then cancel the purchase. My Cannes Coke cost in excess of three dollars but the facilities were more than worth the inflated price. It was now time to return to my friends and their VW.

At Eastern Mountain Sports in Boston I bought a portable shower consisting of a plastic bag and an adjustable shower head. The clear plastic bag filled with water could be placed in the sun, providing the user a warm shower. This was the perfect container to transport water to my outdoor bedroom. A brazed-on attachment on the front fork was the ideal "hook" to carry the container. So it seemed.

This plan worked well until we approached a bend in the road heading in a counter-clockwise direction. The bike leaned to the left, a very natural maneuver for this sort of turn. At that moment my water container also leaned to the left, entering the spokes. The Globetrotter and I were immediately on the surface of the road in a pool of water, as the plastic bag became destroyed between the wheel and the fender.

It was my good fortune that there was no traffic, nor was I injured. I was also fortunate in having this accident at the exact location where a group of Italians was caravan-camping. In an instant they helped me bring the tandem to a place of safety. We then evaluated the damage. The front fender was distorted beyond repair and the portable shower but a memory. There was no other damage to the bike or its passenger.

One of the campers produced a toolbox with assorted wrenches, another held the Globetrotter as we removed the damaged fender. I was then able to proceed to the VW camper where Thom, Eric, and Laititia were waiting for me with a cup of hot bullion. Needless to day, I tried to express my gratitude, speaking both in French and English as the campers replied in Italian. Soon after my return I was sleeping soundly beneath the stars as the gentle tide bathed the beach below. A full moon illuminated my natural bedroom.

Cannes, a large city, is built on the side of the mountain and extends the full length of the beach. Similar to Fréjus, the entire population of Cannes relaxes on the beach. The office of tourism gave me directions to the Castres Museum perched on the top of a hill along with the Cathedral of Esperance. Below I saw the docks of Cannes and a glorious view where pleasure boats fill the harbor.

As a precaution against theft, I carried my handlebar bag with me. The Globetrotter was securely locked, but I did not want to leave the bag that held my tools, camera, and miscellaneous equipment out of sight. I planned to check the bag within the museum so I wouldn't have to carry it. It was at that time I met the Grants, an English couple. The Grants had visited the US but not Boston. I asked if I could take their photograph. I placed the bag on the ground where it remained, forgotten by me but not unseen by others. The Grants and I entered the museum at 3 PM, the official opening time. Sometime later, I remembered my handlebar bag. Was it gone forever? How could I have been so careless?

A native of Cannes saw the bag, picked it up, and went through its contents looking for identification. Finding none, he was in the process of turning it over to the police when I arrived on the scene. My relief was overwhelming when I learned it was in concerned hands. Thanking my benefactor, I returned to the museum where it remained safe behind the counter. Do things run in threes? In St. Tropez I lost my cycling gloves. In Cannes my portable shower self-destructed in the front wheel of my bike. Now at the Castres Museum, I almost lost some of my most valuable equipment. Was I becoming careless? Do things run in fours? Has senility set in?

Camping Terry, the only campground in the vicinity, was listed as a two-star facility. I wonder what the difference might be between a no-star campground and Terry. The only redeeming feature is that it was there. Located on a main highway, the road noise was unbearable, as were the sanitary facilities. The absence of any vegetation created a dusty situation, adding additional discomfort for the campers. Since I had no choice other than a hotel, I tried to make the best of it. Fortunately, the friendship of two Spanish couples made the poor conditions more bearable.

Nice, surrounded by the foothills of the Alps-Maritimes, is magnificently situated some 30 km from the Italian border. The beaches are not sandy as seen in St. Tropez and Cannes, but have a rocky texture. Guiseppi Garibaldi, the hero of Italian independence, was a native of Nice. The painters Dufy and Matisse are buried here. Promenade des Anglais, a wide avenue, follows the coast the width of this great city. Many elegant and luxurious buildings are found along the Promenade.

My fifteen rolls of Kodak film purchased in Cambridge were now exposed and ready for processing. Unfortunately, Kodak film manufactured in the US can only be processed there or in Switzerland. I had no choice but to mail them home with the hope they would not be lost or affected by low-level x-radiation by customs officials. My camera was new, with no way of knowing if the photography was up to standard. With fingers crossed I switched to Fuji film, a highly recommended brand that is cheaper than Kodak. Fuji film can be processed locally throughout Europe and the Middle East.

It became obvious that I did not want to leave France and now I had an excellent excuse to stay a few days longer. The Picasso Museum in Cannes Mer, with its excellent campground as well as the Renoir home and museum, were on my "must see" list after touring Nice. They were close enough to be reachable by bicycle but far enough from Terry to preclude a round-trip. In addition, I did not want my last campground in France to be a disappointment, especially since most were superb.

On a plateau below Mont Gros are extensive remains of the Roman town of Cemenelum, with the remains of the baths and an amphitheater that seated over 5,000 people. This climb was well worth the effort, especially as the Marc Chagall museum is located at a slightly lower level. The baths consisted of a hot, warm, and cold bath, with an adjoining swimming pool. A Roman toilet with running water and a seat carved of stone authenticates the Romans' creativity. The baths' attendant, George Gonard, is a composer and friend of John Williams, former conductor of the Boston Pops Orchestra. George visited the United States and stayed at the Boston YMCA while in New England. He gave me a personal tour of the baths.

My luncheon companion, Peter Robertson from Auckland, New Zealand, is a forest ranger and computer programmer. We met at the Roman baths and spent considerable time together. Vermont, the Kryptonite bicycle lock, and the United States are familiar to Peter. In Barcelona he visited the Olympic opening ceremony and in 1996 Peter plans to attend the Games in Atlanta. We exchanged addresses. He headed for the Archæological Museum and I for the Chagall Museum a few minutes pedaling away.

The blue-carpeted Chagall auditorium accentuates the artist's beautiful stained glass windows that expose daylight through an entire wall of glass, creating a feeling of "life." On the small stage at the front of the auditorium stands a clavichord painted by the artist in his characteristic Russian peasant art. Non-flash photographs are permitted. The museum and auditorium prepared me for the world-famous stained glass windows in the synagogue of the Hadassah Medical Center in Jerusalem. Prior to leaving Nice, I visited the Raoul Dufy exhibition at the Musée Massena located on Promenade Anglais, in addition to the Archæological Museum where photographs and Roman artifacts explain the significance to Cemeneleum. Roman locks and keys made of iron are totally fascinating.

At the beach on Promenade Anglais, I placed a credit card call to the Girodets at a public phone located at the entrance to a bath house. Inadvertently I may have put the small address book on a shelf above the telephone when I reached for my credit card. In spite of repeated visits to the bath house, hopeful that the book would be turned in to the attendant, I finally gave up the search.

An International Festival of Art in the Grimaldi Castle was located in the town of Cagnes. Grimaldi Castle was perhaps my most impressive piece of medieval architecture up to that time. Following a winding cobblestone street, I found the castle at the top of a mountain. On the first floor of the structure is a huge olive tree that has grown beyond the second floor level, seeking light from a huge skylight above. Thirty-three countries, including the United States, were represented at the Festival.

Each visitor to the exhibition was asked to submit a first, second, and third choice; the winner to be announced at a later date. My first choice artist comes from South Korea. Her painting focused on a tree in the foreground with the sun highlighting different areas of the bark. The trees of the forest in the background are "misty" as if the camera is out of focus. In spite of the fact that I did not expect to learn if my selected artist won, it was fun voting.

I almost left the area without a unique experience: the Renoir Home and Museum. Auguste Renoir spent his last days in Cagnes where he attempted sculpture for the first time. Three pieces were done by the suffering artist, the others done by his assistants under his direction. Renoir endured debilitating arthritis toward the end of his life, working from a wheelchair.

The Renoir studio (atelier) was exciting to see. It gave me the feeling of *hallowed ground* situated away from his home on a beautifully landscaped estate. I felt privileged to have this experience.

In the old city of Antibes near Cagnes, I found another Pablo Picasso Museum in addition to the one in Barcelona. This museum is located in a medieval chateau with its courtyard and tower overlooking the Mediterranean. Sculptures of other artists complement the gardens and walks. The difference between the Barcelona museum and that in Antibes is the abundance of ceramics and pottery at Antibes. I found cubism in pottery easier to appreciate than cubism on canvas. A unique feature in this museum is what I term "Braille in art." The title as well as the outline of each painting is in Braille. I feel confident that other museums have similar access for the blind, but this was my first introduction.

Photographs of Picasso as well as Renoir in their working environment give authenticity to these visits. The piercing eyes of Picasso as a young man as well as the aged, bald artist that we know so well demonstrates the intensity of this individual. In no way am I suggesting that I understand either one.

Lost again! Using my compass as well as my eyes, I headed for Grenoble, selecting the wrong road. At 10:30 we retraced our steps to Terry Camping and the correct route. This gave me an opportunity to have coffee with my Spanish friends at their campsite. The routing problem concerns a toll road to Monaco restricted to motorized vehicles.

Promenade Anglais follows the coast the full distance to Monte Carlo. Words can hardly describe the grandeur of the scenery: the Alps originating at the water's edge, the road carved out of solid rock, the ocean liners, the pleasure boats, the hills, curves, downgrades, small ports with their fleets of pleasure boats, the cliffs, the barren rocks, the flowering trees, and the sun—they were mine to enjoy to the fullest.

Baedeker's France recommends a visit to the medieval town of Eze situated on the very top of a mountain, an impossibility for me and the Globetrotter utilizing human power alone. A shopkeeper directed me to a bus connecting the top of the mountain with the main road. He was agreeable to watching my equipment during this excursion to the summit. This bus serves the entire community relative to the mountain and its inhabitants.

A formal wedding was in progress at the cathedral at the summit. The bride and guests willingly climbed the cobblestone steps to the church in spite of their formal attire. The young women in the bridal procession were very chic with sun-burned skin and white mini-skirts. The men wore tux and tails. I spent a worthwhile hour and a half in *le village* before returning to the main road.

Goal number four was within sight: Monaco, the home of the Monte Carlo auto races, the gambling casinos, and the residence of Princess Grace, formerly the American movie actress Grace Kelly.

Chapter 7
MONACO

The very beautiful movie actress from Philadelphia, Grace Kelly, is memorialized at the highest elevation on Princess Grace Boulevard. I could see the Mediterranean through the trees beyond the monument. I'm certain those of my age would have the same sensitive feelings I had when I read this memorial to Princess Grace. I felt especially fortunate being the only person there at the time. It was almost like being with one's own family.

Entry into Monaco was without incident. There were no customs, border gate, or police. A small sign indicated that I had arrived in this principality closely connected to France. Both the language and coinage are French. To my disappointment, there are no campgrounds within its borders. Cap Martin to the east provides the necessary amenities: a campground, restaurant, and stores where food can be purchased. Unfortunately, we arrived at the exact time the stores were closing. This meant I could eat at the campground restaurant or seek my meal elsewhere. Fate again played its hand as I began walking in the direction of a sign leading me to a Chinese restaurant.

For unknown reasons, the restaurant did not materialize. I then began to walk down a steep grade toward the beach, hoping to find my supper near the water. Again I was disappointed. This area is strictly residential. It was nearing sunset when I decided to challenge the mountain on foot, intending to return to the campground and restaurant.

Approaching the summit, I noticed a beautiful young woman looking out toward the Mediterranean. Exquisitely attired in silk, she appeared to be alone. I felt I had two choices: I could walk past this vision of loveliness or try to engage her in conversation. "Do you live here?" I asked in French. In perfect English she replied, "No, my parents have a vacation apartment across the road. Our home is in Torino, Italy." Alessandra locked herself out of her apartment and was waiting for her parents' return. Being gallant, I of course could not leave her alone until her parents arrived. We quickly became good friends. She gave me her name, address, and phone number in Torino. "If you have any problems while in Italy, be certain to call. Of course if you got from Paris to Cap Martin without incident you must be very self-reliant." I almost wished I would have a problem so I could call for assistance. The signaling of the apartment lights meant I must say goodnight to my new friend. I must admit I have not forgotten Alessandra Sartorio from Torino. Why did I not think to invite her on my tour of Monte Carlo the next day? Perhaps I thought it would be boring for her. Perhaps I did not think!

The return ride to Monte Carlo was mostly uphill; the Exotic Gardens and Anthropologic Museum were my first stop. Tropical gardens of huge and exotic cactus as well as flowers follow the stone walls as they traverse up and down the mountainside. Spectacular views of the Mediterranean seen through the cactus fully two stories high tempt the photographer in every spectator with a camera. The paths lead into underground caves that descend into the bowels of the earth where stalactites and stalagmites have been produced over eons of time. This grotto is known as The Observatory Caves.

The Museum of Prehistoric Anthropology, a visit to the Royal Palace and Museum, and the Aquarium (largest in the world) were well worth the price of admission. Changing of the guard and the casino are on every tourist's agenda. One casino will not admit visitors unless they are properly attired. The other let me in in walking shorts with the insistence that I check my cap and bag. I put aside a small amount of money, hoping to increase it at the roulette wheel. At St. Martin in the Caribbean I walked away with my winnings and hoped to do likewise here. An emotional problem presented itself: all the games are operated electronically rather than by humans. My incentive to gamble vanished immediately. In Alexandria, Egypt, some months later, the desire returned.

A visit to the Cathedral and site of the enterment of Princess Grace is another tourist "must" as well as The Museum of Napoléonic Souvenirs and the Collection of the Palace Historic Archives. *Souvenirs* in French refers to memories and mementos. An amazing collection of Napoléonic memorabilia such as weapons, art, documents, medals, photographs, and military attire are on display. Once again I saw Napoleon in his Roman toga accepting the crown in the presence of the clergy. At Napoleon's request, a death mask was made of his face and cast in bronze.

In the Aquarium, fish have the same problem as humans annoyed by flies. Small "pilot" fish incessantly follow the larger fish that are constantly trying to "shake" them but with little success. One species of fish carries the fertilized eggs in her mouth until they are hatched. Upon birth, the young fry leave the safe haven of the mother's mouth but return to her oral cavity if frightened. They are never swallowed.

I made an effort to call my friend Alessandra but the number she gave me was her Torino number. Breakfast for two at the campground restaurant before my departure for Italy would have been a fine idea. My only other alternative was to stop by her home in the morning with the hope of seeing her to say goodbye.

My call to the Girodets finally went through. I talked with both Paul and Margo. The news: the dollar has fallen again. Six hundred thousand people have been evacuated from Miami due to hurricane warnings. New England is suffering from an excess of rain. The rental for a boat slip in St. Tropez is $1,000 per day. In Monaco the cost is $1 million per year. Also, "Ralph, get a haircut." It was nice to know that someone cared. Tomorrow I will be in Italy.

My bill was paid and the Globetrotter fully loaded. I was at the side of the road. Again, I had two choices: number one, proceed in the direction of Genoa, number two, visit Alessandra. I chose number two.

I fully expected Mrs. Sartorio to answer the door and to question the propriety of someone my age visiting her daughter, twenty-six. Fortunately, Mrs. Sartorio and her husband were back in Torino, leaving Alessandra to care for herself. We drank coffee, took pictures with my self-timer camera, and visited in the beautiful gardens overlooking the sea. This particular view overlooking the city of Menton is a favorite of Michelin in the Michelin Guide. Finally it was time to leave. I reluctantly waved goodbye and headed toward Genoa with directions from Alessandra. She advised the coastal road instead of inland as my map suggested. If I were forty years younger! Oh well, at least I can dream.

The Italian customs office supplied me with the tourist information I needed: a map of Italy, a folder on Genoa, and a special edition concerning the 500th anniversary of Columbus. When I asked if they had any information on Italian art they handed me <u>Art in Italy</u>, a wonderful guide with color plates as well as excellent narratives. This guide and my art history book proved invaluable as we headed for Genoa.

Chapter 8
ITALY

The Italian Riviera, a continuation of the French Côte d'Azur, gave a different impression the moment we crossed the border. Traffic intensified and the bicycle became a nuisance to the motorist rather than being part of the French *mélange*. The countryside, though not dirty, was lesd pristine than in France. Rocky beaches beginning in Nice continued on toward Genoa, Italy. Needless to say, the blue Mediterranean and the Alps are equally beautiful in both countries. My first campground was an indication that prices are high in Italy.

This campground is located on the beach beneath the main train tracks leading from Nice to Genoa. Conversation comes to a halt as the trains create a thunderous noise. The sound of the surf, a much more pleasant sound, then takes over. My single-tent site cost $16. Hot water for showering was an extra charge.

Until this time, I planned to visit Greece and Turkey on the way to Israel, where hopefully I would obtain a volunteer job lasting several months. This would put me in Israel about the month of January, a cold and rainy time of year in that country. These plans were altered later, taking me to Malta, Egypt, and Jordan before entering Israel along the Red Sea. The Greek Islands, Greece, and Turkey were then ready for exploration at the ideal time of year, summer and early fall. Genoa, my short-range goal, was now within a day's ride.

During the night, the trains, if there were any, did not hamper my drugged, drugless sleep. By and large, bicyclists sleep soundly after a day's ride. A camper directed me to an alternate route to the main road, sparing me an arduous climb.

Savona, a rather large industrial city, serves the marine and auto industry. Fiat is manufactered here. Moored in an area reserved for pleasure craft and docked for repairs was the most modern, sleek vessel I've ever seen. Even though the work area was closed to the public, the workmen permitted me entrance to photograph this incredible vessel. To whom does it belong? I longed for the ability to speak Italian. The flag at the stern identified it as an Italian vessel.

At a rest stop, I met the son of the owner of one of the many small hotels that follow the shoreline. Michael, a surfer, not a biker, would like to turn professional. According to him, surfing is not a major sport in Italy, with limited economic possibilities. He also talked about the discontent of the Italian youth because of the lack of opportunities, predicting some sort of revolt not too unlike the present conditions in Yugoslavia.

At first the roads were very busy and of rough texture, followed by a limited-access highway with the usual signs: no farm machinery and no bicycles! This was definitely not my choice of road, but I had little choice to do otherwise. Fortunately, the police were not on the highway at the same time as I. Such was not the case a few years ago while tandeming with a friend in Hungary.

We missed our sign on a secondary road on the way to the small town of Tatabanya. The wind was at our backs and to again quote my cycling buddy, John, "We never turn back." The limited-access signing did not indicate that bicycles were unwelcome. It merely showed the picture of a single type of vehicle, the passenger car. Within a few kilometers of Tatabanya, the blue lights going in the opposite direction stopped. The occupant, a man in street clothes, boldly walked across the divided highway. Traffic stopped in both directions. He waslked up to us with his palm extended. "Two hundred *forents*," said this man obviously representing the legal system of Hungary. I engaged him in conversation.

134

"We do not understand the language. We are Americans....." and so on. Without hesitation the officer said, "One hundred *forents*." This was good news! Were we going to be able to talk him down to zero? He finally got tired of listening to me and my excuses. "Passports!" he demanded. We produced the 100 forents. I then asked him what we should do now since we were no longer permitted to pedal. With his fingers and in sign language he indicated that we could walk or it would cost another 100 forents. "You are not in America, you are in *Hongery!*" We walked.

Once we entered Genoa, signs indicated the direction to the home of Columbus, but as time passed the signs began to disappear. At least I was able to find the Columbus exhibit at the Palazzo Ducale the following day. This Palace, a huge structure, is indeed fabulous, with high ceilings that have been restored to their original grandeur. The frescos painted on the ceiling must have required an entire cadre of artists, all working on their backs. Original clothing, tapestries, charts, and hand-written notes in the journals of the day relating to Columbus' first two voyages were on display. Hand-painted globes referred to the portions of the known world that were documented through exploration. Africa, England, Ireland, Scotland, and Europe were well known by 1492. Is it little wonder that a South American country is named Colombia, and Hispanola, now the Dominican Republic, for Spain? The 500th year after the discovery of America was the cause for this celebration.

In the old city of Genoa, where the buildings are tall and the streets narrow, the sun rarely reaches street level. This creates a coolness that is so necessary in these warm climates. It was an ideal place to enjoy a lunch of barbecued chicken and fruit. It was also an ideal place to nap! The important thing for me in this country where I don't know the language is to avoid getting lost.

The narrow streets and bustling traffic of Old Genoa is a moped-motorcycle zoo that barely avoids collisions with pedestrians. I have never seen so many watches for sale in one location and so few customers. Even the barber was patiently idle, reading his newspaper. Should I get that haircut that Margo Girodet recommended? "Ralph, if you hope to be attractive to women, you must get your hair cut."

I visited Italy for the first time in the early seventies. It was a dental school junket that landed in Pisa and then bussed to Florence where we spent the night. On the way to a drug store in Florence I walked past a barber shop. That barber was also reading his newspaper due to a lack of customers. "I think I'll get a haircut." The language barrier prevented the barber and me from conversing. When finished, I paid him in lira, a new form of coinage to me, plus a tip of ten lira. This was the denomination of a small coin in my pocket. The barber smiled and graciously thanked me as I headed for a drug store. At the drug store I learned the value of the Italian monetary system. To my chagrin, I had given the barber a tip of one-tenth of one cent. Returning to my hotel to dress for supper, we again passed the same barber shop. This time he was properly rewarded for his services. We both laughed.

The wind was at my back. In spite of a gradual increase in elevation, the wind eased the climb. The Italian Alps are ever-present in the direction of Milan. Soon I met my greatest challenge with the Globetrotter, requiring that I walk the bike. At one point the grade was so severe that I had difficulty keeping my feet on the pavement and the "Volvo" erect. Intensity of the summer sun at a higher altitude made the going even more difficult. The summit of this mountain, Passo Dei Giovi, was a welcome relief, followed by the city of Tortona about one-third of the distance to Milan. A huge basilica with an all-gold Madonna and Child at the top of the dome dominates the town. I prepared my supper in the courtyard of the basilica, where the fountain is functional.

At the entrance to the toll road to Milan I asked permission to use the facilities but was refused. Had I gained permission, a grassy spot nearby would have been an excellent location to set up camp. By this time it was quite dark, requiring lights on the bike and making it hard to find a campsite. Fortunately, I was able to use the facilities of a restaurant before seeking what is termed "free camping."

Thinking I was undetected, I began erecting my tent in the dark on a grassy area with an attached garden belonging to an apartment complex. The watchman informed me that I was camping on private property. Without undue persuasion on my part, he willingly permitted my stay for one night. That was all I needed. In the early morning, tomatoes from the garden and apples picked from a nearby tree were part of my breakfast. Except for clothes washing and a shower, I felt prepared for the day with a late afternoon arrival in Milan. This was a Saturday, and I had no plans until Monday morning: my next major goal of the trip, goal number four, a visit to the Cinelli Bicycle Works.

In 1970, we adjourned the winter Board of Directors meeting of L.A.W. and then visited the International Bicycle Show in New York. It was there that I saw what I wanted so badly: a Cinelli bicycle ordered directly from Italy. Inasmuch as I was going to Italy in a few months, I decided to order the hand-crafted Super Corsa with the request that they deliver it in Italy, preferably Rome. The measurement process was routine. This was going to be my first custom bike. I was excited.

The scene now shifts to a hotel room in Rome. I am talking to Mrs. Cinelli in Milan by telephone asking her to put my new purchase on the night train to Rome. Mrs. Cinelli said to me in excellent English, "We want to put you in the saddle." If Mrs. Cinelli is that concerned about my satisfaction, the least I can do is go to Milan. What I did not know was that her husband suspected that I was measured improperly by their New Jersey representative. The bike frame as ordered was awaiting my arrival, but with their experience they did not want to take the risk that the frame would be too small for me.

While my tour group visited Rome, I took the night train to Milan. A taxi drove me to the Cinelli Works. Two days later on my test ride toward Venice I realized it was time to return to Rome. If I did not rejoin my tour group, I'd be trying to find them enroute to Naples, a virtual impossibility.

The Cinelli family could not have been nicer, especially André, their son, who speaks English. He was assigned to me as an interpreter. André showed me the custom frame his family built for me, explaining that I was measured improperly: the frame was too small. He suggested an alternative that would please his father, a past Tour de France competitor as well as a perfectionist frame builder. "If you will accept a standard Cinelli silver grey frame we will 'build' a bicycle for you while you're waiting," said André. "In the meantime, you can look at our complete line of clothing and accessories." We came to an immediate agreement.

In addition to an Italian racing outfit in bright red and racing shoes with cleats, I purchased two Cinelli racing caps. One was reserved for immediate use and the other I kept as a memento. Once back in Boston, I put the insignia of the Charles River Wheelmen on the cap with a rubber stamp and put it away for safekeeping. It was this cap that I stowed in my saddlebag with plans to give it back to the Cinelli family, goal number four of 1992. I did not know that the Cinelli Works and its name were sold to non-family members. André is now in a different location with a bicycle business of his own. Mr. and Mrs. Cinelli, both wonderfully hospitable people, are deceased.

Mrs. Cinelli invited me to their home for the noontime meal at the conclusion of their work on my behalf. The bike, now completed, was ready for a test ride around the circular drive reserved for that purpose. Stopping periodically, I would return the bike to Mr. Cinelli who made minor adjustments to the saddle and stem height. The last word in world-class bicycles was now completed. I leaned my newest toy against a tree, awaiting my return from the Cinelli home where they convinced me to head for Verona and perhaps Venice, a two-day test ride, before returning to Rome and my tour group. Mr. Cinelli noticed that the tree left a dark smudge on the white handlebar tape when I leaned the bicycle against it. He returned to his office, selected a pencil with a rubber eraser, and removed the imperfection. His little gem was now ready for delivery. "This bicycle will last you a lifetime," said Mr. Cinelli in Italian.

The Italians have their largest meal at noontime, with a siesta thereafter. Nothing was spared as I shared the pasta and wine with the family. During the entire time Mr. Cinelli and I talked bicycles, with André solving the language barrier. Being in their lovely apartment and sharing a small piece of their lives was one of my life's great experiences. I could hardly wait to return home and my bike club to tell some of these stories.

Mrs. Cinelli and André drove me to a sporting goods store to purchase a backpack in preparation for departure. We then returned to the factory and my new purchases. Dressed in my bright warm-up suit, I thanked them for their hospitality and personal attention and followed a hand-drawn map leading me out of this large city. Were they especially nice to me because I was national president of the League of American Wheelmen or are they this cordial to all visiting bicyclists? I preferred to think the latter.

My first objective now that I was back in Milan, this time on a bicycle instead of in a taxi, was to find the Cinelli Works. A few questions and the telephone book enabled me to locate the factory without difficulty. I planned to camp as close as possible so that Monday morning the new owners would have an unexpected visitor carrying a 1970 Cinelli *capella* as a gift for them. It was now time to locate my campsite and a place to shower and shave.

I selected a secluded spot behind a small municipal shed in the park as a safe place to erect my tent after dark. Later I learned that the parks in Milan are not considered safe, but that is another story. The nearest swimming pool and bath house provided the necessary facilities for washing myself as well as my clothes. To my displeasure, I waited over an hour for the next scheduled pool opening. Everything is much more regulated in Italy than in America, including a bathing cap requirement. The cost of two hours of pool time is seven American dollars. At least I was now clean and refreshed.

A rainstorm and a cold spell added to my evening's discomfort. I had not yet erected my tent and was hungry. This is one of the few times that I felt more like a vagrant than a tourist. A hotel would probably have been a better choice but I was determined to use the tent. The rain continued well into the evening before I could leave the shelter of a mall-type building. Fortunately, I found some gourmet Italian cuisine nearby as well as friendly management. We visited until their closing time. I still ask myself why I didn't ask them for a night's shelter at their home.

The following morning, I was still in the itinerant mode, ready for breakfast and a visit to the *Duomo*, a magnificent Gothic cathedral in the center of the city. The street people provided me with the best method to stay warm and have my breakfast awaiting the cathedral opening. Steel grating over the subway supplies the necessary warmth. Fortunately, my small temperamental portable stove was in a cooperative mood.

Hot Nescafé was satisfying and warming. By example I learned that the steel grating and warmth from the subway can serve as an excellent clothes and towel dryer.

Biking in the park this Sunday morning was more interesting than the buildings, except for the cathedral. Now that the sun was out, the walkers, bikers, and children were enjoying nature's bounty. I joined them and Vincent Riccardi. Vincent was enjoying a rest stop at the time we met. He and I spent the afternoon biking, eating, and socializing. Vincent asked me where I planned to sleep that night. When I explained that I had a tent and expected to sleep in the park, it was he who warned me of the possible dangers of free camping in Milan. Closing one eye and leaving the other open, Vincent explained that this is the way I would have to sleep if I hoped to survive the night.

My campsite that night was a grassy spot in the park near a small stream. After dark, it appeared safe. We were located near a fountain providing fresh frigid water for early morning bathing and coffee. Joggers in the morning greeted me as they stopped for a drink, or waved as they passed by. Not only had I survived the night, but within a few minutes I'd be at the gate of the Cinelli Works.

The gate was open but the absence of people indicated that they were still on vacation. A car followed me into the parking lot, driven by Ivana Cappelletto, a freelance designer artist working for Cinelli. Ivana was my sole contact but a pleasant one. We hung the cap on a wall in a room filled with bike frames of varying sizes and configurations. Hopefully it is still fulfilling its destiny. I learned that the anticipation of delivering the bike cap was more important than the actual event.

Before leaving on the road to Bergamo, Brescia, Verona, and Venice, I decided to sample a portion of Milan that might be of interest to the average tourist. The Archæologic Museum was my choice, and a good one. A superb collection

2 WHEELS, 2 YEARS, AND 3 CONTINENTS

of Dutch paintings reminded me of a previous trip on the Globetrotter to Belgium and Holland, especially the van Gogh Museum and the Anne Frank House in Amsterdam. Pleated collars, swashbuckle boots, beards, and mustaches were in style at the time of these paintings. It was the Rembrandt period. Roman and pre-Roman sculpture nearby identify the Roman emperors by name as well as the dates they were in power. Two huge identical tapestries also hung in the gallery.

The road to Bergamo again reminded me of my first visit with the Cinelli family. Dressed in my bright red warmup suit and backpack, I headed for Venice. The pack carried my clothing worn on the night train from Rome as well as a few toilet articles. In addition, I was carrying an assortment of Cinelli clothing and two bicycle caps purchased at the Cinelli boutique. My most prized possession, the ten-speed Cinelli racing bike with its sew-up tires, literally flew down the road.

"Was this bicycle so special that I hardly had to pedal to make it fly, or was I going downhill? Should I take up racing once I return home? Was I dreaming, only to awaken to the fact that I was back on my Dawes Double Blue in Lexington, Massachusetts, instead of following the Italian Alps into Chianti country on the way to Venice?" A traffic light solved my problem. I was biking with the wind at my back, it was that simple.

Darkness dampened my spirit, especially since I had no lights for illumination or safety. I felt totally insecure with the headlights of overtaking vehicles showing me the way. As a safety measure, I faced the oncoming traffic, clearly a violation of the law. Each time an oncoming car came into sight I pulled off the road, waiting for another period of safety. In this way I knew that at the very least I was safe. The lights of a small town were my indication to leave the highway and seek shelter. This town is named Bergamo.

Seeking a hotel, I walked about this medieval-appearing town with no success. Some young boys tried to help me when I asked for the location of a hotel. They took me from place to place, particularly restaurants, where I tried to communicate with the management. "Dormi" I would say, putting my hands against my tilted head indicating sleep and at the same time holding up my wallet with the words "dollars," "lira." In all cases this effort was fruitless. The boys finally left me to my own creativity. It was a cool night in April and one I was not prepared to spend outdoors unless as a very last resort.

My next attempt was the local rectory. "Surely the local priest will take pity on me and provide shelter, being a good Christian." Unfortunately, he was out in his *autobus*. The lady of the house made certain that I did not go beyond the threshold. I could hear dogs barking due to my presence. At that time I learned that in Italian the word for priest is *papa*. What next?

"Perhaps the church is open, I'll try there." Being locked, I next investigated the covered market. "Anything would be better than sleeping in a field." It was then that I became aware of the local citizens. I could see them looking out from their curtains yet keeping themselves concealed. "Who is this person dressed like the devil himself in our little village?" they were probably asking themselves. My fortune then began to change.

A man opened his garage in preparation for storing his small Fiat van for the night. A light was glowing inside, revealing several bicycles. "This must be the local bicycle repairman with all of those bikes in his garage." I stood in front of his car with the Cinelli Super Corsa in front of me, preventing his progress unless he decided to run me over. We became acquainted. Again I went through my "dormi" routine but without success. He knew what

I wanted but was unwilling to give in. Just then a man carrying a small doctor's bag walked down a path leading from his office. He became interested in me and my problem. Again I tried the "dormi" routine but was unsuccessful. Finally in desperation I said to the doctor in mixed languages: "Usted doctori. Moi dentista." He replied, "Ah, dentista," raising his right hand in pantomime of a dentist pulling a tooth. I then replied, "No, orthodontista." We became immediate friends and colleagues as he escorted me to his small pediatric office. We visited for a short time examining teeth that the doctor extracted, as well as my passport. He then bid me adieu, leaving me in the warmth of his office for the night. I blocked the door so I would not be locked out, seeking a supper of spaghetti and red wine. A blanket in a back room kept me warm as I spent the night sleeping on his examination table. In the morning after washing my face and writing my colleague a letter of gratitude, I again headed toward Venice. It was a beautiful morning and I was at the peak of my personal joy.

Verona with its lovely Coliseum and flower gardens became the end of my journey. Time did not permit further adventure in the direction of Venice, at least not at this time. I boarded the night train to Rome by way of Bologna, arriving in Rome at two o'clock in the morning.

"If I am going to be on the same road leading to Bergamo, wouldn't it be a great idea to stop in to see the doctor who spared me from sleeeping outdoors on a cold April evening in 1970? Perhaps I can take him to lunch as a gesture of reciprocation." Unlike that first day on my Cinelli Super Corsa, the Globetrotter did not "fly" quite so fast.

To my dismay, Bergamo is a city of moderate size with a train station, hotels, and a busy downtown area. Where was I in 1970 when Bergamo appeared to be a village centered around a church, convent, and central market?

Unfortunately, I was unable to locate my benefactor, the pediatrician. People speaking English, as well as the police, tried to be of assistance. "You must give us more information if we are to help you." I headed east toward Brescia and Verona with my cherished memories of a previous visit to Bergamo, Italy.

The road was narrow and the wind stronger than usual. The draft of a truck traveling in the opposite direction flipped my cap into the middle of the road. I stopped. Under ordinary circumstances the passing traffic would have ground road dirt into the cap prior to its recovery. In this instance, every passing vehicle blew the cap closer to the Globetrotter until it was laying at my feet begging to be picked up. Holding the tandem with one hand, I bent down, picked up the cap, and continued on my way.

Iseo, a small town with a well-equipped campground, is located at the foot of the Alps. Green and forested with excellent facilities and a private pool, the cost was only 8,000 lira per night. My first thoughts were to spend an extra day here relaxing in the beauty of the region and writing letters or rereading my book Zen and the Art of Motorcycle Maintenance. The weather, especially the wind, changed my mind. At 6:30 in the morning the wind was of such intensity that I feared my tent would collapse. I retreated to the wash house with the tent, bike, and clothes that for some miraculous reason did not blow away. As long as I was now under cover with all my gear, I decided to pack up and continue the journey. Waiting for the wind to abate, I decided to write to my friend and primary physician Robert Mellors back in the US, telling him that to date I have pedalled over the Alps on three separate occasions and that my knees have not felt this good in years.

The hurricane force of the wind subsided and the sun returned with barely a cloud in the sky. This was a day of perfection to cycle or just to be alive. I felt exhilarated. Being in no hurry, I stopped to cut a bunch of white grapes with my new

Swiss Army knife previously purchased in Genoa. Italian and Sicilian farmers have no objections so long as the amount of fruit taken is for personal consumption. I later learned in Israel after picking oranges, grapefruit, fresh peppers, and pomegranates that it is a felony to pick a single piece of fruit. These grapes are of the same quality as those we purchase in the finest fruit market. At a nearby roadside stand I bought 1,000 lira worth of calamari to be eaten standing up. The calamari lady threw in two fried fish with their heads and tails attached. Delicious!

The foothills of the Alps soon disappeared and I was on a divided highway leading to Brescia. On my previous trip I bypassed this city of clean buildings and friendly people. Lago Di Garda, a magnificent freshwater lake at the base of the mountains, was my next scenic stop, a short distance from Brescia in the direction of Verona. Here the usual placid water was quite turbulent. The storm of the previous night affected Lago Di Garda. "This will surely be one of my better photos."

Usually my arrival at a campground is late in the afternoon or early evening. Verona was the exception. A German couple, Holger Gayer and Barbara Wein, became my newest campground friends. They were using a Whisperlite camp stove almost identical to mine and with the same problems. Fortunately, mine was operating efficiently for a change while theirs generated a yellow carbon flame producing little heat and a blackened pot. We shared my stove. At a later date I thought I had solved the stove problem and was just about ready to write to Holger and Barbara with the news so they could share my good fortune. Unfortunately, it was a false alarm. Another German couple was also exceptionally friendly. Labine and Ludger had been in the United States twice, but not in New England. They were traveling with a caravan and their bicycles. Instead of biking long distances, they use their vehicle and caravan. We enjoyed each other's company.

Holger and Barbara rode the bus into Verona; I biked.

146

Together we walked the town and toured the Coliseum where, as previously mentioned, theater is still being performed. It was fun being with these young people and sharing our experiences. On a previous visit, Holger attended an opera where each entrant received a cushion to sit on, and two candles. At the appropriate moment all the candles were lighted, producing a spectacular visual effect. Leaving Verona, I noticed a street named Campagnolo. "Is there a connection to the famous company Campagnolo in Vincenza, manufacturers of top quality bicycle accessories?"

The town of Vincenza enjoys a history dating to Roman times. At the beginning of the 15th century it sought Venetian protection, enjoying great prosperity at the same time. Vincenza is embellished with an amazing number of palaces. My choice was the Castlevecchio after establishing myself at a four-star campground that services people from a nearby NATO base. I would have attempted entry to the Campagnolo factory but was previously advised that visitors are not welcome.

The archæologic museum is located in Castlevecchio where Roman artifacts are in abundance. A Roman scissors resembles old-fashioned grass shears, being in one piece with spring bronze at the end opposite the tip of the blade. By squeezing on the blades they will cut and when released the scissors return to the open position. George Washington's false teeth operated on a similar principle. When George closed his jaws the two springs connecting the upper and lower denture were under tension. When our first president opened his jaws the teeth opened at the same time. Today we have sports guards of plastic that operate in a similar manner. A medieval sword of enormous proportions without a plaque to explain its origin or use is at least five feet in length. Was it used for ceremony or was the owner a huge person? Interesting, yet not unusual, are the Roman safety pins with their single helix acting as the spring to keep the pin under tension when closed. The Romans undoubtedly knew the technique of tempering metals.

The city of Padua, with a banner across the street, was my next stop and an important one. Frescos by Giotto dating to 1304 located in the Scrovengi Chapel illustrate the lives of the Virgin and Christ. They are considered Giotto's masterpieces. In a leisurely fashion I read the English explanation as others read in their native tongue. These frescos are considered one of the greatest monuments of figurative art of all time.

The Municipal Gallery is equally interesting, with rich holdings of Egyptian, Etruscan, Roman, and pre-Roman history. Venetian works as well as those of Giotto date from the 14th to the 18th centuries. An entire set of Roman tableware with dishes and bowls that nest within each other gives further evidence of the advancement of the Roman culture. One painting depicts Rome as it originally appeared in all its magnificence rather than the remnants of this great era that we usually see. The pillars that we see in our museums, of course, supported complete structures for everyday living.

Taking a break, I met a young Japanese cyclist with his loaded touring bicycle in front of the museum. Last year he toured Thailand, this trip Germany, France, and Italy with his 28x28-inch gearing in the Alps. I then returned to the religious art in the museum, making plans to cycle to Venezia (*Venice* in Italian) even if it was during darkness.

Camping Fusina is located about 15 km from Venezia at the terminus of the water taxi taking passengers into the city. I do not know why I decided to pedal instead of enjoying the convenience of the water taxi except that I always prefer to bike if possible. This time my error became obvious. It was too late to correct the mistake on my first day in Venice, a city that I looked forward to seeing since my 1970 visit to Italy.

Camping Fusina is huge, with a store, restaurant, night club, and banquet hall. Except for the cost of registration, the price of everything is outrageous. As an example, a can of spaghetti costs five dollars.

The bike ride to Venice was a total mistake, giving me the wrong impression of the city. At least four sets of railroad tracks, an expressway with an elevated ramp, and a causeway that seemed to go on forever were my obstacle course of the day. The pedestrian walk was the safest route even though the surface was a combination of cement and roofing material, diverting the front wheel without notice. At one point while traveling faster than conditions warranted, the Globetrotter went out of control, crashing into the guard rail. Fortunately, only my pride was damaged. Finally I, and a lot of other people, arrived at Piazza Roma, the stopping point for all traffic going into Venice. From there we walked due east toward Piazza St. Marco through narrow streets lined with expensive shops. Venetian glass and the jewelry in the shops were exquisite. A hand-painted mask would have been a great gift for my granddaughter Rachel but shipping was a problem the shop could not handle. They were unable to estimate the cost of mailing.

Piazza St. Marco in reality is less impressive than the paintings in the many museums I have visited. Pigeons are as plentiful as they are at the Duomo in Milan. The Basilica, under restoration at that time, was at first closed to persons wearing shorts. Finally after I explained to the attendants that others with shorts were being admitted, permission was granted. Originally St. Marco was intended for the wealthy parishioners; common people were excluded. Four wooden horses over the entrance signify wealth rather than the religious aspect of the church.

Saint Marco never lived in Venice but was selected as the patron saint of the wealthy. Beheaded in Alexandria, he remained buried there for 800 years. At a later date, Venetians successfully brought his body to Venice with a load of pork, knowing that the Arabs would not go near pork. The entire episode is represented in a beautiful mosaic to the right of the altar and toward the ceiling. St. Marco's coffin is in the center of the altar behind a golden screen.

The entire ceiling and dome of the Basilica are done in gold mosaic, a rather remarkable achievement for any period. This dome represents the heavens, leaving little doubt in the minds of the parishioners that their future lay in the glory of the hereafter. Of equal beauty is the floor in different color stones. I was gratified that my bike shorts did not prevent this visual experience.

The Grand Canal is another favorite of both painters and photographers. It is very wide and very busy with small boats, restaurants, and shops lining it. Steps going up and down would have made the Globetrotter or any other bicycle a nuisance. Older people and mothers with carriages had difficulty negotiating the many steps they were forced to climb. People arriving with their luggage travel by water taxi to their hotels. Some of the more prominent hotels provide their own small boats for that purpose. These boats tie up to the pier and discharge their passengers and luggage directly onto the pavement even though there are steps leading from the pavement to the water's surface.

At one point I decided to rinse my right hand in the water. A chocolate ice cream cone on this summer day was the reason for this maneuver. As usual, I wore my waist pack carrying my passport, money, and personal effects, in addition to the camera, over my right shoulder. As I began to descend the steps toward the water, I learned the hard way why passengers step directly from the boat to the pavement without using the steps. The moss-covered stone steps are as slippery as if they were covered with grease. Why I did not fall into the less-than-clean water of the Adriatic Sea I will never know. A young Chinese tourist watched the entire contortion in amazement. "I don't believe it" were her words.

The next day the water taxi renewed my fantasies of Venice. Included in the round-trip fare to and from Camping Fusina is a gondola ride across the Grand Canal as well as a reduced rate to the Peggy Guggenheim Collection of Modern

Art. The weather was perfect, in contrast to a rainy ride the previous evening. I was again in Piazza St. Marco with plans for the day. The Ducal Palace, Peggy Guggenheim Museum, and strolling completed my tour of Venezia.

In addition to the Golden Stairway of the Ducal Palace and its magnificence, an exhibit of the works of Hieronymus Bosch was on display. The entry was darkened so we could enjoy the slides from three projectors showing Bosch's work in totality as well as in sections. Bosch, a Dutch artist, appeals to the viewer's interest in the world of dreams. Birds, fruit, and the like are symbols or metaphors. The artist depicts life on earth as an unending repetition of the original sin. His interpretation of purgatory would have made an atheist into a believer. Salvation to the artist appears to be out of the question. We are all doomed! Finally, the Peggy Guggenheim Museum.

It was refreshing to regain the feeling of my own country. This museum was originally the home of Peggy Guggenheim. Can you imagine yourself looking out your windows at gondolas gracefully transporting passengers to their destination? A special act of the government of Venice as well as the Guggenheim Foundation established this willed entity. In addition to the unique Venetian seascape, the gardens surrounding this air-conditioned building are hidden from view by narrow winding streets. The museum exhibits works of Dekooning, Chagall, Mondrian, Paul Klee, Picasso, Wassily Kandinsky, Max Ernst, Miro, Gorky, Jackson Pollock, Dali, and others. It is truly a jewel within a unique setting. The painting by Dali brought back memories of my recent trip to Spain.

Now that I was getting ready to leave Camping Fusina and Venice, the campers began to take an interest in me. A French-speaking family in a caravan near my tent site showing no interest whatsoever were now ready to become friendly. "Oh, you speak French! Where do you come from? We live in St. Brieux in Brittany" and so forth. An English couple riding their 1968 BSA motorcycle rode the water taxi with me from

Venice to the campground. This machine is one of 26 in their collection.

My first stop, a short distance from Camping Fusina, is the town of Malcontent. Here is the history surrounding this unusual name. The wife of an important official in Venice was perpetually dissatisfied, complaining to everyone with whom she came in contact. Her husband, in desperation, banished her from Venice to this location, now bearing evidence through its name. I wonder how the town of Intercourse in Pennsylvania got its name.

Shortly thereafter I met my newest friend, Giuseppe Cucinotta from Messina, Sicily. Giuseppe, Joseph in English, was resting alongside the road in his tiny two-cycle Vespa car with its door open. He appeared equal in size to his mobilette, which is so small that it does not require a license. Vehicles that displace less than 500 cc. are exempt from taxes and licensure in Italy, and perhaps all of Europe. He and I were both on the road an equal length of time—three months. In Italian Joseph suggested that we stop at a trattoria for coffee. Limited French was our common denominator. To the casual observer we must have looked like the "Odd Couple." Joseph was overweight, with his tiny car, and I on the slim side from all my biking, rode an unusually large bicycle. Giuseppi gave me his address and an invitation to visit him and his family in Messina, Sicily. This was the first time I thought about touring the island of the Mafioso. This island is also the country of origin of the Manguso family, Dorothy's roots.

Until now I planned to ferry across the Adriatic from Italy to Greece, eventually arriving in Israel. The idea of biking the length of Italy along the Adriatic, where the coast appears level on the map and campgrounds are abundant, became an excellent plan. "Perhaps I can take a ferry to Greece from a port in Sicily and thus follow my original itinerary, adding an additional country to my experience. It will be fun as well as educational."

South of Venice is the small port of Chioggia that dates from ancient times. Chioggia reminds me, on a smaller scale, of Venice with its own grand canal, bridges, and fishing boats. Seeking less-traveled roads brought me to this town and a dead end. The narrow winding streets of Chioggia are interesting, but the cobblestones make cycling less than enjoyable. To artists with their easels it is probably idyllic.

Approximately 80 km south of Chioggia, I experienced "bicycle mania" in Ravenna, with its wonderful mosaics that adorn the interior of the ecclesiastic buildings known to be the finest in Europe. People of all ages and of both sexes in Ravenna use their bicycles instead of the automobile for transportation and shopping. Mass parking for these machines creates the appearance of utter abandonment. No less orderly are the streets and piazzas where cyclists pedal in all directions without concern for the orderly traffic patterns of the four-wheeled polluters. To be perfectly candid, I felt less safe in this melee than I do on the Italian roads and highways. When I finally parked the Globetrotter and became a pedestrian I felt even less safe. Bicycles came at me from all directions with their wobbling front wheels that give no indication as to the direction they are heading. For the first time I began to lose the concept of an all-human powered society.

During the third century, the water table in Ravenna rose so dramatically that elevation of the churches was necessitated. In one rather large church the original submerged floor can be viewed by walking down steps from the present altar to the lower level.

Three miles south of Ravenna the Basilica of St. Apollinaris in Classe, a tourist's delight, comes into view. Postcards highlight the basilica begun in 534 and consecrated in 549. My half-hour wait for the opening was spent with some very interesting people, especially Olga and her husband, Russian citizens and members of an international peace movement. Olga was the president of the organization. Their host, a very knowledgeable Italian, opened a bottle of Chianti for us to enjoy. During our conversation I mentioned to Olga that it seems that Madonnas are in overabundance in Italy, located in some of the most unusual places. "You can never have too many Madonnas," remarked Olga.

The mosaics within the basilica, a simplicity of composition and harmony of color, are full of symbolism portraying Christ the Savior and the Transfiguration. Twenty-six arches supported by marble columns are so soft and beautiful in appearance that I had the urge to touch them. The same is true of the mosaics forming the dome. This is religious art at its finest. My newest friends and I bid each other adieu as I headed south toward Ancona.

Ancona Campground became my destination for the night, arriving there twice and with an extra 23 km to my credit. My first arrival at this campground, sandwiched between a main road and a railroad, had very little appeal, especially as it was still early in the afternoon. A divided highway, a long uphill climb, and two tunnels brought me to an incredible descent into North Ancona and an intersection where I had two choices. After catching my breath I opted for the left turn where the terrain is much flatter. To my utter amazement, I was back at Ancona Campground.

Along the Adriatic, the coast resembles the blue water of the Côte d'Azur. I traveled with the wind at my back and high spirt in my soul. At the top of a long climb my knife purchased in Genoa once again came in handy as I cut a bunch of grapes for my own consumption. Toward one o'clock I decided to stop at a food shack for lunch. The owner was preparing a meal for a Belgian couple on vacation. They invited me to share their wine and I invited them to share my grapes. My sandwich was replete with salami, cheese, and mayonnaise. The Italian bread reminded me of the North End in Boston.

The town of Fano, with a population of 52,579, is a

typical old city with its large piazza, narrow streets, and stores. Merchandise in the stores is perhaps atypical for a small coastal town but not for New York's Manhattan. Somebody was obviously spending a lot of money for items displayed in the store windows. I found the Questo Teatro under restoration, where remains of frescos were interspersed with white paint. The theater itself is being completely renovated. The ceiling and balconies were freshly painted in delicate shades of brown and off-white in preparation for the forthcoming season.

Signs directing me to the museum proved fruitless. I found myself in the newer industrial portion of the city terminating along the Adriatic. Signs here indicated that Rome and Bologna are to the west. Port St. Giorgia to the south was more inviting, especially the hardware store there. My not-so-new tent was beginning to show signs of wear, especially under moist conditions. Invariably I found the bottom of my luggage and the end of the sleeping bag dampened by rain or dew. Oil cloth bought in St. Giorgia served as a ground cover. Though a bit on the heavy side, it protected against the penetration of stones as well as moisture through the tent floor. Another positive use of the ground cover is the ability to cover all my gear with little effort in the shortest possible time during a rainstorm.

Ancona was not fun! I felt I climbed every hill in town looking for the Duomo and the archæologic museum. Fortunately, I found the old port with its open-air market as well as a store selling barbecued chicken. Though it was only 10 AM, a full meal of chicken, potatoes, and an ice cream cone satisfied my need for food. From there I found the port where I spent one-half hour staring at the largest passenger ferries I've ever seen. These ships, with at least four passenger decks above and a lower deck reserved for cars, trucks, and bicycles, were destined for Greece. Three times a day a ferry will leave for the the 36-hour journey to Piraeus, where passengers travel inland to Athens. Had I not changed my plans, I could have left Italy from Ancona. Michelle, a campground friend in Port

St. Giorgia, gave me the above advice as well as discussing her experiences in Greece and Turkey.

She and her friend Steve from New Zealand left their van at the campground and then traveled to Greece and Turkey via public transportation. "If I had to make a choice," said Michelle, "I would skip Greece and go directly to Turkey. Turkey is much more interesting!" They gave me their Turkish phrase book and a map of Istanbul, with the comment that the Turkish people are extremely friendly, treating tourists like family. "Such is not the case in Greece."

Without realizing it, I had become a near-vegetarian. It was true that some of the soups had meat, but without a frying pan or cooking oil, most of my food was either prepared in the market or was non-meat products tentside. Not only was cleanup simple, but my meals were healthy. The purchase of a small frying pan and some margarine did add the variety that my taste buds sought. Margarine serves many purposes.

The use of oil to remove grease may come as a surprise, but it works! Following bicycle repairs or the changing of a tire, one's hands invariably become the color of the chain— black. Grease is not soluble in water but it is in oil or an oil-based product such as butter, cooking oil, or margarine. Once well lubricated with a petroleum product, a paper towel will remove most of the mixture, leaving the hands ready for soap and water. The final results are nothing short of miraculous.

One thousand more kilometers and I would be touring the island of Sicily. In mileage that translated into just 600 miles from the small port of Pescara, an area that was fun to visit. It's an active port with very little antiquity to visit. Admission to the nautical museum is free. Turtle shells, a whale skeleton, and huge clam shells are on exhibit along with Grecian ceramic jugs that were used to transport oil and wine. Many of these jugs brought up from the bottom of the sea are encrusted with dried barnacles. The tapered contour made them easier to store in the holds of ships than if they had flat bottoms and parallel sides. It was in Pescara that I weighed the Globetrotter for the first time.

The grocery where I bought my lunch had an industrial scale in their storeroom. Before asking permission to use the scale, I learned the word in Italian for scale, or balance. Phonetically the word is *bilanga*. "May I use your *bilanga*?" Permission was granted. To my amazement, the tandem and its gear at that moment weighed 180 pounds, or the equivalent of another person on board without the saddle and pedals.

While reading in the wash house, where there was an electric light bulb, I learned that Sicily is rich in history as well as beauty. Etruscans, Greeks, and Romans inhabited the island, contributing to the Sicilian culture.

The next day's ride was both hilly and hot with few redeeming features, especially following the sudden partial loss of my right pedal when the front section and toe clip fell to the tarmac. Fortunately, the shaft of the pedal was still attached to its crank, permitting limited pedaling. Much of the day was spent looking for a bicycle shop. During the process of looking for a town, a van passed me, stopping alongside the road near a cornfield. At least eight young men descended on the field, picking corn at a furious rate prior to the arrival of the farmer. In moments the youths were speeding downt the road to escape apprehension. Had I picked corn for myself he would not have objected, but this was, of course, a different situation.

A sign to a campground attracted my attention with the name of a nearby town, Marina Lesina, without an indication of the distance. After all of my camping experience, I was amazed at being "suckered" by this sign. Twenty kilometers later we arrived at a resort area and Albatross Camping, where one night's camping cost 20,000 lira. When I complained about the price, especially "after season," they explained that they are a four-star camping resort. They and I arrived at a compromise price of 10,000 lira, or about ten dollars, after considerable haggling. The next morning I retraced the wasted twenty kilometers heading toward Foggia. The pedal was still broken.

In the United States, a pepperoni pizza is a pizza with slices of that spicy meat called pepperoni as a topping. In Foggia the pepperoni pizza becomes a work of art, where fresh red and yellow peppers are the topping for a deep-dish pizza. The second choice is pizza topped with fresh onions and anchovies. There was little more of interest for me in Foggia than the local pizza. The duomo was unimpressive and the museum was closed until 5 PM. At least I was able to replace my broken pedal with a used one so I could again use the toe clip. Unfortunately, the threads for the replacement were different from the original French threads, creating a problem many months later when the mismatched pedal fell off on the way to Tel Aviv.

A 25-mile-an-hour wind blew me south in the direction of Bari, a major port along the Adriatic coast, where ferries travel to Greece. A major freeway became my only route and an uncomfortable one at that until an exit toward Barletta appeared. After becoming lost and then found and without supper, darkness began to approach. I was forced to make my plans for the night in an area that was totally isolated from any population centers. As always, I carry a supply of edibles, such as they are, to be eaten in case of emergency. Olive groves bordered either side of the road.

The sound of running water was my key to a successful night's sleep. I could shower then and shave in the morning. The full moon revealed the source of the water as well as a small stone shed across the road. The source of the water was overhead irrigation for the olive groves. The farmers perforate their plastic hose in such a way that streams of water irrigate where needed. The interior of the shed with a deteriorated roof was illuminated by the moon. Except for the mosquitoes, this "free camping" was perfect.

After removing my clothes, I walked across the road with a bar of soap and a towel seeking my night's shower, one that may be the very best of my entire life. The warm water was so soft I had difficulty removing the soap from my skin. Under the illuminated sky and after a long day's ride, I luxuriated for as long as I wished before returning to the stone shed and the mosquitoes. As a last resort to escape these evil creatures, I crawled into my tent without erecting it, zipping it closed.

At 6 AM I was up and so were the farmers even though it was Sunday morning. It was a relief to leave the little stone bedroom without having to explain my presence, especially where the language barrier makes communication difficult. Except for the basics such as toothbrushing and shaving, I decided to delay my other chores until I reached the small town of Canosa. A restaurant with a bathroom could provide all of the necessities, plus breakfast. Looking for a spa, I accidentally wandered inside the private residence of a very elderly man. On his wall was a framed photograph of Benito Mussolini of World War II infamy. He directed me to the proper location, a good place to linger, do some writing in my journal, and also visit with the owner Emanuele, his daughter Isabella, and a patron in the store. Emanuele discouraged me from heading toward the mountains and Potenza. He and Isabella were good enough to pose for a photograph before I headed toward Bari and the Adriatic. Most of our conversation was in French, a subject Isabella was studying in school. The wind was again at my back.

Bari is a huge city and one I had no desire to visit, especially as the museums are closed on Mondays. An elevated highway was the perfect solution. Was it legal? I have no idea. Were there police to inform me? Fortunately, no! My total experience in Bari was from an aerial view.

The last 20 km to Cassano were hard, with frequent rest stops. An uphill climb in the heat of summer made me long for the olive grove of the previous night. Except for ice cream and a Fanta at a cost of five dollars, there was no food to be bought in Cassano. My complaint about the exorbitant cost fell on deaf ears. They had me at a disadvantage and they knew it.

Camping Canosa at the beginning of the boot of Italy was a welcome site, with good facilities except for the lack of grass. Fortunately, my recent purchase, the ground cloth, protected the bottom of my North Face tent. Everything I used, except for my sleeping bag, including my cycling shoes, went into the automatic washer. A supermarket nearby provided food instead of more ice cream and Fanta. Sausage fried in butter tent-side, buttered toast, fresh grapes, and coffee were gastronomic. In a short time the heat of the sun dried my clean laundry.

Now that I had arrived in southern Italy, a new and unpleasant experience began to prevail. Mountains of trash, the breeding site for flies and rodents, are located at the entrance and exit of every town and/or community. Discarded washing machines, stoves, toilets, and you-name-it border both sides of the road, leaving a disgusting impression of the humanity of southern Italy. Flies attracted by my perspiration were able to keep up with the speed of the Globetrotter. I had to contend the previous night with mosquitoes, and this day I was introduced to flies for the first but definitely not the last time. Throughout Sicily, Egypt, Greece, and Turkey these insects are a constant annoyance. They also prevail in parts of Israel, having developed the ability to bite at one's ankles and painfully draw blood. In areas where the wind is strong and constant, the flies have developed strength in their wings, enabling them to fly into the wind in pursuit of their victims.

The mountain route saved a lot of mileage but the uncertainty of what lay ahead caused this cyclo-tourist some concern. At times there was a total absence of civilization as we traveled along what seemed like endless fields of freshly cultivated earth. Fortunately, the mountains themselves were less rugged than I expected. Finally the town of Materna with its excavations on an enormous scale came into view. A huge catch basin in place for the collection of rain is so large that it defies one's imagination. At that time the basin was dry. A ten-mile descent toward the Gulf of Taranto was my reward for the day. The police in a patrol car helped my decision process with the advice that I should avoid the mountains and head for the town of Ginosa. With my compass and their advice, I finally discovered civilization. Ginosa, however, "dematerialized" permanently. After the third attempt, some friendly property owners permitted me to wash my hands and face and fill my water bottles in preparation for "free camping" if necessary. Night was fast approaching with absolutely no plans for setting up camp. The perfect solution then presented itself in a most unusual manner.

Parallel to the superhighway, the secondary road terminates at the edge of a farmer's field. Except for workers at a considerable distance in the field, I felt completely isolated and relatively safe. Waiting for darkness so as to be undetected, I prepared my meal and then erected the tent on the hard surface of the dead-end road. At 6:30 in the morning the farm workers in their trucks awakened me from a deep sleep as they drove past my tent. Fortunately, I erected the tent at the side of the road or the trucks would not have been able to pass. Obviously, I was not as isolated as I thought. Refreshed, I continued in what I thought to be the direction of the Gulf of Taranto.

These coastal roads are similar to those intersecting Route 1 in Maine. There are no continuous coastal roads except for the inland main highway. Eventually I ended at the exact point I started, my dead-end sleep site. By noon, except for being well fed and clean, having found a local spa, I had made zero progress.

Following the Gulf of Taranto, the landscape with its olive groves and vineyards began to disappear. Mountain ranges came into view. For a period of time a newly constructed highway was so well graded that gear shifting was unnecessary. Then the unimproved highway with its hills returned, presenting a moderate challenge as well as signs indicating the presence of a campground. At Camping St. Maria a camper, Ken Westwood, advised me that I would have a two-day ride before finding another campsite. He and his lovely wife Maggie, with their two dogs, were comfortably equipped with their Volvo station wagon and attached caravan. Of English origin, this couple resides in Greece in their mountain villa overlooking the Gulf of Corinth. Ultimately at their invitation, I visited them following my tour of Athens.

Camping St. Maria became one of the nicest campgrounds of my two-year experience. The owners as well as the Westwoods made this visit a memorable one. Looking down the length of the property and through a gateway, the Gulf of Taranto comes into view. Excellent facilities and a store stocked with cold beer added to the enjoyment.

Ken lived in Spain for 27 years, where he traveled extensively. He was agreeable to looking at my maps of Greece and Turkey with me. We made an appointment to meet that evening following their supper. It was then that I met Maggie and her two dogs. Ken and I talked over a beer about Greece, Turkey, the Peloponnesians, the weather, and Sicily. "There is no ferry service to Greece from Sicily," said Ken. "If you want to travel to Greece from Sicily, you'll have to return to Italy and then take a ferry from the port of Brindisi." Ken suggested the train as an alternative from Reggio Calabria at the tip of Italy to Taranto and then an easy bike ride to Brindisi. When I told him of my desire to visit Israel, fate took over!

"Sicily is the natural jumping off point to go to Israel," explained Ken. "From Trapani in Sicily you can ferry to Malta and from there you can go directly to Haifa. On your return trip to Turkey and then Greece you can visit us in our mountain home near Athens. This will put you in Israel before winter and Greece in the spring of the year. What could be more ideal?"

That night I had difficulty sleeping with these new plans turning over in my mind. "How fortunate could I be? I'll now be able to tour Sicily, visit my new friend Giuseppi Cuccinata in Messina, and become acquainted with the land where the Manguso family at one time lived." Before leaving Sicily, however, my trip took on a different meaning that I sum up as follows: information/misinformation and adventure/misadventure. The explanation will be forthcoming as the story unfolds. The Westwoods and I had a quick farewell as they prepared to leave Camping St. Maria. "Write when you arrive in Israel," they said. I then decided to pedal toward Reggio Calabria.

Following the coastline, the area is rather desolate, with tremendous mountains to the right. How glad I was that I did not choose the inland route! Olive trees were in abundance but the grape vineyards had vanished. By this time farmers to the north had harvested their crop, leaving only the remnants for people such as myself. What a wonderful grape season it had been for me. Not only are grapes refreshing on the road, they are a great wake-up call in the morning and an excellent dessert following the evening meal.

Entering the town of Ciro Marina, I inquired about a campground. I was advised to "follow the signs to the beach." The campground was there but it was closed for the season. Located 200 yards from the *compeggio* I investigated a beautiful beach and pavilion suitable for camping if I could find water. Although the handle was removed from the outdoor shower, my crescent wrench solved the problem. I now had an unlimited source of water for drinking, cooking, dishwashing, clothes washing, and bathing. By 9 PM I was asleep in my tent.

At about 7 in the morning, I was greeted by a local townsperson. We visited for a few minutes and shook hands before he returned to his car. "Take your time" was his only comment.

Thursday, September 19 was my longest distance to date, covering 138 km with the wind at my back. Usually around 10:30 in the morning I relax, taking my mid-morning break with a cup of coffee American and croissant. Coffee American consists of a slug of espresso in a large cup filled with hot water. This particular morning I tried two slugs of espresso in one cup, a real eye-opener. During this break a truck driver remarked, "Do you remember me? We met in a gasoline station last Sunday in Bari." It is remarkable the number of flashing lights, waves, or honks I receive from people previously seen or met. On one occasion a stranger greeted me with "You are an American going to Sicily." How did he know?

Camping Catazzaro Lido, open year-round, came as a surprise. I was given a private bedroom with an overhead electric light and a circulating fan. How does one accept this sort of luxury after tenting for 3-1/2 months? To be truthful, I prefer my tent, except that in comfort I wrote a long letter to my friend Alessandra telling her of some of my experiences enroute. Alessandra was my inspiration without my knowing it.

To be sure, the grape season was nearing its end, but there were still a few grapes remaining to enjoy even though some of their juice and flavor had diminished. Housewives were busy drying tomatoes on their tables, melons were being sold road-side, and the limes were just about ripe enough for picking. This day I cut open a cactus pear to see what it looks like inside. The cactus pear, a delicacy to some, does not appeal to me. I did the same with a lime. All the lime needed was a little gin, some tonic water, and ice. I had a sense that there would be an abundance of fresh food in *Sicilia*—if I say "Sicily" no one knows what I'm talking about.

This day's cycling was rather uneventful, climbing a few rather long well graded hills and passing through several tunnels, none of which were appealing. If I can see light at the end of the tunnel, I go on the supposition that motorists can see me. If the tunnel is too long or if a bend prevents light being seen at the end, I stop, turn on my generator light, and proceed. The thought of not being seen in a tunnel is not exactly my choice of pleasurable cycling.

The coastal town of Siderno in southern Italy near Reggio Calabria became especially important to me in an unexpected way. The memory of Siderno and Dominico shall remain in my memory for as long as I remember this trip. Domenico Antonio, eating an ice cream cone, called to me from the sidewalk as I passed him. His English was excellent. This 26-year-old Italian bicycle champion was walking back to his shop where he is the sole proprietor. A smiling and very handsome young person, Domenico was champion of all of Italy in 1985. He is now the proud owner of a bicycle shop where only quality equipment is for sale. He and I immediately became fast friends. Soon his mother, a part-time employee, entered the store. Although Mrs. Antonio speaks only Italian, she and I understood each other. When I suggested to Domenico that perhaps his mother and I should become better acquainted he reminded me that I would have to discuss the matter with his father.

Though money did not change hands, Domenico insisted that he sponsor me on the remainder of my journey. A new water bottle, two new bicycle caps, and decals were my gifts to wear and use. Ultimately I wrote the names of the countries I visited on the panels of the caps and then mailed them back to my sponsor, hoping for a reply. The only reason I can think of for lack of a response is that Domenico can speak English well but he does not write the language. I would have gladly settled for a letter in Italian. Mrs. Antonio photographed her son and me before I reluctantly said goodbye. Darkness was falling and I had not located a campsite. The site Domenico recommended 500 meters south of his store was, unfortunately, closed for the season.

At Boralino Marino south of Siderno, some young people with their mountain bikes suggested that I erect my tent on the beach. They pointed to an outdoor shower nearby. This was my first but certainly not my last experience tenting on the beach. To keep sand from entering the tent, I erected it on the asphalt and then carefully carried it to the beach. In the morning I reversed the procedure, shaking the sand off before dismantling.

Coffee, buttered toast, and grapes provided the energy I needed to reach Reggio Calabria. I had plans to visit the archæological museum, purchase maps of Sicily, locate a place to camp for two days, and seek advice concerning a ferry to Haifa.. One hundred fifty kilometers this day exceeded my previous record by twelve.

A sign came into view that I had been waiting to see for a considerable time. The sign, "Reggio Calabria," deserved to be photographed, having chased it for approximately 1,333 km from Fusina Camping in Venice (all recorded distances are estimates, since my computer was returned to Massachusetts).

A food store was closed but next door a store selling soft goods was open. This was a possible opportunity to purchase a pillowcase for my small travel pillow. Mr. and Mrs. Monoriti were the store owners. Ermine, their son, a law student, and his fiancée Francesca were also present. We discussed the matter in English and sign language. The word "pillowcase" held no meaning for these people. I then tried "pillow slip" without success. To Italians, a slip is a piece of feminine apparel as it is in English. When I tried the words "pillow sac" the floodgates of conversation were opened.

Francesca, a petite and beautiful young woman, appeared radiant. Perhaps it was her straight teeth and lovely dark brown eyes that made her so striking. She and Ermine explained that on their honeymoon they will be visiting an uncle in Calgary, Canada.

Tiberius, the father, though shy, spoke the best English of the four of them. His wife behind the counter offered me a cold beer which I had to refuse. The hills surrounding Reggio Calabria were much too steep for me to challenge after drinking beer. We settled for a Coke before exchanging addresses. They now have an invitation to visit me in Cambridge anytime after the summer of 1994. Although I did not find a "sac" for my small pillow, I did find a wonderful family who by chance knew my bike shop owner-friend Domenico Antonio from Siderno.

Following some steep grades and a few tunnels, I was finally in the center of Reggio. The wind at my back was very helpful. Now that the days were getting shorter, I had a limited amount of time to seek a campsite before dark. The campground nearest Reggio is 15 km to the south, with few possibilities to the north. Having just arrived from the north, I had no interest in re-climbing the hills out of Reggio. Poor road surface was another deterrent to further travel. If possible, I hoped to settle in close to the archæological museum as well as the ferry to Sicily. This was time for further ingenuity.

Most of the beach was occupied by private clubs with signs indicating that only members are welcome. One club with an adjoining restaurant was a possible alternative, with private cabanas and outdoor showers. A grassy spot would have been ideal for my tent. Unfortunately, the management did not share my enthusiasm when I discussed the matter with them. Even when I explained that I could pitch my tent after their closing time and vacate early in the morning they remained steadfast in their refusal. At least the restaurant was available.

Next to the beach club with the restaurant a group of local fishermen have their own private beach where they tend to their boats and nets. It all appeared to be more a social entity than a commercial enterprise. This may have been their answer to the "nagging wife" syndrome.

Language was no barrier when I asked permission to erect my tent on their property. Welcoming me for as long a time as I wanted, they would accept no money. As luck would have it, I even had my own shower. The photo of these men with their nets is another of my favorites. This was my night to enjoy the comforts of a restaurant in contrast to cooking tent-side. A second meal came as a surprise as I sat on the steps of a fast-food shop writing in my journal. The owner, a lady with her children, brought me a fried rice cone as a gift. We visited as I ate. She saw me around the area earlier in the evening and wanted to know where I would be sleeping. I tried to explain that this was my secret.

At first I tried to sleep in the open, the weather being quite warm. The mosquitoes soon changed my mind. Without the fly of the tent, I enjoyed insect-free sleeping as well as the sound of the surf as it massaged the shoreline. Without a doubt I had the best of all worlds. I was near the museum and the ferry as well as being among friends.

In the morning the fishermen returned to their sanctuary, having caught but a single small octopus. The size of their catch did not make a difference to them nor did it detract from their enjoyment of life in Reggio. Giungo Vineergoand and Ficora Paolo are two of the fishermen. They wished me well as I headed for the National Museum and then the ferry to Sicily.

Museo Nazionale is a modern museum in the center of town containing an important archæological collection covering the history of Magna Greece. This museum has been selected to house the Riace Warriors dating from the 5th century B.C. These well-preserved bronze sculptures were found off the coast of the small island of Riace and were shipped to Rome for restoration. They are now on permanent display in Reggio where they exhibit an imposing appearance. I was fortunate in being able to photograph one of the sculptures before being told that photos are not permitted. Though the origin and identity of the sculptor is unknown, there is a remarkable likeness to the Greek god Poseidon.

In addition to the many fascinating items dating to the ancient Greeks, a pair or bronze hands delicately clasping one another attracted my attention. A Hellenistic coin collection is located on the first floor of the museum. Street vendors outside the building were selling postcards and miniatures of the statues, but there were no slides available for purchase. Though the admission price to the museum was 6,000 lira, I talked my way in with my Harvard card. This became almost a game as I entered national museums in the countries I visited. Later in Eilat, Israel, following the theft of my wallet, this form of recreation terminated.

Another point of interest in Calabria is the Duomo, located on the main street. Mass was being held at the time of my arrival. Some people on the street in front of the duomo took an interest in me and my overloaded tandem. Even with a language barrier we were able to communicate.

The distance from the duomo to the ferry was no more than 2 km. Every hour on the half hour a ferry leaves from Reggio for Messina, Sicily, my destination for the night. I expected a drive-on ferry but settled for one that transports only passengers. With assistance from the crew, I and the Globetrotter headed for the next adventure, Sicily. A one-way ticket for myself and the bike cost 3,500 lira.

Sicily

Chapter 9
SICILY

Messina is a beautiful city without a history, having been destroyed by an earthquake in 1908 and rebuilt into a modern city, presently the third largest in Sicily. It's the provincial capital with a population of 260,000. This is the place where trains, cars, and bicyclists embark on Sicilian soil.

The immediate objective concerned the location of my Sicilian friend Giuseppi Cuccinata, the man driving his Vespa Mobilette south of Venice. After numerous inquiries, I located his house high on a hill, tucked away on a narrow and quiet street. Neighbors confirmed this address as belonging to Giuseppi but, unfortunately, he wasn't home. Looking through the gate, I saw a small piece of garden that would have been perfect for my tent had my host been home. The guard dog on the other side of the fence had a different opinion. I wrote Giuseppi a short note and tucked it securely near the lock so he'd be certain to see it. Unfortunately, I was unable to make another attempt to meet Giuseppi due to lack of campground facilities. This is another example of misinformation. Messina does have a campground bordering the Mediterranean.

In Reggio di Calabria the opportunity to camp with fishermen was ideal, but in the modern city of Messina there was no opportunity for me to even try to duplicate this bit of ambiance. I had no other choice than to head west in the direction of Palermo, seeking lodging enroute.

Following a sign to a pension, I investigated but continued west in search of a campground. Supper at a restaurant and the return to my pension was my only recourse with the onset of darkness. My host at the pension, Giuseppi Di Pietro, wears a full bears similar to the Riace Warriors in the museum on the mainland. He also bears a striking resemblance to the Greek god Poseidon. This is confirmed by his wife Nancy, an employee of the Regional Museum. A printed guide in the museum given to me by Nancy explains that the preserved art was housed in a convent during the 1908 earthquake. That convent is now the principal location of the museum. From a corridor visitors may enter the courtyard where fragments of architecture following the earthquake are on exhibit.

The biking, the beer, and the Sicilian meal, as well as a bed with a mattress were all I needed for a prolonged nap. At 10 PM, I was unexpectedly invited to join the family for the evening meal by Davida, the pension owner's son. "Is there an extra charge for the meal?" I asked Davida. The answer was negative. To avoid any misunderstanding, I wrote the question on a piece of paper. Had I realized the joy of breaking bread with these people, including the grandmother; I would have accepted the invitation at any cost. Our meal consisted of a complete fish per person, wine, vegetables cooked in olive oil, and a lot of healthy conversation. One big issue was the Italian cookie that resembles a waffle called a *pizzelle*. After a lot of hearty laughs, I finally made myself understood.

Packed and ready to leave the pension the next morning, I was informed that I owed an extra 15,000 lira for the previous evening's meal. Davida was nowhere to be found. To prevent an unhappy situation I paid Giuseppi the full 15,000 lira even though by no stretch of the imagination did I owe it. Being a gentleman, he returned 5,000 lira to me. We parted friends.

The exit from Messina followed the coastline with the wind at my back. Shortly thereafter I began to feel the fury of the Sicilian mountains, a stern warning to stay close to the shore. At a nearby post office I mailed a letter to my friend Alessandra in Torino, but was unable to mail a package containing film and brochures to my daughter Amy. The reason for the refusal of the package is still unclear. The postmistress kept repeating the word "Messina." That meant I'd probably have to wait until my arrival in Palermo.

172

At an Atala bicycle shop I asked an unusual-looking youth the location of a campground, or *compeggio* as it's written in Italian. The threat of rain and the disappearance of signs to a campground prompted this inquiry. "I will show you," he said as he pedaled in an erratic fashion toward the beach. Finally we arrived at a rundown hotel where he introduced me to the owner. Nothing appealed. I was looking for a place to camp, cook my meal in the open air, and enjoy the feeling of complete freedom.

A climb to the summit of a small town named Bivio Tindari proved to be an exciting experience. Starting at sea level and with a workable grade, I was able to reach a monastery at the very top ready for an incredible descent in search of a compeggio. It was my good fortune that there was none to be found. Back at sea level again, I arrived at the tiny medieval town of Mongiove. The main street of Mongiove follows a beach with a depth of at least 150 yards. A stone and cement wall approximately four feet high separates the road from the beach. It was here that I prepared my supper in full view of the citizens of the town. At the town pump where I located fresh drinking water, the older men of the town were gathered. They shared my contentment with "bon appétit" and assurance that I would have no problem putting my tent on the beach. Supper consisted of cream of something soup, panini, salami, coffee, grapes, and cookies, purchased at a small grocery facing the beach. While eating, local fishermen pulled a large boat onto the beach and unloaded their catch of tuna, known in Italian as *thon*. I was invited to use an outdoor shower for my personal hygiene by an elderly couple whose summer home faces the beach. At 9:45 in the evening and with the aid of a street light, I made entries in my journal. Sleep followed quickly.

My impressions of Sicily are a bit different than anticipated. The northern coast of the island is very beautiful, giving the impression of a certain degree of wealth. The towns are cleaner than in southern Italy and appear well cared for. Like southern Italy, though, trash has accumulated along the roads, a breeding site for the common housefly. The beaches and mountains are exquisite.

Sicilians are a friendly people, easy to know, with no evidence to the outsider of the Mafia. When I did talk to some of the young people they expressed discontent with the unemployment situation as well as the power of the Mafia.

Cycling is a popular sport in Sicily for people of all ages. Bicycles and cycling clothes in full fashion include those rakish sunglasses seen in the US. Many of the cyclists were friendly, returning my greeting, while others ignored the gesture. Noisy mopeds ridden by men, women, and children of all ages are a favorite means of transportation for Sicilians.

The elderly people who gave me permission to use their shower bid me adieu as they headed for an outing in the country. It was 6:30 in the morning. Rather than attract more attention at the town pump, I decided to use the back yard of these friends to prepare my breakfast. The nearby store supplied the necessary food, with an invitation to again use their facilities. I left Mongiove clean, shaved, and well fed.

The shore road of northern Sicily can only be compared with the Côte d'Azur of southern France, except that traffic is much less intense. As I climbed and descended the hills of the shore road, the cliffs to my left plunged into the water's surface. After several miles of cycling, small towns would suddenly come into view near the sea, with its marina on the water, and then disappear as I continued south. The hot autumn sun accentuated the azure blue of the Mediterranean. How glad I was that my friend Giuseppi recommended Sicily. At the summit of a steep climb, I enjoyed my lunch at a small grocery, followed by my usual nap.

Rested but groggy, I headed back onto the road to again challenge the mountains and seek a night's lodging. Marina Di Caronia, an upscale beach resort, was the perfect choice. It was four in the afternoon, with ample time to make the right decisions. Rather than wheel my heavy Globetrotter down the steep grade to the beach, I decided to leave it at the side of the road and explore Marina Di Caronia on foot. My objective was to camp on the beach, but to ask permission from the local police, known in Italian as the *carbiniere*.

"How long do you plan to camp on the beach?" asked the officer. Before I had the opportunity to reply, a small red convertible with the top lowered came upon the scene. The owner, Michael Piscitello, asked if it was my bike that was leaning against his mother's house.

"You are not going to camp out tonight," said Michael. "You are going to stay with me and my mother. I have an extra apartment that is vacant, and you can stay there as long as you wish." Needless to say, my conversation with the carbiniere was concluded. We put the Globetrotter in the apartment and by automobile went visiting friends of Michael. The entire incident was so sudden that I felt a bit overwhelmed.

Michael, a musician, and his mother Nancy live in Sicily half the year and in Philadelphia the other half. Unfortunately, at the time I visited Philadelphia on my return to Boston I did not have his local address. I tried all the Piscitellos in the telephone book but without success. Completing the circle, as I did with other new acquaintances, would have been particularly satisfying. I would have been able to meet Michael's wife and their daughter who live in Philadelphia year-round.

Michael's invitation could not have come at a better time. Rain struck with such fury that I'm certain there would have been water in my tent had I camped on the beach. When the sun returned and the sky again became clear blue above the Mediterranean, my thoughts and memories returned to Jamaica. All that was needed was someone singing "Yellow Bird" to the soft music of a guitar.

Speaking of the guitar, Michael is an accomplished musician, playing the electric guitar and accompanying it with his deep mellow voice. In the evening at his favorite kiosk he and his friends sang and socialized the evening away. In a matter of a few minutes his friends became my friends.

It was hard to leave the hospitality of Michael and Nancy, but I had many miles ahead of me. "Stay until the weather improves," said Michael. "The overcast sky suggests more rain." His prediction was more accurate than I imagined.

Within sight of Marina Di Caronia the sky opened with a deluge of rain. My only recourse was to seek shelter in a nearby barn filled to capacity with cows. A thin wooden path divided the backsides of these animals in such close proximity that their swishing tails came into contact with one another. Holding the Globetrotter in an erect position on the path so it would not get bogged down in the detritus, I too felt the impact of the swishing tails. Michael's apartment would certainly have been more comfortable than my situation at that time.

The only solace I could muster during this period was the knowledge that if the rain started, eventually it would stop. In the meantime I moved from place to place, allowing the bald and bow-legged farmer owner, wearing rubber boots, to do the necessary mucking. He and I were both glad when the rain subsided. Unfortunately, the sun did not return, indicating that we were destined to face an all-day rain.

During this waiting period, I found myself thinking about some of the people I met in Marina Di Caronia. Enzio, a discontent and unemployed truck driver, is anxious to move to the United States where jobs are "plentiful." Mario, a butcher, drinks too much because he has too little work to do. His major complaint is Mafia-related. Unwilling to "pay" the Mafia, his customers are discouraged from buying at his store for fear of reprisal. The owner of the kiosk, appeared happy. He prepared great sausage sandwiches for all of us. Lastly there are the Orlandos, a father and son team. The young son and I played the Italian game of table hockey, where fast movement and dexterity are required. I lost. I also had the opportunity to think about an insect bite on the ventral surface of my foot. This mild annoyance proved to be a source of a medical problem that persisted for several months. I suspected it was from the sting of a scorpion.

The next cloudburst occurred in a small town specializing in the manufacture and sale of ceramics to tourists. At a nearby food stand I covered the entire bike with my waterproof ground cloth, borrowed a chair from the owner, and again waited out the storm. At least in this location I could buy prepared food and drink hot tea to ward off the feeling of hypothermia. Feeling pain in my left foot and shaking from the cold, I covered myself with the ground cloth and fell fast asleep. Finally the sun emerged, much to my delight. I thanked my hostess for the prolonged use of her chair and again set out seeking a campsite in the direction of Palermo.

International Camping Rais Gerbi, located near Finale Di Pollina, was a perfect location to recover. This newly constructed tourist center is located 12-1/2 km from the lovely resort town of Cefalu. It was post-season. I chose a location next to an immaculately clean wash house with a solar water heater that provided as much hot water as needed. The restaurant nearby belongs to Vincent, owner of International Camping Rais Gerbi. I recall entering the restaurant the first evening unable to walk down a flight of stairs to the men's room. By this time my ankle was swollen to twice its normal size. I knew that once I removed my shoe it would be impossible to put on.

The wait-staff gave me permission to hang my wet sleeping bag on a long wooden paddle near the pizza oven while I enjoyed a large pizza and beer. By this time I was almost unable to walk. In place of the wet sleeping bag, the restaurant owner loaned me two large tablecloths to use as blankets. This was the end of a very difficult day.

The next morning it was obvious I needed medical attention. My first thought was to seek a physician in nearby Pollina. With great difficulty, I put on my shoes and headed for the town not more than a mile away. To my amazement, though unable to walk, I could pedal. It was then I decided to go to the nearest hospital under my own power. I was informed at the bank in Pollina that the hospital in Cefalu would care for my needs. They also explained that a bank in Cefalu would honor my Mastercard; I was in need of cash.

The ride to Cefalu even under these difficult conditions was enjoyable, following the contours of the coast. Time passed quickly. Soon the town, situated at the base of a huge rock, came into view. Its cathedral dominates the view of the town but a rock, 270 meters high where prehistoric and ancient settlements were located, dominates the scene. Cefalu, incidentally, is in the Province of Palermo. A sign indicated the direction of the hospital.

I was seen by the doctor within five minutes of my arrival at this clean and well-run facility. Fortunately, I brought my passport with me. A product of socialized medicine, I was not expected to pay for this visit. The doctor gave me a prescription for an antibiotic, advising that I rest for three or four days. "You will then be well enough to travel." I swallowed my first pill at a restaurant after limping to the nearest pharmacy. Food and a cold beer diminished the discomfort but not the weakness. I felt unable to attempt the return ride to my campsite without additional rest. A visit to the local museum was appropriate even though walking was almost impossible.

The museum Museo Mandralisca contains Greek vases, including a piece with a decoration depicting a tuna seller. Many of these barncale-encrusted vases came directly from the sea. The masterpiece "Portrait of a Man" by Antonello da Messina, dated 1465, hangs in the gallery. It is the most significant of the paintings. There is also a painting of St. Marks Square in Venice as it appeared 200 years ago, and one of the

Grand Canal. My pain and weakness by this time were talking loudly: "Go home while you're still able."

The ride back to the campground was not as easily accomplished as the one in the morning. With great difficulty, I walked the Globetrotter instead of trying to climb the hill out of Cefalu. Weakness and an unsteady feeling almost caused me to lose my courage, but fortunately, I made it back to the campground under my own power. My tent was a welcome sight.

In due course and after repeated soakings the infection began to come to a "head" at the site of the wound. Additional courage was now required. I carefully washed my Swiss Army knife before lancing the wound. Within a few hours the pain and swelling began to diminish. I had opened an escape route for the infection. This is exactly what we would do in the dental office, except that at Rais Gerbi I did not have the convenience of sterile equipment. "The antibiotics in my system will probably take care of that matter as well as the initial infection!" A booster tetanus shot prior to my trip gave me an additional sense of security.

Foot soakings, rest, and some walking began to prepare me for the continuation of my journey. Except for flies, the day was exquisite. These insects look like the common housefly but they take great joy in biting through one's socks, leaving a telltale trace of blood. This is exactly what my infected foot did not need. In desperation to avoid them I moved my chair into the middle of the parking lot, but with little success. They found me.

This reminds me of a previous bicycle camping trip. John Vanderpoel, my cycling buddy from Concord, Massachusetts, and I were returning to Bar Harbor, Maine, after touring Nova Scotia. John had a tent with fly screen and I had none. When we camped for the night it made very little difference. The wind was blowing too hard for the little varmints, the mosquitoes, to harass us. Such was not the case in the early morning when the wind subsided. The mosquitoes attacked with such fury that I picked up my sleeping bag and gear and headed for the middle of the road post-haste. My friend John slept on. At that moment I promised myself I would never travel without netting or fly screen to protect against insects. Today tents are so light there is no excuse not to protect oneself.

Compeggio Rais Gerbi had almost become my home during this period of recuperation. Owner Vincent Cerrito was friendly as well as interested in my plans. "Why didn't you ask me to take you to the hospital?"

His campground is nicely laid out in a magnificent setting bordering the Mediterranean. In addition to a first-class restaurant, he provides two tennis courts and a pool that any country club would be proud to own. The shrubs are well cared for and the gardenias were in bloom. Unlike most campgrounds, this one is open twelve months of the year in spite of the fact that few campers patronize the facility in the off-season. I left reluctantly in the direction of Cefalu and the hospital.

At the hospital, I asked the doctor to prescribe additional antibiotics. When he asked to see the wound he knew that I had taken matters into my own hands. Though he spoke Italian and I English, he made it obvious that he disapproved of my course of action. Fortunately, I did get the prescription.

My foot now felt good enough to pedal the many up-hill grades. The antibiotic kept the infection in check but it did not cure the condition. Finally while in Egypt two months later, when I changed the medication from ampicillin to tetracycline, the infection disappeared.

I planned to stop for the night short of the city of Palermo and then in daylight seek out a campground that Vincent recommended. Before I knew it we were within the city limits of Palermo. Several parks along the way looked suitable for emergency camping but none had running water. It was now necessary to use my generator light and begin to ask directions using the word *compeggio*.

My newest compeggio was situated along the sea with huge solid rock mountains behind me. A market, restaurant, and bus service into Palermo added to the convenience of this site. Even after a 100-km ride my foot enjoyed improvement, though walking was still difficult. An overhead electric light gave me all the comforts of home. Well, almost!

The bike ride into Palermo was challenging due to the intensity of cars, motorcycles, bicycles, and mopeds. The noise level in the downtown area is high enough to give a person permanent hearing loss. Defensive cycling was the only possible solution to this vexing problem. This city, nesting between two foothills in a beautiful bay, is the undisputed cultural, economic, and political center of the island. Although Palermo has the lowest per capita income and the highest unemployment in all of Italy, it is also a city of superlatives: Byzantine mosaics, Arabian domes, and the graves of Norman kings and German emperors can be found here. In 1860 Garibaldi took Palermo after four days of fighting, uniting the island with all of Italy. Sicily then became autonomous in 1946 following an act of the government of Rome.

Three young perople in front of the opera house were selling season tickets to the opera. They wanted to be friendly and at the same time practice their English. I then left them to visit the cathedral under reconstruction, the pier with its immense ferry, and finally the archæological museum. Etruscan, Greek, and Roman art that I had seen before were also in Palermo. Numerous oil lamps from the Roman period have their own individual decorations. Also from the Roman era, lead pipes with built-in shutoff valves were especially interesting. A huge bronze sheep, obviously of Greek origin, was being shown to a German group by a docent of the museum.

I decided to pursue the idea of taking a ferry from Sicily to Malta and then another ferry to Haifa, Israel, as suggested by my friend Ken Westwood. Here is the "bottom line":

Twice a week, on Wednesday and Sunday, a ferry leaves Sicily from Catania or Siracusa for the island of Malta. There is no information concerning a ferry from Malta to Haifa. Passenger aircraft do not fly that route. The only way for me to obtain additional information is to actually sail to Malta. Under any circumstance this idea appealed, as I had no schedule to keep.

It was now dusk with a distance of at least 20 km to my campground. The generator light was helpful on this return trip. I then prepared a tasty supper and fell fast asleep in my clothes. In the middle of the night I was awakened by the growling and fighting of dogs quarreling over my leftover food. My two-cup mess kit was now reduced to a single cup; the other cup was chewed beyond recognition.

The port of Castellamare and Trapani on the western coast were now within cycling distance, with two choices of highways: one route penetrates the mountains while the other follows the coast. I chose the coastal route until reaching Alcamo. Without consulting the map, I began to follow the mountain route. Most of these roads are well graded until I hit the "wall." This road is so steep that it took all my strength to keep the Globetrotter erect and moving in an upward direction. At the summit the road fortunately joins one of normal width and grade. For a short period of time I felt that this was my "mission impossible."

The climb from Castellammare del Golfo, an attractive harbor town where I spent the night on the beach, to the highway, was substantial. From this vantage point I was able to photograph the beach where I camped as well as the medieval structures ringing this natural harbor. East of town there is a long stretch of beach while rocky cliffs dominate the scene elsewhere. Our climb continued for most of the morning, followed by a fantastic descent toward the water and Trapani. The Globetrotter with its well balanced load tracked perfectly.

Trapani is a beautiful and lively provincial capital with large ships and ship repair facilities on the eastern side. On the western side a road following the sea affords a panoramic view of the area. One ship had its gangway lowered and the officer of the day on duty explained that it was destined for Tunisia. There were no other ships of interest.

Looking at my map, I became aware that I was less than halfway around the island of Sicily. Should I book passage to Tunisia as well as seek out a route to Egypt and ultimately Israel, or should I continue to challenge the mountainous roads of Sicily? Using the convenience of the railroads was out of the question: Sicilian railroads do not carry bicycles.

I spent the night in Lido Valderice, a jewel of an area about 15 km west of Trapani. The town's lights reflect in the shimmering water. In the mountains overlooking the Lido is an entire city. This city boasts a world-famous institute of physics. Fortunately, the compeggio was not closed for the season. I was the only guest.

When I returned to the campground in the evening I found the main gate closed and locked. No amount of shouting brought assistance. This was a time for further creativity. Building a stepladder from a broken door nearby, I could come and go at will, but without lighting I was unable to make entries in my journal. In the dark I made my plans to return to Trapani in the morning where the problem of future transportation could be explored in detail. Travel to Tunisia as well as Egypt would probably require a visa.

In the morning a travel agency cleared up some of the mystery but also contributed to my storehouse of misinformation concerning a ferry to Haifa as well as the trains in Sicily.

Bicycles *can* be shipped by train but they cannot go on the same train as the passengers. "Yes, there is a ferry from Malta to Haifa." With this misinformation, I decided to bike to Catania, irrespective of the terrain, so I could ferry from Malta to Haifa, located in northern Israel. From there I would seek transportation to the port city of Eilat on the Red Sea where I planned to spend the winter.

The Trapani museum is located in a very large villa with a garden in the center. Rather than being a typical archæological museum, it concentrates on local Trapani art. In a section of the museum devoted to coral art, a piece of tapestry under glass has coral woven into the design, giving it an unusual texture. An original guillotine with a metal basket designed to catch the head is gruesome, to say the least. At first I decided to photograph this machine of death but then decided that a brief mention in my journal would be more than adequate. Mentally conditioned to do the entire island, it was time to move on toward Marsala and Agrigento on the southern coast.

Fortunately, the terrain is rather flat in and around Trapani. When I arrived at Marsala with its numerous one-way streets the sun was again shining. By pure chance I ended up at the entrance of a very beautiful and new Museo Archeologico. The director, Angelo Vita, was in the process of giving a guided tour to Italo-Americans from Westport and Norwalk, Connecticut. His spacious mansion, an obvious tourist attraction, is located on the water. Angelo welcomed me into the group.

On display is a collection of Greek ceramics as well as bottles taken from the sea. Greek coins, lead anchors of huge dimensions, and beautiful mosaics are but a part of the collection. Angelo turned the Greek vases upside down so we could view the designs on the bottom. There are also photographs of the objects taken at the site of their discovery.

Several times I stopped to escape the rain, heading in the direction of the Greek temples of Selinunte dating to the 5th and 6th centuries B.C., as well as a compeggio. My main concern was leaving the main road by mistake and having to bike in the dark. Signs to a campground would materialize and then quickly disappear, bringing us closer to darkness as well as a foreboding storm. Using hindsight, I have come to the conclusion that the campgrounds are along the beaches and not on the highway leading to Selinunte. I vividly remember fighting the wind and rain as I crossed a long bridge spanning a deep ravine wondering if I would get to the other side before the fury of the storm struck. No sooner did I arrive on solid ground than the storm, threatening the entire day, began in earnest. A parking area along the side of the road became my campsite for the night. Fast action was required.

I covered my gear with the ground cloth and then furiously began erecting the tent in the dark. As quickly as possible I put the tent on top of the ground cloth and threw my gear and myself inside. When the wind struck it came with such fury that I suspected that it and I would be blown away. My only recourse was to brace the sides of the tent from the interior with my hands, being grateful that my weight and the weight of the gear held the tent to the ground.

To my chagrin, I did not erect the tent properly. One side was done correctly but the other drooped in such a way that rain seeped in, dampening me and my gear and drenching the sleeping bag. Conditions during this storm were the worst I encountered, including the storm in the mountains near Marseille, especially without food except for a chocolate cake. In addition to the other discomforts, I became smeared with chocolate while devouring the cake in the dark. I had no one to confide my discomforts to or give me encouragement; I was left to my own survival techniques.

At daylight I began to assess the situation. The rain abated but the entire area was as wet outside the tent as I was within. To my utter amazement I had pitched my tent beside and partially on top of one of the many trash dumps alongside the roads of Sicily and Italy. Cars passed me so closely that their tires threw water in my direction, adding to an already uncomfortable situation. Fortunately, I had enough fresh water to brush my teeth and shave. It was definitely time to move on!

Within the hour I arrived at a restaurant that serves as a bus stop for passengers in need of food and toilet facilities. The cloudless blue sky and a bright sun gave no evidence of the tempestuous conditions of the previous night. Before entering the restaurant I spread my sleeping bag out on the warm asphalt to begin the drying process.

My plan was a simple one: I decided to order breakfast and then wait until the bus passengers left the restaurant before using the bathroom. To my surprise I had the use of a shower with as much hot water as I needed to wash myself and my clothes. Finally, the chocolate of the previous night was but a memory. I was clean and fed, ready to again head in the direction of Agrigento, a distance of approximately 60 km from the restaurant.

Agrigento, the provincial capital and bishop's seat, is situated in magnificent hilly countryside with buildings of medieval as well as Baroque architecture. A modern graded highway with immense bridges crossing the valleys below made our entrance to the city relatively easy as well as spectacular. Agrigento the city is literally built on the top and sides of a mountain. The beach and campground are within sight in the valley. This is definitely a walking city and not one to tour by bicycle.

The bus and train station provided secure parking for the Globetrotter and the luggage checking area accepted my baggage. It was there that I met two young Germans, Petra Liepold and Eva Matner, waiting to take a bus to the museum.

They invited me to join them. Unfortunately, the museum was closed for the day. We took pictures, shared addresses, then went our separate ways. Petra and Eva had seen the Greek temples, a relatively easy walk from the museum, and I had not.

The Temple of Concordia, built around 425 B.C., ranks among the most perfectly preserved Greek temples in the world. In its original condition it would have been colored and covered inside and out with stucco instead of the present oxidized red sandstone. This temple was ultimately converted into a Christian church before becoming a national monument in 1748.

Within sight of the Temple of Concordia, the Temple of Olympian Zeus completed my touring for the day. This temple is a mass of shattered stone blocks and pillars, destroyed by an earthquake. Its buildings have been scattered over an area of 6,000 square meters. The most original and the most unfathomable creation of the Greek world, the Temple of Olympian Zeus is said to be even larger than the Temples of Selinunte.

My walk back to the Central Station in the dark gave me a feeling for the area with its hundreds of stone steps that join one level of the city with another. I was grateful for the fact that my knees were now in much better condition than when my trip began. I retrieved my baggage, secured it on the bike, and with great care followed the road into the valley below in search of the compeggio. A strong wind was blowing off the Mediterranean.

In the morning I decided to use bus transportation rather than try to climb the mountain by bike. Threatening sky helped me make this decision. The Museo Archeologico Regional, previously closed, was my principal objective for the day. This modern museum contains archæological finds that date from prehistory to Roman times. In a two-storied room devoted to the Temple of the Olympian Zeus one of the original 38 Atlas figures used to adorn the temple is reconstructed. The head of another Atlas as well as some fragments are also on display. These immense *telemon* are without a doubt the most exciting exhibit in the museum. They were originally designed for placement between the Doric columns to give the impression that the telemon are holding up the roof.

After leaving the museum I "auto stopped" back to the city. Auto stop is a synonym for hitch-hiking. My host, in addition to being a very interesting person, took me directly to a bank. I knew from my map that I would be biking inland in the mountains and would probably need more funds.

The following day became my longest ride to date, having covered 144 km. Marina di Ragusa, a fishing village in the process of becoming a seaside resort, became my objective. There was little else to do this day except ride. I selected a longer route to Siracusa, but at least it was along the shore instead of being in the mountains. The grounds, the tropical foliage, and the facilities of my compeggio were excellent. I could again hear the surf and at the same time erect my tent on grass instead of sand. A young man on a Vespa scooter led me to this site when I asked for directions.

The next day with the wind at my back I easily covered 115 km. At a restaurant where I enjoyed a prepared meal, one of the patrons, the driver of a camion, became especially friendly. The tandem bicycle was of special interest to him. He insisted that I accept his cap as a souvenir even though it had no redeeming features. He also wanted me to take his auto compass as well. I thanked him for the cap but showed him that I too had a compass.

At the outskirts of Siracusa I stopped two women tourists and inquired about the location of a compeggio. Their tour book did not list a campground in Siracusa but verified that Fontaine Blanche 30 km back toward Ragusa did have such a facility. Upon my arrival there I discovered that it was closed for the season. This long and useless ride added to my disappointment. Fortunately, a restaurant and hotel across the street from the campground was still open even though the tourist season had ended. A night's lodging at the hotel would have cost me 82,000 lira. When I refused their offer, the price was lowered to 70,000. That price did not appeal, either. The attendant then asked me where I was planning to sleep, since this was the only hotel in the area. I avoided his question.

I used the toilet facilities of the restaurant and then walked the bike across the street to the entrance of the compeggio where I pitched my tent and fell fast asleep. Leaving this improvised campsite in Fontaine Blanche in the morning, I stopped for breakfast at a bar and petrol station along the road. The station attendant brought my attention to the front tire. The sidewall had worn to such an extent that the inner tube and plastic "tire saver" were exposed. This was my first tire problem in five months of touring.

The "tire saver" is a hard strip of plastic that is placed between the tube and the inner surface of the tire. It was recommended by my friend Michael at Ace Wheelworks. "This will add a bit of weight to your wheel," said Michael, "but it will save you from the flat tires you would usually encounter." I took Michael's advice and profited from his experience. Utilizing the same tube and my spare tire, I headed for Siracusa and the nearest bicycle shop. Without a spare I felt vulnerable.

For reasons I cannot explain, I spent very little time exploring this city that dates to the 10th century, B.C. Perhaps I was becoming anxious to reach Catania and the ferry for Malta. In 212 B.C. the Romans attacked Siracusa, taking it in conquest. The mathematician Archimedes was killed at that time. Cicero vividly describes the city as "so big one might think it was made up of four giant towns put together..."

I did, however, seek out the Archæological Museum, located in a circular building, using a simple floor plan to display a wealth of ancient treasures. Photographs attest to the presence of human skeletons as well as the treasures placed within the burial sites. Ceramic jars were so brightly decorated that I wondered if they were repainted during the process of restoration. A bronze statue of a dog has a head at either end of its body.

From the museum I gravitated toward the Archæological Park at Siracusa where I was greeted by Ethyl Ronald, an 81-year-young woman, a member of the Cyclists Touring Club of England. Ethyl heard that "there was a cyclist about" and she sought me out. A dance teacher, biker, and hiker, Ethyl gives the appearance of being 61 instead of 81. We visited for at least an hour, had a cold drink together, and shared addresses. To our regret, her group was preparing to leave, terminating this unexpected and pleasant meeting. She sealed our meeting with a kiss on the lips. Now that I've returned home, Ethyl and I are pen pals. I look forward to seeing her in Boston one day.

Had I known that there was a compeggio in Siracusa I would not have had to retrace my steps to Fontaine Blanche. This fully-equipped facility is open year-round. To my surprise, Eva and Petra, whom I met in Agrigento, were also camping there. They took the bus, stopping off at the popular mountain town of Enna, where theatrical performances are held. We had a fine reunion.

Before leaving Siracusa I pedaled to the old city to have a final look and to also seek seek out the silver altar piece of S. Lucia, virgin and martyr, located in the cathedral. A priest gave me a postcard showing the details of this work of art, with the advice that it can only be seen on special occasions such as Christmas. I then decided to head toward Catania.

Unlike the northern shore, the southern shore of Sicily is quite industrial, especially between Siracusa and Catania. Oil refineries and major highways as well as a headwind made my progress slower than usual. After 58 km of hard work I began looking for the impossible, an open compeggio. A large sandy beach with showers presented itself as a poor alternative. I felt uneasy about my safety near this large metropolitan city, especially as I was the only camper. In spite of my concerns it became the last resort. Fortunately, I had no problems except for the mosquitoes. I must have brought them with me from Siracusa!

Instructions at the ferry in Catania concerned a one o'clock sailing on Tuesday. This gave me enough time to bike to Taormina where Mt. Etna can be seen. I attended Etna High School in the town of Etna, near Pittsburgh, where a sign at the entrance indicates that it's named for Mt. Etna in Italy.

The terrain was again that of the Sicily I prefer, with gradual climbs and shorter descents, finding myself continually at a higher altitude. The towns enroute for the most part preserve their paving block main street. The purpose may be to slow traffic or perhaps to retain something of the past. In any event, it slowed me to a crawl. Though the weather was cloudy I could now see Mt. Etna, with volcanic smoke emitting from its mouth.

Taormina, with its lush vegetation and mild winter climate, has been the most popular resort in Sicily since the 19th century. The history of Taormina goes back to 396 B.C. when a fortress town was established. The train station is at sea level, with the town at the summit of a small mountain. My choice of campground was situated about one-third of the distance to the top, overlooking the very beautiful Gulf of Catania. A full moon added to the romantic effect as I viewed the lighted city below. Fortunately, the mosquitoes were busy tormenting the folks at a lower level. I slept well.

Two Irish lads, Ken and Frank, as well as an American living in Germany with his girlfriend, were camping nearby. Not only were Ken and Frank friendly, they wanted to share their barbecued chicken with me. They ate, drank, and sang until late in the evening. The log fire as well as the alcohol provided the needed stimulation. Then an amazing thing happened!

The moment I crawled into my tent, my newest friends became very quiet. Sleep came easily. In the morning I expressed my gratitude to Ken and Frank for their concern. "In Ireland we call it respect." Was it respect for my age or respect for me as a human being? I preferred to think the latter.

Leaving my gear at the campground, the climb to Taormina on my Globetrotter was almost effortless. The early morning sun as well as the spectacular view made this experience one of pure joy. Hotels, boutiques, mini-markets, churches, restaurants, and a Greek theater at the summit are all in excellent taste. I had ample time to enjoy the experience before returning to my compeggio and friends. The narrow and winding road as well as the length of the tandem made this ride hazardous. Drivers in the opposite direction gave me as much room as I needed on the curves so I could cross the center line without feeling I was endangering myself as well as others.

Ken and Frank reminded me of a tour of Ireland that Dorothy and I did when the Globetrotter was new. We ordered it from England with plans to fly to Ireland for a two-week vacation. Less than a week before our planned departure, the box and its contents arrived at Logan Airport in Boston. This gave us a very short time to become acquainted with our newest toy.

We stayed in Killarney for one night before biking the Ring of Kerry. Halfway around we stopped at the Ring Motel for the the night where a wedding reception was being held. The pool table and chairs were moved aside to provide room for dancing. Two bars were set up for the hotel patrons as well as the wedding guests. The lines to both were endless. A three-piece orchestra played American swing music.

To our amazement, the younger people were dancing with their older relatives and friends. One elderly woman used her cane as support so she could dance around it. A child of approximately ten was her partner. "Go on and dance," they said to Dorothy and me. This encouragement was all we needed to join them with our American style of swing dancing. Would this have occurred in the US? Probably not!

I said goodbye to Ken and Frank and headed in the direction of Catania, my final stop in Sicily. A small archæological museum at sea level in Catania presents both Roman and Grecian artifacts. An elaborate Greek scale with its accompanying weights as well as a small loom were displayed. Weights were not only used with the scale but they were also used to keep individual threads in place during the weaving process by weighting them down.

Some 3.5 km beyond Catania I located Camp Jonio before the onset of rain. Mt. Etna was completely fogged in, preventing a last look before heading toward the island of Malta. After erecting my tent, I went in search of a restaurant. Upon my return I was greeted by Frank Hagen, a young German cyclist. Frank and I met in Palermo. We went out for ice cream before turning in for the night. The pineapple ice cream dessert was very tasty until we received the bill. Each dessert cost $8 American! Two letters the next day at a local post office cost $8.50. I wonder how the ordinary person in Sicily can survive the high cost of living.

Finding a post office was not easy, even though black and yellow signs with the letters "PT" indicate the presence of such a facility. PT stands for "poste" and telegraph. Following the signs took me nowhere. I then asked and asked and asked some more. Finally I discovered a small postal annex in a building of identical architecture to the others and without a PT sign. To quote my granddaughter Rachel, "Give me a break!"

Catania, a provincial capital and the second largest city in Sicily, has a population of 400,000. Its university is the oldest on the island. Catania was founded by Ionian Greeks in 729 B.C. Evidence of severe bombing during World War II are non-existent due to the intensive building that has since ensued. Prior to that, destruction by earthquake in 1693 leveled the city. Uzeda Gate, located at the end of Etna Street, is built of volcanic lava and white stone, making the entrance from the west very impressive. Vast public gardens that are well cared for are located in the center city. In addition to a floral clock, the name Bellini is spelled out with flowers, as is the G clef, suggesting music as the theme. Every day the date is changed by rearranging the plants. These plants growing out of the lava appear permanent even though they are moved daily. Bellini was an operatic composer born in Catania. Teatro Bellini nearby is one of the most beautiful opera houses in Italy.

A Roman amphitheater with an open gate is located in the center of the city. As expected, the remains are of volcanic rock. The passageway where the lions were directed into the arena is still in existence. Stone seats and stairs are in disrepair in this small yet impressive structure. I photographed the arena and a Baroque public building in the background.

Half a rotisserie chicken, french fries, bananas, and grapes satisfied my hunger at noontime. I ate in a public park near the Duomo where all of the statues have their heads broken off. There is undoubtedly a story about this but my tour guide did not mention it. I decided to try to research the matter upon my return to Cambridge. To date I have no explanation.

I stopped at a nearby supermarket to replenish supplies, including toilet tissue, which is sold in a plastic wrapped package of six rolls. The most I can carry on my Globetrotter is two. I knew if I asked for only two rolls the stock answer would be "Impossible!" My Swiss army knife did its work. At the cashier I created a seemingly unsolvable problem. The cashier could not believe her eyes as she summoned the manager. Meanwhile the line of customers was ever-growing. Finally the manager in desperation sold me the two rolls so the checking-out process could continue.

As I was preparing my supper, a couple looking over the bay near my tent began to visit. She is English and he Sicilian. We talked until well into the evening as well as the next day. Our conversation became so intense that I decided to forego my planned visit to the museum in Catania. Her name is Joan Darling and his is Salvo Micieli. This visit was better than one additional museum. Before parting, Salvo asked me to do him a favor when I arrived in the old city of Jerusalem. "Please write a prayer on a piece of paper for me and put it between the stones at the Western Wall." This wall is frequently called the Wailing Wall. It is said that a prayer placed between the stones will go directly to heaven. I can attest to the fact that Salvo's prayer was answered, for when I returned at a later date the piece of paper was missing, with a different prayer in its place.

Before going to the port of departure for Malta, I bought another lunch of chicken and french fries to be eaten on the ferry. The Globetrotter and I were then safely on board and underway in the direction of the Port of Siracusa and finally Malta. The sun was bright and the day a good one to be alive. Though the cargo bay carried a few vehicles, one immense trailer carried sheets of cut marble while another had manufactured steel items as its load.

To pass the time, I read my travel guide on Israel even though I was now convinced that my friend Ken was incorrect about a ferry service to Israel from Malta. Walking the passageways of the ship, I looked for an unlocked bathroom. My perseverance paid dividends by providing me with all the hot water I needed for a relaxing shower. We arrived in Malta shortly after midnight.

MALTA

Chapter 10
MALTA

A woman passenger on the ferry suggested the southern shore rather than the northern, but she strongly advised a hotel. "In Malta we do not permit free camping. The only camping that is permitted is at St. Paul's Bay. That is a considerable distance from the port and you would be permitted to stay there for one night." I thanked her as we went through separate lines at customs.

"Let me take you and your bike to a hotel in Valetta," said a taxi driver.

"Thank you, but I prefer to cycle, and besides, I plan to camp tonight."

"Then get the f___ out of here." I thought for a moment I was back in the US.

Without a map but with my compass, I headed in a northerly direction toward St. Paul's Bay or a campsite nearby. The prospect of cycling in the dark in unfamiliar country was not especially appealing. The absence of fences and security, however, made my quest that much easier. "Surely I will find a campsite without too much difficulty where I can be hidden as well as comfortable." To my dismay, the location I chose was neither hidden or comfortable.

I selected a parking lot belonging to a church and an adjacent building that appeared vacant. Except for a brisk wind that stirred up the dust of the parking lot, I felt I'd be unseen and comfortable until morning. In the dark, I erected my tent that was now marked with a ball-point pen in such a way that with the aid of a small flashlight I could always thread the flexible poles through the proper eyelets, avoiding the problem I had on the previous rainy night in Sicily. My bike was securely locked with all my baggage inside the tent. I began to ready myself for sleep. Suddenly a window directly overhead opened followed by illumination of the room. This vacant building obviously was not vacant. Two cars pulled into the parking lot nearer to the church than to the tent. Moments later the lights were turned on in the church. Additional cars also arrived, shining their lights in my direction but parking near the church. "Have I been detected? Will the police be the next to arrive?"

Taking a fatalistic attitude, I pulled my sleeping bag over myself, using it as a blanket rather than as a bag, and slept soundly through the night. Early the next morning, perhaps at 5 o'clock, I heard an alarm clock ring. The building I thought to be abandoned houses people of a religious order. I concluded that I was surely detected and that it was time to vacate the premises.

The turbulent wind of the previous night was beginning to increase in intensity. I sensed a storm would soon strike and probably with great fury. For two reasons time was now of the essence: the occupants of the building, and the impending storm. Leaving the parking lot, I headed toward the port, seeking protection from the rain wherever possible. When I entered a tunnel leading to Valetta, the capital of Malta, the storm reached its climax. The rain was so intense that some of the cars were forced to pull over to the side of the road while others entered the tunnel, splashing me as they drove through. For two and a half hours I was forced to endure the discomfort of the wet and cold. "Was this the Malta I looked forward to visiting?" Travel brochures report an annual rainfall of 20 inches on the island. I estimated that during the time in the tunnel I was witness to approximately one-fifth of the annual total. Finally the rain abated and I headed in the direction of Valetta and breakfast.

Ronnie Soler, manager of the travel agency Cassar and Cooper, confirmed the fact that there are no ferries from Malta to Haifa. His suggestion—a very good one—was for me to book a flight to Cairo later in the week. From there I could easily work my way north into Israel through the Sinai peninsula. I would then be on the Red Sea at the port of Eilat where I planned to spend the winter. This, he explained, would place me in Egypt during the cooler fall and winter months when bicycle touring is much more practical. "In all likelihood in Egypt you would be unable to bike in the intense heat of the summer, especially in the desert," explained Ronnie. The purchase of a one-way ticket to Cairo as well as an Egyptian visa were now necessary to complete my plans. Fortunately, the Egyptian Embassy is not far from Valetta in the town of Tarxien.

Enroute to the embassy I noticed a sign for a bed and breakfast inn at the Savoy House in the town of Sliema at the reasonable rate of $16 per night. Two sisters operate this friendly inn within biking distance of Valetta and the airport. The Savoy House became my residence until my midnight departure on Sunday for Cairo. This was much more practical than camping at St. Paul's Bay, particularly as I planned to do some serious sightseeing. Malta, with its rich history and strategic location at the crossroads of the Mediterranean, was a bonus I did not consider when I planned my two-year trip.

In spite of its small size, Malta has played a vital role in history since early civilization. Two periods of history, the Neolithic and the period of the Knights of St. John, stand out from the rest, except, of course, for the role Malta played in the Allies winning back North Africa during World War II.

Originally the Egyptian pyramids were thought to be the oldest architectural monuments in the world. Recent research has revealed that the earliest Neolithic temples on the Maltese islands predate the famous pyramids of Giza by as much as 1,000 years. The temple of Ggantija on the island of Gozo is thought to be the oldest building in the world. It was built by piling huge rocks on top of each other, fitting very closely together but without any decoration. Carving and decoration came later. Equally fascinating are the cart ruts found on many of the rocky ridges of Malta, thought to be made by primitive slide-carts that were used before the invention of the wheel. Phoenicians, Carthaginians, Romans, Arabs, Normans, and Castillians also colonized the islands at different times.

In 1530 the Knights, the soldiers of Christ, withdrew from the island of Rhodes, forced out by Suleiman the Magnificent of Turkey. They chose Malta as their new homeland. Tenure was granted by Emperor Charles V. There they quickly built new fortresses and hospitals. Trade and commerce under the Knights began to flourish. In 1565, assisted by the people of Malta, the Knights of St. John defeated an invasion of Suleiman after a four-month siege. The golden era of Malta ensued, with the building of attractive buildings and the new fortress city of Valetta. Its fortifications, art treasures, museums, and churches are the work of the best European engineers and artists of the time. The palaces and other treasures led Sir Walter Scott to describe Valetta as "the city built by gentlemen for gentlemen." Two hundred sixty-eight years of rule by the Knights ended when Napoléon, on his way to Egypt, seized Malta without firing a single shot. French rule was shortlived, however, when Nelson, under the British flag, drove the French garrison out of Malta, thus starting 160 years of English domination. In 1964 Malta gained its independence and in 1974 adopted a republican constitution, gaining status as a nation.

Medina, the original capital of Malta, is an uninhabited medieval town located at the crest of a promontory toward the center of the island. It is referred to as the Silent City. Walled and complete with a moat, there are narrow and winding streets at the entry designed so that only two horses could ride abreast at the same time. The winding streets prevent an enemy from shooting directly into the fortress. Medina, occupied by Arabs as well as others, was damaged in the earthquake of 1693, after which rebuilding began. Piazza San Paul is the location of the Cathedral Museum, which is open to the public. Though the Cathedral is Baroque and the two houses next door are of

Gothic architecture, they are in harmony with each other. The Museum of Natural History is hardly an example of excellence, at least at this time. The taxidermy is so old that the animals appear dusty and shopworn, with the seams of the hides separating. A collection of vertebrates, however, ranging from fish to mammals, is exceptionally well done. Skeletons of fully grown chickens, their chicks, frogs, rabbits, and cats represent mammals that hop or leap.

A Roman villa outside the walls of the Silent City is being used as a museum. The Roman cemetery is located behind the villa. Original pillars and a mosaic floor give authenticity to this building that houses both Greek and Roman artifacts. Items of particular interest that I had not seen previously are a baby's feeding bottle made of terra-cotta and a rattle of bone. Bone hairpins, bronze brooches, and soldering iron, as well as an olive crusher with two conical shaped stones of lava used to grind wheat into flour gives evidence of the advanced civilization of the Romans. I was pleased that my travel agent Ronnie Soler recommended this area, especially as the entire length of Malta is no more than seventeen miles.

I became friendly with an English couple at a nearby craft center where Quonset huts built for the military during World War II are now being used for making and selling local crafts. The ex-GI husband discovered that his barracks is now one of these buildings. He mentioned that during the bombing of Valetta by the Germans the children in that city were moved to Medina for safety.

Is it possible to compare Malta and Bermuda, both small islands with a strong British presence? Bermuda is presently a resort island catering to the American and British tourist. Driving on the left side of the road is common to both, as is a British accent. Malta, on the other had, has converted from being a naval base to a sea-related economy. Shipping and ship repair are well represented. Malta gives me the feeling of bigness while Bermuda appears small in comparison.

St. John's Church in Valetta has four original Carvaggio paintings, one of which was stolen but later recovered. This is the painting of St. Jerome with his quill in hand that is so well known in both Catholicism and art. Victor Buttigieg, an attendant, and I became friendly. Victor explained the meaning of a very large tapestry entitled "Time Unveiling Truth" taken from a Peter Paul Rubens painting in which Faith in white and Trust in blue are conquering, while at the same time Calvin and Luther are being crushed beneath the wheels of a chariot. Catholicism in 1697 was the enduring religion. While we were visiting, he advised me to be concerned about my safety when I cross the border from Egypt to Israel. When he made the crossing, he and others formed a convoy to ensure the group's safety. Now that I have maps of both Egypt and Israel, I'm able to gain a sense of the relationship between the two countries.

"The Malta Experience" is more than a movie. It is a must for the Maltese visitor. Five thousand years of history are viewed and listened to through headsets in the language of the visitor. Overriding the headsets is the universal language, music. The film begins with the Stone Age, ending with our present era. Pictures of the German destruction of Valetta are almost unbelievable. The loss of life and property was so great that Malta became known as the "unsinkable aircraft carrier." King George recognized the valor of these indomitable people with the highest civilian award possible. The Malta Siege Memorial, opened in 1992 by Queen Elizabeth, commemorates all who died on Malta during World War II and the convoys sent to relieve this stricken and besieged island.

Once a week the Royal Palace, where inner offices as well as the Halls of State are located, is opened to visitors. Knights in full armor line either side of the Halls—an excellent "photo opp." The paintings on the ceiling are applied on fabric and then glued to the surface. During World War II they were removed and put in storage for safekeeping. Most of the frescos painted on the walls 500 years ago have been saved, except for one room that was totally destroyed. Tapestries that adorn the rooms appear new. Keeping them in a darkened room has preserved their original quality.

At the National Archæological Museum, I was introduced for the first time to Stone Age artifacts. One object, a huge stone cup with one handle, I called "Coffee American." We Americans seem to prefer our coffee in a large cup.

The War Museum is devoted to all wars, but especially to World War II. In addition to military objects, photographs give additional evidence to the vast destruction of Malta by the Germans. The hard-working Maltese, who speak English as well as their own language, are also intensely proud that they prevented the invasion of the Turks even though they were greatly outnumbered. Their language is partially Semitic, dating to a period when the island was occupied by Arabs.

Careful planning of my last day on Malta was a necessity. I wanted to visit the island of Gozo and also bike to the airport that evening for my flight to Cairo. The owners of the Savoy House were helpful in this matter. They not only permitted me to store my luggage until the evening, but provided bathroom facilities so I would be showered and shaved before leaving for the airport. They could not have been nicer.

The ride to the western coast of Malta is challenging, with its steep hills and brisk wind. "Well, at least the wind will blow me back to the Savoy House in the evening." I enjoyed passing through St. Paul's Bay where camping supposedly is permitted for a single night at a time. This sophisticated city does not lend itself to camping. At the port of Cirkewwa it was pleasurable to wait in the sun for the next ferry that would transport me and my Globetrotter to the island of Gozo. A young German and I conversed as we both waited. He was in Malta endeavoring to improve his English. I was probably a good subject even though my English is American with a Pennsylvania and New England accent. His recent experiences in Egypt gave me an insight into the country next on my list.

The Megalithic Temples of Ggantija provide an excellent example of the prehistoric monuments found on the Maltese archipelago that were built of huge stones 3,500 to 4,000 years before the birth of Christ. It is still a mystery how these early people were able to assemble stones weighing several tons apiece into the outer wall, reaching as high as six meters in some places. According to an old myth, a female giant named "Sunsuna" carried the rocks on her head to the building site. Some are convinced that Homer's famous poem "The Odyssey" is located on Gozo. With my guide book in hand, I tried to identify the different altars and structures. Dorothy and I did the same thing when we visited England and Stonehenge, another prehistoric temple of mammoth proportions.

Located within the walls of the Citadel at the highest point on the island, I visited the small yet impressive Gozo Archæological Museum. The Citadel itself with its mounted cannons meant business protecting the Maltese from the Arabs, Turks, and Barbary pirates. The pirates used Gozo as a base.

Malta Airport is new and impressive, serving only Air Malta. My early arrival gave me the opportunity to seek out the proper person to ensure the bike's safety, since I had no box to protect it from damage. Ronnie Soler had already alerted him to my needs. He assured me that my property would be well cared for. The midnight flight to Cairo left on time, arriving in Cairo at 3:15 in the morning.

In the Cairo airport, a porter wheeled the Globetrotter in my direction as I waited with the other passengers for my luggage. "Check the bicycle while I am here so its safe arrival can be reported back to Mr. Soler," said the porter. I then knew that Ronnie had done his utmost to help me. Yes, it was in the same condition as before. I reinflated the tires, loaded the baggage on the racks, and tried to decide my next move.

Mohsen Ebrahim, an engineering student working at the airport as a tourist aide, came to the rescue. When I use the word "rescue" I am using it literally. The other tourist aide was looking for only one thing—money. As an example, he was trying to sell me a complimentary map of Cairo for $20 American. Fortunately, I had no money except for four Maltese coins. Until I reached the Cairo Hilton with an American Express office, I had travelers checks but no currency. Mohsen provided me with the name of the Cairo Youth Hostel and directions to the Hilton. We planned to meet that evening near the hostel.

It was my good fortune that I headed for Cairo, a distance of approximately 26 km, before the onset of the serious traffic that this unconventional city presents. With compass in hand I headed south toward the Nile and the Hilton. Even at 5:30 in the morning, traffic police were on duty at the intersections. In locations where there are no police, traffic lights are meaningless. Huge lorries, antiquated cars, and taxis that date back to 1938, as well as donkey carts with their male occupants share the road with bicycles, mopeds, and motorcycles. It was somewhat of an early morning zoo! At no time was it necessary to ask directions; my compass was my guide. Needless to say, the Nile was a welcome sight. Shortly thereafter I discovered the Cairo Museum and the Hilton nearby. My mission was accomplished: I was in Cairo, Egypt.

EGYPT

Chapter 11
EGYPT

The unusually beautiful Nile Hilton with its Egyptian motif and lovely gardens became my central headquarters, while at the same time the Cairo Youth Hostel served as my bedroom. Bicycle parking was available with a smile at the hotel! Had I been an Egyptian on a bicycle I would not have been afforded the same courtesy, but would have been escorted beyond the walls of the hotel where I became shocked by reality. Nestled under the bushes and against the wall, mothers with their babies and begging for *bakshish*. Some of these women are severely handicapped, while others use the presence of their children to bring attention to themselves and their plight. Needless to say, the contrast between either side of the wall is light years apart.

Looking for things to do before the opening of the hostel at 2 o'clock, I visited an Egyptian coffee house for the first time, where Egyptian men smoke their water pipes and drink sweetened coffee so typical in the Arab world. Fortunately for me, English is the second language in Egypt. Even though the street signs are in Arabic, I felt comfortable asking directions from the friendly pedestrians or taxi drivers. Passing a fire station, an elderly fireman invited me to join him for a glass of tea. His companions joined us, asking questions that became routine for the next month: "What is your name?" "Are you married?" "How old are you?" I was always asked those questions and always in that order.

My friend serving me tea suddenly pointed to the street so I would be certain not to miss an unusual sight that was beginning to unfold: a herd of camels with a large brand on each animal's thigh was being driven through the city on the way to the camel market. They were recently transported to Cairo from the Sudan. These ungainly animals became a part of the traffic mix of Cairo along with the donkeys, bicycles, horses, and motor vehicles. I'm sure the camels negotiate the sand and potholes better than I, especially after a recent earthquake that temporarily brought Cairo to its knees. One of those potholes proved too much for the Globetrotter's front fork.

I shared a room at the hostel with four other tourists. One had his camera stolen. Another, Hassan Douan, a young Moroccan, and I became quite friendly. We exchanged addresses. One year after my return to Cambridge I received a letter from Hassan. "Do you remember me?" he asked. Hassan was working at the time in the food industry in Tangiers where he is a buyer of pork products. Even though the Moroccans, like the Jews, do not eat pork, they serve it in their restaurants for the tourists.

The Cairo hostel is located on Manuel Street, a short bike ride along the Nile from the Hilton. Small shops, restaurants, and businesses such as auto repair line the street. The tools required for the repair as well as the complete restoration of an automobile are locked up in sheds bordering the sidewalk, while the actual work is done on the street, curbside. Automobiles dating back to the 1930s are completely disassembled and then rebuilt within view of pedestrians. These cars serve the taxi industry as well as the private owner. A clone to my 1938 Plymouth coupe went chugging up Manuel Street.

Some of the eating places are not restaurants in the true sense of the word, but are of the vendor type with push-carts or small sheds where food is prepared and sold. Many of these vendors specialize in different varieties of macaroni generously prepared with olive oil. This type of establishment became my favorite eating place in spite of the myriad flies and masses of people. In short order the local people came to know me and I them. Lamb kabob, salad, a Kaiser roll, and mineral water cost approximately $4 American. Breakfast consisting of a hard-boiled egg, tea, and cheese was complimentary at the hostel.

At a restaurant where I stopped for coffee, the owner said that he would arrange for a permit so I could camp at Giza, site of the Pyramids. His family would provide for my meals. This is just one example of the friendly nature of Egyptians. My roommate Dave Cheeseman, whose camera was stolen, met a man on a bus who invited him to a wedding reception. Not only did Dave attend the reception, he slept there as the man's guest. His accommodations were rather basic but this added to his impromptu experience. "The toilet was a hole in the ground," said Dave.

The Museum of Egyptian Antiquities is centrally located near the Hilton, north of Midan Tahrir. More than 100,000 relics are located in this huge building, representing almost every period of ancient Egyptian history. The exhibits are chronological from the Old Kingdom to the Roman Empire.

I parked my Globetrotter in the Hilton parking lot, visited the American Express office in the hotel, then purchased a copy of the "Lonely Planet Travel Survival Kit" entitled Egypt and the Sudan. The authors of these travel guides present their material in an interesting and informative manner. With book in hand, I felt ready to spend the entire day in the museum, with special emphasis on the Tutankamun exhibit that was on a world tour several years ago. We viewed these priceless relics at the Boston Museum of Science.

The ancient Egyptians, in preparation for the next world, not only put the possessions of the deceased in the tombs, but also interred sacrificed slaves and animals. Skulls of horses with holes in their cranium are on display, giving evidence to the sacrificial nature of these highly spiritual people. Funerary treasures of New Kingdom Pharaoh Tutankamun are especially important, since this tomb was not robbed. It was found intact by the English archæologist Howard Carter in 1922. The young King Tut, as he is referred to, ruled for only nine years before his untimely death. The incredible contents of his rather modest tomb makes one wonder about the fabulous wealth that must have been interred with Pharaohs of greater importance. Seventeen hundred items are on display throughout twelve rooms of the museum. Golden sandals, a solid gold coffin, and precious jewels are but a few of the items there.

Even though visitors are forbidden to take their cameras into the museum, superb color slides are available for purchase in the gift shop. These slides and those from the Athens Museum showing the masterpieces found on the island of Santorini are among my favorites. The lovely grounds outside the museum, where picture taking is permitted, are open to the public. Considerable antiquity is on display in the gardens for one's enjoyment. I lingered there after the museum closed.

Within sight of the hostel and in the dark I hit a pothole with such force that the front forks buckled beneath me. Fortunately, the fractured parts were still attached to one another, permitting me to align them in their original position. A skilled welder would not have to guess about their proper alignment. My task was to find a willing and creative welder. "Surely if vintage cars can be restored, my Globetrotter will not be too great a challenge."

"No problem," said one of my street acquaintances when I showed him the Globetrotter. He stopped working on his immediate task and began to set up the equipment for the brazing operation with silver solder similar to the process used in the fabrication of bicycle frames. He ignited his torch, protected his eyes with dark glasses, and began brazing the forks with the wheel in place. I learned that his reason for keeping the wheel in the forks was to prevent distortion and a lack of alignment when the task was completed. There was one problem that he and I did not consider: the tire began to smoke from the heat of the torch. A tap on his shoulder brought this to his attention. He then put me to work spinning the wheel while he did the brazing. This prevented heat from the torch from being concentrated for too long at any single place on the tire. The repair was then completed with satisfaction.

"How much do I owe you?"

"Six Egyptian pounds," or about $3.25 was his reply. I gave him ten, remembering that in France a similar repair in Toulouse cost $70 and a four-day delay of my travels. Under the circumstances I considered myself very fortunate, not realizing that this repair was not intended to be permanent. Had I known that several months later while touring the Golan Heights in Israel when the front fork permanently self-destructed, I would have begun a search for a new fork without delay. Giza and the Pyramids were now my goal for the following day.

Looking south from Cairo, the Pyramids are easily discernible when viewed from the upper floors of buildings. In my judgment, all that was necessary to reach Giza was my compass. Similar to an experience in London, where I followed my compass toward the Tower of London, I missed the Pyramids by a few kilometers, ending up in Memphis, the ancient capital of Lower Egypt. In London I missed the Tower and discovered the city dump. "Standard deviation" is the problem.

Memphis itself is a bit of a disappointment, but the baby sphinx of Ramses I made of alabaster was an excellent subject for my slide collection. Facing east, as do all sculptures done by the early Egyptians, one side is badly worn from the weather. One of the reasons for my disappointment in Memphis is the removal of the ancient stones by local peasants to build their homes. Many of these stones are inscribed with the hieroglyphics of the day. Fortunately, antiquity is protected today, preventing further pillage.

A shop nearby demonstrates the making of papyrus. The papyrus art work in that store is, of course, for sale, and at inflated prices. Naturally growing papyrus is cut and soaked in water for six days, with the water changed daily. It is then pressed and dried. Strips of the dried material are laid out in a "cross patch" fashion and again immersed in water. When removed, they are pressed and dried into the final product upon which drawings are made. Fake papyrus is made of banana leaf instead of the authentic material. Buyer beware!

Located near Memphis is the Sphinx Carpet School where carpets are hand-made by children. These young girls with small and agile fingers are capable of tying the knots that their elders cannot. They work four hours a day and go to school four hours. Many are permitted to create their own designs, while others follow a predetermined pattern. They enjoyed being photographed even though they are female. Their mothers, aunts, and grandmothers would have denied me the opportunity of bringing back these memories on film.

In the 27th century B.C., the Pharaoh's chief architect Imhotep designed the Step Pyramid of King Zoser in Saqqara, the necropolis of Memphis. This was the largest stone structure ever built and the inspiration for Egypt's future architectural achievements. I found the pyramid quite easily on my ride back toward Cairo. Unfortunately, the entrance to the Pyramid was closed to the public. At one site in the desert of Saqqara four pairs of feet have been preserved where the second toe is characteristically longer than the big toe. These sculptures are thought to be the feet of the Pharaoh, his wife, and their children.

My ride back to the hostel was in darkness, giving credibility to my total enjoyment of the day. Naturally, I was lost most of the time until I found the Nile and then the Hilton. The ride from the Hilton to the hostel was routine in spite of intense traffic. Biking defensively usually makes city traffic bearable. That night, though, an impatient taxi driver touched my rear wheel but, fortunately, I did not crash. While mentioning my favorite means of transport, I'm reminded of the Egyptian children and their interest in the Globetrotter. They are attracted to the tandem as a moth is to a flame. Any time I stop, they run out to touch the bike, many of them holding on to the rear rack.

At the same time, of course, they are shouting *bakshish*, or "money." I wonder if they realize they are putting me at risk when they reach for the bike. Eventually I had to work out a technique to avoid this constant quest for bakshish. It was out of necessity that I learned how to fool them every time, especially when I was traveling south toward Luxor and Aswan.

Swarms of children come running across the fields shouting "bakshish" as they climb the embankment onto the road. They will then wait for me to come by so they can play their little game of "trick or treat." If I do not give them money it's fair game for them to play a trick on me. As mentioned, they try to grasp the back of the bike, or on some occaions they will attempt to thrust sugar cane sticks into the spokes of the wheels. If I pass this test safely, I will then receive a barrage of stones, with many reaching the target. I could never carry enough money to satisfy this mob of children.

Here is my technique: I will slow down as I approach these young people, giving them the impression I plan to stop. They become complacent, quietly waiting for me. With superhuman strength I accelerate so rapidly that they are left wondering how they could have been fooled so easily. Even their stones fall short of the mark.

At times, adults will act in a similar manner for the same reasons. I remember one Egyptian male dressed in his long cotton coat and sandals running down the road at top speed trying to catch me, his sandals flapping on the road behind me. It was a close call but I outdistanced him.

Even the Egyptian post office is an experience, especially if the sender wishes to mail a package, as contrasted to a letter. The contents must be placed in an almost tissue-thin envelope but not sealed except in a postal clerk's presence. I was certain none of my brochures and mementos would reach the US without being lost. The clerk will then seal the package with the stamps purchased for that purpose. To avoid this problem, I found a heavier weight envelope but was refused at the post office. My joy! The package arrived safely.

After learning firsthand about the Egyptian postal system, I went in search of the Cairo Tower, a focal point of the city. My "Lonely Planet Travel Survival Kit" was my constant companion. From the top of the Tower I identified Ramses Square and the Island of Gezira below where a soccer game was under way. The Island is devoted to sports.

Ramses Square is an incredibly busy concentration of roads and people. I had the experience of arriving there by biking the elevated highway that criss-crosses the Nile. "If the donkey carts can do it, so can I." My return was by way of the sandy, rutted, potholed, and highly trafficked local roads leading toward the Hilton. The recent earthquake left the roads of the city in deplorable condition, giving ample evidence to the fact that Cairo is built on top of the same desert as Giza and the Pyramids. One pothole was so deep that I felt certain my front fork would again self-destruct. Except for the rim being forced out of alignment, there was no other visible damage. I trued the wheel at the Hilton parking lot using the brake block as my guide.

The following day was Friday, the Moslem sabbath. At six that evening I was 40 km south of Cairo and the Pyramids looking for a hotel and restaurant. Darkness forced me to turn on my generator light to avoid hitting the donkeys and/or pedestrians quietly walking along the side of the road. My "Lonely Planet Guide" indicated that 80 km to the south I would find a hotel. I had leisurely toured the Pyramids and the Sphinx without regard for my evening necessities. "One way or another I will solve my eating and sleeping needs when the time comes." The time was now!

A very basic unpainted wooden structure with an outdoor prayer rug came into view. A canvas roof of a sort was constructed over the rug where someone was kneeling in prayer.

A kerosene lamp illuminated several tables and chairs, suggesting that I was looking at some sort of restaurant. At that moment we were south of the small village of El Badreshein. A plan immediately began to formulate: "If I stop here for my supper and get to know the owner, he may give me permission to erect my tent on the prayer rug. This would be a perfect place to spend the night."

Using a small hand pump for water, I washed my hands and face before ordering my food. The owner's grandson pumped the water at his grandfather's instruction. A meal of eggs, cheese, bread, and tea, the only items on the menu, was served by the youngster. Using sign language, I asked for a knife by showing him my Swiss Army knife. The result: a second platter of eggs, cheese, and bread.

I then approached the owner, again using sign language, explaining my need for a place to sleep and the possible use of the prayer rug as my tent site. He understood. His alternate suggestion proved much more practical as well as being safe. He brought the Globetrotter inside the structure and then pointed to a wooden cot nearby, an excellent location for my air mattress and sleeping bag. It is my understanding that at times he sleeps at his restaurant using this cot. My air mattress, in the past, made the ground as well as sagging beds at hostels reasonably comfortable. This, I felt, would be no exception.

Members of the owner's family, including his wife, came to visit. A son who served in the Egyptian army spoke enough English to converse in a limited manner. The family talked in great length in Arabic, discussing me as well as the contents of my handlebar bag. The Swiss Army knife with its Swiss cross on the handle caused quite a bit of discussion. One of the men present said in a loud and contemptuous manner "Christian." I tried to explain that the cross had no religious significance. They then became cruious about my religion. I was obviously not Moslem and perhaps to them I was denying that I was not Christian. Although I understood the word *yahuin* in their conversation, I acted as though I did not comprehend the question. Egypt and Israel had been at war and Egypt suffered badly. I had no intention of losing my makeshift motel room because of ideology.

In the morning, the grandson greeted me before leaving for school. His grandfather followed soon after. He prepared hot water so I could shave, served me a tasty breakfast, and accepted payment for the food but not the accommodations. During these few moments a donkey and cart arrived. A tank was mounted on the cart with a small bucket hanging from the spout in the rear. The driver replenished the owner's kerosene that he uses for his stove and lanterns. His older son then arrived with a dish of dates and honey as a gift for me, and a farewell handshake. I felt overwhelmed.

Beni Suef, my next destination, a distance of 80 km, gave me ample time to reflect on my visit to the Pyramids. Watching the horses and camels galloping across the desert surrounding the Pyramids reminded me of the movie "Lawrence of Arabia." The young men and boys riding their mounts enjoyed themselves to the fullest. A solar bark belonging to the Pharaoh Cheops occupies its own museum. The boat is designed to accommodate 48 slaves. Half of them rowed while half slept. I wondered if 48 slaves were sacrificed to ensure the safe passage of their king to heaven. The ship constructed of Lebanese cedar in which all the parts are united with hemp. There are no nails in this 5,000-year-old original bark reconstruction. When the hemp becomes wet it shrinks, bringing all the pieces into contact.

Some tourists leave Giza unimpressed with the Pyramids, while others such as myself are left in awe. The Pyramids, in my opinion, are truly worthy of being known as one of the seven wonders of the world. I probably would have gone inside the Great Pyramid of Cheops except for concern for the safety of my possessions that were attached to or hanging from the bike. On my second visit to Cairo and Giza I threw caution to the winds and joined the tourists up a narrow passageway to the top of the Cheops.

The Sphinx in Arabic is *Abu Hol*, meaning the father of terror. The Abu Hol is carved from a single piece of limestone. It was left in the quarry from which Cheops had his stones cut for his pyramid. During their occupation of Egypt, the Turks used the Sphinx for target practice. The nose and chin that were shot off reside in a museum in London. Negotiations are said to be under way to have the parts returned to Egypt, their rightful owner.

My hotel room in Beni Suef, such as it was, was located on the third floor across the street from the train station. After the long and hot ride, the stairs with my baggage were a challenge. My knees healed, permitting comfortable bike riding, but I still had difficulty with stairs. Two other problems persisted without letup: flies and children. Horse, camel, donkey, sheep, goat, and human dung in Egypt serve as a breeding ground for those tenacious flies. The thought of the diseases they carry is almost beyond comprehension. One fortunate fact is that flies go to sleep once the lights are turned off. The unfortunate fact is that at night the mosquitoes take over where the flies leave off. The other problem is children crying out for "money, money, money." At times adults will restrain them, especially when I appear hostile.

Was the reinfection of my foot caused by the infestation of flies or was it that the infection was not completely healed? Needless to say, I was concerned, giving some thought to the possible discontinuance of my tour. Fortunately, I was able to purchase ampicillin without a prescription. Though the infection was never eliminated, I was able to prevent it from becoming acute. "When I reach Israel I will avail myself of some good Western medicine and seek a cure." The following day was one of rest and relaxation. I slept most of the day, giving my entire body rest. The infection or the antibiotics may have induced sleep.

Beni Suef was the perfect location to register with the police and have my passport stamped. Travelers to Egypt are given seven days for this routine method of keeping track of the tourist population. Those who choose to ignore this requirement put themselves in jeopardy when they prepare to leave the country. This routine procedure at the police station took over an hour of bureaucratic nonsense. Each officer shuffled through the pages of my passport and then passed it on to the next person. Finally I was told that my passport was in order and that it did not require further handling. At no time did I receive the necessary rubber stamp. Several weeks later, when I wanted to leave Egypt and enter Jordan, the police's error became evident.

Motorists in Cairo drive with their horns, while in Beni Suef they are much more relaxed. Here the roads are dirt, with deep and rough tracks caused by horse-drawn cabs that are much more suited to the roads than a narrow bicycle tire. Balloon-tire bicycles of the one-speed variety made in China are better adapted for the roads of Beni Suef than my Globetrotter. One such bike sounded like an eighteen-wheel tractor trailer instead of a bicycle. The owner, a young male, attached a truck air horn to the rubber squeeze bulb of his bicycle horn, giving it the sound of great importance. Until I realized that I was not being forced off the road by a truck, I quickly moved over to the right.

Drinking water is plentiful along the Nile. I noticed that many store owners hose the sidewalks in front of their stores while others frequently wash their cars. The desert environment deposits a crust of sand and dust on everything. Potable water, fortunately, can be found three or four feet beneath the ground's surface.

Some Western clothing is worn by young men, with razor sharp creases in their trousers. The older generation wears the traditional long cotton frock that buttons in the front, resembling a woman's dress. Some of these frocks appear immaculately clean while others probably have never been washed. Many men wear sandals, while others prefer to go barefoot.

The women cover themselves in black so they won't show the shape of their bodies. Many keep their head and face covered, with a small opening in the front. They can see out but others cannot look in. One such woman walked down the street wearing high heels and the traditional all-black costume. In stores I noticed that women show considerable interest in lacy undergarments that can be enjoyed yet not seen. For the most part I tried not to look at the women, since their men were looking at me. It was easier that way.

Farm machinery is unnecessary in Egypt as long as there are a myriad of children and women to do the work. The short-handled hoe is the major farming tool. Tomatoes and corn were being harvested at the time. In some places gasoline powered pumps are utilized to raise the level of the water from the canals to the earth's surface, while in other more primitive areas donkeys are employed. A donkey is blindfolded and then tied to the handle of a rotating pump handle, the pump being at the center of the circle. Once the donkey is struck on his rear he will begin to walk in a circle, thus pumping the water. Another form of employment is the making of bricks from camel or donkey dung. Women in their black costumes sitting along the road with a small dish in their hands collect the dung and fashion it into the shape of a brick. I could not help fantasizing when I saw this for the first time. "Dear, let's build an addition onto our house. Perhaps we should build a game room at the same time. How about a garage?"

At an intersection I saw a sign in English directing me to Maydoun Pyramid and Oasis. Maydoun was not in my guidebook but was within sight of the road. It deserved investigation even though the sun was exceptionally hot. Being covered with limestone, this pyramid appears different from those at Giza. At one time the Great Pyramids were similarly covered.

An Arab at the oasis came out to greet me with the information that they had a cafeteria inside the hut. This was great news until I discovered that, to him, cafeteria meant tea. Fortunately, I had some processed cheese and bread in my panniers. This would have been an excellent location for camping except that food was unavailable. I was also concerned about being a distance from humanity with the chronic infection in my foot.

My early departure from the hotel disturbed three of the employees sleeping fully clothed on the lobby couches. One of them refreshed himself for about one minute, returning with a broom. He began to sweep the sidewalk outside the hotel, using his hand for a dust pan. The others continued to sleep. I headed for the Nile.

At this point the river is exceptionally wide, with a bridge spanning it in the distance. Barbed wire prevents human access to the Nile. Apparently it is permissible to use the Nile canals, but not the river itself, for human purposes. Women wash their clothes and cooking utensils in the canals. Water buffalo keep themselves cool in the same water that people use for bathing. The shallow wells with their hand pumps provide for potable drinking water. It is interesting to see the heads and horns of the cattle with their bodies submerged.

Women, horses, and donkeys are the beasts of burden in Egypt. The donkey has short ears and a face more like a small horse than a jackass. The women take care of the family, work in the fields, and carry huge burdens on their heads. It is not at all unusual to see a man riding his donkey while his woman walks behind carrying a huge burden on her head. In the fields, some of the workers bend over to do their work while others squat or sit with their hoe between their legs. Every plant receives individual care. Beans, tomatoes, cotton, corn, and zucchini were being harvested locally. Most of my riding was along the canal instead of the Nile.

A motorcycle carrying three men passed me. One of

them hit me on my back with such force that the memory still lingers. Later on, a 17-year-old male on his bicycle rode along with me. His name was Usama Motasseum Ahmed. This intelligent and friendly youth more than made up for the earlier assault. Usama confided that his goal in life is to study medicine in Cairo or in the town of Minya. We stopped for lunch. I took a photo of Usama and a horde of children before continuing. He said goodbye, asking me to promise to invite him to American upon my return. "Address all correspondence in Arabic," said Usama. He wrote his name and address in my address book in both English and Arabic.

El Minya, 347 km south of Cairo, is a center for soap manufacture and sugar processing. The tree-lined Corniche, or promenade, along the Nile is a pleasant place for a picnic or a ride in a horse-drawn hantour. P.L.M. Hotel Nefertiti, a beautiful and modern hotel with a room rate of $65 payable in U.S. currency, attracts the upscale American tourist. Attached to the hotel, take-out food is prepared and sold. The hotel dining room was too fancy for this "grubby" cyclotourist. In the morning at a roadside restaurant I was asked if I wanted an omelette. I explained with gestures that I preferred two eggs over light. Will I never learn? My breakfast consisted of three hard-boiled eggs.

Back to the housefly: we have all seen photographs of third-world country children who are covered with flies. Yesterday while stopping for a cola, I was witness to a small boy who looked up at me and smiled. His face was covered with flies. He had flies in the corners of his eyes and in his ears, in addition to the usual places. Believe it or not, this youngster made absolutely no effort to chase these insects. He was immune to the common fly.

I was going to describe the town of Mallawi, 48 km south of El Minya, as "seething," but a better term is "pulsating." The people, and there were a lot of them, are busy making things. Mallawi is a stopping place for trucks and truck repair. Auto and truck engines are rebuilt on the street, with tool sheds lining the sidewalks as I saw in Cairo. Bodies of cars and trucks are removed from their chassis in preparation for complete restoration. A fully restored 1941 Desoto reminded me of our family car in 1941.

The horses and hantour cabs are immaculately adorned with brass decorations. Some carriages are even equipped with turn signals. Manure in the street is removed at regular intervals, leaving the odor of horses but with very little evidence of their manure. I liked Mallawi.

Magdy Mohammed Emara and I became friendly at the local commercial hotel where he and his driver friends were staying for the night. Magdy practically begged me to take his photo. They invited me to go out with them for coffee and entertainment but I was discouraged by the hotel management who gestured: pickpockets. Regretfully, I refused their invitation. If I could relive that night, I know I would join them for an evening of enjoyment. By coincidence, I met Magdy again several days later; I was resting alongside the road trying to recover from the heat. When Magdy saw me he stopped his truck to investigate. He was concerned that I was ill and perhaps needed assistance.

Wednesday, the 28th of October is not what one might call a usual day in the life of a cyclotourist. In addition to putting salt instead of sugar in my tea, I was struck in the back of the head by a passing fun-loving Egyptian male and ended up being transported 40 km by the police. Oh yes, I was also hit in the back with a rock thrown by a child and was chased by a man-eating dog. This was, of course, in addition to the usual encounters with children begging for bakshish and their grabbing onto the back of the bike.

A pickup truck carrying a load of human cargo passed. These trucks serve as buses for the local population. One of the passengers reached out and struck me with his hand, hitting me at the back of my head with such force that I had a headache for most of the day. Fortunately, I was able to keep the Globetrotter under control. When I discussed this incident and others with the police they tried to assure me that their brothers meant no harm. It is their little joke they are playing on me. Fortunately, aspirin is readily available in Egypt; packets are often given as small change in the stores.

At 9:15 in the morning at one of the many road checks, I was stopped by the police supposedly for five minutes. "The bus will arrive in five minutes to transport you and your bike," said the officer. He gave no reason for his actions. I then learned that an Egyptian five minutes could be five hours. "Why are you detaining me?" I asked after an hour's wait.

"For your own safety," said the officer. He then brought me a glass of tea. I waited patiently.

In desperation I finally spoke to the young officer again, asking him if I could be taken through the troubled area in a police vehicle. "Impossible" was his reply. Shortly thereafter, the police put the Globetrotter in the back of a police Jeep. I was then invited to join the young officer up front. At a speed of 100 km we sped past cars, trucks, people, donkeys, and camels, the horn barking its warning that someone of importance was coming through. We did not hit a single obstacle!

At a roadside stand the officer stopped to purchase two Pepsi Colas which we drank as we drove the final distance to another roadblock 10 to 15 km north of the city of Asyut. "You will now be safe," said the officer. He and I unloaded the bike, shook hands, and went our separate ways.

Asyut, settled on a broad fertile plain during times of the Pharoahs, is the unofficial point where Upper (southern) and Lower (northern) Egypt meet. It is the chief agriculture center of Upper Egypt, dealing in camels, cotton, grain, and carpets. For several centuries the Forty Day Road from Darfur

province in the Sudan ended in Asyut where the camel caravans traveled, bringing these animals to market. Today Cairo
is the final destination.

The entrance to Asyut is impressive, with its wide and
clean boulevard passing Asyut University and its buildings.
The Nile comes into view shortly thereafter. This exceptional
view precedes the center of the city. Taking my lunch at a small
outdoor spa, I left the city in the direction of Luxor.

The police assist brought me to Asyut sooner than anticipated and too early to stop for the night. Sahag, 57 km to
the south, seemed to be the only prospect for any sort of accommodations. I now had another reason for an earlier departure from Asyut: the local museum was closed until Tuesday.

I thought I was seeing a mirage instead of a campground 27 km south of Asyut. This would be the first and last
camping I would do until I reached the Sinai Peninsula and
Red Sea. This meant also that for the first time in Egypt I would
not have to deal with flies and mosquitoes. Unfortunately, the
restaurant dealt a blow to my digestive tract. I should have
known better than to eat the meal that was placed before me.
The meat that was prepared hours, or perhaps days, before was
not only indigestible but unappetizing. I would have been safer
had I eaten the canned tuna in my pack.

"Welcome to Egypt" is a common phrase spoken by
shopkeepers and people on the street. The next day I was "welcomed" by being struck in the back with stones, having children try to jam sugar cane between my spokes, and having my
panniers unzipped. My favorite bungee cord and water bottle
were now an Egyptian child's favorite possessions. The chilren
are totally undisciplined. They are spoken to by their elders
and/or parents but enforcement is totally absent.

The Ramses Hotel recommended by a townsperson
was closed. An inch of dust and sand had deposited itself on

the floor, railings, and stairs. My second choice for accommodations was not much better. Upon entering, I walked through rubble to a darkened stair that led to my room on the third floor. The door was secured with a padlock. Two iron beds and windows that had probably never been washed describes the room with its cold water sink and tub. The toilet was a hole in the floor. This was the sort of accommodation I would think twice about before housing my pet, much less a human.

In search of water, an elderly Egyptian approached, offering coffee and any assistance I might need. This, of course, set off a warning in my brain. In a small room off the main street that he calls his office he made me coffee and insisted on buying me a breakfast of rolls and goat cheese. He accepted no money for this kindness. I then discovered that he wanted me to invite him to the US where he offered to work for me even though he knew I was a retiree. "Egypt is not a good place to live. I receive too little money per month," was his reply. He then wrote his name and address in Arabic on an envelope so I would have no excuse not to write.

Sixty-two kilometers north of Luxor is the provincial capital of Qena, at the intersection of the main Nile road and the road across the desert to the towns of Safaga and Hurghada on the Red Sea. It is also a railway terminus on the route from Cairo to Aswan and the Aswan Dam. I became better acquainted with Qena and its hotel than I had planned. The hotel was directly across from the train station, an easy spot to find when I returned from Luxor the following day to recover my passport from the desk clerk. He neglected to give it to me when I paid my bill the following morning, and I forgot to ask for it.

I secured the bike at the hotel, closed the door to my room behind me, and fell asleep fully clothed on the bed. At midnight, without supper, I turned off the ceiling fan and fell asleep again. No food was better than the prepared food such as at the previous campground where the sauce and meat were prepared hours or days before. Macaroni at the pushcarts is, of course, different. It is fresh and tasty, the only problem being that it's prepared with an overabundance of olive oil. My breakfast consisted of packaged cookies and a large glass of mango juice. The outdoor market displayed pomegranates, bananas, dates, onions, and tomatoes. Unfortunately, they were all fly-infested. Dates immersed in honey were not appetizing, particularly where they were uncovered.

The mosque in front of me is the tallest structure in Qena. I knew I was missing great opportunities, but photographing people was usually impossible. Many Moslems, especially women, do not want their picture taken. As usual, I was not without friends even though I preferred being alone. Everyone wanted something: money, my watch, my pen, or they wanted to ride the bicycle. On some occasions, in contrast to "no pictures," men and boys asked to have their picture taken even though they knew they would never see the photo.

It was interesting to observe camels as working animals. They are so burdened with sugar cane that only their heads are visible. Often a cart will be drawn by one donkey and one horse, a strange looking pair. A donkey was being ridden by a man and a child while the woman walked behind with a large burden on top of her head.

The children appear quite attractive, with ready and open smiles, but the older people are drawn and aged in appearance. On occasion a male dressed in western clothing with shirt and tie appears on the scene looking very businesslike. The fundamentalist women in their black habits and veils occupy a portion of the scene as well.

Penicillin kept the foot infection under control. Without it I would have had to head for a Western-type hospital. The affected area was still red and moderately swollen but at least I felt able to walk and pedal. My limited first-aid kit now contained an additional supply of ampicillin. I felt fortunate to be able to arrive at Luxor under my own power.

While looking for the budget hotel St. Mark's Pension, as recommended by the "Lonely Planet Guide," Honey Tarek, riding his bicycle, found me. I looked at a campground belonging to the YMCA but it had very little appeal. Honey promised to take me to the New Home Pension, a budget hotel that he assured me was among the best. We covered every dirt road in Luxor before arriving at what appeared to be a very nice small hotel. When Honey asked me for my passport I then realized I had left it at my hotel in Qena. "What shall I do now?" I knew that eventually this sort of thing would happen!

Honey volunteered to return to Qena with me via surface taxi so I could retrieve my passport. A surface taxi is a motor vehicle that leaves one parking area for another if and when all seats are filled. The cost is very reasonable, allowing the local citizenry to go from place to place for very little money. I was the only non-Egyptian aboard our particular taxi. The trip that took me most of the day by bicycle took one hour by taxi, to a part of Qena I did not recognize. "Where is the hotel?" asked Honey.

"It's near the railroad station, within view of the mosque." This required hiring a hantour that took us to an exact address, rather than the surface taxi that only goes from one fixed point to another. The owner-manager of the hotel, instead of apologizing, merely asked if I was staying another night. I was mildly angered.

Upon our return to the New Home Pension, I met Cheryl, a young American woman who, unfortunately, was bedridden with intestinal problems. Cheryl, a resident of Tahoe, California, lived in Israel for several months working as a waitress at Eilat. She was planning to return there and begin work at an all-new hotel. When my friend Klaus and I later stopped at the all-new Princess Hotel a short distance from the Egypt-Israel border, I asked for Cheryl but she was not known by the management.

2 WHEELS, 2 YEARS, AND 3 CONTINENTS

The attention the Egyptian men paid Cheryl was short of amazing. They bounced in and out of her room just so they could take another look. The code in Egypt is so strict that the sexes do not come into contact with one another until after marriage, leaving the male population sexually starved. This may also be true with the women but I cannot comment from my own experience. Egyptian women are fully clothed so that their arms and legs are hidden from view. Cheryl in her nightgown was a vision that was more than these men could handle.

My first full day in Luxor was one of zero cycling and an abundance of relaxation. Tours of Luxor or Karnak Temples did not start until 3 PM. At 1:30 I returned to the American Express office for the start of a tour of the Luxor Temple. Due to non-participation, the tour was cancelled. This gave me an opportunity to discuss my plans with the manager, seeking his advice. It was unlikely that I would bike across the desert from Qena to Safaga on the Red Sea, a distance of 200 km with no towns in between. A bus was my only other alternative. It was now dark—an excellent time to visit Luxor Temple.

Luxor Temple was built by the New Kingdom Pharaoh Amenophis III on the site of a previous temple. It is a strikingly graceful piece of architecture, particularly at night, on the banks of the Nile. The lights, palm trees, moonlit sky, and majesty of the Temple create a wonderful atmosphere. The romance of the evening should have been spent with a special and beautiful woman. It was an evening for holding hands.

This temple has been added to over the centuries by Tutankhamun, Ramses II, Nectanebo, Alexander the Great, and the Romans. Excavation work has been going on since 1885, exposing a part of the Avenue of Sphinxes, a remarkable sight, especially at night. At the entrance are colossal statues of Ramses II and a pink granite obelisk. At one time there were a pair, but today its twin is at the Place de la Concorde in Paris. Now that I visited the illuminated Luxor Temple at night, I made plans to return in daylight to take my photographs.

Luxor Museum is a wonderful little museum about halfway between the Luxor and Karnak Temples. The well-chosen collection of relics from the Theban temples and necropolis are superbly displayed. A finely carved statuette of Tuthmosis dates from at least 1436 B.C. This sculpture is considered one of the finest of ancient Egypt. On the first floor, a well-preserved cow-goddess head from the Tutankhamun tomb is given special prominence. Egyptian coins, dishes, hinged pitchers with their lids, and a statuette of the God Amun of Karnak with facial expressions of King Tutankhamun are a few of the marvelous objects to be seen at the Luxor Museum.

Karnak Temple was built, added to, dismantled, enlarged, and decorated over a period of nearly 1,500 years. The original sanctuary of the Great Temple of Amun was built during the Middle Kingdom period. A light and sound show in the evening interested me, especially after my existential experience the previous night at the Luxor Temple. An easy bike ride to the Karnak Temple and the ticket office prepared me for the evening's performance. My return took me past the beautifully situated Nile Hilton bordering the river. In the hotel gardens I met two English widows. I could very easily have become interested in one of them. We talked at some length but did not exchange names and addresses. One of the ladies stated that she was spending the tax her children would have had to pay on their inheritance. She appeared to enjoy spending it!

Standing in line waiting to enter the Karnak Temple that evening, I became aware of an English-speaking couple in front of me. "English is spoken," I said out loud, intending for them to hear me. Don and Toby Galinsky and I became instant friends. Take the *sky* off the end of Galinsky and we are almost cousins. Don and Toby's home is Toronto, Canada. The show itself is a bit overdone. "When the show is over," said Don, "we would like you to join us for dinner at the Hilton where we're staying." A buffet supper and imported beer added to the evening's enjoyment. We agreed that I would reciprocate in Aswan.

Don and Toby had reservations on the "Nile Goddess", the luxury cruise ship owned by the Sonesta Corporation, scheduled to sail from Luxor to Aswan. We planned to meet the following Sunday at the Sonesta pier in Aswan.

Karnak, the Great Temple of Amun by day, is well worth the visit. Perhaps I prefer the Luxor Temple because it the first ancient Egyptian temple I visited. A canal at one time connected the Amun and Montu enclosures, with the Nile providing access for the sacred boats on their journey to the Luxor Temple during the Opet Festival. A paved Avenue of Sphinxes linked the Amun and Luxor Temples. Most of this 3-km avenue lies beneath the paved roads of modern Luxor. Only one of the four obelisks is still standing at the entrance of Karnak, while parts of the others lie in the court. I was shown a temple with two interesting statues on the Karnak site. A hole in the ceiling permits the sun to enter the temple one day each year: for a short time on December 20, the sun illuminates the two statues.

The West Bank of Luxor is the necropolis of ancient Thebes, a vast City of the Dead. During the New Kingdom this necropolis was inhabited by a living population who attempted to protect the tombs from robbers. Artisans, laborers, and priests also lived on the West Bank. The secrets of tomb building, decoration, and concealment were handed down through the families. Even though there was only one entrance to the Valley of the Kings, few of the well-concealed tombs escaped the vandalism of grave robbers.

Fortunately, I did not hire a donkey but relied on the Globetrotter and my own foot power to tour the area. I would have had a lot of riding with little time for tomb visiting. Following a light breakfast, I headed for the Nile ferry. There was a great deal of activity at the terminal, particularly by young people representing themselves as guides. A guide, in my opinion, is not necessary, as the tombs are well marked. My "Lonely Planet Guide" was my source of information. The incredible heat and mountainous terrain made the day's expedition both a joy and a challenge.

A massive pair of statues known as the Colossi of Memnon are all that remain of the Temples of Amenophis III. These statues are the first objects of antiquity to be seen, located just before the ticket office. One of the most magnificent of Theban temples, the Temples of Amenophis has now, for the most part, returned to the earth.

Close to the Valley of the Queens, the Ramesseum, raised by Ramses II for his ultimate glory, lies in ruins. Dedicated to the god Amun, it was intended to be an eternal testimony to the greatness of this king. The faceless statues of Ramses II weigh over 1,000 tons each.

I returned to my Globetrotter in preparation for a tour of the Valley of the Kings. The thought of theft or vandalism in this remote area never entered my mind. To my dismay, the Presta valve pump was gone. To the non-cycling reader, this may seem insignificant: "Buy another pump." The word "Presta" is the key; it is the valve and pump of choice for European racing and touring bicycles, but not in Luxor, Egypt. In spite of this knowledge, I planned to visit bicycle shops in Luxor on the outside chance that I'd be lucky.

Entering the Tomb of Seth Nakhl, I was aware that except for the attendant, I was the only visitor. The attendant, a man older than myself and wearing the usual Egyptian costume, greeted me with open arms. I gave little thought to his kissing me on both cheeks. This form of greeting is not uncommon in Europe. Kissing me on the mouth was more than I was ready for. His hands, I might add, were as active as his mouth. This was just one more experience with Egyptian males.

Daniel Barre and I met on the way up the mountain overlooking the Temple of Hatshepsut. One of the natives led us up a steep path to the summit, a high and desolate place.

Daniel, a postman on the Isle of France, and I exchanged addresses. Since then we have been pen pals. He writes to me in French and I reply in English. When we parted, I headed for the entrance to the Temple of Hatshepsut but was disappointed to learn it was closed to visitors. From the outside, it resembles a train station more than a tomb.

At the Luxor Bicycle Shop I found what I thought to be a Presta valve pump. It was not the same quality as the one stolen, but that made very little difference. "Now, if I choose to bike across the desert from Qena to Safaga, I at least have a pump for that possible emergency. Wasn't I fortunate to find such a product in an out-of-the-way place?"

Nick, a guest at the New Home Pension, and I arranged to meet in Aswan. A civil engineer from England, he was traveling for eighteen months. While touring Israel and just about out of money, Nick became undecided about his immediate future. Should he seek employment or return to England? Working in Israel as an alien meant that he would be working "under the table" at a low level and for a very low wage. An incident then changed Nick's future as well as the way he looks at things such as fate. He found six thousand US dollars without identification on the street! No, he did not turn it in to the police. We enjoyed a lunch of grilled fish and rice pilaf.

Kom Ombo, located approximately 165 km south of Luxor, was a greater distance than I wanted to pedal in one day, but I had no choice. Kom Ombo is the nearest town that supports a hotel and restaurant. My arrival was destined to be in the dark. Leaving Luxor, I stopped at the Sheraton Hotel complex and then headed south. Though nice, the Sheraton does not compare with the Luxor Hilton.

The vegetation is verdant on the Nile side of the road, while the scene on the other side began to look and feel like desert. Sugar cane and bananas are the major agricultural products. Men and boys, chewing sugar cane as I passed, offered me some. It is little wonder that the teeth of these Egyptians are so badly decayed. Soon both sides of the road became hot and dry, taking on the appearance of a lunar landscape. In its stark nature it was also very beautiful.

Fortunately, I brought some emergency rations along. The few stores along this route sold only cold drinks and sweets. A meal of pilaf and meat was being prepared at one stopping place, but I wasn't hungry. Desolation set in as I penetrated the desert in quiet solitude.

A young boy with his donkey and cart appeared on the opposite side of the road. He was wearing the usual full length costume I was accustomed to seeing. In his cart were fresh oranges and a portable scale. He weighed my selection of fruit by holding his scale in one hand and added weights to the other until the scale balanced. I then discussed my taking his photo while he held the scale. Canned meat was the incentive that closed the deal. At the last moment, when I pointed my camera in his direction, he covered his face with his hands. This slide, in spite of the outcome, is one of my favorites, especially when I think of the desert conditions where this youngster and I met.

Biking in the dark on the way to Kom Ombo convinced me not to try a night ride through the desert from Qena to Safaga. One pothole and my party would be history. If the Safaga road compares to this one, such an accident was almost a certainty. I then made a firm decision: from Aswan, I will train to Qena, staying overnight in a hotel. Arising at 4 AM, I will then experience sunrise on the desert as I bike the full distance in a single day.

The Cleopatra Hotel in Kom Ombo was not worth more than the five Egyptian pounds I paid. The mosquitoes were vicious but the people delightful. A cafeteria in front of the hotel was the center of activity where most of the townspeople gather. I received the usual "What is your name?" "Are you married?" "How old are you?" Adel, a mathematics teacher, speaks excellent English. He and I discussed at some length the problems of the Middle East. Though Adel is Catholic, he and his school observe the Moslem sabbath on Friday. His problem, like most of the Egyptians I met, is lack of money. "I don't get paid enough," he said.

The absence of screens made the infestation of mosquitoes inevitable. At first I closed the doors and windows but could not endure the oppressive heat. In the morning my body was a mass of welts. Fortunately, the hotel in Aswan provides the necessary protection—tight-fitting screens.

The Temple of Kom Ombo stands at a bend in the Nile where in ancient times the sacred crocodiles basked in the sun on the river bank. The temple is 2 km from my hotel but not readily accessible due to the sandy condition of the road. Walking part of the way, I found this dual temple of Kom Ombo. Architecturally, everything is doubled and perfectly symmetrical. There are twin entrances, twin courts, twin sanctuaries, etc. There may have been a twin priesthood. The left side is dedicated to Horus the Elder, the falcon-headed sky god, and the right side to Sobek, the crocodile-headed god. The temple was begun in the early second century B.C. and later added to by the Romans. Mummified crocodiles are on display in a small stone building nearby. They were dug up from the animal cemetery.

Leaving the temple, I found improved roads leading toward Daraw. Camels are brought up in caravans from the Sudan on the Forty Mile Road to Daraw where they are auctioned off every Tuesday at the camel market. Merchants come from Cairo to buy these animals and ship them back by train. From the station they drive them through the streets of Cairo past the firehouse where I drank tea with the firemen. Even though I missed the camel market, I did have the good fortune of seeing and visiting with a camel caravan along the Forty Mile Road near the Temple of Abu Simbel south of Aswan.

A surface taxi left our hotel in Aswan at 4 AM with seven passengers and a driver in a small station wagon. We were headed for the Temple of Abu Simbel, 283 km to the south, near the Sudan and the Aswan Dam, the world's largest manmade dam. The Temples were destined to be swallowed up by the flooding of the dam were it not for the rescue operation of UNESCO. In the 1960s UNESCO launched a worldwide appeal for the funding of this salvage operation. The money collected by children helped accomplish this remarkable achievement. Massive structures were dissected and moved to higher ground at a cost of US $40 million. They were then reconstructed so carefully into an artificial mountain that the more than 2,000 blocks weighing from 10 to 40 tons each appear as though they had never been moved. This project took just over four years to complete; it officially reopened in 1968. Attached to the outside of the Temple is a brass plaque on which the Egyptian government permanently gives the Temples to the world.

We crossed the High Dam at Aswan and did not stop until we were well into the desert. The driver asked me why I was not bicycling to Abu Simbel. "You biked from Cairo to Aswan, didn't you?" The answer was obvious: except for an occasional discarded truck tire or empty oil barrel, we looked at sand, sand dunes, and more sand. Our rest stop was in the middle of nowhere. This was a desert stop without the frills: a covered pavilion serving cold drinks, one toilet, and three oil drums filled with water provided for our basic needs.

Shortly thereafter we came upon a camel caravan on its way to Daraw. The animals, covering a rather large area, were resting in preparation for the next leg of their journey. Our affable driver agreed to stop on the way back from Abu Simbel.

Huge statues of Ramses II support the roof of the Temple while reliefs on the walls exemplify in a symbolic manner the exploits of Ramses at war. There are offerings to the gods as well as funeral scenes with the solar barques. The sanctuary was reserved solely for Ramses II and the high priests. Statues of these gods sit on their thrones waiting for the dawn on February 22 and October 22 of each year. The first rays of the sun penetrating a hole in the ceiling illuminate these figures. Unfortunately, these sculptures of Ramses II, Ra-Harakhty, Amun, and Ptah are somewhat damaged.

The smaller temple at Abu Simbel is the Temple of Hathor fronted by six massive figures. Four represent Ramses while the other two are of his beloved wife Nefertari. In the sanctuary there is a statue of a cow, the sacred symbol of Hathor emerging from the wall. This preservation of antiquity is truly remarkable.

Those who choose to visit Abu Simbel but not take the time to drive the 283 km have the option of going by air. Had I flown, I would not have had the opportunity of meeting Eissa Mohamed, one of the caravan drivers doing what he enjoys most. A graduate of Cairo University, Eissa prefers to be in the desert with his companions and the camels. I must confess that at the drop of a hat I would have paid my own way to join the caravan. The bike and a lack of clothing made this thought but a fantasy. We took pictures and visited with Eissa. He speaks excellent English. The High Dam was the last stop before our arrival at Aswan.

Egypt, a Moslem country, prohibits the selling or drinking of alcoholic beverages except under controlled conditions. If a profit is to be made, they do not mind selling spirits to visitors. The Police Rowing Club in Aswan is one of those establishments where liquor is served. The desert experience made me long for a tall cool glass of beer! I decided to eat supper at the Rowing Club and enjoy some liquid refreshment. This Club is within walking distance of my hotel.

On the Club roof waiters were ready to take my order. I found the chilling evening breeze too uncomfortable for a lengthy stay. Sherif Halin Mikhail had the same feelings. We met casually and began to talk. He and I enjoyed a cup of Egyptian coffee before leaving for his favorite restaurant, located in the *souk*, or outdoor market, of Aswan. Naturally, I relied on Sherif to do the ordering but felt guilty when he would not permit me to pay for my meal. This is just one more example of Egyptian hospitality. Even though my host was an assistant manager of the five-star hotel on Elephantine Island, the Aswan Oberoi, he prefers the native food of the souk. Sherif recently graduated from a two-year course in hotel management. We talked about the social aspects and policies of Egypt, Israel, and the Middle East, as well as our loves past and present. Before parting, he invited me to visit the Aswan Oberoi "after eleven any evening;" Sherif is the night manager of the hotel. "Take the hotel water taxi directly to the hotel," said Sherif.

USA Today was on sale on the Corniche for six Egyptian pounds, or $2 American. After reading the paper from cover to cover, I was convinced I was caught up with the news back home. Clinton won the election, the recession was still rampant in both the US and England, and Dan Quayle is out of a job.

On Elephantine Island, I visited the five-star New Cataract Hotel, with a long drive lined with palm trees and exquisite grounds. The hotel is designed and decorated in colonial style. From the verandah I watched the *feluccas* with their large sails gently cruising on the Nile. My only disappointment was that I was unable to strike up an acquaintance at this upscale hotel.

My first visit to the Aswan Oberoi hotel was during daylight, the second was to see my friend Sherif. I heard that the view of the Nile from the hotel roof is an outstanding experience, especially at twilight. The day manager was briefed about the American on a bicycle. He was as cordial as Sherif. At 5 o'clock the elevator was unlocked so guests interested in supper and/or cocktails could be served. Shortly thereafter the sun began to set. At the same time, lights from the city of Aswan reflected in the water of the Nile. On Elephantine Island I saw the river divided by the island and then rejoin into a single body near the High Dam. Feluccas were lazily cruising, giving a completely carefree appearance. I felt badly that I was unable to photograph this scene so that others might share it with me. There is, however, a feeling of gratification in being able to describe this experience.

In the morning, I wrote to my friend Ken Westwood telling him of my good fortune in touring Egypt at the cooler time of year. Our visit along the shores of the Adriatic in Italy set me on a path that was both unpredictable and exciting. Looking back, I became acquainted with Sicily, Malta, and now Egypt because of Ken and his advice. Perhaps that is when I coined the phrase "Information/misinformation, adventure/ misadventure" that fit my lifestyle to a "T."

It was then time to locate the Sonesta pier where the "Nile Goddess" and the Galinskys would soon be docking. This luxury liner was just arriving. Toby and Don were standing on the upper deck watching the docking procedures. We met shortly thereafter, visited their stateroom, then went ashore. A sumptuous Sonesta luncheon and tuna on the road were part of my experience.

The Hotel Aswan Oberoi is separated from the rest of Elephantine Island, which probably got its name from the large gray granite boulders partially submerged around the island. Most of the Pharaohs from the fifth dynasty come from this area. Today the Aswan Museum, the Nilometer, the Temple of Khnum, and the Nubian Village are of interest to tourists.

I paid my fare on the water taxi felucca bound for Elephantine Island and boarded with tourists and local Nubians. Soon we wer sailing gently across the Nile. A young woman, obviously one of the Nubians, motioned for a passenger to pass her a soup can that was on the bottom of the boat. She nonchalanty dipped the can into the Nile and quenched her thirst with its contents. Had I tried to do this I probably would have been sent home on a stretcher, or worse.

A sacred mummy with its gold-painted mask is the highlight of the Aswan Museum. After a lot of cajoling, and of course bakshish, the attendant let me take my photograph. The only requirement was that I must wait until the room was empty, and, of course, "no flash." The Egyptians mummified baboons, rams, crocodiles, people, and who knows what else. Several slate palates have been preserved and put on exhibit. These palates were used for grinding paints. All the pigments used by ancient Egyptians came from the desert: copper, phosphorus, iron, manganese, gold, and silver. Egg yolk was the medium in which the colors were mixed.

Many of the mummy cases in the museum are highly decorated. A priest is depicted with a beard on his gold-painted mask. His wife's mummy case is identified with a lotus flower design. Two jackals stand guard at her feet just above the ankles. The bearded husband is shown wearing gold sandals on his feet. His toenails are painted gold.

The Nubian Village is a sun-drenched, poverty-ridden group of brick and mud dwellings. Piles of trash and garbage produce the smell of poverty. I was pleasantly surprised that some of these homes are furnished and electrified, unlike other areas where creature comforts are absent. The Nubians appear reasonably comfortable.

A Nilometer is a device invented by the Egyptians to measure the height of the Nile. They were restored by the Romans during their occupation and can be seen at various places along the river. This concluded my visit to Elephantine Island, except for a walk through the remains of the Temple of Khnum. It was time to return to my hotel and preapre for an early departure by train to Qena.

Two young Egyptians met me as I was preparing to leave the Corniche. The Globetrotter was locked there for half a day. I had met one of them previously near my hotel. To my disgust, the mirror and a small bike bag were stolen in my absence. In the bag was a small tripod that I used to take time exposures or time-delayed self-photos. I felt glad I was leaving Egypt.

The two young men were what we would call homosexuals. In the Egyptian culture where the sexes are separated until marriage, this may be merely a state of convenience. In any event, I was given the hard sell, not taking "no" for an answer. They both knew that if they were seen by the authorities bothering a tourist they would be severely punished, yet they persisted. Finally, I disappointed them by heading back to my hotel.

A single train track connects Qena and Aswan. This requires numerous delays by sidetracking one train so another can pass. Finally, we arrived in Luxor and then Qena, where I had previously left my passport. I decided to stay at the same hotel as before but to take responsibility for the passport instead of relying on the management. It was then that Gamal Nasser and I met.

Gamal, age 21, is studying tourism and hotel management in Asyut. Perhaps this is what brought us together. We arranged to have supper together. In friendship, he gave me a small photograph of himself with a personal note on the back. Following a meal of *shish ka bob* at a rather nice restaurant, we adjourned to a tea house—tea for both of us and *shishi* for Gamal. Shishi is the Turkish water pipe. Sharing his shishi with a complete stranger, Gamal explained that all Egyptian men are brothers. "You would share your shishi with your brother, wouldn't you?" he asked. We then returned to my hotel. Gamal smoked while I messily ate a pomegranate. My day ended on an upbeat note, with plans to arise at 3 AM and leave the hotel at 4 or 4:30 for the ride of a lifetime across the desert to Safaga on the Red Sea, a distance of 154 km. I was emotionally charged. Incidentally, *Gamal* in Arabic is "camel."

The ride across the desert was made possible due to the false security that I had a working pump in case of a flat tire. The true nature of this error was not discovered until the following morning in a hotel room in Safaga. At 3 AM as planned, I made a complete breakfast in my room using the small stove for the preparation of my Nescafé. Inasmuch as the sink and toilet were beyond redemption, I neither shaved nor washed my clothes, but did use the spigot under the shower for tooth brushing. At his request, I awakened Gamal to say goodbye, leaving Qena under cover of darkness at 4:30. Fortunately, the road surface was excellent and traffic was light as I began to penetrate the desert. A full moon illuminated the road in the cool freshness of the early morning.

The sun soon began to rise, revealing a desert devoid of vegetation. On one side rather tall mountains can be seen, while on the other side volcanic eruptions dominate. The wind was at my back. At about 9 or 9:30 I stopped at a pumping station for a rest, a call of nature, and a photograph. Two large gasoline engines working in relay were used to pump fresh water from the Nile to the Red Sea. Hussein Hassan Dokrony from Qena supervises this operation. Squatting in front of his small stove, he prepared tea for us both. We shared my cheese. When I asked Hussein the location of the toilet he pointed to the desert.

The two photos I took show the engines and their pumps and Hussein preparing tea. A photo that is missing would have shown the small vegetable garden near the pumps where water leaks onto the ground. "Enjoy one of my tomatoes," said Hussein in excellent English. Growing in the sand were watermelons, mint, and tomatoes. I tried to be gracious when I refused to accept one of his precious watermelons. His desert-growing tomato was one of the tastiest I've ever eaten.

At the halfway point, I discovered a rest area and restaurant serving cokes, tomatoes, and falafil. Using my waist pack for a pillow, I stretched out on a bench. Sleep came easily until I was awakened by the ubiquitous flies. My journey then continued.

The next rest stop was at 3 PM in the middle of nowhere at the top of a steep grade. A huge boulder shielded me from the road, providing complete privacy where I enjoyed an especially tasty lunch. I then knew that a nap was in order even though this delay would place me in the desert after dark. Will I be sleeping in the desert or biking to Safaga in the dark? The answer at the time was irrelevant.

My grass mat served as a ground cover and the waist pack again as a pillow. There were no flies as I slept in complete isolation for as long as I wished. Awakening, I stopped at a native's hut to ask for additional water in case I would be camping. Their water is stored in metal drums similar to the drinking water at the desert rest stop near Abu Simbel. Egyptian generosity prevailed.

My desire to camp was very real, especially with the awesome beauty of the mountains of volcanic rock and sand as level as though someone had put a spirit level on the earth's surface. The Egyptian desert wind levels the sand, unlike the desert between Las Vegas and Hoover Dam. In that desert the terrain is hilly and irregular. The one common feature is the tranquility of pedaling along in silence, except for the sound of the chain. I remember stopping to photograph a desert flower on the way to Hoover Dam. The absence of noise was unbelievable to one such as myself who lives on busy Massachusetts Avenue in Cambridge, where road noise is continuous.

At six in the evening I was surrounded by complete darkness even though a full moon had illuminated the road that morning. It was not until I left the mountains that the moon again came into view. Too early for sleep, particularly after my lengthy nap, Safaga became my destination regardless of the distance. My generator light served nicely to illuminate the road, except for the times I pushed the Globetrotter up the steeper grades. Occasionally an automobile or truck temporarily illuminated the highway. Finally, after considerable effort, the mountains were behind me as I came back into the desert. The glorious full moon of the previous morning again illuminated the road. Except for a long and smooth descent, my mission was accomplished when the shimmering surface of the Red Sea greeted me.

Finding accommodations in the upscale town of Safaga was difficult, especially when price is considered. One young man I asked was especially interested in helping me. He has a friend who owns a small hotel approximately one kilometer from where we met. His offer to go with me in hope of finding a vacancy at a reasonable price was a bit strange. To my dismay, he ran alongside the Globetrotter as I pedaled slowly. We reached the hotel, he made the deal with his friend, we shook hands and parted. Except for my gratitude, he accepted no payment. Can you visualize a pedestrian running alongside your car to personally show you the location of the local Holiday Inn?

Fully rested in the morning, I decided to head north toward the port city of Hurghada, the location of a ferry to the Sinai Peninsula. I would then be out of Egypt proper and on soil that was previously considered Israeli-occupied territory. From there I planned to cycle to Eilat, the southernmost city in Israel. My original plan to spend the winter in Eilat began to unfold.

This was an excellent time to "top off" the pressure in my tires with my newly acquired pump. The intelligent thing to do with a new pump would be to try it on a spare tire first. That morning in my hotel I confess to not being very intelligent. I unscrewed the small inner valve of my front wheel Presta valve and began to attach the small brass fitting of the new pump to the tire valve. The rest is history! Trying to attach an ill-fitting brass connector to the valve caused immediate deflation of my tire. Yes, I had bought the wrong pump in Luxor. In trying to bring my tire up to pressure I created a problem that was almost insurmountable.

The possibility of finding a Presta valve pump in Safaga was less likely than in Luxor. This new town consists of new hotels and a very small shopping district. In all likelihood I would not find a bicycle shop, much less a European-style pump.

In my pack I kept the business card of the bike shop owner in Malta specializing in sophisticated bicycles. "Should you have a problem in Egypt you can use my fax number to order the necessary part or parts," said the owner. "I will ship them to you immediately." This became the last card in my deck of solutions. Not only did I have no desire to spend at least a week or two waiting for the replacement pump, but the thought of Egyptian bureaucracy trying to recover the item became overwhelming. There had to be a better way.

"If I cut off the improper fitting brass connector, perhaps I can attach the hose of the pump directly to the valve stem, and at least get enough pressure into the tube so I can continue. Nothing will be lost in cutting off the offender since it doesn't fit."

The idea was valid but the results disappointing. The small volume of air I was able to pump into the tube rapidly dissipated when I removed the hose from the valve. My front tire was as flat as ever. My ego was almost as flat as the tire. "Is there another way? Perhaps if I unscrew the hose from the body of the pump, the male fitting of the valve stem might just mate with the female fitting of the pump. It's worth a try."

To my utter joy, the fit was perfect. The threads matched perfectly, permitting me to inflate to a full 90 pounds of pressure. I was so amazed and pleased with this accomplishment that I decided to pump up the rear tire as well. How could I have been so lucky? Later, while biking in Turkey where I met the number two bicycle racing champion of New Zealand, I told him the story of my fortuitous discovery. "We always do that in New Zealand," said this man from "down under."

I learned by word of mouth that two female tourists were shot the previous day by fundamentalists in Qena. These people believe Egypt should return to the days of separation of the sexes in the same way Iran has returned to fundamentalism. European women who wear clothing that reveal their limbs or their shape are a target for this form of reactionary thought and violence. Though still a third-world country, Egypt has come a long way in adopting western attitudes and culture. There is a battle between the old and the new, with female tourists caught in between.

European women find it very difficult when they travel without a male escort. Egyptian men shout disgusting obscenities at them as they pass within hearing range, while others constantly annoy them, asking for sexual favors. Either way, the Western woman is put at a terrible disadvantage. While in Alexandria some months later, I boarded a trolley car without paying attention to the fact that only women occupy particular cars. I was informed by the female occupants that I had entered a car reserved for women only. It was almost the same thing as walking into the ladies' restroom in error. This is obviously a method developed to spare the female population from sexual harassment.

Sixty-five kilometers to Hurghada was an easy goal until I discovered the hills and wind. Even though the wind was in my face, making cycling difficult, the beauty of the Red Sea to my right and the desert to my left created an unforgettable scene. Fortunately, the day was relatively cool. I stopped to rest at the halfway point. A fruit drink and cookies energized me. Until this time the absence of humanity and the desert scene gave this part of Egypt the utmost of authenticity. The natural beauty of the desert was exquisite until the scene suddenly changed.

Some 15 to 20 km south of Hurghada, new construction of hotels began to take form, the first one open for occupancy. Workmen were busy laying sod while others were planting palm trees. The supervisor in his electric golf cart directed operations and the guests rode the paths on rented bicycles. German was now the second language. Was it possible that all the water needed for these hotels was being pumped from the Nile, a seemingly impossible task?

Shacks were being erected for occupancy by the workmen and their families across the road, opposite the seaside hotels. An absence of vegetation or any amenities stood in stark contrast to the upscale resorts facing the beach. Humanity was in the process of trying to conquer the desert, with the financial assistance of the oil-producing countries and the sweet water of the Nile. The development of these five-star hotels is named Palm Beach. Perhaps this is the reason for the planting of palm trees. Hurghada, a small diving center on the Red Sea, was becoming a vacation resort overnight.

My accommodation, the Egyptian Youth Hostel, was directly across the road form the sumptuous Sonesta. For five Egyptian pounds I had a private room, comfortable surroundings, and easy-going and friendly management. Breakfast and supper were served at the hostel. Membership in the world-wide hostel movement is a requirement. My life membership card was always cordially received in the many hostels where I stayed; the Hurghada hostel was no exception.

The average Egyptian on the street shows a great deal of affection for the US and its people. They watch television avidly and are anxious to emulate the West. They know that violence from the fundamentalists will discourage tourism, the lifeblood of their economy. For the most part they enjoy being at peace with Israel and will talk about it without hesitation. The fundamentalists, on the other hand, predict the destruction of the State of Israel.

My first day in Hurghada was one of leisurely bicycle touring, locating the various points of interest. The circular Sheraton Hotel located on the shores of the Red Sea was on my agenda. An English-language newspaper printed in Britain brought me up to date with the news, British style. The garden courtyard of the Sheraton, with tables, chairs, and a central fountain became the perfect place for early morning reading.

I then continued on into the port of Hurghada and its ferry terminal. While there, I booked passage to Sharm-el-Shaykh for the following Monday, giving myself ample time for a snorkeling adventure at and around Gitton Island. Sharm-el-Shaykh, the southernmost port on the Sinai Peninsula, is also spelled Sharm-el-Sheikh. Sharm, as it is referred to, is reputed to be one of the finest diving centers in the world. That day I learned more news about the shooting in Qena. Not two, but six, women were shot.

Snorkeling was not the "piece of cake" I thought it would be. At the Sports Center we were issued masks and flippers and assigned to a boat. Stephan, a German, and Judy, his American friend, became my companions for the day. Stephan is a diving instructor but Judy, like myself, is a complete novice. Fortunately, I learned the basics from Stephan before entering the water. The boat anchored offshore near a coral reef and it was then every person for themselves. Except for Judy and myself, the passengers were swimming in deep water without apparent difficulty. I hung on to the anchor line trying to expel seawater from my mouth and mask.

Finally after becoming acquainted with the equipment, I struck out for the coral reef where I could stand or swim, as the situation required. This reef is a virtual natural aquarium hosting some of the most beautiful tropicals I've ever seen.

2 WHEELS, 2 YEARS, AND 3 CONTINENTS

The snowflake moray near my flippers looked exactly like the one on the identification chart I bought the previous day at the Sheraton. I was also able to identify the green chromis, the blacktip soldier fish, the parrot fish, and several other species. They were magnificent in their natural habitat.

Living coral is perhaps more exciting to me than the tropical fish, since most coral we see is the dried skeleton of the living animal. These coral are undulating living sea life, creating a virtual garden salad of tropical creatures. They are protected by law so they may be enjoyed by future visitors.

We then enjoyed a lunch of grilled fish, rice, salad, and Pepsi on the boat before migrating to the beach where friendly people and tropical surroundings contributed to the enjoyment of the day. I inquired at the Sports Center about the source of fresh water in Hurghada. In addition to the sweet water that is transported from the Nile to Safaga and then to Hurghada by way of pipelines, Hurghada also has a desalinization plant. That night I biked to the location of the Egyptian immigration offices to obtain an extension to my visa and at the same time have a correction made on my passport. The immigration officer in Cairo wrote the correct day and month but the wrong year. I wanted to have it corrected before leaving the country to avoid unnecessary delays. At the Department of Immigration I was told to return the following morning. It was too late in the afternoon for this type of work.

Forms, a photograph, ten Egyptian pounds, and then more forms were required. Each time I inquired about the delay, I was told "five minutes." Finally all the paperwork was completed. All that was needed was a signature form the officer in charge. The wait continued. "Five minutes," I was told.

In desperation after a three-hour wait for work that required no more than five minutes, I walked up to the window, brought my fist down on the counter, and shouted, "I want my passport!" From the inner office an officer immediately came over to the counter, signed the passport, and handed it to me. I then began to leave the immigration offices. The same officer motioned for me to come into his office, offering me a chair. "Tea or coffee?" he asked.

"To be truthful, I would prefer to leave. I have an appointment."

"Tea or coffee?"

"Coffee."

I then learned that drinking tea or coffee is always a preliminary to a social or business engagement in Arab countries. The officer wanted to know why I was so unhappy. Had he come out of his office two hours earlier instead of smoking and drinking coffee I would not have been unhappy. We parted with a handshake. Fortunately, there was still time for my luncheon engagement with Mahmoud Attia.

Mahmoud and I met outside the entrance to the Sheraton, he on his bike and I on mine. A resident of Cairo, Mahmoud works at the reception desk of Arabia Village, a hotel in Hurghada. We visited at the side of the road and then agreed to meet again at his place of work. He was pleased to see me.

We walked the lovely grounds of the hotel and then refreshed ourselves with non-alcoholic drinks. Being an employee as well as of the Moslem faith, Pepsi-Cola was the chosen beverage. We then made arrangements to meet again at my hostel. Mahmoud has tapes of American music that he wanted me to listen to and interpret the lyrics. Some of the words were unintelligible to him. When we met that evening he was disappointed to learn that I too could not understand some of the words due to different dialects that are found in America. He thought we all speak alike even though we are of different races and geographical locations.

Before parting, Mahmoud presented me with a magic ruler as a gift. I accepted it with the comment, "I have received far more than I have given." His reply was, "Of course."

A civil engineer by training, Mahmoud is studying German so he can translate books on engineering into Arabic. We got along quite well until the subject of religion arose. I became aware that my newest friend was a Moslem zealot, a true believer in the Koran, and unable to see beyond his own personal experience. Spirits, the devil, etc., were in his belief system. On a lighter note we said our goodbyes. I again thanked him for my gift, a very interesting device that enables the holder of a pencil to make intricate designs without effort. He asked me to write to him when I return to the US.

Shauky, the director the Hurghada hostel, gave me a letter of introduction to the hostel in Sharm-el-Shaykh, as well as brief directions. He and I agreed to save our goodbyes until the morning after breakfast. At 7 AM I was the only person awake in the entire building. I had to awaken Shauky to unlock the front door for my departure. I enjoyed a buffet breakfast with a bottomless cup of coffee at the Sinbad Village Resort where a yellow miniature submarine is docked. While I was looking out the restaurant window the crew boarded the Sinbad and headed for the Outer Harbor. Had I known that shortly thereafter my wonderful breakfast would end at the bottom of the sea I might have eaten less.

The ferry was small and the sea turbulent. At first I thought I could handle the situation but the sea finally took its toll. Three young people on the top deck ate, drank, and smoked with abandon. They had a nerve to be laughing while I sought a place to lie down and sleep. As long as I was horizontal the pitch and roll of our small vessel made little difference. Shortly before dark we arrived at our destination.

Having no map, I followed a sign to Sharm-el-Shaykh but was told I was going in the wrong direction. Reversing direction and with very little hope of finding the hostel, I headed north in the direction of Dahab, Egypt, and Eilat, Israel, passing four- and five-star hotels but no campgrounds. At one new and still unopened hotel I asked permission to camp but was denied. Their kiosk was open, serving food and cold beer. One of the divers, a Canadian, suggested that I bike to a campground in Sharks Bay about 8 km to the north. By coincidence, he is a member of the Cyclists Touring Club of England. The CTC and LAW (now LAB) share the same wings and wheel emblem. My supper refueled my burner; I felt ready to challenge the darkness of the evening enroute to Sharks Bay.

A short distance from the kiosk, the main road takes a sharp left turn away from the Red Sea toward the port of Dahab. Had I not been biking in the dark, I probably would have seen this turn. Unfortunately, I forged ahead into unknown territory that reinforces the concept of adventure/misadventure. For the next sixteen hours I experienced more of both than I bargained for. The hostel, and now Sharks Bay, were out of the question. I challenged the darkness.

A native civilian stood guard at the lighted entrance to a small compound. Lights in one of the houses indicated that there were people nearby. "May I camp here?" He escorted me to the house.

Civil engineers, all Egyptians, were using this house as their headquarters. Their workday over, they were watching color television. I introduced myself to the obvious leader of the group. "Tea or coffee?" he asked. We visited, drank tea, and talked about America, football, hockey, and soccer. The younger men then entered the conversation, turning it into a discussion about sex. The problem of the young Egyptian male again rose to the surface.

"Of course you can camp here for the night," said the leader. "We have a house down the road with a caretaker. You can spend the night with Hamdi." One of the men directed me to a pickup truck, indicating that I should follow him so I wouldn't become lost once more. Shortly thereafter Hamdi prepared coffee for both of us.

The house, previously lived in, was illuminated with a single electric bulb. Hamdi slept on an wooden cot in one room, the other room was mine. My inflatable mattress converted the wood slats into a comfortable bed but the overhead light became a problem: it attracted both flies and mosquitoes. When I reached up to shut off the light Hamdi appeared upset. I waited until he was asleep. Now that the light was extinguished, Hamdi and I slept without being bothered by the ubiquitous flies. All the plumbing in the house was disconnected; steel drums of water provided for washing or cooking. The great outdoors was the bathroom.

Oranges, tangerines, cake, and Nescafé from my panniers served as our breakfast, leaving little food for emergency supplies. A Westerner's breakfast probably pleased Hamdi. I then asked him, partially in sign language, if I was heading toward Dahab, approximately 100 km to the north. He nodded in the affirmative, not knowing the question. I then headed into a strong headwind, waving goodbye to this gentle and friendly person. With perseverance, I felt I could reach Dahab before sunset.

Following the contours of the shore, I had absolutely no concept that I was on the wrong road. When the local airport came into view, I stopped to replenish my food supplies. Security conducted by the military was extremely heavy. Finally after a careful passport check and interrogation I was permitted entry to the snack bar where the selection was very limited. At least I had a feeling of confidence that even under the worst conditions I could feed myself.

The condition of the road began to deteriorate, becoming more and more sandy as we headed into the desert. Naively I thought that perhaps the closer to Israel I got, the poorer road conditions would be. After all, the two countries had been at war with each other and even in peace the armistice was referred to as the "cold peace." In the distance a village or perhaps an army encampment began to materialize.

Soon the hard surface disappeared completely, making cycling especially difficult. "Should I turn around or forge ahead toward the settlement? If I can reach the settlement and if I'm on the wrong road, perhaps someone can transport me to the main road. If it's a military base I can surely ask for assistance." I decided to forge on.

When the hard surface of the sand disappeared I was forced to dismount. Pushing with great difficulty, the bicycle with its heavy load imbedded itself in the sand. Occasionally I returned to the saddle when the surface became firm. Jeep tracks from the military base tend to create a semi-hard surface that I tried to follow. Finally, nearing exhaustion, I reached the barrier separating the base from the desert.

The passport check and questioning were conducted by the guard on duty as a formality rather than a military urgency. He then invited me to follow him to the canteen where I was given a cold Coke. We talked in English. Pointing to a jeep nearby, I asked if I could be taken to the main road."Impossible," said the enlisted man. "The jeep belongs to the general and he is asleep."

"May I wait until he awakens?"

"That will be in two hours."

"May I eat with the soldiers while I'm waiting?"

"That will be in three hours."

An officer appeared out of a military hut with a set of keys to the jeep. Without delay, the Globetrotter and I occupied the rear as the officer and one enlisted man sat up front. We headed down a sandy road parallel to the beach, penetrating the desert rather than veering to the left and the main road. At one point I overheard the enlisted man say the words "sixteen kilometers" to the officer. "Do you want to take pictures?" asked the officer as we continued. I was more interested in the main road than in taking more pictures of the Red Sea.

The jeep then stopped and I was asked to assist the enlisted man in removing the Globetrotter. Pointing in the direction of the main road, the officer indicated that we were 2 km from it, an easy ride on what looked more like a camel path than a road. It became obvious to us both moments later that I was unable to push the bike and its load in the loose sand. We put the bike back in the jeep and continued deeper into the desert. This time when the jeep stopped the officer told me I would have no further problems, pointing to jeep tracks in the sand. I thanked him for his thoughtfulness and watched the jeep turn around as it headed back to the military installation. I was now alone in the desert.

Soon the sand became so soft that it was impossible to pedal. I dismounted and, as before, began to push my heavy load against what seemed like impossible odds. At the same time, the sun at high noon began to concern me. It was then I decided that under no circumstances was I going to eat my meager rations until I was out of the desert and onto the main road. Water would be limited to an absolute minimum. I remember saying, in a voice that only I could hear, "Oh no," as though this time I had bitten off more than I could chew.

My first thought was to temporarily abandon the bike and gear, walk to the main road, and then seek aid in recovering my property. Instinctively I knew that this was not the best solution to my problem. I could not see the Bedouins in the desert but they could see me. If I left my gear, that would be the last time I'd see it. There had to be a better way.

I then unloaded the bike and wheeled it approximately one hundred yards toward the road. Putting the baggage on my shoulder, I then carried half the load to the bike, making a second trip for the rest. When everything was in one place, I repeated the procedure over and over, progressing toward what I thought to be 2 km but at the same time remembering what the enlisted man said to the officer: "sixteen kilometers."

At some point in this journey of futility I began to feel the sun's effects. I was beginning to feel faint, but not defeated. A miracle then happened: out of nowhere a four-wheel-drive vehicle appeared beside me. Two young men approached, introducing themselves as Canadians and divers. They stopped at the military installation and were told of my plight by the enlisted men. The officer, new to the area, was unfamiliar with the territory, but the enlisted men knew I was out there and in trouble. They put my equipment in the back of the vehicle and prepared to drive across the expanse of sand toward the road. "You have pushed and walked eight of the sixteen kilometers toward the main road," said the Canadians. We rapidly covered the additional eight.

Back on the hard surface of the road leading to Dahab, my rescuers gave me the option of going back to Sharm with them and starting out again the following morning, or if I "was crazy" I could continue on toward Dahab. My reply was that "I am crazy."

The parting words of the driver were "Just remember that you were rescued by two Palestinians!" This was the beginning of a scenario that ultimately brought me to the House of Grace, a Greek Catholic-Palestinian halfway house and shelter in Haifa where I spent four of the most interesting months of my life. Did my rescuers know I was Jewish? Is that why they said what they did? I will never know.

I leaned the loaded Globetrotter against a boulder and sat on a smaller one eating half the food I bought that morning at the airport. A fresh orange kept in reserve from the previous night served as my dessert. Eighty-five kilometers later I was in Dahab on the Gulf of Aqaba and looked for the Bedouin Village, the part of Dahab that attracts young people as well as those on a low budget. It is well described in my "Lonely Planet Guide."

The Hilton Camp Village, commonly called the Hilton, provides less than sumptuous accommodations. My all-cement motel room with a cement sleeping bench had one small over-head bulb and one screen-less window. Bathroom facilities are in a separate building, in true Hilton style. I was awakened in the morning by the braying of a donkey outside my window. For some reason, I was not bothered by mosquitoes or flies.

Mohamed, the Hilton owner, is a gracious man, as is Said, a guest who's in the oil drilling business. He has worked and studied in Texas and Chicago. Said provided me with a lot of information concerning my planned visit to Israel. He is the second person to discourage my biking in the Negev Desert, the first being Louise, Dorothy's cousin. She lives in Holliston, Massachusetts, and has traveled extensively in Israel. The cold weather at night and the hostility of the people concerned Said. In spite of these warnings, I did bike the Negev without incident the following April.

Ninety kilometers to the north lay Nuweiba, a beach resort town that is one of the Sinai's most popular tourist areas. It is also the site of a ferry terminal connecting Egypt and Jordan. Between Dahab and Nuweiba I was virtually alone in the desert. This time, though, I was well stocked with provisions and water. Except for a small amount of sagebrush and a beautifully striped melon that grows in the sand along the road, vegetation was absent. This melon or gourd eventually turns brown, with its seeds retained inside. As a souvenir I stored some dried ones in my pack and made the mistake of tasting a green one. This was before I discovered that this product is poisonous. The taste is so vile that even if poisonous, very little entered my system. Some of my precious water helped wash away the taste as well as my roadside lunch. Except for the wind, the silence of the desert prevailed.

A dead camel lay rotting in the sun while two others roamed unattended looking for food. The entire area was very desolate. At a police roadblock 35 km from Nuweiba, a road goes west toward St. Catherines while the road to Nuweiba begins to climb. I asked permission to rest at the police station. "Impossible," said the officer as he continued to read his newspaper. "In Nuweiba you can rest."

To my surprise and amazement, a structure with the word "CAFETERIA" on the side became visible at the crest of a mountain. The closer I came, the more I was aware that this "deserted" cafeteria was open. The proprietor, a most unusual and interesting person, greeted me with open arms. Jahquv Ben Yamanthou, a black American Jew with a Rastafarian hairstyle and an engaging personality, brought out a bottle of Jim Bean whiskey with two glasses. We celebrated the occasion as well as life in general. Jahquv had been celebrating one thing or another for many hours prior to my arrival.

In addition to the Jim Bean, I enjoyed fresh coffee, a marvelous garden salad, and a Pepsi. "Stay here tonight," said my host. "We have plenty of room and there is no charge." As a matter of fact, Jahquv would accept no money for my lunch until I insisted. "You are a wayfarer," he said.

I learned the reason for the existence of the cafeteria as well as the source of the Jim Bean. The UN peacekeeping forces nearby patronize the cafeteria. The soldiers also keep my newest friend Jahquv well supplied with liquid refreshment. Military vehicles arrived and left during my relatively brief stay. This cafeteria is not as remote as I thought. At a later date, when my German cycling friend Klaus and I visited the St. Catherine Monastery, we stopped at the cafeteria to renew this friendship with Jahquv. Then months later when I returned to Egypt he was no longer there. I was told the Egyptian government deported him for passport violations. Jacob told me on my first visit that in the three years he operated the cafeteria he was no farther than a radius of 50 feet from the building.

Reluctant to leave yet anxious to reach Israel, I headed down the mountain, using my brakes the entire distance. Signs warned of the steep grade, advising low gears and a speed not to exceed 30 mph. This continuous descent finally leveled off after 20 km near the port city of Nuweiba. Approaching darkness, I found a campground near the beach on the Red Sea.

A woman tourist greeted me at the reception area. She saw me in Sharm-el-Shaykh as well as from the window of her tour bus near Nuweiba City. "You must go to Petra in Jordan. Don't miss it," she said. She also invited me to have supper at her camper bus with its attached "chow wagon" trailer. The trailer is a complete kitchen on wheels, with at least one cook. Though I was not especially hungry after my meal at the cafeteria, I could not pass up the freshly boiled potatoes with butter and tuna fish.

In the morning the German tour bus crew served breakfast promptly so the bus and trailer could leave. Gerlinda Belda, my hostess, and her companion Isabel Aney, with braces on her teeth, said goodbye before boarding. "Don't forget to visit Petra," repeated Gerlinda.

For the first time I found it necessary to buy bottled water for drinking. All other water has a saline taste. The water was not impure, but with a salty taste even coffee was unpalatable.

On top of the mountain at the cafeteria I could not wait to get back on the road, seeking the Israeli border as my most important destination. Now, at the beach and only a day's ride to Eilat, I was ready for some rest and recreation. The urgency was no longer urgent. I decided to bike to Nuweiba

Port, buy some food, investigate the purchase of a visa for Jordan, and look into the possibility of a camel trip in the desert. A New Zealand acquaintance gave Jordan high praise. My only problem was one of reality: Jordan at that time was technically at war with Israel. For obvious reasons, Jews were unwelcome in that country. Should I overlook this technicality and follow Gerlinda's advice, or stand on ceremony? I could rationalize the matter by saying "It isn't my war" even though emotionally it was my cause. At the ticket office when I bought a round-trip ticket to Jordan, the agent said, "I suppose that when you return to Nuweiba you will be going to Israel?" Had I said yes, he would have refused to sell me a ticket.

"Oh no, I am returning to Cairo."

A group of Australians, New Zealanders, and British tourists arrived at the same time; all expressed an interest in snorkeling. We met at the dive shop and were outfitted with the necessary equipment and given brief instructions. Had they given me instructions in Hurghada, my initiation would have been much easier. We even had the opportunity of trying on different size masks and flippers. The cool water temperature and a strong breeze made a full morning of snorkeling enough for me, especially after I put my left hand on a sea urchin in an effort to keep from falling. I left the water with nine separate poisonous sea urchin barbs deposited in my palm. Experienced divers told me that until each barb is removed, the area will be painful. A clean needle and a strong will were needed.

Klaus and Crystal Baeger were vacationing on the beach with their caravan. Crystal found the necessary needle. I had to find the courage. They helped the cause by serving me hot, fresh, *real* coffee instead of my usual Nescafé. Klaus, a man with a sense of humor as well as an eye for pretty women, introduced me to Ruth, a diver. She came to Nuweiba from Dahab to explore the underwater sea life. I suspect she had other motives as well.

She and I were both disappointed with the tropical life at Nuweiba, as compared to Hurghada and Dahab. Ruth had been in the water at Dahab and I at Hurghada. We hit it off like old friends even though she was 22 years younger than me. I walked to her bus with her; we kissed and hugged. It was then all over. Oh well! I had the trip to Jordan and Petra to look forward to the following day.

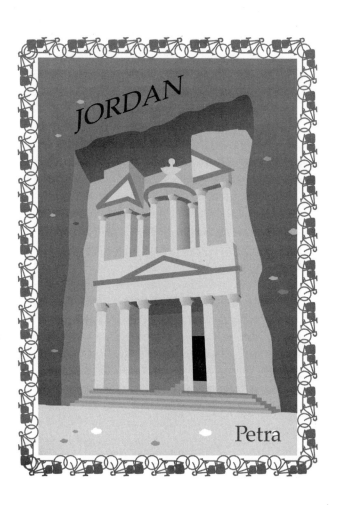

Chapter 12
JORDAN

Though a short distance, the boat ride from Nuweiba to Aqaba, Jordan, took an entire day. Loading the hold of the ship with trucks and their cargo took much more time than processing the passengers. I shared my seat with some Egyptians and they shared their food with me. Highly seasoned steak and *kufta* ultimately did me in. By the time we left the ferry and customs I began to feel ill. In spite of my digestive problems, I pedaled to Aqaba in search of the Petra Hotel recommended in my "Lonely Planet Guide." Parking my Globetrotter in a safe place, I slept around the clock, except for two interruptions. At midnight the management made me a glass of tea. The Moslem call to prayer at 4 AM reminded me that I had to use the facilities.

By noon I felt well enough to head for Petra, especially in the sunshine. The weather report, however, indicated that snow had fallen the previous evening in Petra. I felt confident that with my tent and sleeping bag I would be comfortable camping in the mountains, even though it was now December. What I did not take into consideration was my weakness as a result of this short illness, or the terrain enroute to Petra. I was in unfamiliar territory. The uphill grade on the King's Highway was more than I bargained for.

I thought the King's Highway may have been named for the present king Hussein, a very popular monarch. My "Lonely Planet Guide" for Jordan indicates that this road originated in Biblical times, linking the East and Middle East. Today, trucks in particular travel from Aqaba to Saudi Arabia and Iraq. The condition of this road can only be compared with the roads of Cairo after the earthquake. They were not intended for bicycles.

Approximately 30 km from Aqaba, I stopped to photograph a sign stating that Saudi Arabia was 2 km from the

King's Highway. The grade by this time was steep and relentless. Seventy additional kilometers to the summit of the mountain was threatening but not discouraging. I was determined to
reach Petra under my own power.

About to mount the Globetrotter and continue the
climb, an immense truck came to a stop at the side of the road.
The driver, Sami Gorpan, lashed the Globetrotter to his truck.
I tossed my gear behind the front seat of the cab and his truck
began to inch its way up the mountain. I have no idea as to the
contents of his load. Sami spoke Arabic. In one way or another
I asked Sami if he minded if I slept. If he was looking for
companionship I did not want to disappoint him. When I awakened it was dark. Except for an occasional Bedouin village or
a rest stop, we were driving in barren and desolate country, far
from an ideal place to camp.

Sami stopped his truck at a sign indicating that Petra
was 35 km to the left. Soon the bike was on the hard top with
the gear back in position on its racks. Sami pointed to a police
station, indicating that I could sleep there until morning and
then bike to Petra in daylight. We exchanged names and addresses. I took his photo before he climbed back into his cab
and headed for Amman, the capital of Jordan.

Less than one month ago, I received a letter from Sami.
"Do you remember me?" he said. "I rescued you in the mountains." Unfortunately, my reply to Sami has been returned twice
because of an incorrect address. I duplicated the photograph I
had taken and enclosed it with my letter. For the second mailing, I cut out his address as he wrote it and taped it to the
envelope. It too was returned. Sami deserves a reply but I don't
know how to pursue it further.

Dressed in summer cycling togs, the cold winter air
produced an immediate reaction: my teeth began to chatter. I
was cold!

Across the road, at the entrance to the police station, a sentry stood guard in his small privy-like structure with its kerosene heater. He was dressed in winter clothing, wearing a coat with the collar turned up, and gloves. The radiant heat felt good as I tried to warm myself. "I would like to sleep in the police station tonight and then bike to Petra tomorrow."

"Impossible," said the officer. "Only the police are permitted in the police station."

"Would you call in to your commanding officer and ask if I can have special permission?"

The commanding officer, a young a very handsome Jordanian dressed in a stylish uniform, arrived at the sentry house a few minutes later. It was obvious to him that I was not dressed for the winter cold; he acquiesced. When I asked permission to bring the bike into the station, permission was denied. I looked forward to digging into my winter clothing and dressing in the warmth of the station. He finally agreed to my request.

Warm-up pants and a wool turtleneck sweater I had bought at the the the Cinelli works in Milan, Italy, on my first visit helped ease the pain of the cold. The officers present were warming themselves around a kerosene heater similar to the one roadside. They made room for an extra pair of hands— mine. "Tea or coffee?" I was asked.

The officer in charge then asked to see my passport. As he was thumbing through the pages he asked, "What is your religion?"

"Catholic" was my immediate response. Had I replied Jewish, I would have found myself in a prison in Amman. The numerous telephone calls that followed were in Arabic. The only thing I knew was that the calls concerned me. I presented the police with a unique problem that required a solution. Being accustomed to unique problems, I instinctively knew that eventually something positive would happen. Inasmuch as the police could not permit my overnight stay in the police station, a different solution was required.

Some time later, a police van arrived. The officers helped me put the Globetrotter into the cargo area. I was invited to occupy the seat behind the driver as we headed for Petra, 35 km distant. Even in the dark I was aware of the difficult downhill terrain that I would be biking had I been permitted to sleep in the police station. The driver stopped at the entrance to a small hotel. We were greeted cordially by the management.

I looked at the surroundings and inquired about the hotel rate. The oriental rugs, the native Jordanian men in their traditional clothing, as well as their beautiful women wearing expensive silk dresses gave me the clue that this was not the usual tourist hotel. The room clerk verified my suspicions. He suggested a tourist hotel nearby. In the meantime the officers were enjoying the tea served to them by the management. We then drove a short distance to the Alanbat Hotel.

At first glance I knew I was in the right place and at the right time. Supper was in the process of being served. Many of the guests sitting on the floor or on cushions were watching a video. Most of them had been on the ferry with me from Hurghada to Sharm-el-Shaykh. I received a warm welcome. Thanking the police for their kindness, I sat down to a meal of soup, chicken, potatoes, and salad. They returned to their headquarters. A hot shower and sleep followed. Amen!

Upon my return, I stopped at the same police station and was greeted by the sentry who obviously knew about me. He called in to the station at my request. The same officer as before came out to greet me. After the usual greeting, I asked the officer, "Why didn't you take me to the rest station in Ma'an, much closer than Petra?"

"You said you wanted to go to Petra, didn't you?" In the police log, the entire incident was recorded as "encouragement of tourism."

The next day my distance covered by bicycle was zero km but by foot it seemed like many miles. We were given transportation by the hotel to buy provisions and were then taken to the entrance of Petra, the capital of the Nabataeans, who dominated the Trans-Jordan area in pre-Roman times. Their elaborate buildings and tombs are carved out of solid rock. This is what my two German friends at Nuweiba insisted that I see. It was indeed unfortunate that Israelis were not permitted to visit Petra, it being one of their secret desires.

The actual entrance to Petra is 6 km from the main road, where tickets are purchased entitling a person to entrance for the day. There the Bedouins are gathered with their horses, offering tourists the 6 km ride. I accepted the offer with the concept that I would be riding one horse and the owner would be riding another. When I discovered that the owner, wearing his flip-flop sandals, intended to walk, while I the tourist had the comfort of a saddle, I decided that upon my return I too would walk. The owner's name was George and his horse was Susie.

Some of the tourists were returning for their second or third day, while others such as myself were new to the area. Each had his own agenda. Some decided to climb Mount Aaron, named after the brother of Moses. My small guide book acquainted me with Petra. Unfortunately, the light at that time did not favor photography.

Khazneh, or the Treasury, is well protected by its surroundings, and has not suffered the ravages of the elements. Carved out of solid rock, Khazneh served as a tomb instead of a treasury. A tale refers to pirates who hid their treasure here in an urn on the second level of the building. The urn is damaged by bullets by those who tried to open it and steal the treasure.

Interestingly, it is the facade of the buildings that are so artistically beautiful. The interiors are merely unadorned square rooms.

A 3,000-seat theater originally built by the Nabataeans was refurbished by the Romans. The colonnaded street, with a few of the columns re-erected, runs alongside the *wadi* with debris of the ancient city scattered on either side. I found a place in the sun to sit and enjoy my lunch stowed in a pannier.

At a higher elevation, I visited a small museum that was well organized. As the only visitor at the time, I was offered tea and a conducted tour by the male attendant. A perfume bottle preserved from the time Petra was a thriving trading center, as well as a female sphinx, were especially interesting. An oil lamp depicting the "Kidnapping of Europe by Zeus" verifies Greek occupancy. Fragments of a plate that was painted with birds pecking at a bunch of grapes, as well as globular ceramic cooking pots, attest to the quality of life of these early people.

A substantial climb led me to what is called the Monastery, where I met two brothers, Ahmad and Mohammed. Ahmad was my guide while his older brother operated an outdoor store with artifacts and postcards for sale. Business was rather slow. We took pictures and walked the area. In addition to money, I gave Ahmad some of my raisins as a gift. He was probably no more than eight years of age. A 5 o'clock departure from Petra to my hotel shortened my visit with Ahmad, a delightful little boy.

Walking alone toward the entrance to Petra, I noticed two young Arab men trying to put a noose on a camel. We place a bit in a horse's mouth to attach the reins, but with a camel a noose is placed over the animal's nose and mouth. This incident bears repetition since it's "my favorite camel story."

No matter how hard these two men tried, they were unable to place the noose over the muzzle of their camel. Every time the drivers tried to apply the noose, the camel would roll his eyes, make a strange "gurgling" sound in his throat, and then throw his head to avoid the noose. I watched three separate unsuccessful attempts.

Without comment, I laid my pannier on the sand and walked over to the camel and the two young men. With my right arm I applied an arm lock on the camel's neck, which I believe is known as a "half Nelson." This maneuver immediately restrained the obstreperous animal, preventing him from throwing his head from side to side. Moments later he was under the control of his masters, with the noose properly attached.

The youngest of the camel drivers looked up at me and in English asked, "At home, you have camel?" Had I the presence of mind, I might have said, "No, at home I have Mustang."

I was not alone walking back toward the main road. The feeling of friendship and camaraderie prevailed as we walked in the twilight, taking our last pictures. One of the guests at our table celebrated his birthday. The hotel produced a cake baked especially for the occasion. Another wrote the events of his day in his journal. Free-hand sketches artistically executed became a part of his entry in addition to the written word. I was impressed with the exactness of his penmanship, mine being little more than a scribble. David Marsh from London also dined with us; we met on the ferry on the way to Aqaba.

"Have you had the experience of an introductory scuba dive?" asked David. "If not, I would recommend it. You will never forget the exhilaration of being able to breathe under water. The dive center at the Alcazar Hotel in Aqaba took excellent care of me and the other first-time divers." How could I ignore a suggestion such as this?

Against the hotel management's advice, I decided to leave for Ma'an and Aqaba the next day. They wanted me to stay one more day and then bus back to Aqaba. Would they have understood my need to bike the distance on the return? Probably not. They reminded me of the steep 35 km climb from Petra to the main road that I barely saw from the back seat of the police van in the darkness of night.

The summit of the mountain was almost in sight as I pushed my heavy load in the warm morning sun. A pickup truck driven by an Arab and his wife stopped to offer me a ride to Ma'an and the main road. I willingly accepted their kindness. Both he and his wife chain-smoked cigarettes in the front seat. I sat in the rear. Without explaining my intentions I tapped the woman on her shoulder and said in a loud voice, "Good morning!" Arab women, by the way, are not touched by men other than their husbands. This lady jumped so high I thought her head would touch the roof of the cab. Anxious to witness the reaction, I finally had the opportunity to do so. At the main road my host helped me remove the Globetrotter from the back of the truck. "May I pay you for your kindness?" I asked.

"If it is your wish."

Most of the return trip was downhill on the rough, potholed King's Highway. Hand brakes and the Phil Wood rear disc brake were a necessity to keep my load under control. Being the Moslem sabbath, traffic fortunately was light except for the oil trucks coming from Iraq. At 3 PM I began to look for some sort of campsite, knowing I would not reach Aqaba before dark. I had no intention of trying to negotiate the potholes or steep grades at night.

Fifty-six kilometers from Aqaba, on the right side of the road, a tire repair and restaurant of a sort came into view. I remembered it while traveling in the opposite directions. Yes, I could sleep there as well as obtain nourishment. As we walked toward a room in the back of the structure, we disturbed at least ten to twelve cats who disappeared into another part of the building. I was shown a mattress on the dirt floor. This was far from gracious living but at least I found a place to sleep in the middle of a harsh and desolate area of Jordan.

My ground cover protected me from direct contact with the mattress, on top of which I placed my sleeping bag and pillow. At about 6 PM I was awakened by the sound of a television. Supper consisted of chicken, potatoes, salad, tea, and then Nescafé. One customer, a truck driver, offered to transport me and my Globetrotter to Aqaba but I politely declined. Had road conditions been worse I would have accepted.

Dressed in my clothes, I slept the night under *very* cold conditions. In spite of my nap, I slept until 6:30 AM, when my Bedouin hosts returned to open the restaurant. A large tank near the entrance provided ice cold water for washing and shaving. In the cool of the winter's morning I felt refreshed.

The sun was warm yet the air was cool, requiring winter biking clothes as I traveled through the desert. Except for an occasional herd of sheep, I was alone with the long stretches of sand and mountains. Women, children, and their dogs were tending the sheep. Surely in Biblical days the scene was nearly identical to that of 1992. Finally, the last range of mountains appeared, with a rapid descent into Aqaba. Improvement in the quality of the road permitted me to loosen some of my control over the machine. At times I passed the trucks and at other times they passed me. My "impossible journey" was safely at an end. I felt content to be back in the warmth of the Red Sea in the thriving city of Aqaba, where tasty Arabic food was available as well as the diving center recommended by David Marsh. "It will be the best money you ever spent," said David. Before registering at the Jerusalem Hotel, I reserved a place for myself for the following morning at 8:30.

The Jerusalem Hotel had advantages and disadvantages. The disadvantage was the absence of hot water. Meeting Klaus was a definite plus. This young German cyclist who was my roommate has since become a true friend. Though a non-Jew, Klaus is attracted to Israel, having worked on a kibbutz on one of his previous visits. Both of his grandfathers were in the German army in World War II. One died in the war and the other in Siberia—the Russians deported him there following the peace.

Klaus and I ate supper together, then walked to the water's edge. From our vantage point we could see the lights of Eilat, Israel, directly across Aqaba Bay. If these two countries were at peace as they are today, the lengthy ferry ride would have been unnecessary. At that time a no-man's land existed between the two countries, separating them by a fence as well as by the military. We stopped at a sweet shop to taste the pistachio pastry and Turkish coffee.

Klaus, a sensitive young man, and I decided to return to Nuweiba and bike together to Israel. We enjoyed each other's company. Klaus planned to take the 12 o'clock ferry and I the 4 PM boat following my scuba experience. We arranged to meet at the campground in Nuweiba, and bus to St. Catherine's Monastery as well as Mount Sinai. From there we decided to return to Nuweiba, a one-day bike ride to Eilat. Had it not been for intestinal problems that delayed Klaus' return by one day, our schedules would have coincided.

Unfortunately, David Marsh and I do not view our first scuba diving experience with the same degree of nostalgia. Getting started took time. We were outfitted with tanks, masks, flippers, and waist weights before being escorted by van to the shore and reefs near the port of Aqaba. There we put on our wetsuits and began to receive instructions. At no time while in the water did my instructor break contact with me. He and I entered deeper water, causing painful pressure in my right ear. In sign language I was told to clear my air passages. About that time I discovered that my waist belt of lead weights had fallen from my waist and was hanging off my legs. Thanks to my instructor, the belt was again in its proper position. We then went in search of the underwater sea life that makes Aqaba popular with divers. Living coral, sponges, and sea urchins abounded in this area, but the amount of tropical fish was limited. The moving, waving, and undulating coral made the experience an adventure. Preparation, plus travel time to the beach, took 3-1/2 to 4 hours. Our actual time under water was thirty minutes. I would have settled for fifteen.

The word "please" does not seem to come through in the translation from Arabic to English. An example of this occurred at the ticket office in downtown Aqaba. The agent said to me, "Sit down." Again he repeated, "Sit down."

After the third time I asked, "Do I have to?"

"Not if you don't want to." We both smiled.

The entire passenger list on the ferry identified three Europeans, all others being from the Arab community. Except for Paul and Margaret Putters and myself, most of the others were chain-smokers, leaving a foul odor in the lounge area. By the time we got underway, many passengers were asleep on their backs, lying directly on the decks.

Paul and Margaret, from Holland, and I soon became acquainted. Our friendship continued when we and Klaus camped at Nuweiba. Two delightful Jordanians who, I might add, were not smokers, also became part of our acquaintance as we waited for the ferry to get underway. Rasmi Mahasneh is an enlightened cinema critic who is very aware of US events, both past and present. His friend Najeh Hassan is a bit more reserved but friendly nevertheless. We had a wonderful time exchanging stories as well as food. One story I told them concerned my encounter with the immigration officer in Hurghada, where the officer, in true Arab form, said to me, "Tea or coffee?"

273

It was perfectly fine for our Arab friends on the ferry to buy us food or beverage, but when we tried to reciprocate they politely refused. Finally in desperation I said to Rasmi and Najeh, "Tea or coffee?" They ordered tea.

The following Christmas season I received a Christmas card and note from Rasmi. Hopefully, he will reply to the letter I wrote after my return in June.

After a late arrival in Nuweiba Port and the arduous task of going through customs, I headed back to the beach and my campground, guided by the desert sky. Except for a bus and a car that passed me, I owned the desert for that short time, arriving at the campground at 3:30 AM. My Jordanian experience had come to an end.

Jordan, by observation, is a country with a certain amount of wealth. In Egypt the Jordanian *dinar* is considered hard currency. The native Arab people in Jordan appear much less aggressive than those in Egypt. Even in Petra, where bottles of colored sand are sold along with souvenirs, it is offered in a much more gentle manner. The same is true of those offering horse and camel rides.

King Hussein and his beautiful European wife are loved by his subjects. Their portraits are seen in most stores and restaurants. The king appears frequently on television, speaking in a very straightforward and rational manner. Smiling, he appears in both military and civilian clothing. Unfortunately, Jordan has found it necessary to straddle the fence when it comes to its common borders with Israel and other Arab countries.

Americans are liked in Jordan, all my contacts having been cordial and friendly. I cannot speak for the Palestinians, as I did not knowingly come in contact with them.

Aqaba is a clean, well laid out city that is a credit to Jordan. Good food at fair prices, as well as hard goods, are easily available in this port city. Materials come to Egypt through Jordan from Syria, Iraq, and Saudi Arabia. Truck traffic on the King's Highway carries oil from Iraq and cement from Amman.

The Jordanian men, who are especially handsome dressed in their military and police uniforms, present themselves as being intelligent, friendly, and virile. They and most of the people I came in contact with speak excellent English.

This unexpected visit to a Middle Eastern country proved to be one more stroke of good fortune as I followed my nose from country to country. In conclusion, I am gratified that Jordan and Israel are now at peace. May it last forever!

ISRAEL

Chapter 13
ISRAEL

Frederick Millet, a journalist for the French magazine "Le Cycle," happened to be on Nuweiba Beach at the same time as I. He saw my bike and Italian racing cap and became interested in my story. I agreed to be interviewed without any expectation of seeing the final product. He took photos of me with my Globetrotter and conducted a detailed interview. Perhaps I asked him to send me a copy of the article, I don't recall. This was the only time we met.

Following my return to Cambridge, I wrote to my friends the Chermats living in Guingamp, France. I had an excellent photo of them that I wanted them to have. Laititia Chermat, who is studying sports physiology at the university, bought "Le Cycle," saw the article and saved it in the hope that I would write to her and her family so she could mail it to me. Not only did I receive the article, but the photo taken by Frederick Millet is now imprinted on my personal stationery. My memory of Nuweiba as well as the Chermat family lives on.

The bus ride to St. Catherine's was uneventful except for a passport check. The Egyptian police, in a detailed manner, check the paid tickets against the number of passengers as well as the tourists' passports. For unknown reasons, one passenger was taken aside by the police. We proceeded without him.

Our bus climbed the mountain out of Nuweiba, passing the cafeteria operated by Yaquv Ben Yamanthou. We were then in a barren and mountainous region. Huge granite mountains appeared hostile to human life and yet it was here that Moses and his tribe of Israelites journeyed. St. Catherine Monastery was built later and maintained in this seemingly inhospitable environment. We arrived there shortly before dark.

An unheated dormitory with one electric bulb and a super-abundance of blankets served as our headquarters. The wash house was located in a separate building some distance away. By 5 PM it was cold and dark. The community supper was scheduled for 7:30. Klaus and I awaited that exciting moment under a pile of blankets in an attempt to stay warm. In warmer weather we would have climbed Mount Sinai to spend the night at its summit, but in December it was even difficult to stay warm at the base. The Egyptians call it "the mountain."

Fifteen Greek Orthodox monks live in this monastery, founded in the 4th century A.D. by the Byzantine empress Helena. A small chapel is built beside what is believed to be the burning bush from which God spoke to Moses. This chapel is dedicated to St. Catherine, the legendary martyr of Alexandria. In spite of the isolated setting, buses and private automobiles fill the spacious parking lot. The only portion open to the public is the chapel, with its collection of icons and jeweled crosses. A room full of bones of deceased monks was not available for inspection.

Klaus and I decided, on one condition, to hire a taxi for the return to Nuweiba: the driver had to promise to stop at my favorite cafeteria. Not only did I want Klaus to meet my friend Yaquv, but I was anxious to renew his acquaintance. We were not disappointed, especially when our host placed three glasses and a bottle of Jim Bean on the table. This was a grand reunion.

In the morning, with regrets we left Nuweiba Camping Village by bicycle. The weather was favorable and the employees were exceptional. Passing Dr. Shish Ka Bob's restaurant, we stopped to say goodbye with a promise to return soon. Ninety kilometers to the north lay Taba, Egypt, the Egyptian-Israeli border, and the Israeli city of Eilat on the Red Sea. Klaus and I were both excited.

We enjoyed a leisurely lunch along the side of the road 30 kilometers south of Taba. Boulders served as our table and chairs. Unattended camels nearby were searching the area for vegetation. The emaciated bodies of these animals mirror the harshness of the desert. When we came into their view, they fled as though they were frightened puppies. Except for an occasional vehicle, these camels probably see few humans in the course of a day.

We passed an Egyptian police roadblock before our entry to Taba and the Taba Hilton. Israel built and owned the Hilton during the time the Sinai was occupied territory. Taba consists of a one-doctor hospital, a few administration buildings, and a mosque, in addition to this luxury hotel.

Customs and passport control into Israel were routine. An x-ray inspection of my luggage aroused questions by the police until I explained that they were looking at a small camera tripod. At numerous times while in Egypt we were asked to show our passports, but it all seemed routine. One Egyptian tourist police guard, however, asked for ten Egyptian pounds, but then returned it. He was probably trying to pad his own pocket but then became fearful. Punishment would have been quick and severe had he been apprehended.

The Israeli police were young, polite, and knowledgeable. Several were female. Being especially courteous, they assisted us as much as possible. We were not required to empty the contents of our panniers, but interrogation was very thorough. "Has anyone given you anything to take into Israel? Are you carrying any property not belonging to yourself? Has your bike or baggage been out of your sight at any time you were traveling so that someone could have placed something in one of the bags, such as a bomb?" These were some of the routine questions asked.

The all-new and luxurious hotel, the Princess, became our first stop on the way to Eilat. Klaus needed to cash a travelers check and I was looking for the waitress I met at the New Pension Hotel in Aswan. Klaus got his money but I was unsuccessful in my search. Perhaps she was at another "newer" hotel.

Coral Reef Camping south of Eilat was perfect for our needs. Klaus and I enjoyed a meal with no holds barred. We ate everything in sight, including an elaborate ice cream dish for dessert. Fortunately, the attendant at the campground asked for my passport, a common occurrence at hotels or campgrounds in Egypt as well as Jordan. That night when I was robbed, at least I did not lose my passport.

Gabriel, a retired Finnish engineer, and his wife were our first acquaintances in Israel. Gabriel is an alien volunteer building a school near the Lebanese border. Though a Christian, he had adopted the Hebrew ethic along with his own religion. He and his Finnish co-workers feel very comfortable in this land of Jacob. They needed a welder as part of their crew.

We talked at some length concerning the possibility of my becoming a volunteer on his project. I had a limited knowledge of gas welding, but a lifetime of experience working with metal. I also had a desire to become a volunteer. We exchanged names and addresses. Gabriel's mailing address is in Jerusalem. It all seemed perfect.

That night before crawling into my tent, I put my fanny pack under my pillow, my usual practice. Not only do I feel safe having my valuables beneath my head, but the waist pack gives additional bulk to my small travel pillow. I had left my campsite twice for a few moments. Upon arising in the morning, my waist pack felt especially light as I went to fasten it around my middle. I then discovered I had been robbed. Everything except for my travelers checks were taken. Egyptian money, Israeli money, US currency, and my credit cards were all missing, as well as those irreplaceable photos and personal mementos. The other immediate problem was a recurrence of the infection in my right foot. I now needed both money and medical attention.

The climb by bicycle to the hospital in Eilat was difficult with the swelling and pain in my foot. A red streak was beginning to extend up my leg toward the region of the groin, indicating blood poisoning. There was no doubt I needed immediate care. I entered the emergency room.

"This visit will cost you 108 dollars, payable in advance," said the admissions person, smoking her cigarette. When I explained that I had been robbed the previous night, it fell on deaf ears. The travelers checks I held in reserve were for such immediate needs as food. I pointed to the red streak on my thigh and in a loud voice said, "I want to see a doctor!"

The antibiotic ampicillin I was given was identical to the one I received in Sicily. I also got a skin cleansing agent. I explained in detail to the doctor that the previous medication helped but had not cured the infection. "In four days you will be as good as new," he said. The hospital admissions person photo-copied my passport. I'm sure she thought the hospital would never see the $108. American Express travelers checks paid for my medication.

Klaus went on to Jerusalem by bus with his bike and gear. I remained at Coral Beach Camping, seeking a more permanent address in Eilat. He and I planned to meet at the Central Bus Station in Jerusalem on December 23, my birthday. In the meantime, the management at the campground was sympathetic to my situation. They agreed to wait for their payment until my new Mastercard arrived. It was a new experience for me to be in debt: I owed Klaus, the hospital, and now the campground, as well as my landlord in Eilat.

I shared a small two-bedroom apartment with a young Israeli working as a waiter during the day and drinking with his friends most of the night. He learned English by listening to American music. For the most part, the apartment, centrally located, served as a single-person residence.

The day I pedaled to Eilat to report the theft to the police and to look for an apartment was a rather cool day, complicated by a fever. My foot infection was taking its toll. At the police station, I became so chilled my teeth were chattering. Then my entire body began to shake. The officers sitting behind their desks were sipping tea as they worked. "I have a fever and am rather ill. May I have a glass of hot tea?" I asked. Had I been in Egypt, I would not have had to ask. My request was ignored. To keep warm I utilized the electric hand dryer in the lavatory.

I had no money and the banks were closed for Shabbat. At a department store I went to the customer service desk, explaining my problem. "Will you cash a travelers check under these unusual circumstances?" I asked. Not only did they require that I purchase something in the store, but the cost of the transaction was 15 percent. In addition to the cost of a tube of toothpaste, cashing a $100 check cost me $15.

That night in my small apartment I lay on the bed fully clothed, sleeping soundly until the middle of the night. I awoke in a pool of sweat. The fever must have broken. From then on I felt better, except for the swollen and sore right foot.

Shifting from a very active and physical life to one of inactivity, especially as I was trying to keep my foot elevated, was a bit difficult at first. I was grateful for my apartment with an abundance of hot water and a two-burner stove. Solar heat provides water at scalding temperatures that requires tempering with cold water. I also had a table and chair that served as my desk and for eating. Lighting was adequate. Unfortunately, central heat here and elsewhere in most of Israel is totally absent. The cement block buildings store the winter dampness, making the rooms feel colder than they actually are. At times I found it necessary to light the gas oven to warm the spaces.

I locked the Globetrotter to an outside railing without concern for its safety. On a quiet residential street with relatively little traffic, I had misplaced peace of mind. That night the bike was vandalized by neighborhood children. What they could not steal they destroyed. As a parting gesture they flattened both tires. At least I was beginning to feel better.

I inflated the tires, put on my cycling togs, and headed for Coral Beach Camping, a distance of about 8 km, to find out if my new credit cards were delivered by express from Tel Aviv. At the time I reported my losses, I was told I'd have new cards in seven days. The only address I could give was that of Coral Beach Camping. Getting back on the bike was like a new beginning. I felt rejuvenated until the final insult: the road was recently resurfaced with fresh tar.

On my next bike ride I avoided the tar and picked up my new American Express card. This enabled me to pay my bill at the campground and to then purchase more travelers checks at the local American Express office. I also paid Itzak my first month's rent. At least I was again solvent. "As soon as my Mastercard arrives I'll be able to obtain cash at the ATM of a local bank." Cash at ATMs is always in the currency of the host country—in Israel it's the *shekel*. I planned to pay the hospital with shekels at that time.

An excellent library within walking distance provided the English edition of the daily Jerusalem <u>Post</u> and a large table of second-hand books for sale at reasonable prices. Any book written in English that remotely related to Israel or the Middle East became part of my library. By the time I left Eilat on the first of April, I mailed home ten books I had read. This first winter of retirement was proving to be one of enlightenment as well as education.

With my new Mastercard, I went food shopping at the nearby supermarket, and bought a bus ticket for Jerusalem at the Central Bus Station for a December 23 departure. I was looking forward to my reserved window seat and the view of the Negev Desert and Dead Sea. The days seemed to pass quickly, with not enough time to do everything. Though Eilat was unseasonably cool, cold weather with snow and floods were being reported from Jerusalem.

One day while pedaling to the border gate between Egypt and Israel, I stopped at the caravan previously occupied by Esko and his wife. A Finnish couple who were friends of Esko now occupied it. I wanted to try my limited Hebrew and at the same time keep in touch through them with Esko, who was then in Jerusalem. Their Hebrew was as rudimentary as mine.

Between Eilat and Ein Gedi there appeared to be little more than desert and rugged mountains. A 20-minute rest stop gave me an opportunity to have a snack and to see this oasis for the first time. Though highly developed for the tourist industry, it was obviously no place for me to spend the winter. Eilat was not only larger, but more cosmopolitan. When the driver said "Twenty minutes" he did not mean twenty-one. Pounding on the door as the bus began to back out of its berth, he finally let me in. This was my first encounter with Israeli bus drivers, but not my last. We passed five-star hotels and a campground on the way to Masada, King Herod's mountain-top fortress. Tourists with backpacks got off there while others joined us for the steep climb to Jerusalem. The aisle of the bus was then filled to capacity. Ever-present in my mind was the question: could I make this trip on the Globetrotter? I had promised Louise, Dorothy's cousin, that I would not bike the Negev, but that did not mean I didn't want to do all or part of the distance under my own power. "Perhaps I can bike to Ein Gedi or Masada and then bus the rest of the distance to Jerusalem." In that way I would avoid the heroic climb from 250 meters below sea level to 820 meters above.

My good friend Klaus greeted me at the Central Bus Station in Jerusalem. Arriving in the dark, I would have had a problem finding the Faisal Hostel in East Jerusalem without him. We took a local bus to the Old City and then walked to the overcrowded hostel. It being both Christmas and Hanukah, seating on the bus as well as beds in Jerusalem were at a premium. I could have sold my bed a dozen times during that particular weekend. The owner Ali did not know how to say "no" even though we were filled to capacity. That night I loaned my air mattress to a younger person who slept on the floor.

Knowing this was my birthday, Klaus presented me with a card, a small gift, and even candles. He prepared our meal that was added to by a tourist, who had more spaghetti than he needed. Outside the hostel, rain was falling steadily on a rather chilly night.

"We are going to do what you want to do tonight," said Klaus.

"Stay in so we can keep warm and rest for tomorrow?"

"No, tonight we are going to do what you want to do. We are going to walk to the Old City."

"Klaus, are you sure this is what I want to do, or is it what you want to do?"

Damascus Gate was a short distance from the hostel. We entered the Old City through that gate and headed for the Western Wall, often called the "Wailing Wall," where Jews for centuries have cried over the destruction of the Temple. Streets were vacant for the most part, with Israeli soldiers posted at key points. Within sight of the Wall, six eternal flames were burning, symbolic of the six million Jews murdered by the Nazis. I felt that Klaus was especially proud to be able to introduce this highly significant area to me. To the left of the Wall we paid a small entry fee and entered a synagogue. Our hats served as head covering in respect for this house of worship. It was the first synagogue Klaus had ever entered. He felt

285

uneasy about being in a place where he might not be welcome. "Klaus, if they don't want us here they will tell us." Klaus explained to me that the Western Wall is considered a synagogue even though it's outdoors. Placed between the cracks of the wall are prayers written on small pieces of paper by those who were praying. Mythology states that these prayers will go straight up to heaven. I remembered my Sicilian friend who asked me to place a prayer in the wall for him.

Writing in Hebrew, I asked God for peace and then placed my piece of paper in a recess of the wall. Would you believe it did go straight to heaven? When I returned at a later date my prayer was gone. Is that not proof enough?

Klaus then insisted that we walk the Old City, for "that is what I wanted." The rain and cold sent me a different message. Finally we returned to the Faisal Hostel owned by Ali and his English wife Pat. I was probably the only Jew at Faisal. Israelis advised me, for my own safety, to stay out of the Old City. In actuality, I felt as safe there as anywhere else.

A family of four consisting of a grandmother, her daughter, and the daughter's two children were semi-permanent guests at the hostel. Lisa, age 8, and Michael, 11, are Sherry's children. At that time, the family was living there without any funds.

Sherry and her mother received a message from their God that they should leave the state of Washington and move to Israel. They probably did not consider the fact that as non-Jews they would not be able to obtain Israeli citizenship. I am assuming that prior to the theft they were financially solvent, having rented an apartment as well as a van. For reasons that are not clear, Grandmother kept the family funds in her purse.

One day while sightseeing, they parked their van near the beach so they could walk on the sand. Grandmother left her purse on the seat of the van. The rest is history: the window of the van was broken and the purse stolen, leaving them destitute. The generosity of Ali and Pat enabled these lovely people to have a place to stay and the opportunity of sharing the holiday season with all of us. The grandmother and I had something in common: the US Treasury would not forward our Social Security checks.

On Christmas Eve, Klaus and I decided to spend the evening in Bethlehem in spite of the cold and rain. We arrived at Manger Square by cab early enough to attend the Lutheran service nearby (Klaus is Lutheran). Though wet, we wore our outer clothing to keep warm. Small heaters mounted on the walls of the church proved ineffective. It was cold! The service was conducted in German and English.

We then stood in line waiting for our turn to pass through the Israeli Manger Square security check. In spite of a heavy downpour and the hour and one-half wait, the spirit of the visitors was high. Each person was taken individually into a small guard house where he or she was frisked and interrogated. Female Israeli soldiers attended to the women while male soldiers examined the men. All non-Europeans were taken to a separate location for examination. Were they permitted entrance? I don't know.

Hypothermia finally set in. My wet and cold body began to shake. Fortunately, we were now within Manger Square, where stores and the post office were open for business. In one souvenir shop an electric heater on the floor became my haven. The owner, seeing that I was so chilled, brought us each a glass of wine and a smile. My only problem was that I stood too close to the heater, scorching one leg of my trousers. Later in Eilat, I had the trousers converted into a pair of walking shorts. Some months later, while visiting Bethlehem for the second time, I visited the same souvenir shop. The owner's wife looked at me and said, "Oh, you're the man who burned his pants on Christmas Eve." Despite the hundreds of people who came and went from their store, she remembered me.

Visiting choral groups from all over the world performed on the outdoor stage. Most memorable to me were the Fiji Islanders who come every year to celebrate in Bethlehem. The following year I was again fortunate to listen to their spiritual songs and to visit with them later in the Old City. On that visit, following the initial peace agreements between the Israelis and Palestinians, security was almost non-existent. A part of the West Bank, Bethlehem will be returned to the Palestinians in spite of the fact that this city is a very short distance from Jerusalem.

At a pre-arranged brunch, Klaus and I visited with Swedish Christians within the Old City walls. In their small apartment with hot water radiators, we enjoyed the fellowship of these people we had met at St. Catherine's Monastery. Conversation centered around the Jewish presence in the Old City, the Arab discontent, the Arab terrorists, and the so-called "Jewish Holocaust mentality." Obviously, these were not the easiest of times. I was now listening to peace-loving non-Jews who did not necessarily share the same opinion as the Israelis. These were sons of Swedish people who had, at risk to themselves, saved many Jews from extermination in the 40s.

Christmas dinner at the hostel was no different than in Hometown USA. Ali prepared a huge turkey with more than enough food to go around. Some of us collectively bought the Christmas cheer. Though the hostel was bursting at the seams with people, we each found a place to sit and socialize. Sherry, with her mother and children, shared in the joy of the event. One year later I had the same pleasure of "breaking bread" at the Faisal Hostel with Ali and Pat. Sherry and her children were still living there, but her mother had returned home to Washington State. She undoubtedly had a sizeable Social Security check waiting for her.

One day during my Hebrew lesson in Eilat I asked Ariella where she teaches in addition to her private students at home. She acquainted me with a club known as "Sheesheem

Plus," *sheesheem* meaning sixty, where she teaches Hebrew to new immigrants. "You are too young for these old people," said Ariella.

"Ariella, I'm over sixty myself."

"Yes, but you ride your bike and stay young while these people who are recent immigrants from Russia appear much older."

I then became a member of Sheesheem Plus, studied at the Ulpan with Ariella, and had my private lessons at her home. Ulpan refers to the study of intensive Hebrew, concentrating on the spoken word. It is offered to all immigrants so they can become part of the community.

In addition to hearing the language, a social life centers around Sheesheem Plus; that was important to me. I became acquainted with many of the people, some of whom speak English. On Friday evenings we were served a festive meal followed by entertainment. Charlie was the master of ceremonies. We then spent the remainder of the evening swing-dancing American style. I recall one elderly lady who, having suffered a stroke, required a cane. With her cane in one hand and the other on my shoulder, we danced to "Mack the Knife."

Now that I started making friends, the people on the street did not seem so unfriendly. Being brusque and unfeeling to strangers appeared to be the way of life in Israel. During Christmas week in New York City, as an example, I could walk down Fifth Avenue without touching shoulders with a single person. In Eilat, unless I was willing to accommodate the other person on the sidewalk, we would be on a certain collision course. With bus drivers, I was always on a collision course.

It was only natural that the members of Sheesheem Plus would want to stop and visit on the street or in the market place. They were retired and for the most part unemployable.

Many of these Russian immigrants have been professional people, such as physicians, stomatologists, or engineers. In Russia a stomatologist is a dentist. These recent immigrants were in the process of trying to become accustomed to their new surroundings yet, at the same time, remember their heritage. Hearing Russian on the streets of Eilat is not unusual.

I spent my time in a productive way instead of playing cards or socializing at the Club. The Eilat Public Library became my principal pastime, especially when the weather was inclement. At times the sun would emerge from Eilat's winter shroud, giving me the energy to again to cycling in spite of the fact that my foot infection was beginning to return. An 8-km ride from Eilat city to the Egyptian border became my routine when weather permitted. The Gulf of Aqaba and the Har Adom, or Red Mountains as they're called in English, were always a welcome sight. These are the barren mountains of Jordan and Saudi Arabia. Often, the wind blowing south from the Negev became my challenge for the day as I returned to Eilat. At other times I headed north as far as the military roadblock and the Elat Kibbutz. In either case, soldiers, tourists, or cab drivers were always anxious to visit. On occasion, I would stop at the Princess Hotel to again become acquainted with the "good life." Their gift shop on the lower level is a source of gifts sent back to my family as well as a stocked paperback library for myself.

One day while pedaling toward Taba, Egypt, located just across the border, my chronic infection became especially aggravating. I remembered the one-doctor hospital located near the Taba Hilton. "This might be a good opportunity to purchase ampicillin at a much lower price than at the pharmacy in Eilat." I decided to investigate and at the same time add to my cultural experience. An Israeli would never buy across the border, but I was not an Israeli. I had previously bought and used Egyptian medicine.

Entering the Sinai from Israel is as easy as writing one's signature and showing a valid passport. Egypt proper, however, requires a visa. On my return to Israel, I was then granted an automatic 30-day visitors visa.

The all-cement Egyptian hospital building painted white was exactly where I remembered it. A hospital aide directed me to the doctor and his surgery a short distance from the entrance.

"Tea or coffee?" asked a rather scruffy-looking man who introduced himself as the doctor. In need of a shave and with fingers yellowed from years of cigarette smoking, the doctor wore traditional sandals and desert clothing. His English was excellent. "I do not have any ampicillin in supply, but if you wish, you can try tetracycline. We have that in stock." In addition to examining the wound, he supplied me with some antibacterial cream and vitamins as well as the tetracycline.

"How much do I owe you?"

"Ten Egyptian pounds." This is about the equivalent of three US dollars.

I then biked to the Taba Hilton in an effort to change Israeli or US currency into Egyptian money. Thanking the doctor for his kindness, I swallowed one of the tetracycline pills and headed back to the border and Eilat before darkness. An incredible thing then began to occur: almost immediately the swelling and redness of my foot began to subside. By the time I had finished my supply of medicine, the infection was almost eliminated. A few more pills were required.

When I returned to Taba for more medicine, I was again granted a 30-day visitors visa by the Israeli border police. Fortunately, the same doctor was on duty. He willingly supplied me with additional tetracycline as well as the other items I received on my first visit. "How much do I owe you?"

"Now that we know each other, you do not owe me

anything." Again I returned to the Taba Hilton to change my money and pay him the same amount as before. He willingly accepted the money.

Some months later when I left Israel and entered the Sinai for the third time, I stopped at the hospital with plans to visit the doctor and give him a gift in appreciation. He unfortunately had been transferred. I knew I was being a hypocrite when I decided that my gift would be one or two cartons of cigarettes. As a past smoker, *je déteste tabac*.

The turn of a key changed my quiet and peaceful apartment into a quagmire of noise, confusion, filth, and loud ethnic music, as well as the local watering hole. The Israeli waiter moved out and three Ethiopians moved in, one being a rather attractive young female. Soon, instead of three, there were six in addition to the many visitors who came but never seemed to leave. Many of these new immigrants are unemployed and on the dole. They occupied their space 24 hours of every day.

Friday night was the beginning of a weekend of drinking. The music and the loud, noisy behavior of these tenants and their guests soon brought complaints to the police. When the police arrived they looked at the Ethiopians and then they looked at me. I was ignored. The Ethiopians were threatened with punishment.

A bus ride to Tel Aviv had two purposes: my passport required renewal and I wanted to get away from my unacceptable apartment mates. Instead of going the same route as the Jerusalem bus, we traveled to Beersheba, the capital of the Negev and the location of Ben Gurion University. The climb from below sea level to above sea level was as heroic, or more so, than my previous climb to Jerusalem. The city of Beersheba gives a pleasant appearance, particularly after many miles of desert travel. This time, though, I saw desert farming where fresh vegetables are grown under plastic so the moisture from "drip" irrigation does not evaporate. Many bus stops are identified as the location of moshavs or kibbutzim. A moshav is a for-profit farm and a kibbutz is a socialistic scheme where all members supposedly share and share alike. It was Ben Gurion, the first prime minister of Israel and a resident of the Negev, who made the statement: "If we don't conquer the desert, the desert will conquer us."

Although it was winter, the road to Tel Aviv revealed beautiful green landscapes with huge groves of oranges. In Sicily the oranges have a green skin, but in Israel they look like real oranges. Broad highways, traffic lights, and the suburbs of Tel Aviv presage the city itself, located on the Mediterranean. Shortly thereafter we arrived at the Central Bus Station, the end of the ride.

Shambo, a hostel within walking distance of the Central Bus Station, became my residence on this, the first of several visits to Tel Aviv. It seems that Tel Aviv held an unavoidable magnetism for me. Many guests at Shambo's are backpackers who have traveled an incredible number of miles as they tour various parts of the world. Some were New Zealanders or Australians as well as those from other countries. Massachusetts and Canada were represented. Though none of these tourists wanted to give the appearance of being anti-Israeli or anti-Semitic, they all deplored the way Israelis treat Arabs. "Why are the Israelis treating the Arabs the same way the Jews were treated in Europe?" was asked continually. Perhaps it has to be kept in context in trying to understand this sort of mentality. The question I asked myself was: "If there was no Arab terrorism, would the Arabs be treated badly? Even though the Jews were not a threat to the safety of the Germans, they were persecuted. Can the two be compared?"

On a lighter note: the day was Monday, January 18, the day I planned to visit the American Embassy for my passport renewal. To my surprise, all US government offices worldwide were closed; the holiday was Martin Luther King Day, a perfect day for sightseeing.

An incident at a local bank enroute to the Central Bus Station demonstrates my naiveté to the problems of the Middle East, Israel in particular. I entered a bank carrying my panniers and sleeping bag stuff bag. These served as suitcases. "Can you direct me to the Mastercard window?" I asked a bank employee. She pointed to an office on the second level in clear view of the first floor. Without giving the matter further thought, I placed my bags on a chair and walked the stairs to the second floor. Time passed. A bank employee came running up the stairs speaking directly to me. "Are those your bags on the chair downstairs?" Had I denied ownership, the police were prepared to take them out of the bank to the center of the street. A robot would then be brought in to blow up the baggage. Fortunately, this did not occur. I had just received a necessary and thought-provoking lesson. One other time in Eilat, when I went from one window to another in the main post office, I unthinkingly leaving my pannier at the first window. The reaction was identical to the one at the bank. This time I apologized profusely, since I knew better than to cause this sort of anxiety in an anxious society.

Rather than hurry back to my smoking and drinking Ethiopian neighbors, I boarded the bus for Jerusalem and the Jasmine Cottage. The Holocaust Museum and Yad Vashem were my principal reasons for returning to Jerusalem. I read about Yad Vashem in my "Lonely Planet Guide" but I knew very little about it or its location. *Yad Vashem* in Hebrew means the hand and the name. Jack, the owner of Jasmine, gave me directions and the numbers of the proper buses going to these two places. I waited at the bus stop.

"Does this bus go to Yad Vashem?" I asked the driver. There was no response. I asked again, louder. An English-speaking woman seated near the front of the bus acted as my interpreter, explaining that the bus does not go to Yad Vashem, it only goes to the entrance. "He (the driver) could have been a little more cordial," I said to the woman, expecting to receive agreement to this statement.

"What should he do," she asked, "Kiss your hand?"

This incident was quickly forgotten as I began to explore, see, feel, and read about the extermination of six million people, one and a half million of them children. The site of this memorial and teaching entity overlooks Jerusalem from an elevated position. There is an outdoor memorial to the children as well as an indoor remembrance where a single candle reflects in one thousand mirrors. The solitary candle is the only illumination within the structure. We walked the passageway in near darkness, listening to a solemn voice over a loudspeaker. The voice recites in a seemingly endless manner the name, age, and country of the one and a half million children. Eventually we were back in daylight, having been touched by reality for the remainder of our lives.

Under the synagogue roof an eternal flame elucidates the names of all the death camps operated by the Nazis. For obvious reasons, silence was observed and felt. Photographs are permitted even though the solemn surroundings seem to indicate the contrary.

An art museum representing works of the victims exhibits art that was smuggled out of the concentration camps, as well as work of contemporary artists. A children's section expresses hope, joy, and pain through their art. Two sculptures captured my sensitivity: one was a pile of shoes done in clay. That was all that was left after the extermination of these innocent people. The other was done in black burlap and two-by-fours. It represented a person with arms raised, facing the wall waiting to be shot. The two-by-fours are the person's arms. I became overwhelmed.

The Yad Vashem Museum is a historical review dating back to the early 1930s with the rise to power of Hitler. Photographs, news articles, and a limited number of tangibles are enough to keep a person occupied for an afternoon. Weapons used in the Jewish resistance as well as concentration camp clothing are also on display. Considerable space is devoted to the Warsaw ghetto uprising. Death permeates the scene as the Nazis tried to achieve the "final solution." Perhaps these experiences, within the memory and lifetime of so many Israelis, account to some extent for the outward attitude of the citizens of Israel today. It is all so very complicated.

Returning to the present, this is perhaps a good time to discuss the military presence in Israel, where both men and women are conscripted. These young people have been trained to shoot to kill, each carrying an automatic rifle with the safety in the "on" position. Dispersed throughout the country, these weapons are a definite deterrent to terrorism. I began to realize that my safety was insured by their presence.

It is said that during military training, the recruit is required to sleep with his gun. I saw young Israeli soldiers dancing and at the same time carrying their guns over their shoulders. Armed civilians accompany children on the buses to protect them from terrorism as they travel to the beaches and recreation areas. These volunteers also ride the commercial buses for the same reason. This may occur only in certain locations or it might be on all buses. I do know that the Eilat bus that travels to the Egyptian border and back carries a volunteer guard. My friend Eva, from Sheesheem Plus, is one of those who volunteers for this type of service. She originally lived in Hungary, having come to Israel via Brazil and Canada.

I spent an entire day at the Israel Museum, a complex of museums and buildings that could rival any general type of museum in any country, and within walking distance of the Jasmine Cottage. Traveling in the opposite direction, I easily walked to the Old City of Jerusalem. The Knesset, or Parliament, located a short distance from the museum, is surrounded by a fence and protected by guard dogs. It appears to be secure outside the fence. An enormous bronze Menorah has been erected at the entrance to the Knesset; this symbolic lamp with its seven candles signifying the seven days of Creation was given to Israel by Britain in 1948.

The "Shrine of the Book" is one of the many buildings of the museum. It houses the Dead Sea Scrolls. The white roof of the Shrine is designed to resemble the clay jars in which the scrolls were found at Qumran, bordering the Dead Sea. Most of the original edition of the Book of Isaiah is on permanent view, in addition to many artifacts of interest that relate to that particular era. Most are in near-perfect condition. Barbara and Bob became my friends for the day outside the entrance to this museum. Before the day had ended we hired a cab to the Old City. I visited the Western Wall for the second time, Bob and Barbara for the first.

In the museum we were provided a two-hour guided tour by a lovely, aged docent who speaks excellent English. Her tour is divided into Archæology and Ethnology. We visited entire rooms decorated as to their country of origin. The wedding scene with its ethnic North African clothing is beautifully displayed. A wooden synagogue from Eastern Europe has been reconstructed within the museum walls. It is perhaps the last of its kind in the world; the others were burned by the Nazis. The Billy Rose Sculpture Garden outside the museum includes works of Henry Moore and Picasso.

Jack, the owner of Jasmine Cottage, recommended that I pay a visit to Mea Shearim, particularly since it's located near the Old City. This tourist attraction is an ultra-Orthodox Jewish district that is the only remaining example of the ghetto that existed in eastern Europe before the Holocaust. The residents dress in 18th century East European clothing, including unusual hair styles for both men and boys, in which their curls are seen below the traditional "flying saucer"-type black hats. These people, for the most part, devote full time to religious studies. They are financed by ultra-Orthodox communities abroad.

The residents of Mea Shearim did not pay any attention to me until I decided to photograph the window of a store displaying religious articles. I knew that taking photographs of people was forbidden, but I didn't suspect that a photo of a store might make a difference. One resident came up to me screaming "Police!" I quickly left the area in fear that my camera would be taken and destroyed. The police, fortunately, did not hear this "call of the wild."

I was on time for a walking tour of the Old City conducted by Menachem, who takes his work very seriously. He does not work for money alone; he attempts to provide information to interested persons. If a tourist appears disinterested, even though he has paid, Menachem will make an effort to ease him out of the tour, or if he thinks there is hope for this person, he will speak harshly to him. At one point while walking with the group, I stopped to purchase a map of the Old City, causing the entire group to wait until the transaction was complete. Menachem thought I was souvenir hunting. After I explained my reasons for stopping, he apologized for his comments. We then proceeded on our two- to two-and-a-half hour tour. I returned to Jasmine Cottage on foot when the tour was concluded, using my map as a guide.

The tour of the Knesset was very worthwhile and in my usual style, a bit unique, keeping in mind that security at the Knesset is of the highest priority. To the right of the entrance is an eternal flame in memory of those who have died in past wars. Our group progressed to the foyer where three beautiful Marc Chagall tapestries are hanging, as well as mosaics designed by this prolific artist. Chagall also did the glass windows of the synagogue located in the Hadassah Hospital in Jerusalem. Most of the stones in the mosaics are indigenous to Eretz, Israel.

We were shown the Parliament, with its seats arranged in the shape of a Menorah. The two major parties sit opposite each other, while the smaller parties sit in the back facing the podium. The balcony where we sat is reserved for visiting dignitaries on one side, and the press on the other. At that point I decided to return to the gift shop instead of remaining with our group, with the intention of buying postcards and a book on the museums of Israel. Things then became complicated: I found myself in an area of the building not reserved for visitors.

Knowing the security mentality of the Israelis, I did not want to be apprehended and interrogated as a possible security risk, but I felt it necessary to continue down the same corridor I had selected as the one leading to the gift shop. Moments later I noticed a well-staffed security office. Entering, I immediately disclosed my identity and the reason for my presence. "How did you get here?" asked the head agent. Following a passport check, he escorted me to the gift shop where we shook hands and separated. Feeling fulfilled, I began to make plans to return to Eilat and my Ethiopian acquaintances. Unfortunately on this trip to Jerusalem, I did not have the opportunity to interview Yael Dayan, a member of Parliament, but there was still hope. "Perhaps on my return with the Globetrotter in April this can be accomplished."

One of the second-hand books I bought at the Eilat Library is entitled Envy the Frightened. Yael Dayan, the daughter of General Moshe Dayan and a very controversial member of Parliament, is its author. Written first in English and then translated into Hebrew, the book touched a nerve. I in some measure identified myself with the main character of the book, Nimrod.

Nimrod was born and raised where survival of the fittest prevailed, particularly with the constant threat of Arab terrorism. He and his companions played the game "who can be the strongest" that became so intense that these young people would secretly steal their way into enemy Jordanian territory and then return unharmed. They did this to prove that they were strong and capable of dealing with the enemy if and when necessity beckoned. At the same time, something was happening to their psyches, especially Nimrod's. He was trading his humility and sensitivity for strength.

A product of World War II and the military, I found a parallel between my life at that particular time and Nimrod's. Civilian life and a peacetime economy eventually eased me back into balance. The near-loss of his only son brought Nimrod to his knees. After his previously non-existent tears, he was able to look back with regret at events such as the death of his mother. He did not attend her funeral. "She was dead. What did it matter?"

I was so impressed with Envy the Frightened that I discussed the book with Israeli mothers at every opportunity. "Are the Israeli youth so conditioned with a need for survival that they have a Nimrod mentality?" I asked. "Is the Arab threat of terrorism so great that an Israeli Jew can see no worth in an Israeli Arab? They both belong to the same land."

These were difficult questions that required more than a simple answer, but in more cases than not they were not answered in a succinct manner. "Our children are given so much love as they're growing up that the military has no effect upon their humility. They are serving their country; they are not life-time soldiers," was the usual reply. When I discussed the matter with the soldiers themselves I often received a different point of view. The Israeli soldier has been trained mentally and physically so that he or she knows "who is the strongest." There is no doubt in the minds of the soldiers that they consider themselves superior and therefore invincible. The possible lack of humility is something that would require much more research than my simplistic questions.

The day before I left Eilat to resume my bicycle tour, I received a package from Jerusalem. Yael returned my book with two inscriptions, one in English and the other in Hebrew! She made no mention of a possible interview. It became obvious that her book, suitably inscribed, would be my only contact with this talented person.

Shortly thereafter, the Jerusalem Post English edition featured an unauthorized interview that Yael Dayan had with Yasser Arafat, the titular head of the Palestinians. Not only was she accused of grandstanding, but also of standing in the way of the peace process. Many Israelis called for her expulsion from the Knesset. Before leaving the country, I read other articles on other issues that concerned this controversial person and one of my favorite authors.

Marc Anderson and Nina Bignell were walking from the Central Bus Station in Eilat with their backpacks and sleeping bags. "Are you looking for a place to stay for the night?" I asked. Our friendship extended over a period of two months. Marc is English and Nina Swedish. They met on a moshav on the West Bank and fell in love. They were on an overnight visit to Eilat and the Red Sea with its sun-drenched beaches even though it was winter elsewhere. I must admit I had a good feeling when I visited with these young people who shared similar values to myself, in contrast to my Ethiopian apartment mates. I also enjoyed being their host, a throwback to my life in the US. They appeared to enjoy the breakfasts I prepared for them as well as my hospitality. One month later Nina and Marc returned to Eilat for another brief visit.

They borrowed a van owned by their employer and drove into Hebron seeking an overnight of rest and relaxation. Their license plates were Israeli, not those of the West Bank. Marc, a veteran English paratrooper, stated that he had never been so concerned for his safety, much less for Nina's, than he was while in Hebron. Perhaps this is the reason I made no attempt to visit Hebron even though I did bike in the West Bank, Jericho, and even Gaza. An invitation to visit my newest friends at their moshav unfortunately never materialized. We have subsequently lost contact with one another.

The very modern Kibbutz Elat is north of Eilat near a military checkpoint. Many times I would turn around at this checkpoint on my morning training ride and let the wind blowing off the desert carry me back to Eilat. Once a week Kibbutz Elat is host to visitors for an evening of dinner and entertainment in their large dining room complex. This facility serves at all other times as the dining room for members of the kibbutz. I decided to become a true tourist and be entertained.

While waiting for the bus to take us from Eilat to the kibbutz, I met a lovely lady who was unattached, at least for that particular evening. She and Nina are both from Sweden, her home being Göteborg. Her son was stationed with the UN peacekeeping forces on the Israel-Lebanon border. Lisa and I spent an enjoyable evening dining, dancing, and being entertained by a French-speaking Israeli. Some of the dancing was American swing and some Israeli folk dancing such as the hora.

The city of Göteborg is the second largest in Sweden and the home of the Volvo factory. Meeting Lisa brought back memories of a bus/bike tour to Scandinavia that Dorothy and I shared. The tour was called "International Weekends." She and I were the only people who showed up with their own two-wheeled transportation.

We pedaled to our hotel in Copenhagen while the others rode the bus. This was our first hotel, the next scheduled hotel being seven miles north of Göteborg. Dorothy and I decided to bike to Göteborg instead of taking the tour bus. Though the bike ride was pleasurable, it does not concern the memories to be discussed. We spent two nights and one day on this adventure before arriving at our hotel under the most unusual circumstances.

At about 3 o'clock in the afternoon she and I decided to bike the seven final miles from Göteborg to our hotel, in time for rest and supper. With only seven more miles to go, we estimated that we'd probably arrive before the two tour buses. Using a road map, we arrived at the city limits of Göteborg and the beginning of a divided interstate-type highway. Obviously, something was very wrong. What was it? We had pedaled at least seven miles, we were beyond the city limits and at the beginning of a freeway, yet there was no hotel in sight. I parked the Globetrotter and inquired at a gun club identified by a sign in English. The answer to our question then became very obvious. Ten kilometers are the equivalent of one Swedish mile. In other words, we were 70 km away from our hotel when we were in the center of Göteborg!

My nervous wife/companion/stoker and I selected the shoulder of the highway as our only immediate solution as we headed toward an airport a considerable distance away. We were hopeful that we could fly the additional distance needed in order to rejoin our tour. To do otherwise meant that we'd probably not see them again until departure time in Stockholm. We would totally miss the tour of Norway and an overnight stay in reindeer country. Is it little wonder Dorothy was nervous?

At the airport, a language problem arose that made communication very difficult. We did not speak Swedish nor did we have a Swedish-English dictionary. Fortunately, an English-speaking employee provided the needed information. "Take the train. The station is only a quarter of a mile from here." Did he mean English or Swedish miles? This solved our problem, as we rejoined our group into Norway and the Bergen Railway above the Arctic Circle. It seems as though someone was looking over our sholders.

Conditions at my apartment had not improved. I was an unhappy camper! My Ethiopian roommates had taken over the apartment, leaving the kitchen and bathroom in the same condition that I visualized the appearance of their tents in Ethiopia. Traditional Ethiopian music in its repetitious manner continued to resonate off the walls. "Should I look for different accommodations or try to adjust to the situation?" Fortunatelly, I had only two weeks to endure this abuse before resuming my travels. An idea then entered my mind: why not take a bus to Beersheba, since I had no intention of climbing the horrendous elevation by bike from the desert road. I was witness to this climb on the bus enroute to Tel Aviv. "This way I can avoid the Ethiopian noise and at the same time see Beersheba, the 'capital of the Negev.'"

USA Today headlines announced a record snowfall in the US, especially along the eastern seaboard. I felt fortunate in being in Eilat instead of shoveling my walks in Cambridge. I should have been concerned about my own property thousands of miles away, but as the adage goes, "no news is good news!"

The 11 AM double-decker bus left Eilat for Beersheba. Reserved seats at the front of the second level provided a wonderful view of the desert. My seat companion, a young French woman, was at first hesitant to converse, but after the "ice" was broken we enjoyed the ride together.

Until after the evening meal at the Beersheba YHA hostel, I was the only occupant of an eight-bed dormitory room. Unfortunately, it was too cold to use the pool, part of this modern facility. I decided to visit the Museum of the Negev, within walking distance. Located in an old Turkish mosque, this attraction is one of three reasons I wanted to visit Beersheba. The Bedouin open market held every Thursday, and an escape from the Ethiopians in Eilat were my other reasons. Although I knew about Ben Gurion University, this was not one of my priorities. By sheer chance, the University became my most important new experience in Beersheba.

To my disappointment, the Museum of the Negev was closed for renovations. This meant I was deprived of seeing the exhibits and archæological artifacts of the entire Negev region, dating back as far as 4,000 years. The section on the Bedouin culture was also closed to the public. A sign on the door indicated that an exhibit on Ethiopian culture in an adjacent building was open. The price was 2-1/2 NIS (new Israeli shekels). Even though I had come to Beersheba to get away from the Ethiopians, that didn't mean I wasn't interested in their culture, particularly as I had little else to do until supper.

The exhibit was small, quiet, and interesting. At the time I entered I was the only person there, except for the staff. A male attendant, without discussing the matter, decided that he would make my visit as authentic as possible. He turned on his tape deck at a volume almost as high as I had been forced to listen to in Eilat. You guessed it, the music was identical to that of my apartment mates.

Most of the exhibit items are copies of the originals located in the Israel Museum in Jerusalem. Women washing the hands of their husbands prior to eating injarra, their native food, and one of washing her husband's feet, part of the religious ceremony, demonstrate some of the culture of these people. Photographs reveal desert scenes showing a barren existence as well as their "child-like" ceramics. Soon a group of children arrived with their mothers. These children did not know that, in museums, objects of art are not to be touched, nor did their mothers instruct them in the proper behavior of a museum visitor. Traditional music and this lack of discipline gave me cause to shorten my visit. Once outside, I breathed a sigh of relief and headed toward Ben Gurion University in the New City.

It will come as no surprise that this university is located on Ben Gurion Street. A large stone is positioned at the entrance identifying the name of the institution. The buildings, less than forty years old, resemble the cement structures at the University of Massachusetts, Boston. I stood there looking at this tremendous accomplishment where the Ph.D. degree is awarded to worthy candidates. Even though I personally had little to do with this achievement, I felt overwhelmed and proud. My gifts to the Combined Jewish Philanthropies could hardly be considered major contributions. A security check was, of course, necessary prior to admission. My US passport was the only document needed. It being late in the afternoon, I decided to spend my time in the main library by starting at the top floor in the stacks and working my way to the first floor. This decision could not have been better.

I randomly removed a book from a shelf and opened it to a section on photosynthesis written by a doctoral student. Though complex, I could understand the intent of the article, written in English. At the end of the article is an obituary of this researcher and author, who died at age 25 in a motorcycle accident. He was a Canadian, family man, and accomplished musician. This was my introduction to the third floor. Dusk was falling but through a window I was able to see the city.

The second floor is what could be called "unexpected ecstacy." What I did not see at the Museum of the Negev I saw here in the library. Discovered by university archæologists are original items found in Egypt and the Negev. Large photographs exemplify the sites where the objects were found. Gypsum masks of the Persian period as well as the Hellenistic and Roman periods were found near the Suez Canal. These masks date to the 5th century B.C. Ceramics, copper, bronze, alabaster, and stone objects were also dated. A set of dishes from the North Sinai nested one on top of the other. Female fertility figurines representing the Middle Bronze (Persian) Period date to the 18th century B.C. A decorated juglet with a Canaanite motif of an ibex and a palm tree identify the late Bronze Period of the 13th century B.C. The ibex is a type of wild goat indigenous to Israel. Small signs with the picture of an ibex along the roads of Israel indicate a nature preserve.

Keith Taylor, my newly acquired roommate, lives in Birmingham, England. He and I awakened at 5 AM so we'd be ready for the Thursday morning Bedouin outdoor market. This market is supposed to be the highlight of Beersheba, but in actuality it's just another market. At one time it was conducted by the Bedouin people but today it's perhaps more an Arab market with Bedouins well represented. Egyptians drive from the Sinai with their salable items. Perhaps the cold and rain of the morning made this weekly event seem less exciting. Keith and I enjoyed Turkish coffee at the market, then returned to the hostel for a full Israeli breakfast. There was good fellowship at the table, particularly with a young Dutch mother of three traveling alone with her backpack. Her children were in Holland with their father.

A World War I cemetery is maintained by Britain several hundred yards south of our hostel. Over 1,300 English soldiers were buried here following the Battle of Beersheba between the English and Turks. The Turks were defeated under the leadership of General Allenby, who is commemorated by the Allenby Bridge crossing the Jordan River between Jericho and Jordan. The cemetery, in my opinion, is a monument to the futility of war.

I began to inquire about the advisability of biking in the Negev. The police station where I reported the theft of my valuables seemed the best place to begin. It was also where I asked for hot tea and was refused. Should I have been surprised when I was answered in one-syllable sentences? Perhaps the chief had other things on his mind, but survival was on mine. I recall that the evening after this inquiry, I was writing to my two children. To cover all bases, I told them that I chose to be buried in Eilat should the need arise. The Eilat cemetery is at the edge of town, elevated above the homes and commercial buildings. It is literally at the edge of the desert. Many graves are decorated with a miniature tank or piece of military equipment to commemorate the death of a soldier in one of the wars since the birth of Israel. I was not anxious to reside there but with the constant talk of terrorism, ambush, and murder, death had to be considered.

My visit with the military at the roadblock north of Eilat produced different and better results, particularly with the young soldiers. They were anxious to give me advice as well as being friendly. One of the young enlisted men referred to me as "Dad." The general consensus was that until Ein Gedi I had very little to worry about, but near Hebron and Arad I should be cautious. "After Hebron, wear your helmet," they said. "They throw stones from the cliffs." They also suggested that I seek assistance from the military in the areas that might be unsafe for a lone traveler. The soldiers smiled when they talked about my wearing a helmet. Before returning to Eilat I stopped at Kibbutz Elat to visit and to reserve a place for lunch the following Tuesday. The Underwater Observatory, Coral Reefs, and Kibbutz Elat were on my list prior to my departure. I was anxious to experience a kibbutz meal that so many people had talked about, where in cafeteria style one can eat as much as he or she chooses. Quality as well as quantity typify an Israeli kibbutz meal.

New shorts, a pair of L.A. Gear shoes, my new one-burner butane stove, and a small portable radio were my newest purchases in preparation for an April 1 departure. Jordache jeans converted into shorts were the work of a local seamstress. The lone remaining unsolved problem revolved around the Globetrotter. I had written to Michael at Ace Wheelworks, telling him of the replacement parts I needed, but they had not arrived. Now that the tandem was vandalized, all its "bells and whistles" were missing. I needed new fenders, a chain, a rearview mirror, and a complete replacement of the lighting system that was stolen. Fortunately, the machine itself was still in good operating condition.

The weather was now improving rapidly, making my round-trips to Taba more frequent and pleasurable. On one of these training rides I visited with an English couple well acquainted with Malta. "It seldom rains on Malta," said these tourists. I was reminded of the time when I stood for two and a half hours in the wet and cold waiting for an incredible storm to abate. We three agreed that Malta is a lovely place, i.e., the people, geography, and its history. While we were talking, an EGED (an acronym for the passenger buses throughout Israel) bus stopped to discharge some passengers. On board in civilian clothes, my friend Eva was doing her volunteer work as a police officer. We talked for a moment before the bus returned to Eilat. I felt like an "old-timer" now that people on the street, as well as Eva, recognized me.

On my return ride, I stopped at the Coral World Underwater Observatory. The sea life, especially the live coral, exceeded my expectations. I was looking at a natural aquarium through the underwater observation windows. The fish swimming by are indigenous to the area, a part of the Red Sea. Electricity generated by an eel in one tank was sufficient to illuminate a 100-watt bulb. The eel is in solitary confinement. In one open-air tank, a sting ray shares space with the tropicals. When fed generously, the fish and rays seem to get along quite well together. Four countries can be seen from the Observatory lookout tower: Israel, Egypt, Jordan, and Saudi Arabia.

In the light-free areas, photographers are asked not to take flash photos that could injure the fish. There, flashlight fish with two flashlights per fish dart around the tank illuminating the area. Below the eye on each cheek is a luminescent patch that the fish can cover or expose at will. The illumination from the flashlight fish is said to attract other sea life searching for food.

My lunch at Kibbutz Elat was sumptuous. Date palms and the view of the mountains from the dining room added to the ambiance. I was pleased that this kibbutz was on my list of things to do and places to visit. A fierce tailwind blowing out of the desert carried me back to Eilat in what seemed to be a matter of minutes. "Is this what I'll have to endure if I decide to bike to Jerusalem?"

The person who sold me my portable radio has experience in the desert, especially in the region of Timna Park, approximately 35 km from Eilat. "A campground 10 km north of Timna Park has tent sites as well as food." I decided to check out this information with my landlord Itzik, a desert guide. From discussions with others as well as with Itzik, I learned that in Timna Valley National Park, the site of Biblical copper mines, a campground is located next to the visitors center. Situated alongside an artificial lake, campers watch the park animals, especially the ibex, when they come to drink. Either of these sites seemed exciting for my first night in the desert.

Itzik and I studied the map together. He advised me to follow the desert road to the Dead Sea, staying out of the mountains. SDE Boker, the retirement home of Ben Gurion, was on my list of especially interesting places to visit, but it would have been foolish for me not to take the advice of this local resident. Itzik strongly advised that I visit Timna Park, an area he knows well.

My last night at Sheesheem Plus was pure fun. I wrote out a farewell speech in English and Hebrew. Charlie, the master of ceremonies, knew of my plan and went along with it. Ariella, my Hebrew teacher, and her husband were my invited guests for this Friday night supper. Unfortunately, her husband was unable to join us. All or most of the membes of our Hebrew class attended. Hilda, my English friend, and Eva, the volunteer policewoman, were there along with most of my Russian friends. Following an introduction by Charlie, I said goodbye to these lovely people in English and then in Hebrew. At the conclusion of this short talk I said to Ariella, "I forgot a word in my haste to do it perfectly."

"They knew what you were trying to say," said Ariella. We took pictures of everyone with my camera. Eva then insisted that I take one of just her. Promising to send the photos after my return to the US, we shook hands, we kissed, and we hugged. My Eilat experience was rapidly coming to an end.

That evening the television was turned on when Eva and I entered her house. President Weizman, the new president of Israel, was being interviewed by the press. This man is my exact age. "Here I am retired from the work world and this man's labor is just beginning." In 1967 he commanded the Israeli Air Force and was responsible for the destruction of the Egyptian Air Force while their planes were still on the ground. A hawk then, he has since mellowed. He talked about returning the Golan to Syria even though at one time this land was declared non-negotiable.

March 30, 1993, was a banner day. My repaired glasses arrived from Jerusalem, having gone to the dead letter box. They were sent from home three months earlier but did not arrive. The postmaster opened the package, found my name and address, and forwarded the package to me in care of my landlord Itzik Belanga. A parcel from Ace Wheelworks containing all the "goodies" I requested was also delivered to Itzik the same day. Last but certainly not least, my autographed copy of Envy the Frightened was again in my hands. It was signed by Yael Dayan in English and Hebrew. I was now ready to plan my departure.

The Ethiopians were history; they were evicted. In their place were three young Israelis, one of whom is a bicycle mechanic. With his assistance we installed the new lighting system. I easily handled the remainder of the repairs. These three young men were visiting Eilat for an annual rock concert. The entire town was invaded by young people from all corners of the country. That night eight females and three males occupied one room and I the other. At 5 AM Itzik's brother-in-law Zvi awakened me as he brought additional rock enthusiasts to the tiny apartment. By 9, I was on the road for Timna Park. Yaffa, Itzik's wife, Zvi, her brother, and I said goodbye as though we probably would never meet again. I photographed them and they me. It is said that "parting is such sweet sorrow." I was truly sad to leave these friends, yet anxious to resume my adventures.

Shifting into the lowest gear, the Globetrotter and I headed into a wind that appeared relentless. Sand caught up in the wind bombarded my exposed skin as we tried to conquer the desert. Timna Park is 35 km north of Eilat and I had the determination to see it through. By noon and with no idea as to the actual distance covered, this determination turned into exhaustion. I turned around and headed back to Eilat.

Needless to say, our return ride was fast and easy. We stopped at the Central Bus Station. I bought a reserved seat to Jerusalem and a ticket for the bike. "Louise, Dorothy's cousin, will now have her wish. I will not be biking in the Negev."

The next morning we arrived at the Central Bus Station in ample time to load the Globetrotter on the bus. To my disappointment, the amount of baggage in the storage compartments prevented me from putting the bike on board. Although I had a reserved seat, there is no such thing as reserved space for baggage. This was the Passover season and it appeared as though the entire population of the country was going somewhere. The dispatcher suggested that I try a later bus. I had a different idea. This time I'll take enough water and food so it won't matter how strong the headwind is blowing. I felt like writing to Louise to tell her that I tried to follow her advice but conditions prevented it. There was no other alternative and I was excited.

The intensity of the wind was no different than the previous day, the only difference being that I knew that, given enough time, I could reach my goal for the day. The road to King Solomon's Mines, a commercial venture, confused me. I thought this was the entrance to Timna. Returning to the desert road, we then continued on an access road to the Park and the admissions gate. That particular night, I was the Park's sole occupant. An entrance fee of 10 NIS will admit one visitor, but it's free for cyclists. I figured out why cyclists are given this consideration: no sane biker would be out here in the desert looking for a campsite.

The restaurant near the artificial lake is owned by a local kibbutz. One of the workers named Scott lives in Connecticut. He graduated from Northeastern University in Boston and was taking time out to be a kibbutznik before getting on with his career. Watermelon, the cash crop of the kibbutz, was being harvested for the first time the day of our arrival. This was the reason for my being given a piece at the entrance gate. Hot and thirsty, I appreciated this delicious treat.

That night I did not stay up to watch the ibex refreshing themselves. I set up my tent near the restaurant, protected by a windscreen that during the day shelters visitors from the weather. A kibbutz member unlocked the wash house. Everything was now ready for a restful night's sleep, my first in the Negev.

A series of sandstone ridges caused by erosion of a 50-meter high cliff is aptly named King Solomon's Pillars. There I met a group of Israeli tourists from Tiberius, near the Sea of Galilee. The driver's last name was Cohen, a friendly person who was nice enough to photograph me with the Pillars in the background. Had my Globetrotter and gear been lighter, I probably would have done more touring in the Park. Heat and hills as well as my planned lunch stop at a resort area called Yotava about two and a half hours north of Timna kept me on schedule. This resort, with a mini-market, air-conditioned restaurant, a pool complete with a huge water slide, and an abundance of vacationers was a welcome sight. Frozen popsicles sold by vendors were a special treat.

The remainder of the day was spent in the desert, with a greeting from an occasional car or lorry. A wave of the hand or the honking of a horn was all I needed to feel at ease with the world. I remember passing a moshav where peppers were being grown under plastic so that moisture from drip irrigation would be retained in the soil and not dissipated into the atmosphere. The peppers come in three different varieties: red, yellow, and green. At the time, I didn't know that the picking of a single piece of fruit or vegetable is considered a felony in Israel, punishable by a fine or imprisonment.

I carefully leaned the Globetrotter against one of the Quonset-like huts and again went to work with the Swiss Army knife. My home-grown peppers in Cambridge, with the assistance of compost, fertilizer, and underground sprinkling were tasteless compared to these beauties. They are so full of water and flavor that they shall remain in my memory as the best ever. Even the paprika in Hungary, a type of pepper, does not compare to a desert-grown red or yellow pepper. Had I known I was stealing, they probably would have tasted even better.

An intersection soon came into view, where the road to the left goes to Dimona and SDE Boker, while Route 90, the HaArava, continues due north to Ein Gedi. This was the moment of final decision. "Do I take the advice of Itzik or shall I be foolish?" I took his advice and was pleased that I did, especially after pedaling 101 km from Eilat.

Kilometer 101 is a desert rest stop of a very unusual nature. It is owned by a man who was previously in the military. He's referred to as "Shahor," or black, referring to his skin color. This oasis in the middle of nowhere is a combination of petrol station, zoo, restaurant, and Bedouin tent. Chickens, pheasants, goats, dogs, and miscellaneous members of the animal kingdom have complete freedom of the grounds. Children ride the donkeys and pet the animals but their parents pay the Bedouins for camel rides. A lone Bengal tiger is the main attraction of the zoo. It is said that Shahor owned two tigers, but the animals didn't get along well with each other. Rumor states that one day he destroyed one of them. There is more to tell about Shahor, but since it is all hearsay, I shall restrain myself.

I enjoyed a prepared meal at the cafeteria and a night's rest in the Bedouin tent. The head Bedouin, a man older than myself, prepares coffee for his guests and sings to them in his native tongue, probably Arabic. My only mistake occurred in the cafeteria. It brought an immediate rebuke. I must have thought I was in my mother's kitchen, where it was always a compliment to the cook when you smelled the soup. It was not a compliment to this cook, and he told me in no uncertain terms. I must say the soup tasted as good as it smelled.

My host the following evening was Marc Kolberg, a professional tennis player who owns and lives in a small apartment at Moshav Nevt Hakikav bordering on the Dead Sea and Jordan. Marc provided the "port in a storm" I desperately needed.

Toward evening, following the desert road toward Ein Gedi, the road became more and more challenging. At times I considered dismounting, but my heavy load was harder to push than to pedal. An alternative solution proved useful except when I had no other choice than to dismount. I would stop for a moment to rest and catch my breath, then continue uphill with renewed strength. Using this technique, since I had no other until I discovered a method of improving my hill climbing ability while in South Africa, I finally came to an intersection with a military presence. The soldiers helped me decide on my next course of action. They directed me to a moshav within sight of the Dead Sea on the Israel-Jordan border. Some of these farm settlements are believed to actually be located on foreign land, but that too is purely hearsay.

A rough textured road terminates at a gate and guard house. This entire moshav is enclosed and protected by a chain link fence, yet the gate was open. Perhaps it is only closed at night. The Globetrotter and I found the village roads primitive as we carefully proceeded toward some dwellings and their occupants. Instead of cars, trucks, or jeeps, the residents prefer three- and four-wheel all-terrain vehicles. One young woman stopped her ATV to answer my questions concerning a place to put my head down for the night. At first she was agreeable to my erecting the tent on her tiny lawn, but a better idea occurred to her. Marc Kolberg was single. Attached to his house is a small annex with a bedroom that she suggested I use with Marc's permission. I followed her ATV to his home.

Entering the house, I could have been in Miami or Boston. A color TV was turned on in the well-furnished living room that looked more like Hometown USA than a border community in the middle of the desert. The program was being broacast in English. Marc had just awakened in preparation for his nightly turn patrolling the moshav. He apologized for not being able to visit with me, but he did have time to escort me to my sleeping quarters and his bathroom with its hot shower. This is the only time I saw this man. "What was a tennis professional doing in the middle of the Negev on a moshav?"

Marc, an Israeli, was granted a tennis scholarship in California where he received his bachelor's degree. Living on Moshav Nevt Hakikav, he teaches tennis to the children and their parents. He also teaches at the hotel resorts along the Dead Sea, some within sight of his moshav.

The following morning I left a note of appreciation to my host in both English and Hebrew and headed for the Dead Sea. Coffee and breakfast rolls from my pannier provided for my needs. The new butane stove was proving to be light years better than the previous gasoline-fueled model. I would have gone shopping at the small mini-market that provides for the fifty homes in moshav Nevt Hakikav, but as luck would have it, this market was closed for Shabbat. Masada, 60 km farther north, was the next available stopping place. As it is a tourist center, I knew food and accommodations would be readily available regardless of the holiday.

My first stop along the Dead Sea was the Dead Sea Works, where chemicals are extracted from salt water. From the bus, the factory was unimpressive, but being within "touching distance," I was curious to know more. "Why did the military prevent me from photographing the Dead Sea Works? Anyone could take a photograph from the bus and no one would be the wiser." I biked a distance out of range of the military and got what I came for: a picture with my telephoto lens.

The five-star Hotel Nirvana located along the salt-encrusted Dead Sea became my lunch stop. There, salt deposits resemble snow glistening in the desert sun. With my American Express card I enjoyed a sumptuous meal and pool-side fashion show. Incredibly curvaceous Israeli beauties presented the latest in swimwear as I enjoyed my Julienne salad, fresh rolls, and coffee. A child no older than eight dressed in her swimsuit strutted with her older companions. She was adorable. At the same time others were bathing in the sea, or perhaps I should say "bobbing" as a cork bobs in the water.

The long and arduous climb to the base of Masada was not without reward. There my life member AYH card admitted me to the hostel at a discount. A very beautiful and well cared for hostel, this facility is near the cable car, restaurant, and gift shop. All trees and vegetation have been carefully planted and nurtured. The remainder of the landscape is a treeless, barren vista of the Judean Desert. This desert in its hostile appearance is foreboding yet magnificent. It is here the people of the Bible wandered.

The luxurious and formidable palace built by Herod the Great in 35 B.C. was inspired by his fear of being killed by Cleopatra of Egypt or the possibility of a Jewish revolt. In this arid location, with its steep ascent and elaborate fortifications, Masada was thought to be impenetrable. A "snake" path used for the transportation of supplies to the palace in 35 B.C. is used by tourists and visitors today. Masada is an absolute must on the list of places to see for those who visit Israel. The summit can be reached by climbing the path or by taking a cable car at any time during the day. The recommended time for the climb, however, is just before dawn so the rising sun over the Dead Sea and the Judean Hills can be appreciated.

Herod died in 4 A.D. without needing to call upon Masada as his refuge. In 66 A.D., a group of Jewish zealots captured Masada from the Romans, who occupied it following Herod's death. This revolt ended in 70 A.D. when the Romans captured Jerusalem and then advanced on Masada, the last Jewish stronghold in Palestine. At that time, 967 men, women, and children occupied this mountain fortress. When the zealots realized their defeat was inevitable, they chose to commit mass suicide in preference to being captured. Reaching the summit, the Roman legions found two women and five children who escaped death by hiding. The fall of Masada and the capture of Jerusalem by Titus of Rome ended the Jewish presence in Palestine.

I originally decided to take the cable car to spare my knees until a fellow tourist suggested otherwise. "You can always return to the base camp if necessary and then take the cable car, but think of the joy in doing the climb and succeeding." I was convinced.

Making friends at five in the morning was easy, especially because I was the only person with a cook stove and coffee. A family from Denmark with two beautiful daughters, and my newest companion, Roger, challenged the mountain together. A baby and the mother of this family met us at the top, having taken the cable car. They are a family of fiddlers, and play other instruments such as the accordion and harmonica. The father, the leader, sings the lyrics, followed by members of his family who sing the other stanzas. In this way they entertain by telling simple folk tales in song. I and others were fascinated by the nose ring worn by the youngest of these fetching females, a natural blonde.

Together we watched the sun rise over the Dead Sea during our sixty-minute ascent to the summit. The views from the top of the mountain were more impressive to me than the remains of the fortifications of Masada. We did look at the remains of dwellings, store houses, the western palace, a lookout tower, and the synagogue. The remnants of the hot baths are called the calderium and the ritual baths the mikvah. A cistern hollowed out of solid rock supplied King Herod and his troops with water collected during the rainy season.

I gave some thought to taking the cable car from the summit to the base camp, but am delighted that I reconsidered. The descent was even more spectacular than the climb, especially as we were at all times looking out over the badlands toward the Dead Sea. Adequate lighting assured us of satisfactory photographs. Our small group dispersed at the base; Roger headed for Eilat and Egypt and I for Ein Gedi.

Except for a car that stopped to ask the direction and distance to Ein Gedi, I was the only occupant on this desolate stretch of road. The desert then began to come alive with vegetation. Ein Gedi Health Spa, Ein Gedi Kibbutz, and then the campground came into view. A restaurant, petrol station, and mini-market associated with the campground were all within walking distance of the Dead Sea. The petrol station appeared to be the perfect place for me to try for a ride to Jerusalem by truck. The other facilities were equally suitable for my needs as a camper.

Friends from the Masada hostel greeted me as I wheeled into the campground and began to erect my tent. We shopped at the mini-market and prepared supper together. While eating, we planned our visit to the Ein Gedi Nature Reserve.

An oasis and animal preserve, the Nature Reserve is strikingly beautiful, in contrast to the barren desert. Streams of water rapidly cascade out of the rocks into pools deep enough for wading. One rather spectacular falls flows over moss-covered rocks before ending in a pool of densely grown reeds. Grottos, caves, and barren rocks add to the beauty.

We watched the ibex in its natural habitat as well as the tiny hydrax that's related to the elephant. At the summit of the cliffs, waiting to be photographed, were the adult male ibex with their sizeable curved horns. These animals were resting in the sun as they unconsciously posed for a tourist with his tripod and telephoto lens. Each of us was invited by the photographer to view the animals through his lens. One male ibex filled the entire lens, making a rather glorious sight. Beautifully executed, this park, as well as Timna, is a credit to Israel and its people. My only unfinished business was a Dead Sea experience.

A young German with her small child occupied a tent next to mine. Being the unfortunate victim of a skin condition, the doctors in Germany wanted to medicate this woman with a drug that had many known side effects. She chose to try the healing qualities of the Dead Sea, with complete success.

My one-time venture into the super-saturated salty water of the Dead Sea was an experience that I need not feel compulsive about a return visit. The water is so filled with minerals that it's actually slimy to the touch, providing extreme buoyancy. It may be possible to swim in the water, but I had no desire to subject my eyes and taste buds to its saline properties. Others and I bobbed in the water with our legs elevated into the sitting position. It was as though we were sitting in a chair without the chair. At least I could say I bathed, not swam, in the Dead Sea.

Bicyclists and motorcyclists seldom have much in common except for being on two-wheeled vehicles, but Otto, a young German, and I got along quite well. Later, he and I saw each other in a campground in Caesarea, near Tel Aviv. I invited Otto to join me for supper. As it was Passover week, the meal included fried matzoh, which I prepared "exactly as Mom made it."

Eva in Eilat had wanted me to stay at least until after Passover, but being compulsive by nature, I felt I had a mission. Both desires seem to have been fulfilled: I was biking in the Negev and celebrating the holiday with a friend. With my watch set for 3:30 AM, I turned in for the night.

Three-thirty arrived too soon. It was early and dark. My plan was simple: after breaking camp, I would pedal to the nearby petrol station where lorries stop for fuel. There I could talk with the drivers who, hopefully, were going to Jerusalem and looking for company. This way my journey would be safe and it would solve the problem of climbing from the Dead Sea to Jerusalem. At 4:15 and in the dark, I found the petrol station closed and a total absence of traffic on the road. Reluctant to return to the campground, I walked the tandem to the nearby Mogen David, the equivalent of a Red Cross emergency station. The door was open but devoid of any EMT personnel during my entire stay of an hour and a half. The recovery bed was mine until six in the morning.

Conditions were identical in the daylight except that I was now well rested. The station was still closed and traffic minimal. "Forgive me, Louise, but it looks as if I will be biking the distance, at least to Jericho and the Allenby Bridge."

A few miles south of Jericho, past my final view of the Dead Sea, I noticed cars entering a nearby park. The swimming pool was the main focus of the park. My thoughts concerned a second breakfast at the mini-market. It should have come as no surprise that all of the day visitors to the park were Palestinians, since I was now entering the West Bank. Arab hospitality to a stranger was no different here than elsewhere. The parents were anxious to share their food and hospitality with me as they watched their children jumping into the natural spring water that supplied the pool. "Tea or coffee?" they asked in the same friendly manner as my doctor friend at the Taba, Egypt, hospital.

Jericho was neither a surprise nor a disappointment. The marker at the entrance makes an excellent photo. Engraved on its surface are the words "the oldest city in the world." The other distinction is the Allenby Bridge connecting Israel and Jordan. Signs directed me there, located two to three kilometers on the other side of the city.

To my astonishment, the bridge was not only closed because of Passover, but there was not a person or soldier in the vicinity. A large sign identifies the area as the entrance to the Allenby Bridge, but the chain link fence prevented my seeing the actual bridge. Even the guard house was empty. Printed on the sign were the words "no photographs." Naturally, I took my picture!

I noticed a distant cloud of sand being churned up by the wheels of a military vehicle. "Might these soldiers be looking for me? Perhaps I should be on my way back to Jericho, since there was little else to see." My intuition was correct.

A moderately large, open command car pulled up alongside me, the machine gunner occupying a position between the front and rear of the vehicle. Two soldiers sat in the front bucket seats. The interrogation then began: "What were you doing at the bridge?" "Where did you go?" "Why were you there since the bridge was obviously closed?" "Let me see your passport."

I considered the incident a bit humorous. I was an American on a bicycle with a passport issued in Tel Aviv. Except for taking a photograph, I felt I had every right to be on the road. One thing I did not take into consideration was the fact that the Arab population was on strike against the State of Israel that particular day. In a nonchalant manner I spoke to the machine gunner: "Please don't point that thing at me." The incident ended as quickly as it began. Obviously they did not know about my camera, or perhaps they didn't care.

A Mercedes taxi was parked outside an open gate within the city limits of Jericho. Inside I saw both Europeans and Arabs gathered in some sort of festivities. The driver,

Mohammed, and his passengers were drinking tea and coffee with relatives of his family. Some family members were aged, while others, especially the young women, were particularly attractive.

Mohammed explained that there were two reasons why he could not take me to Jerusalem. He would be at risk since the West Bank was on strike. If he moved his cab, he would be guilty of violating the solidarity of the Arab community. The other and more pressing reason was that he already had passengers he was planning to transport to Jerusalem. At the same time I was introduced to his family, and of course offered "Tea or coffee?"

His passengers convinced Mohammed that he had room for one more passenger and that the Globetrotter could be carried on the roof rack without damage to his cab. This vehicle cost Mohammed in excess of one hundred thousand dollars; he was in no mood to have it damaged by my bicycle. We took the scenic tour to Jerusalem, stopping at Wadi Qelt and St. George's Monastery.

Wadi Qelt is a nature preserve with a natural spring and pool located under a waterfall. It's near a Roman aqueduct that delivers water to St. George's, built into the cliff face of a canyon. We enjoyed the panoramic view atop a huge stone precipice near the road.

We arrived in East Jerusalem and the end of my cab ride. Perhaps Mohammed was fearful of driving in a non-Arab area when he made it clear to me that I was at the end of the line. Until I insisted, he was unwilling to accept any money for my fare. Apparently the others hired him for a set charge and, in his mind, I was part of the package. At the side of a narrow and steep street we unloaded the Globetrotter and its gear and said our goodbyes. Not only had I avoided the climb from 250 meters below sea level to 820 meters above, I had an unplanned scenic tour with exceptionally friendly people.

Back in East Jerusalem and near the Mount of Olives I began to see places I recognized from previous visits. With map in hand, I found my way to the Jasmine Hostel on Bezalel Street. A place for the bike, a place for me, and a hearty meal made Jasmine an excellent choice. The Old City and a tour of the Rockefeller Museum in East Jerusalem were my plans for the next day.

Within sight of Damascus Gate and the Faisal Hostel, I was heading toward the Rockefeller Museum. A voice calling "Ralph" drew my attention to the hostel and the people on the second floor balcony. "We have mail for you," called one of them. They recognized the tandem and knew it was mine.

What a grand reunion I had with Ali and Pat, the owners, as well as Sherry, with her children Michael and Lisa. The mail was a postcard from my friend Klaus from Germany. He assumed I would be staying at the Faisal hostel and would enjoy receiving mail. He wrote about a volunteer job he had near Haifa with a Palestinian group before returning to Germany. He worked with Father Elias Chacour, a Palestinian Christian at his school in the all-Arab town of Ibillin. I didn't know then that I'd soon be affiliated with Kamil Shahade, a close friend and colleague of Fr. Chacour at the House of Grace. It's interesting to look back and see how the pieces were beginning to come together. The first piece of the puzzle was my being saved by two Palestinians in the Sinai desert. "Remember that you were saved by two Palestinians," said my benefactors. The following December 23, my birthday, I visited the volunteer quarters in Ibillin as a volunteer at the House of Grace. Christmas carols were being broadcast over the loudspeakers to the students and staff of the school where Klaus was a volunteer. For reasons I can't explain, one of the songs they played was "Happy Birthday."

Sherry, Michael, and Lisa were still living at Faisal with the generous support of Ali and Pat. By this time Sherry was an employee of the hostel and in this way able to cover her own expenses to some extent, but not able to take her children to a restaurant. We ate as my guest at the restaurant of their choice. Naturally, it was an Italian restaurant with pizza on the menu. This was perhaps my best pizza ever, watching Michael and Lisa as they had their fill, in addition to a "doggy bag" they took back to the hostel.

Twice I had been to the entrance to the Dome of the Rock and twice denied admission. Tourists are permitted in the mosque or on the grounds at times other than during prayer. Temple Mount is a walled-in area within the Old City walls that is holy to Jews, Muslims, and Christians. It is here that some consider the site of Abraham's sacrifice and some believe that when God said "Let there be light" that the light first shone over this area. It's also the location where Mohammed is said to have ascended to heaven on his white horse. Unfortunately, the gold dome of the mosque was under repair, with scaffolding marring its beauty. I decided to supplement my own photographs with purchased slides that showed this central holiest of holy places in its most pristine condition. Finally, my arrival coincided with acceptable hours for tourists.

I locked the Globetrotter near the entrance to Temple Mount and passed through the Israeli military presence into the grounds surrounding the Dome of the Rock and the El Asqa Mosque. Open lockers are provided for shoes; they are prohibited within the walls of the mosques. Running water was available for washing feet, but that was not mandatory prior to entering. The floors of both mosques are fully carpeted.

Returning to my Globetrotter, I was greeted by the owner of a nearby shop, an Arab. Had he not intervened, I would have been writing to my insurance company concerning the theft of my means of transport. Some young Arab men were discussing their plan among themselves: they were going to carry the bike to their homes where they would attempt to cut the Citadel bar lock that locked the front wheel to the frame. Fortunately, the shop owner overheard the conversation and spoiled their plans. In gratitude I offered to buy something in his store even though the religious articles were of no interest to me. Again, Arab hospitality became obvious when he refused to accept my money.

An art store on the Via Dolorosa displayed two huge oriental brass coffee urns, one of which was enameled. The price of $1,900 included shipping for both of these pieces that stood at least four feet high. The obvious question was what I would do with them if I did make the investment. At home I was trying to downsize rather than add to my modest antique bicycle collection and miscellaneous art objects. The owner graciously let me photograph both. This was the next best thing to ownership.

The bicycle gave me a lot of mobility as I visited various parts of Jerusalem, including Mount Herzel and the Herzel Museum. A lovely park surrounds the buildings and military cemetery. This impressive area honors Theodor Herzl, the founder of politcal Zionism. A replica of his Vienna study, library, and furniture is in the museum. Nearby Yad Vashem beckoned me for a second visit.

My walk through the Children's Memorial was as impressive the second time as it was the first. It is beyond human comprehension to visualize or understand that children as young as four, five, and six were exterminated as part of Hitler's "final solution." From a distance and at a lower level I could see the Hadassah Hospital, built with money raised by Jewish women of the world. The stained glass windows of the synagogue of the hospital executed by the famed artist Marc Chagall became my next goal. I knew my children, being members of Hadassah in the US and extremely proud of the accomplishments of the Jewish women in their communities, would question me about the windows.

Unfortunately, this day of bicycle touring was rapidly coming to a close. I parked the Globetrotter at the bottom of a rather steep mountain and inquired about the tour of the synagogue and its windows. To my disappointment, the last tour was concluded and the area closed until the next day. One of the docents who learned that I pedaled my way there expressed her personal regrets. "If I were permitted, I would give you a private tour," she said. "Come back tomorrow!" The thought of repeating this steep climb seemed out of the question at that moment. By the next day I reconsidered. "My children would not forgive me if I left without seeing the Chagall glass."

My return to the Jasmine hostel in late afternoon included a climb up the mountain from the hospital to the level of the city of Jerusalem. Within sight of the Old City walls, the King David Hotel was my last stop for the day. Across the road from the hotel is a huge YMCA, appearing rather new with its attached restaurant. With a swimming pool, tennis courts, and gardens, the King David provides the ultimate comforts for those who not only can afford but desire them. Jewelry stores in the hotel display exquisite works of art in precious metals.

Following a satisfying breakfast, I was again on my way the next morning to the Hadassah Hospital and the Chagall windows. Now that I knew the location, the distance seemed shorter. Though it was cool, the sun was bright and the day invigorating. It was good to be on the bike without its heavy load. As I entered the synagogue, an English-speaking guide immediately began her talk. The windows came alive.

At age 72, Marc Chagall was asked by the women of Hadassah if he would do the twelve windows in the synagogue. He replied, "I was wondering if I would be asked." Except for the cost of materials and the payment to others for their labor, the artist donated his skills. He considered these windows the crowning achievement of his entire career. The project took two years to complete and was then on display at the Louvre in Paris. Finally they were shown at the Museum of Modern Art in New York before being installed here. Having seen Chagall's work in his museum in Nice, France, I thought perhaps these windows might be redundant, but they were not. They were each radiantly magnificent.

Damaged by gunfire in one of Israel's wars, the blemished windows, except for one, were sent back to France for restoration and repair. The one bullet hole remaining is a vivid reminder of the Israeli struggle for survival.

The tour ended following an explanation of the meaning behind each of the windows, representing the twelve tribes of Israel. I then went in search of the hospital cafeteria and gift shop. A sign on the cafeteria window read "closed for Passover," an eight-day holiday in Israel. I had no intention of waiting for the doors to reopen. Fortunately, the gift shop stocked color slides of the twelve windows.

Bullet-proof glass prevents the viewer from appreciating these windows from the exterior of the building. It also protects the art from external elements. The Kennedy Memorial and the Rubinstein Pavilioin at the top of the mountain became my next objective.

At the highest point on the main road on the way back to Jerusalem, an arrow points to the summit. Though steep, I was able to make the climb without dismounting. During this difficult challenge, several cars passed me with a wave of the hand or the honk of their horn. Feeling encouraged by their greetings, I had added determination to go the distance. Waiting patiently at the entrance to the Kennedy Memorial stood four people approximately my age.

"Where are you from? Why are you riding a tandem bicycle? How far have you traveled? What is your name?" Unlike the Egyptians, they didn't ask my age or marital status. Naomi and her husband Philipp Leitner are Israelis. Their friends Ruth and Alex Meisels live in Switzerland. To my surprise, the Leitners lived in Medford, no more than four miles from me. For ten years Philipp was associated with MIT.

"When you come to Rehovot on your bike we want you to come and visit with us," said Naomi. "Rehovot is the home of the Weizmann Institute of Science established in 1890 by Polish Jews." I had not heard of Rehovot before. Looking at a map of Israel, I learned that Rehovot is not far from the Mediterranean coast near the Biblical towns of Ashdod and Ashkelon, an area I intended to explore. We made tentative plans to see other each at a later date.

At a level lower than the Kennedy Memorial, the Artur Rubinstein Panoramic View presents an excellent location for photography. The forested hillsides are a tribute to the thousands of people who gave financial support to tree-planting projects here and elsewhere in the country. Because of deforestation, these hillsides were once barren. It was Artur Rubinstein's wish upon his death that his remains were to be cremated and the ashes scattered over Israel.

Jasmine Hostel owner Ya'acov (Jack) Halpert has a hobby: he takes pleasure in leading tours of Bethlehem every Shabbat, making the area come alive with his unique and personal manner. I'm especially pleased to have spent the day with Jack and other hotel guests who had the foresight to join our small group. When we parked in Manger Square, Jack gave us a briefing. "We are in occupied territory. Do not use your Hebrew vocabulary and do not be alarmed if you get teargassed. Don't be fearful but keep alert." We then walked through an Arab market, perhaps the busiest and most authentic I had seen. From there, Jack escorted us to the home of a Palestinian family.

On a previous tour, Jack and his group were the unexpected recipients of a tear gas attack. In desperation, they entered a nearby home, the same home we were presently visiting. We were each served tea by the family of Almad Balboul, a barber and the spokesman. In a friendly manner, Almad invited us to discuss any of the political or military aspects of Palestinian residence in Israeli occupied territory. As a youth,

Almad was a terrorist. Jailed on numerous occasions, he spent a total of seven years in prison. At the time of our visit, he represented himself and his family as peaceful citizens who feel that through time and negotiation far more can be accomplished than through terrorism.

The Church of Nativity, the oldest Christian church in the world, was the center of our activity. On Christmas Eve it is impossible to enter this church without an admission ticket, but on this sunny day we spent as much time as we wished. It is built over a cave where Christians believe Jesus was born. Emperors Constantine and Justinian, the Crusaders, Saladin, and the Mamelukes each had an influence on this citadel-like structure.

In addition to other places of interest, Jack took pride in showing us the site of Rachel's Tomb, revered by Muslims, Christians, and Jews. The matriarch Rachel was the wife of Jacob and mother of Benjamin. Her plain whitewashed shrine was built by Sir Moses Montefiore in 1860.

Climbing the bell tower in Bethlehem, we saw the Jerusalem Hilton as well as Herodium, a city that King Herod built within the crater of a volcano. Thank you, Jack, for a great day and a great tour.

The bicycle fork repair that was done on the street in Cairo began to show wear and tear. Further repair or replacement became a priority. I don't know why I didn't search out a bicycle shop with the likelihood of locating a new fork. Further repair was the only thing that entered my mind, even though as an orthodontist I had a broad knowledge of the properties of metal. I knew that heating the fork during the repair process made the metal brittle. Later, when the fork finally fractured while in the Golan, I wished I had been more creative.

Within walking distance of the hostel, David, an expert welder, repaired the previous weld with the assurance that

I'd have no further problems. His claim to fame is that, next to his father, he is the number one welder in all of Israel. I felt confident to continue on my journey. David's total charge was about nine dollars American. There was no charge for the Turkish coffee.

Now that the Globetrotter was again operable, I continued to visit various places in East Jerusalem and the Old City. The Garden of Gethsemane was built in 1924. The first church on this site, in the 4th century, was destroyed by an earthquake. Some of the world's oldest olive trees are in the Garden, the popularly accepted site where Jesus was arrested. A road to the summit of the Mount of Olives connects with Mount Scopus. I looked out over the Judean Desert toward Jordan from a panoramic pavilion. The Dead Sea was visible in the distance. The Hebrew University and Jerusalem came into view in the opposite direction. A gold reflection occurs at dusk when the sun shines on the Jerusalem stone.

I visited for some time with the assistant manager of a small Hyatt Regency Hotel atop Mt. Scopus. His educational fantasy is an MBA from Harvard, but finances prevent him from fulfilling this dream. I gave him my address.

A sign on the way to the Rockefeller Museum directed me to King David's Tomb, located behind an iron grill in an active synagogue. Decorated with blue and gold cloth, the Torah on top of the tomb memorializes an event dating back 3,000 years. My instincts told me not to take flash photos, but desire overcame prudence. Returning to the Globetrotter, I discovered it was again vandalized. The lights I recently replaced were damaged beyond repair. "Was this the price I paid for two color slides?"

The Room of the Last Supper is on the second floor. The family that sheltered Jesus lived on the first floor. Inasmuch as second stories were seldom used except for storage, Jesus and his disciples felt reasonably safe from being discovered. There are no basements in Old City buildings even though the rock beneath the first floor has been hollowed out. These areas are used for storing water during the rainy season.

Fortunately, the Rockefeller Museum was open. Designed and built in medieval architecture, it is well protected by the military. The museum is organized according to time periods, the oldest objects being closest to the main door. Neanderthal Man, known as "Galilee Man," interested me from an orthodontist's point of view. This skull dating back 100,000 to 120,000 years exhibits a full dentition, including third molars, commonly called wisdom teeth. Heavy supra-orbital ridges suggest early man. An absence of a Simian shelf in the jaw demonstrates that the individual was human and not simian. This skull was found in Wadi Amud in 1925 or 1926.

Another skull dates to 10,000 B.C. in what was called the Natutian Period. The dead were buried in a "contracted" state, with the head decorated with seven strings of ornaments called dentalia shells. Following decomposition, the bones were dug up and the skull reconstructed with clay to resemble the features of the deceased.

Anthropoid coffins made of ceramic and dating back to the Iron Age standupright approximately 6-1/2 feet high. The head of the deceased is sculptured in clay, with the hands high on the chest. Jewish coins from the Bar-Cochba War (135-132 B.C.), when the Jews revolted against Rome, display views of the Temple façade, palm trees, clusters of grapes, and beautiful harps. I felt gratified that I lingered in Jerusalem long enough to be able to tour this remarkable collection of history.

My final gift from the city of Jerusalem was to again visit the Israel Museum and the House of the Scrolls. There was so much more to see but my mission was not yet complete. I felt compelled to resume my travels and search out as many interesting places as possible.

In the Museum I tried to concentrate on art of Judaica instead of archæology. Ceremonial dishes, silver spice boxes, illuminated *Hagada* and Torah decorations are some of these artworks. Traditional wedding clothing of Jews worldwide validate the dispersion of these people. Mannequin brides from Yemen, Tunisia, and Algiers were among the most beautiful. A collection of the masters such as Impressionists and post-Impressionists and Dutch art was substantial. These galleries are impressive.

Leaving Jerusalem was uncomplicated until I reached the vicinity of the central bus station. A bomb scare caused confusion in the area, but the matter was, fortunately, settled in short order by the experienced Israeli police.

The Tel Aviv highway follows the land contours, with dramatic descents and uphill grades that required walking. Being in no hurry, I allowed nature to take its course. Pine forests at first cover the mountains on both sides of the road, soon giving way to fertile fields and later desert-like terrain.

A military installation came into view in the distance. An army tank atop a cement platform some 20 feet in the air suggested the possibility of a military museum. I had come upon Latrun, a historical site, now an armored car museum of considerable proportion. Visitors are encouraged to climb aboard captured enemy tanks or photograph any of the equipment. The admission fee of 6 NIS entitled me to a personal guide, young and attractive Sharonn't ("Sharon") Yehod, an Israeli soldier. We toured the grounds and viewed a film in English in the air-conditioned auditorium. Sharon explained some of the details of Latrun and its significance during the 1948 War of Independence. She pointed to a location where the enemy had turned off the water supply to Jerusalem, and to the Burma Road that allowed urgently needed supplies to be brought into the city at a time when it was almost ready to fall into enemy hands. Suddenly it all began to take form in my mind and memory. One of the books I bought and read while in Eilat, O Jerusalem, told the story of the city's liberation and the capture of Latrun from the enemy, the Jordanians. On a wall, the names of over 4,000 Israeli soldiers who died in the Armored Car Corps since its inception are inscribed. A computer in Memorial Hall will retrieve the vital statistics and photograph of each soldier.

Back in the oven-like outdoors, I viewed Israeli and enemy tanks. All of the latter, primitive as they are, were manufactured in Russia. The Charioteer is an all-Israeli tank designed by a soldier and made in Israel, at a secret location. Everything in its construction is designed for the soldier's protection.

I planned to sleep in the town of Ramla and then bike to Rehovot where I would visit with Naomi and Philipp Leitner. I was unsuccessful in finding accommodations in Ramla, but when I phoned the Leitners and found them home, I went to their house. Had I not met this lovely couple, I might have missed visiting the Weizmann "White House" and Weizmann Institute.

Willed to the State of Israel, the Weizmann home is a true mansion, with the State's first swimming pool. Following her husband Chaim's death, Vera Weizmann, a pediatrician, used the property as a children's rehabilitation center. A custom Lincoln limousine parked under the canopy outside the house was given to the President by Henry Ford II. The only other of its kind was presented to US President Truman. Dr. Weizmann evidently preferred his smaller and less ostentatious car, so the Lincoln was seldom used. "It is too big and too hungry," remarked the President.

A photograph of Albert Einstein and Vera Weizmann hangs in the library of the house, in which Einstein is playing the cello and Vera the piano. The piano is bleached to match the decor of the room. An interesting art object is a 2,000-year-old Chinese ceramic horse that at one time had a mane and tail.

During World War I, Chaim Weizmann developed a process in England for making acetone used in smoke bombs. This gave him international importance. A friend of Balfour and Lord George, he introduced the concept of Zionism to the British. It is said that at one time Weizmann predicted the Holocaust.

The Canadian Institute of Solar Energy, part of the Weizmann Institute, is equipped with solar panels that concentrate energy from the sun and project it into the atmosphere. The result is an artificial sun. Any bird that flies into that energy beam will be converted instantly to "Kentucky fried chicken." I was pleased that my photograph of this artificial sun turned out well.

Had I known about the slide show explaining the Institute's activities, I would have attended. Unfortunately, I also missed a guided tour mentioned in my "Lonely Planet Guide." My limited tour of the Institute and grounds proved inadequate. The large campus is beautifully landscaped with tropical trees and plants. Beds of petunias were in bloom. The landscaping is as carefully designed as the buildings. Common to most campuses, I noticed a profusion of bicycles which casually dressed people pedal from building to building. After lunch at a local Chinese restaurant, I followed Philipp's directions that led me to the Gaza Strip in the West Bank.

Located on the Tel Aviv-Ashkelon road, Ben and Jerry's Ice Cream added a touch of Vermont. The B&J's sign is in Hebrew and English; the picture of the black and white Vermont cows require no translation—they spell "Vermont."

Within a few kilometers of Ashkelon, a sign brought instant recognition. In English and Hebrew, it identifies the entrance to Kfar Silver, an industrial school for young Israelis. When my youngest daughter Terry was in high school she lived at Kfar Silver for one year as she attended the Molly Goodman School during her senior year of high school. This discovery was so unexpected and exciting that I immediately changed my plans. "Perhaps I can put up my tent on the Kfar Silver campus and meet some of the people at Molly Goodman." I did not know at the time that the American school was closed and an industrial school opened. The school director informed me that for insurance reasons I would not be permitted to erect my tent. He was sympathetic to my needs, especially since my daughter had been a student at Kfar Silver. Shortly thereafter, three boys about the age of 15 escorted me to the guest quarters where I was shown my own small apartment. They encouraged me to make myself comfortable until supper, when they would call for me. I don't know if these boys were assigned to me or if they took it upon themselves to be my hosts. I do know that Nir, Reuben, and Oshri made my visit to Kfar Silver a highlight of my trip.

A calf born that day had not learned to suckle from its mother. The boys were trying to open her jaws and insert a huge baby bottle, with a nipple at least eight inches long. This reminded me of "my favorite camel story." "Let me see if I can do it," I said. Being a dentist, I had a technique that was successful in getting reluctant children to "open up." "Perhaps it will work on calves!"

In moments the calf emptied the bottle, the beginning of her learning cycle. We did some mechanical milking before touring the farm, where the indoor vegetable gardens are covered with plastic. The modern henhouse is limited to four hens per unit, with a trough at each unit. The trough delivers unbroken eggs to a central collection area.

My newest friends called for me in the morning so we could eat breakfast together before saying goodbye. At the entrance to the school, I noticed a pay phone. I was determined to call Terry in Moab, Utah. It was almost midnight Utah time. "Terry, guess where I am! I'm at your old school, Kfar Silver!" A sleepy voice replied, "Do you know what time it is?" I could hardly be faulted for wanting to share this experience with her.

Whether the city is pronounced Gaza in English or Aza in Hebrew, this ancient city south of Ashkelon is part of the occupied territory of the Gaza Strip separating Israel and Egypt. It is said that Gaza has been taken and destroyed in war more often than any city in the world. First mentioned in the Bible as a Canaanite city, it was here that Samson was imprisoned and died. I look back and wonder why I felt compelled to visit a city that has a reputation for extreme hostility and terrorism. The excuse that I used to satisfy this need and the reality of my desire may in fact be two different things. I am certain of one thing: I did not have a death wish!

I was entering a Moslem area on a Friday when most of the people were praying in the mosque. Arab children from past experience were fascinated by the Globetrotter and this American traveler who might be a source of *bakshish*. No adult would shoot into a group of Arab children in an attempt to kill a stranger. Lastly, Americans are usually well liked by the Arabs, especially in Egypt. Could our generous foreign aid have anything to do with this friendship?

The Israeli military at the border crossing warned me adequately of the possibility of my being injured or killed. "Why do you want to go to Aza? Don't you know the people are armed? Don't you know that you could be killed by going into enemy territory? We cannot stop you from going, but we strongly advise you not to cross the border!"

"I have seen the best and now I want to see the rest," was my reply. "I know there is a risk, but I am willing to take it so I can make my own observations rather than listen to firsthand comments from others." Had I been at Gaza a week later, I might have heeded the soldiers' warning. An Israeli lawyer representing a Palestinian Arab, crossed the border in an effort to aid his client. He was killed before he could be of service.

My predictions were correct: most of the adult population in Gaza City was not visible. They were probably praying at the mosque. The conditions of Gaza, compared to Israel, are striking. Referring to my journal, my comments are that the area gives the appearance of what might be left "after the bomb." This reality was not a new experience, but it was a shocking contrast to the highly developed area of Israel a few kilometers to the north, where farming, industry, and tourism exemplify prosperity.

Within moments of crossing the border, children on their bikes or walking began to crowd around me, each trying to touch the bike as they bombarded me with questions in English: "What is your name?" "How old are you?" "Are you married?" These were the identical questions I was asked in Egypt. At the same time they had their hand out asking for *bakshish*. I slowly began to penetrate the city proper. One child in particular was my guide as we went in search of Coca-Cola for the children. Small bonfires of trash and rubber tires were burning in the middle of the glass-littered street.

Was there any point in my continuing farther? We located the Coke from a nearby vendor, with enough bottles to satisfy a small army of children as well as a child on his donkey. Considering myself fortunate to have seen a small part of Gaza without injury, I took the child's photo and headed back toward the border. Taking pictures of the Gaza devastation would have been in bad taste. It might also have precipitated stone-throwing or worse. As I was leaving, one child bent down as though he was going to pick up a stone, but it was a false alarm. A newspaper reporter interviewed me and other returnees from Gaza at the border, asking our impressions of the area. I then headed toward Ashkelon, a city on the Mediterranean near Kfar Silver.

Ashkelon is popular with vacationing Israelis because of its sandy beaches and an adjacent park near the water. The history of Ashkelon involves conquerors of many nations: Philistines, Israelites, Greeks, Romans, Crusaders, and Muslims have dominated this area at one time or another. Under the

Philistines, Ashkelon flourished as an important caravan stop between Syria and Egypt. This trade route was the Via Maris.

Prior to leaving Ashkelon, I did visit some of the excavations in the park dating back 4,000 years to the remains of the Canaanites. Greek civilization is represented by Nike, the Goddess of Victory standing on a globe supported by Atlas. It becomes obvious that the Greeks knew the earth to be round. The Goddess Isis (Greek) is holding the Child-God Horus (Egyptian).

The YHA Munich hostel, given to Tel Aviv by the city of Munich, became my objective for the night. Using a map and compass, I came within a few blocks of the hostel. It was now dark. A small, elderly woman walking out of her apartment became an obvious person to ask for directions.

"You are almost there," said my newest acquaintance, Edna Kessler. "You can walk there with your bicycle instead of riding in the dark. If you would like a cup of coffee, come up to my apartment and I will prepare one for you." This was one of several visits with Edna, the most recent being her telephone call to my home in Cambridge in response to one of my letters. In addition to coffee, I drank copious amounts of water and ate one of Israel's sweet grapefruits.

Edna, though elderly, still works as a musician in addition to taking care of a neighbor older and less able than herself. She turned on her television to show off her granddaughter, a news commentator. Edna, a commentator of sorts herself, enjoys telling stories.

One of the stories originally told by Yiddish humorist Sholom Aleichem concerned an Eastern European man who decided to walk from his ghetto to the ghetto in Prague, a long journey on foot. When he stopped to rest, he removed his shoes and pointed them in the direction of Prague, so that upon awakening he would know the proper direc-

2 WHEELS, 2 YEARS, AND 3 CONTINENTS

tion to continue. While he was asleep, someone
saw his shoes and turned them around. Following
his shoes after awakening, the man unknowingly
returned home. "Oh, Prague has a ghetto just like
mine," said the man. "Look, Prague has a house
just like mine! Would you believe that the woman
in this house looks just like my mother!"

Another Edna Kessler story concerns a man who died
and was desirous of entering the Pearly Gates. St. Peter gave
him a challenge. "Identify Adam among all the persons inside
the Gates and you may remain forever." How did the man recognize Adam? The answer: not born of woman, Adam had no
navel.

The next morning, I knew I had become dehydrated
the previous day. During Hamzeem, the fifty hottest days of
the year, Israelis try to remain sedentary as they consume as
much water as possible. In the desert near Ein Gedi, an Israeli
asked me how much water I drink each day. "A lot," was my
reply, "I probably drink a liter or a liter and a half while I'm
pedaling in the desert." He explained that as an absolute minimum I should drink six to seven liters a day and that I should
stay out of the sun. Mad dogs and Englishmen!

Except for visiting one museum, the Haganah I.D.F.
Museum, I spent the day resting in my roon. Haganah, the
military force prior to Israel's independence, later became a
part of the I.D.F., or Israeli Defense Force. That night Edna
and I talked until 1:30 in the morning.

This must have been the time for storytelling. Two
brothers from New Zealand were touring the battlefields where
their grandfather fought with General Allenby against the Turks.
We shared a room at the hostel. They researched the area with
maps obtained from Cambridge University in England, as well
as with photos given to them by their grandfather. These brothers had a vast knowledge of Palestine history during World
War I. As an example, they explained to me that the site of the

Munich Hostel was a battle ground where the English and Turks fought. Here was their story:

> The Pope and a lawyer were trying to enter the same Pearly Gates. St. Peter decided to show each where they would be permitted to enter. The lawyer was shown a palatial home with exquisite gardens, fountains, and beautiful arches. The Pope was shown a dilapidated shack with a leaky roof, window sashes hanging from the structure, and nothing but desolation around him. "Here I am Pope and look at the meager digs you are going to provide me, while a mere lawyer is going to live in a palace," said the Pope. "Why?"

> "Well," said St. Peter, "this is the first time that we have had a lawyer."

A modern highway crossing the Yarkon River connects Haifa and Tel Aviv. I planned to have a full day of cycling that would bring me to Haifa if the wind and weather permitted. All signs of fatigue from my previous riding disappeared. I was ready to move on! Haretz Museum, in the direction of Tel Aviv University and a part of the Israel Museum complex, interrupted these plans. Gregory Vinitsky and his colleague from the photography department made me feel like a celebrity as they took candid shots from all directions. We then retired to Gregory's studio where he prepared coffee for us. He then asked me if I would be agreeable to an interview by the press. An appointment was then scheduled with a correspondent from a Russian newspaper. I explained to Gregory that I was not interested in publicity, that this was my own personal adventure, but I would be pleased to cooperate with him and the press. In the meantime, with the Globetrotter safely stored, I spent most of the day visiting this magnificent institution. The grounds near the entrance are terraced so visitors can sit on the grass and watch the performance being conducted on an outdoor stage beneath them. During my visit, children glee-fully rolled on the grass as they descended from one terrace to another.

Maxim Reider, the Russian journalist, is a cyclist. He tape-recorded our interview. I headed for the seaside resort of Netanya, said to have replaced Antwerp as the diamond center of the world. Maxim promised a copy of the article following publication, even though it could serve only as a souvenir.

Netanya is much larger than I anticipated, with tall, substantially built buildings giving it an air of permanence. I took an immediate liking to Netanya. A restaurant in the center of the city appealed to my senses. Faith Bloome Krupnik and her husband Asher were waiting at the entrance for the owner of the bicycle to return. Asher, an avid cyclist, was es-pecially curious when he saw this overloaded tandem designed for one person instead of two. The conversation on our first visit was not especially long, but it started a friendship that has endured. Faith, a professional person, was born and raised in Springfield, Massachusetts. Asher, a piano tuner, is in compe-tition with immigrant Russian piano tuners who will work for less money than he. This gives Asher more time to ride his bike but less money in his pocket.

"When you return to Netanya," said Faith, "we want you to come to visit us. We are not like Americans who say this but do not mean it. We really want you to stay with us!" Had I a bit more *chutzpah* (nerve), I might have asked them for accommodations that night. At that moment, I had no plans except for the fact that my tent was securely strapped to the Globetrotter. We exchanged addresses and went our separate ways. I began my search in earnest for a campsite.

Tucked away from the road, behind some bushes, I found a secluded spot on a precipice overlooking the beach and the Mediterranean that could not have been more suitable, especially after finding a residential hotel nearby, whose management gave me permission to use their bathroom facilities. Artificial light from nearby apartment buildings provided enough illumination for me to set up my tent without a flashlight. In the morning, I discovered I was not as secluded as I had thought.

Awakened by a local resident taking his dogs for their early morning stroll past my test, I became aware that I had erected my "home" in a "fish bowl" completely surrounded by apartment buildings, in addition to the pedestrian walk at my front door. It made little difference to me as long as I did not have to explain my presence to the police. The color photo of this beautifully located campsite is one of my favorite slides.

I looked forward to my next visit to Netanya when I would get to know Faith, Asher, and her family. At that time I didn't know that Asher and I would meet on the road early one Sunday morning while I was on my way to the Rothschild tombs.

Caesarea, pronounced "kasaria," one of Israel's most important archæological sites, is located between Haifa and Tel Aviv. For almost 600 years Caesarea was the Roman capital of Judea. Herod the Great established this city in about 22 B.C. On at least three separate occasions, I camped at Caesarea as I traveled the Haifa-Tel Aviv highway. The distance is no more than 50 km, but fierce headwinds turned the journey into an all-day event.

At a make-do Caesarea campsite with barely the basic necessities, my German friend Otto Muller and I met once again. He is the young man with whom I shared my fried matzoh at Ein Gedi.

The Roman theater at Caesarea, restored for contemporary use, is situated with the stage facing the sea. Caverns beneath the stage were and are used for dressing rooms. Even though this theater is restored, it has not lost any of its original

Roman charm. Within the walls of the Caesarea Crusader City, a tourist attraction is being designed and funded in the best possible taste by Edmund Rothschild. The attractive stores and restaurants are artistically situated within sight of the excavations.

Protected by a fence, archæologists and volunteers can be seen as they go about their work. Shovels, hand picks, and brushes are their tools. Dirt is carried from place to place in large canvas bags. An archæologist confirmed my suspicions that the standing arches have recently been rebuilt.

Before my trip, I inquired at the Harvard Center for Semitic Studies about becoming a volunteer at a site such as this. At that time I was told that the cost for doing this type of work is approximately $350 per week. "Do I pay you or do you pay me?" I asked. Guess! I quickly decided that my two wheels would take me from interesting place to place with much more variety and less cost than sifting sand in the desert sun. The startling discoveries, I learned, are found by the seasoned experts and not by the volunteers.

A very strong headwind made my progress slow and laborious as we traveled toward Haifa. I stopped for lunch at a cafeteria enroute to Zichron Ya'acov, the burial site of the Rothschilds, and Tiberius on the Sea of Galilee. The city of Nazareth, only 18 km away and in my direction, was a good stopping place for the night. Within 2 or 3 km of Nazareth I noticed a sign pointing to the left, indicating that an inn of some sort lay in that direction. The sign showed a crossed knife and fork and the symbol of a bed. It was now late in the afternoon. I decided to follow my nose. A steep grade eventually leveled off to a plateau of a sort, the location of a high-tech industrial park. There was no inn within sight!

A parked motorist explained that the inn was closed, but at the very top of the mountain a kibbutz would provide accommodations as well as food. I proceeeded to climb until the grade became so severe that I was forced to dismount. It seemed strange that a kibbutz would be located in such a desolate and distant place, but having seen kibbutzim in such places as Masada, nothing came as a surprise. Nearing sunset, the kibbutz, a modern complex of buildings and grounds, came into view. I began making inquiries concerning permission to camp as well as use the dining room. A telephone finally connected me to the director's office.

The member in charge was totally unsympathetic to my needs. She would not permit camping, she had no accommodations, and I was not welcome in the dining room. If I wished to go back down the mountain "you will find hostels in Nazareth." I then became angry.

"I followed a sign all the way to the top of this mountain with my bike looking for a night's lodging or campsite only to find that the inn is closed. It is now dark and I refuse to endanger myself by returning to the main road in the dark. If you knocked on my door in Cambridge, Massachusetts, with a similar problem, you can be certain I would not send you away. I need assistance and you can provide it, if you are so inclined."

The person on the other end asked me the location of the telephone. She advised me to wait for someone to greet me who would be able to help. Soon Zachary, an avid cyclist, arrived with a key to one of the apartments reserved for visitors. He explained that I would be dining with his family within the hour, giving me time to shower and rest. Identical to my experience at Kfar Silver, he indicated that he would return for me in about an hour. In contrast to the director, Zachary, a Ph.D., scientist, and cyclist, could not have been nicer.

A baked chicken dinner with stuffing was one of my best meals in Israel, made more enjoyable in the company of Zachary's kibbutz family. A noted archæologist eating at an adjacent table was more than agreeable to discuss the archæology I had seen as well as possible sites yet to be seen.

Zachary arrived in the morning at my door with his racing bike wearing the latest fashion in bike togs. We ate breakfast together prior to our steep descent into Nazareth. Like so many Israelis, Zachary was in a hurry. "I have a car. Call me if you have any difficulties while in the area," said Zachary. We exchanged addresses.

Was Nazareth of little interest or was I disinterested? The "Basilica of the Annunciation" looks a bit like a misplaced lighthouse even though it is one of Christendom's most holy shrines. Nazareth is said to be the only city in Israel where the Sabbath is celebrated on Sunday instead of Saturday. Before leaving in the direction of Tiberius, I photographed the Arab market, an authentic appearing souk where a ditch runs down the middle of the cobblestone path with markets on either side. During the rainy season this ditch is a necessity, draining the path. Fortunately, I was not criticized for taking photos of Arab women shopping on this busy Saturday morning.

Tiberius and the Yam Kinnert, or Sea of Galilee, was a welcome sight, especially from my elevated vantage point, where I could see the entire Sea. This freshwater lake, feeding the Jordan River, is the source of water for all of Israel; Jordan also draws from it.

In a well developed recreation area at Kibbutz Hittin, I had my own cottage near a mini-market and restaurant. Tenting is not permitted there. My only problem was a human one. A vagrant, who aggressively tried to become friendly, caused me concern. I had the feeling that my property was soon to become his. He asked for my knife, my food, and my time. Delinquent in paying his rent, the management eased him out the front gate. I felt relieved.

At 9 PM a memorial service was conducted throughout the State of Israel. Air raid sirens reminded the citizenry that one minute of silence would follow the cessation of the sirens. A solemn service was then conducted by young people at a local synagogue, both indoors and out, to commemorate the loss of life of those fallen in previous wars. This service was concluded with the singing of the National Anthem, "Hatikvah." Independence Day to follow was then celebrated with joy and the flying of flags. To get in the mood, I bought a small flag of the size displayed on automobiles. It extended from the back of the Globetrotter, being secured beneath a bungee cord that strapped my sleeping bag to the rear rack. This flag and a friendly family eased my distress in the Golan, following the fracture of the front fork a week later.

Leaving most of my baggage in the cottage, we descended to a beach on the Kinneret. I did not look forward to the inevitable climb back up the mountain in the evening to Kibbutz Hittin, but that price was to be paid later in the day. It was now time to enjoy being in an area known and discussed in a book written over 2,000 years ago, the Bible. It was also an area popularized by Jesus' ministry in the New Testament.

At a kibbutz named after the founder of the kibbutz movement, A.D. Gordon, I parked the Globetrotter in a safe place and walked toward the beach, passing through an opening in the fence. Families were enjoying the day by doing what families do best: having a picnic. In true Arab hospitality, I was invited to join in the festivities. I felt reluctant at first but soon discovered that being a stranger, I was expected to join them. Young attractive Arab women were especially attentive, as were their mothers. When the families began to get ready for their return home, the women kissed each other on the cheek. To show my appreciation for their hospitality, I moved in the direction of one of the maiden's cheek, with an instant reaction similar to the Arab woman in Jordan whom I tapped on the shoulder. Men do not touch unmarried women! They laughed and joked about the forward advance from this stranger obviously not an Arab.

On our return to Tiberius we came upon the Kibbutz Ginnosar, the location of a 2,000-year-old boat under restoration. In 1986, with the water level of the Kinneret at its lowest level in many years, an ancient boat was found buried under an exposed portion of the lake near Kibbutz Ginnosar. It has been dated to somewhere between the 1st centuries B.C. and A.D. Once discovered, its removal to a safe site on land attracted large numbers of people who enjoyed watching the delicate operation of wrapping the boat in fiberglass so it could be safely removed from its watery grave. A separate building on the grounds of Kibbutz Ginnosar has been built to house this historic relic that might have been sunk during a sea battle. A model of the 27-foot wooden boat with mosaics depicting the superstructure, and a documentary video are available in the main kibbutz building. The price of admission to the video is used to defray the cost of restoration. One theory suggests that this boat was sunk during the Jewish revolt against the Roman soldiers of Vespasian. The nine-year restoration project was obviously well underway before I arrived. Following completion, this piece of history will be available for public viewing.

Capernaum, the home of Jesus when he began his ministry, was my goal the following day. Having climbed from Tiberius to Kibbutz Hittin without dismounting, I felt at ease knowing that the grade either appeared steeper, or perhaps I was getting stronger. In any event, I was anxious to continue my tour of the entire lake.

Six miles north of Tiberius, on the lakeside road, a sign identifies a small white domed shrine as the birthplace of Mary Magdalene. The town noted on the sign is "Magdala," named for the defense tower protecting this fishing village. Extinguished candles within the shrine indicate previous worship.

Beautifully situated in a garden setting on the water nearby, the Church of the Primacy of St. Peter was my next important discovery. It is here that Jesus is believed to have appeared for the third time following his resurrection. Steps cut out of the rock outside the church encourage visitors to wade in the warm water of the Galilee. The altar shaped in the form of a boat in this black basalt church built in 1933 alludes to Peter's occupation as a fisherman. The flat rock in front of the alter is believed to be the table where Jesus and his disciples ate.

Capernaum in Hebrew is Kfar Nahum, the village of Nahum. There are numerous references in the New Testament to Jesus' teaching in the synagogue at Capernaum. Known history of the town dates to the 2nd century B.C., with a strong Christian presence in the 2nd century A.D. It is believed that Jesus moved here because of his converts Peter and Andrew.

The Franciscan open-air archæological museum at Capernaum, purchased in 1894, includes ruins that have enough detail to permit precise drawings of the synagogue. Decorations of the Star of David carved in stone are still visible, as are those of the menorah. A wine press with its stone accessories and equipment used to crush the olive is located on the nearby grounds. Olive oil was used as the fuel for lighting the menorah and in food preparation. So valuable was this oil that not a single drop was lost in the crushing process. Human or animal power turned the wheel that crushed the olives. Modest dress is required within the grounds of Capernaum.

Wednesday, April 28 was my last day at Kibbutz Hittin. A group of 500 young boys and girls from the city of Arad in the Negev invaded the campground. The quiet reserve of the area instantly converted into a rock-and-roll playground. The volunteer soldier protecting the children is a cyclist; he introduced himself to me. By strange coincidence, Pistrov Giora, this cyclist, father, and amateur soldier, in a car saw me plodding along in the Negev on my way to Jerusalem. We have since become pen pals.

My departure the following day could have been better: walking backwards, I tripped over a metal waste receptacle. Bruised and bleeding, I gave the appearance of having fallen from my bicycle. Later that afternoon while being chased by a man-eating dog, my front wheel caught in a rut in the road. My 180-pound load and I landed on the ground. Shortly thereafter and for the first time in my cycling experience I was directly in the path of a bird's dropping. "Oh well, it could have been worse. A lot worse!"

Pistrov and his daughter came to say goodbye. They were returning by bus to Arad. My clothes were clean, the bike was well lubricated, and I was ready to leave Kfar Hittin, named for the battle of the Horns of Hattin, when Saladin defeated the Crusaders in 1187. Seriously damaged by numerous battles and earthquakes, Tiberius went into decline. Kfar Hittin overlooking the Galilee could not have been a better choice as a base camp for exploration of the eastern shores of the Kinneret.

The Ernst Lehman Museum is named for one of the founders of Israel's banking system and long-time chairman of the board of the Tiberius Hot Springs Co., Ltd. located across the street from the museum. High concentrations of sulfuric, muriatic, and calcium salts in the springs are reputed to have curative powers. Stone Age people 10,000 years ago benefitted from these waters, as did Biblical people. King Solomon has been given credit by some for the creation of the springs and Jesus is acclaimed to have cured many with these waters.

Hammath Tiberias National Park includes the Lehman Museum and the ancient synagogue of Hammath, with its mosaic floors said to be the most beautiful in all of Israel. This synagogue was built in the 4th century A.D. The upper portion of the mosaic contains the holy ark and two candelabras, and the lower the zodiac. In each of the four corners are women representing the seasons. Helios is shown riding his chariot. Artifacts from the Lehman collection, such as ancient oil lamps and Roman glass, are displayed. The Lamp of Tiberius Synagogue, with its seven branches, is alternately decorated with flowers and pomegranates. Concavities on each branch are designed to hold olive oil for illumination. In the Park, hot sulfurous water with its strong odor heated the Jewish baths in Biblical times, and the pools in modern times. This water, too hot to immerse one's hand, emits steam.

Kibbutz Degania, located enroute to the Jordan River, is the world's first kibbutz. A museum of natural history dedicated to the founder of the movement, B. D. Gordon, is on the kibbutz grounds. Most of the wildlife species in Israel are represented in this museum, in addition to some amazing embryos in jars. There are twin human female fetuses, who would be in their fifties if living, as well as the fetus of a horse with its feet tucked under its body. Strangely, I saw only one ibex in the collection. Another unusual human fetus is contained within its amniotic sac being nourished by its umbilical cord at the time of termination. The reason for the inclusion of these unborn is not given.

Archæological findings in the Museum date back over one million years. Stone Age chopping tools, crafted stones for throwing, fertility figurines, and stones made into male and female sex organs are a sample of the objects to examine. A gold pendant 4,500 years old, a copper ax, and ceramic jugs are identical to those found in Egyptian tombs. I said goodbye to the curator Samuel, an elderly man, paid my 6 NIS, and headed for Ein Gev, a very sophisticated kibbutz on the Kinneret.

Established in 1937, Ein Gev is renowned for its 5,000-seat amphitheater, vineyards, banana plantations, date groves, and fishing. It operates a ferry service on the lake, providing a 45-minute crossing from the kibbutz to Tiberius. A huge restaurant caters to the guests of Ein Gev and visitors from other nearby vacation sites. Unfortunately, camping is not on the list of amenities.

Steve Amdur and I met quite by chance on Kibbutz Ha'on near Ein Gev. When I asked directions to a campsite of a woman whose English was limited, she pointed to Steve to help me. I discovered that Cambridge, Massachusetts bonds us together: Steve was born on Sycamore Street in North Cambridge before moving with his family to nearby Belmont. He now resides in Israel. In addition to inviting me to join him for supper in the kibbutz dining room, he gave me advice that I was unwilling to accept.

"Tomorrow is the beginning of Hamzeem, the fifty hottest days of the year. You have a lot of climbing to do if you are going to go to the Golan. Wait until the temperature begins to moderate. Whatever you do, Ralph, be sure to carry a supply of water. Drink water continuously!"

The Holiday Village of Kibbutz Ha'on nearby provided excellent facilities at only 12 NIS per night. Had I decided to take Steve's advice, this would have been an excellent place to camp. I had access to excellent showers, a restaurant at reasonable prices, and pleasant grounds. The only problem was my desire to push on. "I had biked in the desert of Egypt. How could this be different?" I decided on an early morning climb to the Golan.

Following the contours of the lake, we intersected Route 87 and began to climb. At no time was the grade unduly excessive, but it was continuous. I stopped occasionally to rest and drink some of my reserve supply of water. At one point I stopped to watch the maneuvers of some Israeli tanks a short distance away. Flatbed trucks were bringing some of these monsters into this staging area, while others were transporting their heavy load toward the summit. Huge belches of diesel smoke polluted the cloudless blue sky.

At one point, the driver of one of these trucks gestured to me to get off the road so he could proceed in an uninterrupted straight line. Although the engine noise blotted out his voice, I fully understood his gestures. With power steering, he could have easily given me the small amount of road space I required without his hostility. I leave it up to you to guess whether I moved or ignored him.

A sign at the summit pointed to the left toward the city of Katzrin, fondly called the "capital of the Golan." Nearing exhaustion from the sun, I decided Katzrin was my goal for this first day of Hamzeem. The interesting scenario is that I did not realize just how close I had come to the physical state Steve Amdur described.

I investigated a historic site a short distance from the city limits. Relief from the sun was immediate once I entered the remains of the reconstructed 3rd century synagogue. Sitting on a bench to recover, I fell into an instant and deep sleep. I occasionally awoke into semi-consciousness, noticing that I was surrounded by tourists. Finally, I felt recovered enough to tour the site before going on to Katzrin. I had learned the meaning of Hamzeem.

The S.P.N.A. campground began to fill shortly after my arrival with an unusual mix of people. They were a combination of Arabs, Christians, and Jews, all with a common purpose: peace and understanding. This "club" meets periodically at different locations with an intentional objective, physical activity. They contend that doing things of a physical nature together breaks down old barriers that have separated these three groups for centuries. They also conduct casual yet structured discussions. Clergymen are well represented in the group of approximately thirty men. Eitan Shishkoff and his son David were especially cordial to me. Eitan, a rabbi in the United States, is both a businessman and peacemaker in Israel. He and David invited me to their home in Haifa. By coincidence, Eitan's wife Connie, a member of my Hebrew class in Haifa brought us together at their spacious home on top of Mount Carmel.

The following morning the group conducted a round table meeting without the table. We stood in an unbroken circle where each person who felt like speaking did so. Finally it was my turn. "I want to thank each of you for your hospitality in this 'chance meeting.' I am privileged to be able to learn first-hand about your altruistic objectives."

Eitan spoke to me privately after the meeting broke up. "Ralph, this was no 'chance meeting.'" I did not reply.

The campground could not be kept open for one person, to my disappointment; I was that person. I would have preferred to stay for a day or so and tour Katzrin. Instead, I visited the Katzrin Archæological Museum, where a multimedia film discusses ancient Gamla nearby.

Present-day Katzrin, established in 1977, was built in the shape of a butterfly, with the body as the center and the wings as the neighborhoods. Though the white cement buildings are monotonous, they provide a high standard of living for the occupants. A park with a small zoo rounds out the city. Mineral water, winemaking, and a military presence are the reasons for its existence. An S.P.N.A. Field School with dormitory rooms and a dining room are the only accommodations, other than the Field School campground where Eitan and his friends and son camped.

On October 12 in 67 A.D., the Romans began the siege of Gamla, a Jewish city overlooking the Golan. Thousands of people had fled there as a result of the Jewish revolt against Rome. Three legions of Roman soldiers massacred 4,000 people, while 5,000 committed suicide at the same time by leaping over the cliff, similar to the events at Masada. Two women survived. Gamla means camel in Hebrew, the contour of the land resembling a camel's hump.

I decided next to visit Gamla on the way to Mount Hermon, Israel's only ski resort. I left Katzrin in bright sunlight with a stiff cool headwind and continued to climb along the desolate road to Gamla. Signs were posted periodically warning of land mines adjacent to the road. Shortly before the sign directing me to Gamla, I stopped to examine a monument where a jeep is permanently entombed. Suddenly, one hundred feet farther on, I found myself on the ground, stunned but unhurt. The twice-repaired front fork of the Globetrotter fractured without warning, depositing me gently on the road surface. Gamla was no longer my immediate objective, survival was!

I found that one fork blade was fractured, the other remained intact. There was no other damage. In order to condense my possessions as much as possible, I broke the other blade and laid the damaged parts on top of the tandem in order to tie the parts together in a more manageable package. I placed my luggage alongside the bicycle and waited.

Occasionally a car or truck passed, but none stopped even though I tried to bring attention to myself. Then my Israeli flag became useful. Waving the flag and pointing to my problem, the next vehicle, a small van, stopped to investigate. This family of three was traveling toward Katzrin. We placed the bike on the car roof rack and my baggage inside. The parents not only returned me to civilization, but they escorted me to the entrance of the Field School, within walking distance of a bus stop. "The 5 AM bus will take you to Tel Aviv where you can get your bike repaired." They accepted no money as payment for their kindness.

To my dismay, the Field School was completely booked for the night. Camping is not permitted on the grounds even though I offered to pay the daily room rate. The S.P.N.A. campground remained closed. Once again I had an unexpected problem that required creativity. "If I go to the police, they might give me permission to camp in the park for one night." The walking distance from the Field School to the police station presented a logistics problem. "Perhaps I will erect my tent outside the campground fence, knowing there will be no toilet facilities." The distance from the bus stop to the campground was another negative consideration.

355

I left the Globetrotter locked to a fence and began walking with my necessary luggage and tent toward the campground. Attendants at the Field School willingly agreed to store the remainder of my gear until the next morning. An opportunity then presented itself.

Moshe was standing outside his house with its small green patch of lawn. I introduced myself as an American, a cyclo-tourist, in trouble through no fault of my own. "Would you give me permission to put my tent on your lawn for one night?"

"I will have to ask my wife," replied Moshe. Soon Hananit came to the front door to investigate our conversation.

"But we don't know you," said Hinanit. "This is Israel and we have to be very cautious when it comes to strangers, especially with our small son." I showed them my passport, explaining again that I had an unusual problem and they could be of assistance if it was their decision to do so.

"We are going to visit friends," said Hinanit. "Join us as we decide what we can do to assist you." That is how I became acquainted with the Loyter family: Moshe, Hinanit, and their adorable 8-year-old son Sagiv. This was the first of four visits with them—three times in Katzrin and once in Haifa.

Returning to the Loyter home, the telephone rang. Galila, Sagiv's grandmother, was calling to tell her daughter and family that she arrived safely back in Tel Aviv after her visit with them that weekend. Shortly thereafter, I was invited to introduce myself to Galila, a retired school principal and amateur artist. Her sculpture in the Loyter home reminded me of the French artist Mailol. "If I can get the bike repaired in Tel Aviv tomorrow, will you have supper with me tomorrow evening? If I have to fly to France for these repairs I will call you concerning my change of plans." It was agreed. At that moment Galila asked if the television was turned on. She was being interviewed on the street by a reporter. I now had a visualization of my "date's" appearance. No, I did not pitch my tent on the Loyter's front lawn.

"What would the neighbors say?" said Hinanit. I slept in Galila's bed.

Moshe and I left the house in the morning, he for work and I for the bus stop. Sagiv had my autographed Israeli flag, and I had an invitation to return to Katzrin to celebrate Rosh Hashanah, the Jewish New Year. "Send me a postcard from somewhere interesting," asked Sagiv the previous night. Although Sagiv spoke only Hebrew, we quickly bonded. My Hebrew was almost as limited as his English.

I explained to a taxi driver in Tel Aviv that I wanted to stop at every bike shop in the city seeking a replacement fork. If none was available, I would then ask him to take me to Ben Gurion Airport so I could fly to France. The bike is of French construction even though it was sold as an English product. My only other alternative was to end the cycling portion of my trip, something I was not ready to do. Bicycle shop number two produced excellent results!

The Cycling Center owned by Eli Samocha not only had a replacement fork and the expertise needed to install it, but at a later date following a car-bike accident near the Lebanese border, he supplied another replacement fork, to be installed in Haifa. Eli loaned me a bike at no additional cost during the time needed for the repair. "Your fork is worth more than this bike," remarked Eli. "I may have your repair completed by 7 o'clock this evening." What luck to be able to find a tandem fork and to have it installed in time for my dinner date with Galila! Someone surely was looking over my shoulder. Galila and I saw each other a second time in Katzrin during the Rosh Hashanah holiday and in Haifa when the Loyter family and she spent the day with me on Mount Carmel.

Following our dinner date, I decided to return to Tel Aviv and the Munich Hostel where I stayed on a previous visit. The estimated distance to the hostel was about 10 km. It was now almost 1 o'clock in the morning. My map and compass eventually brought me to the Mediterranean near the city of Jaffa and eventually back into Tel Aviv. I then knew my way to the hostel. Well past 2 in the morning I found a secluded spot behind a building opposite the hostel, erected my tent, and slept comfortably in preference to checking in at that unseemly hour. Tel Aviv residents probably would not advise such a decision.

Headwinds the next morning were so ferocious in the direction of Haifa that small cars had difficulty staying on the road, much less myself on the Globetrotter. By this time I had developed a certain mentality relative to wind and hills: shift to a lower gear, take your time, and smell the roses. Biking against the elements in the Negev was tedious, but on the Tel Aviv highway where I had company it merely took a little longer.

Twenty-five kilometers south of Haifa, I found Kibbutz Newe' Yam and a campground. By this time the weather had changed into a driving rainstorm, so severe that a tent would have been impractical had I not found a shelter large enough to accommodate my bike, tent, and gear. Kibbutz Newe' Yam and its guests could not have been more hospitable. A severe electrical storm during the night might have given me cause for concern in an open field. A strong tailwind the following morning brought us to Haifa for the first time.

Beth El Hostel, a Christian-oriented hostel in Haifa at the base of Mount Carmel. provides clean facilities and a cordial atmosphere. Stores and restaurants within walking distance are plentiful. A short distance from the hostel, a road connects Mount Carmel at the top with Haifa and the Mediterranean at the base. One-third of the way to the top is an access road to the Baha'i Shrine and Gardens, the world headquarters of the Baha'i faith. Strategically located, the Shrine is a focal point for the entire city of Haifa. In all cases, clothing must be modest, one's legs must be covered, and shoes must be removed prior to entering the sanctuary.

My first visit to Beth El Hostel was for one night, with plans to return following a trip to the north at Rosh Hanikra and the Israel-Lebanon border. I decided to then return to Haifa, seek a volunteer job, and leave for a bicycle tour of the Greek Islands, Greece, and Turkey. My thoughts at that time centered around a volunteer position in a hospital or dental facility where my 42 years of orthodontic experience might be needed and wanted. Until then I had not heard about the House of Grace.

Acre (Akko) and Nahariya, two towns of interest, were merely stopping places for food or directions but not for visitation. I was determined to see Rosh Hanikra, with the hope of setting foot on Lebanese soil. The continuation of the rainy season postponed these plans. North of Nahariya, I began to pursue a nearby campground prior to the onset of a storm. When I found the campground closed, it was raining lightly. At the entrance to Molitan Threads, owned by Jonathan Moller, it was raining much harder. Those inside were as surprised to see me as I was to be in a perfect location at the ideal time.

Jonathan's son, Eitan, cordially invited me to use the kitchen facilities while waiting out the storm. Prepared for the unexpected, I was well fortified with provisions. Until this time I had not met Jonathan.

"Would you like to sleep here tonight and escape the rain?" asked Jonathan. "You can sleep in the bomb shelter where there are mattresses and a full-size pillow. We also have toilet facilities. I then learned that every industry, kibbutz, and institution of learning in Israel must provide a bomb shelter. Conditions in the Middle East warrant this protection.

A bus driver and I became engaged in conversation at a kibbutz near the border. "We must not do what we did with

Sadat and give it all back," he said. "Give some of the Golan back so Asad can save face but protect the Kinneret at all costs." A veteran of the Golan campaign, the driver is of the opinion that there is one more war to be fought.

A cable car at the border gate descends into what is known as the Grotto. Waves crashing beneath the earth's surface have created a cave-like grotto. The thunderous noise of the water and the nearby white chalk cliffs are a unique area in Israel. At one time a train connected Haifa and Beirut through a tunnel in the Grotto. In the War of Independence, the Palmach of Israel blew up a bridge in the Grotto to prevent a possible invasion by the Lebanese army.

A seaside metal sculpture on the Mediterranean shore attracted my attention. After taking a photo of the sculpture, I walked the Globetrotter across the highway to the hostel to use the toilet facilities. I then mounted the bike, pointing the front wheel toward Rosh Hanikra to the north. When the road appeared safe for a U-turn, I began to make a gradual swing toward the opposite side. It was then I heard the screech of brakes of an oncoming car, followed by the smell of burning rubber. In 30 years of adult cycling I have never smelled burning rubber prior to a crash or near-crash. A moment later the bike and I were on the pavement. Fortunately, I corrected my steering to the right when I heard the brakes, making the blow a glancing one instead of a side-on collision. This car must have been traveling at a high speed to have been undetected in my mirror. I assured the woman driving the car that the fault was mine and that I was uninjured except for road tar on my fallen side. The bike also appeared undamaged. She left the scene talking to herself.

The Globetrotter was not undamaged, as I thought. My spanking new front fork installed by Eli Samocha was bent, making steering difficult but not impossible. I knew I could pedal back to Haifa. I called the Cycling Center from a nearby phone booth. "Eli, do you have another new tandem fork?"

"Of course. Why?" Following a brief explanation, Eli agreed to send the newest fork to the Beth El Hostel in Haifa so I could have it installed in that city.

"You are lucky," said Eli.

"Eli, I do not feel lucky," I said jokingly.

A Holocaust Museum is located between Nahariya and Akko, within walking distance of Kibbutz Lochamei Hagetaot where I spent the night. My original plan to climb the mountain to the mystical city of Safed was aborted because of the damaged front fork. Finding and exploring this museum, established in 1949 and named the Ghetto Fighter's House, was a valuable opportunity to learn more about the Holocaust and the Jewish resistance movement. Former resistance fighters from the ghettos of Germany, Poland, and Lithuania built the museum and furnished it with artifacts related to the Jewish communities in these countries. The artists Elsa Pollack and Ella Liebermann Shiber, both Holocaust survivors, contributed their vivid art, identifying the atrocities they witnessed. With the Museum's permission, I placed the open page of the painting by Shiber "On the Edge of the Abyss" on a flowering bush outside in the sunlight and photographed it. I prefer not to elucidate the atrocities.

The Akko Youth Hostel was an excellent choice in the picturesque Old City within sight of Haifa. Minarets, domes, and Crusader remains of Acre (now known as Akko) make it a must on a tourist's itinerary. One of the world's oldest towns, Acre is mentioned in Egyptian sacred texts of the 19th century B.C.

The Akko hostel is in what was originally the home of the Turkish governor. A cordial Arab-Christian family operates the hostel, which has extremely high ceilings. Two other guests were a rather unlikely couple, Joel and Sheena.

Joel is a Canadian with Jewish heritage on one side of his family. Sheena, his common-law wife, is a United States citizen born in India. Each are professional people who met in the Negev while touring separately. Both visited Masada, King Herod's winter palace, and each planned to return to Jerusalem by bus. By coincidence, Joel and Sheena selected adjoining seats on the same bus. Two days later they purchased rings and held a private civil marriage ceremony. We became immediate friends and spent a great deal of time together. Sheena and Joel were planning a formal wedding at the Canadian Embassy in Tel Aviv the following Friday. "We would like to have you stand up for us at our wedding," said Joel.

At first I declined the invitation, having made plans to leave Haifa by ferry to tour the Greek Islands. I reconsidered. "Of course I can attend your wedding if I want to. All I need to do is change my plans. I even have a necktie shirt I can wear." The shirt was reserved for extremely hot desert cycling, to protect my forearms. Joel told me not to buy a tie; his best man would have an extra. We agreed to meet at the Greenhouse Hostel on Dizengoff Street Thursday evening.

Traffic into Haifa was intense and I felt a bit "gun shy." The damaged fork and my memory of the accident left me apprehensive. This was, fortunately, my last encounter with an automobile for the remainder of the trip. At 3 PM I left the bike and its newest fork at a bike shop and by 5 the installation was completed. I was now prepared to bike to Tel Aviv for the wedding of two unusual people.

David Friedman, a recent medical school graduate from Detroit, and I became friends at the Beth El hostel. He borrowed the money for a trip to Israel as a graduation gift to himself. David assured me that the swelling of my ankles was not due to cardiac insufficiency, but was probably related to arthritis. He was amazed that a person his father's age could pedal a 180-pound load around Europe and the Middle East. We agreed to stay in touch, especially after my next visit to

Rosh Hanikra. David wanted me to photograph a sign at the border showing the distance between Jerusalem and Rosh Hanikra. We talked about The Source by James Michener and its relevance to the Akko-Safed-Haifa area. Michener placed Tel Makkor between Acre and Safat (Safed) for his convenience in his historical novel. I learned that Makkor, meaning "source," was actually Tel Gezer, located within sight of the Ben Gurion Airport near Tel Aviv. Though I had read The Source, I decided to reread the book. We laughed about a sign in the hostel men's room: "No hand washing in the sink." It obviously meant that guests are not to do their laundry in the sink.

Now that the Globetrotter was again operational, I decided to seek the elusive "volunteer job" that I hoped to find before leaving Haifa for Rhodes. The hospital Rambam, having an orthodontic department associated with the department of oral surgery, was my first choice. Professor Lauder, the department head, was not available but his cheerful secretary arranged an appointment later in the day. Putting this time delay to good use, I visited the Dagon Museum, the only wheat museum in the world. Attached to the museum is a huge grain elevator that accepts grain from incoming ships and transfers it to silos, from which it is loaded onto railroad cars or trucks. The entire procedure is done by computer.

In the small yet very complete archæological museum at Dagon, a petite mummy made of wheat in the shape of a human is placed in a mummy case. This discovery was made with the aid of x-ray. Authentic beer mugs made of clay are on display, with their built-in strainer to strain off the barley during the pouring process. At that time I did not know that I'd be making one of these mugs in ceramics class at the House of Grace. A mother with two of her children was visiting Dagon at the time. I later learned that she was Agnes Shehade, wife of Kamil Shehade, the director of the House of Grace.

Professor Laufer, his secretary Carmella, and the dental specialists at Rambam were friendly and mildly interested in my quest for volunteer work. I had the feeling a position would be found even though I was not actually needed. Orthodontia was of less importance here than oral surgery. The other factor I was not yet aware of is that with the immigration of Russian Jews, stomatologists are in great abundance in Israel.

A dental facility with an active orthodontic department near the Beth El hostel also presented job possibilities. The director, a woman, introduced me to her technician and the staff doctors. She did not discourage me, but suggested we meet another time when she was not involved with clinic patients. It was then I decided to look for volunteer employment in a field other than dentistry. I practiced my profession for 42 years; wasn't it time to do something else? What might it be?

My climb to the Baha'i Shrine was not without difficulty. I pulled a pair of gym pants over my bike shorts, removed my shoes, and entered the sanctuary. A young woman kneeling in prayer with her head on the carpeted floor and I were the only people present. I then understood the requirement for long skirts. Two exotic oriental vases were displayed behind a screen. This was obviously a place for prayer, not elegance. I then waited outside the sanctuary for the woman. "I apologize for talking to the attendant while you were worshiping. I didn't realize I was in the sanctuary until I saw you kneeling. Please forgive me."

The young woman was neither Arabic or Baha'i. Ann Marie Herrera is an American Catholic whose home is Ventura, California. One of five children, she was a volunteer at a shelter-halfway house known as the House of Grace, located a short distance from the beach in Haifa. The more we talked, the more interested I became in her association with this Arab-Christian institution associated with the Greek Catholic church. "Have you had lunch?" I asked.

Our Arabic lunch was enjoyable and informative. Ann Marie talked with such enthusiasm about the House of Grace and Kamil, the director, that I expressed an interest in meeting him regarding becoming a volunteer. She explained that in addition to the resident street people, recovering drug addicts, and distressed women, they accommodate prisoners in the process of being released from the custody of the Israeli court system. The House of Grace also gives assistance to over 700 families in the Galilee and Upper Galilee. All the money needed for their operations comes from donations. Even though some of the residents are detained by the courts, the State of Israel does not contribute to their support. Kamil Shehade raises the needed funds through personal solicitation in Europe. Ann Marie and I walked the short distance from the restaurant to 10 Palyam Street. I pushed the Globetrotter, trying to avoid the throngs on the sidewalk, a combination of religious and ethnic diversity representative of Haifa.

"Have you eaten?" asked Kamil as he poured Arabic coffee into small white cups without handles that are so characteristic of the Arab world. The rich sweet coffee was identical to that in the restaurant. We made an appointment to meet and discuss my becoming a volunteer.

Ann Marie and I toured the facility and the volunteers' quarters. She introduced me to the staff and Agnes, Kamil's wife. "I saw you at Dagon the other day," said Agnes. She then introduced me to her four young children, two of whom are twins. A congenial atmosphere prevailed.

It took three visits on my part to convince Kamil. Reasons were given such as "we have other volunteers scheduled to arrive and there might not be enough room," or "we are fully staffed at the present time." I explained that I wasn't interested in starting until September 1, and that I would stay until the following April. He finally accepted my offer without giving the actual reason for his reluctance.

In the Arab world, senior family members are revered and doted upon. They do not work! As a potential member of the family of the House of Grace, Kamil could not visualize my being of use as a volunteer. In spite of his reluctance, he welcomed me and assured me of a bed on September 1. By that time Ann Marie had returned to California. I now felt enthused about the forthcoming Cody-Singh wedding in Tel Aviv.

Caesarea again became my overnight campsite. I was anxious to renew my friendship with Nancy, a young woman working in the gift shop. To my disappointment, Nancy had returned to her native Sweden. I purchased a wedding gift at the Eretz Israel gift shop at Caesarea, which the ladies behind the counter gift-wrapped. I then pedaled to the Munich hostel, near Edna Kessler's home. Edna invited me to her apartment, where she provided an iron and ironing board. I wanted my white shirt to look its best. Before our visit ended, I ironed Edna's clothes as well. She was amused and pessimistic: "There will be no wedding!" I then went in search of the Greenhouse hostel and my pre-arranged rendezvous with Joel and Sheena.

They were not registered at the hostel as they indicated. The management felt this was not unusual, since they have very few rooms for married couples. We did not see one another that night. In the morning, wearing my white, long-sleeved necktie shirt, I arrived ahead of schedule at the Canadian Embassy. "Where are the people? Oh well, perhaps it's still early." As time passed it became obvious that there was a glitch somewhere. Not a single person knew about this wedding except for one telephone operator who received a call from the bride's father concerning his wedding present. There was no wedding!

Giving Joel and Sheena the benefit of the doubt, I felt obliged to wait longer than necessary. Edna reminded me that her prediction had come true. "Would you like a gift from your friend Ralph?" I asked. The wedding gift is now hanging on her wall. She told me of her supernatural powers.

While on vacation with a lady friend, she visited a casino where a portly gentleman at the roulette table had a pile of chips in front of him. "Play number 39," said Edna.

"How did you know I would win with number 39?" he asked.

"Well, I am Jewish and I live in Israel. We Jews have a special connection with the patriarchs of an earlier time." He then asked her to give him another winning number. "I am sorry," said Edna, "I have lost the connection." She then asked him if she might have one chip from his winnings. Playing her lucky number 39, she won enough money to pay for two nights at her hotel. Is this story true? Ask Edna.

At 17 Ben Gurion Boulevard, near the Mediterranean, the home of Israel's first prime minister, David Ben Gurion, is open to the public. Had I not made an unscheduled trip to Tel Aviv, I might not have toured this historic home, now owned by the State, nor would I have stayed overnight with my friends the Krupnicks in Netanya.

The Ben Gurion home is maintained exactly as it was at the time of his wife Paula's death. A 20,000-volume library and the prime minister's correspondence is partially housed here. A letter written in 1964 to Charles de Gaulle predicted that in ten to fifteen years Russia would become a democratic nation is on display.

I camped overnight in Caesarea and headed for Haifa in the morning. A restaurant at the intersection of the road leading to Zichron Ya'acov was not the only welcome sight. Asher Krupnick was on his early morning fitness ride and also in need of nourishment. I had stayed with Asher and his family in Natanya and now we had the opportunity of becoming better acquainted. This was just one more "chance meeting."

Asher returned to Netanya and I proceeded toward the Israeli Gardens and crypts of the Rothschilds, an extremely steep climb. Rather than walk my heavy load, I decided to tour on foot. At the same time that I asked directions to the Park, the driver of a new Mitsubishi stopped to inquire its location from the same person. Ilya Etlis, a chemical engineer from Haifa, was on a day's outing with his parents. "Would you like to join us?" asked Ilya, a Russian immigrant. Two hours later he and his parents dropped me off at the base of the mountain. We enjoyed each other's company and the magnificence of the manicured park. I reinflated my rear tire and headed for Haifa. Two days later I was aboard a ferry for Cyprus and Rhodes.

Much of my free time in Haifa was spent doing bike repairs. A shop selling the necessary parts permitted me to use some of their tools to replace worn gears, a worn chain, and both tires. I decided to test-ride the Globetrotter to be certain it was ready for two months of strenuous cycling in the mountainous countries of Crete, Greece, and Turkey.

Chain number 1 self-destructed near the top of Mount Carmel. Chain number 2, a French Sedis chain, was like meeting an old friend. I knew I had quality equipment that would last. We headed for the Druze villages of Daliyat al Karmel and Isfiya in a very mountainous region beyond the highly developed commercial and residential areas of Mount Carmel.

The Druze have a reputation for being extremely friendly to strangers. Male elders are recognized by their thick mustaches and distinctive robes. Most of the women wear the traditional long dark dress and white headdress. The owners of an art store in Dalyat, Younis and Hagma Alkara, who are probably not Druze, showed me an oil painting of the Old City of Jerusalem. I decided at first to buy it as a gift, but my second thought was to buy it for myself. It arrived in perfect condition in Cambridge and is hanging on my wall, not on someone else's.

Rhodes

Chapter 14
HAIFA to CYPRUS to RHODES

Our first stop at Cyprus was limited to a few hours, permitting the unloading of cargo at the port of Limassol. Not unloading my bike for transportation was indeed a mistake. Most of my time was spent walking as opposed to exploring—an error I promised myself would not happen again. Sailing was scheduled for 1:30 but we didn't get underway until 2:00. Underestimating the distance, I boarded at 1:45.

Robin and her two friends were "kibbutzniks" on vacation from their volunteer jobs. A graduate of Brandeis University in Waltham, Massachusetts, Robin and I had things in common. Soon we four were playing a dice game to pass the time. Robin, or Rifka as she prefers to be called, contrasted me with her father. She considers her dad "very straight," trying to make a living with all its stresses, while I was doing what she and her friends were doing: leading a carefree life without a need for the "superficial amenities" associated with the United States.

I tried to explain to Robin that I was older than her father. I worked for 42 years, leading a lifestyle similar to her parents' before embarking on a two-year adventure completely out of character to my previous existence. "With a credit card and a line of credit from the bank, it's very easy for me to lead the life of what I term a 'professional bum.' If I were still working, I'd probably be as straight as your dad." She was visibly disappointed!

Rhodes was a welcome sight. Robin and her friends continued on the *Harmony of the Poseidon* to the islands of Santorini and Crete. Ultimately, they planned to reach Greece, 260 nautical miles away. I biked in to Rhodos, the capital of this "Island of the Sun," the fourth largest Greek island. The medieval windmills on the pier of St. Nickolas greeted me as I pedaled into this very busy tourist center with an American Express office. The check I cashed in exchange for Greek currency haunted me for the next year. I inadvertently wrote the bank number on my check instead of my account number. This error caused my bank to refuse payment to American Express, with the untimely cancellation of all check-cashing privileges. The matter was finally resolved months after my return, but meanwhile my only source of credit was Mastercard.

The 17-km ride to Faliraki Camping passed the Citadel in Rhodos as well as the port and medieval windmills on the pier of St. Nickolas. From there the road follows the coast southward toward Lindos, the site of an ancient Greek acropolis. Winter rates still prevailed. Faliraki offers complete facilities, including a separate building with a kitchen-dining area. A plethora of ants living in the sandy soil was the only problem to us tenters; we learned very quickly to keep the flyscreens securely closed.

The owner's pet, a German shepherd, gave birth to a litter of pups while I camped at Faliraki. Until the delivery, this docile animal was everyone's friend. She selected her birthing nest in a tool shed where I had access to the tools. "Stay away from the tool shed. The pups have just been born," said the owner. I was of the opinion that the dog considered me her friend. "I'll have no problem borrowing a hammer." The dog felt otherwise as I withdrew from her territory. Two months later on my return trip to Haifa, I revisited Faliraki Camping. The dog no longer had her pups; they were given away. When I reached out to pet my old friend, I thought I was going to lose my right hand. She remembered!

A car rally in the center of Rhodos introduced me to the town. The area was marked off with cones to establish an obstacle course for the sports car drivers. The difference in driving ability and the quality of equipment was remarkable. I fully expected to see a car end up on its side.

Nothing is remaining of ancient Rhodes. Architecture constructed during the period of the Knights dates to 1190 A.D. Nike of Samothrace, the masterpiece of a Rhodian artist created in approximately 190 B.C., is preserved in the Louvre in Paris. Today the walls of the Old City (Chora) enclose walks, roads, restored buildings, gardens, and a multitude of shops and restaurants. The mixed architectural designs represent the Gothic, Byzantine, and Turkish cultures. A stroll along the flagstone walks leaves one breathless. In addition to the medieval facades, trellis windows, loggias, and minarets contributed by the Turks, a conglomerate style is created that probably cannot be duplicated elsewhere in the world.

I had the good fortune of finding a well equipped bike shop with a piece of equipment I sorely needed in preparation for the mountains of Greece and Turkey. A 28-tooth freewheel at the rear was not adequate for the coming weeks, but that was the best I could find in Haifa. Mike, the shop owner, generously loaned me the necessary tools to make the switch. I now had the hill climbing ability I wanted and needed. Lindos to the south, where the original Temple of Athena was destroyed by fire in 342 B.C., became my next goal, with plans to travel the entire perimeter of the island prior to departing for Crete.

Traveling alone, I arrived around noontime at Lindos and its azure blue harbor. At first I decided to be a true tourist and ride a donkey to the site of the Citadel and the remains of the Temple of Athena at the summit. The weather was pleasant and the tourists congenial. Compared to the "snake path" leading to Masada in the Negev, this hike was a "piece of cake." The Citadel, originally the Acropolis of Lindos, is on the highest point overlooking the Bay of Lindos. Greek construction began in 200 B.C. and continued until 20 A.D. During the Middle Ages, the Byzantines occupied the Acropolis, followed by the Knights.

According to plan, I spent the night at the southernmost point of the island at the small village of Katavia. The

Prasonisi Club there has very modern rooms with an adjacent restaurant. We settled for 3,000 drachmas instead of the asking price of 5,676.

A motorcyclist warned me about the unpaved roads on the western side of the island. "I would not try it on a motorcycle, much less a bicycle!" he commented. I had to find out for myself and soon learned this was "mission impossible." The contrast between the eastern and western sides of the island was beyond my imagination. I was now in the wilderness trying to keep erect on a road that would challenge the tires of a jeep. After a 5-km struggle, we turned around and headed for Katavia, Lindos, and finally, Faliraki Camping.

At a roadside stand selling freshly picked oranges, I met Roman Matzke, a fellow cyclist from Germany. A doctoral student in computer science, Roman carries photographic equipment weighing more than his bike. In spite of the weight, this fit and vigorous new friend patiently waited for me at the tops of hills. My Globetrotter weighed more than the combined weight of his bike and equipment. We both camped at Faliraki. I made breakfast for both of us in the morning before we went our separate ways. Roman was on his way to another Greek Island in the Sun and I planned to see more of Rhodes before departing for Crete.

Much of the following day was spent in the Old City. Nikos Balaskas greets patrons beneath a huge ficus tree at his outdoor restaurant, The Oasis. The friendly atmosphere as well as his singing fills the tables while restaurants nearby are relatively empty. I looked forward to the guided tour, where beautiful mosaics of Roman origin were imported from the island of Kos. Our guide explained the method used for recovering mosaics and their transportation to a new site.

A cloth the size of the mosaic is glued to the surface prior to the mosaic being unearthed. It is then rolled up as one would roll up a rug so the mosaic can be moved without being disturbed. It is then placed on a bed of fresh cement at its new site.

An extension of the Castle is the Castle of St. Nicholas that protected the ancient Rhodians as well as the Knights. There, three remaining windmills of unusual design greet visitors to Mandraki Harbor. These round structures built of stone support the windmills with their conical wood roofs. At one time the spokes of the wheel-like windmills were draped with cloth as a wind-catching device. At a distance of perhaps a quarter of a mile from the Castle, the US aircraft carrier Frank*lin D. Roosevelt* was anchored. Between six and seven thousand sailors aboard the *FDR* were escorted by small boat to this island for rest and recreation.

Until then, I had not met a single acquaintance from the US. On two separate occasions I met people who live or lived in Cambridge, but I didn't know them prior to my trip. "I'm going to make myself comfortable in view of the sailors who are coming ashore with the hope of seeing someone I know." An hour later I gave up this futile attempt.

The following day, I was back on the pier fully packed and ready to board the ferry enroute to Crete, the home of the Minoans. In addition to the ferry, the *F/B Daliana*, a cruise ship of the Cunard Line was tied up nearby. Passengers from that ship were sunning themselves on the pier.

A man wearing sunglasses and a baseball cap walked toward me. Marvin Reisman, a cyclist from White Plains, New York, was interested in this fellow cyclist using a tandem without a partner. We began to talk. I then turned toward Marvin, a man approximately my age, and said "Pakatakan Lodge!" Pakatakan Lodge was a cyclist's haven in the Catskill Mountain where the New York Cycle Club gathered once or twice a year. I remembered that Marvin Reisman, a Madison Avenue lawyer, and I biked together while staying at Pakatakan Lodge several years previously. That was the first and last time I rode with Marvin. Needless to say, he on the pier and his wife on the upper deck were stunned when they learned of our previous mutual experience. I then boarded the *Daliana*. Several weeks later, while living as a volunteer at the House of Grace in Haifa, I received copies of the photos taken by Marvin and his wife. My favorite showing the Globetrotter and myself in "true form" using a plastic bag of food attached to the rear rack is on the cover of this book.

Crete

Chapter 15
RHODES to CRETE to SANTORINI

The *Daliana* docked at Herakleio, Crete, at 8:30 in the morning. From the pier, I biked to the Lions Fountain, the center of tourist activity of Crete's capital. A sign directs visitors to the nearby Youth Hostel of Herakleio. It was refreshing to take a shower even though there was no hot water, and to fall into bed following a restless night aboard the ship.

The Herakleio Archæological Museum, founded in 1883, is unique, containing only exhibits from Crete dating from the Neolithic period to the end of the Helleno-Roman era. The exhibits are arranged in chronological order, allowing me to learn the history of Crete without prior knowledge. The jewelry, frescos, and exceptionally beautiful vases of the Minoan era are more than I could have imagined. A fresco from the Minoan Temple of Knossis, the "Ladies in Blue," is a masterpiece. A faience ibex dating to 1600 B.C. reminded me of the ibex of today's Israel. Ivory figurines relating to the bull-leaping ceremonies, with the figures in motion, along with other finely crafted objects are, as mentioned, spectacular! I left at 6:55, five minutes before closing time, with a collection of slides bought at the gift counter. Because the museum is closed on Mondays, it was unlikely I'd be able to return.

Knossis, a Minoan palace, is Crete's most famous monument, located 5 km from the capital. It is around this palace that the Minoan civilization grew and prospered. King Minos, a descendant of the mythical Minos, sprang from the union of Europa and Zeus. He was the founder of Cretan naval power, the scourge of pirates. The king was a wise legislator and head of the Minoan religion.

An English-speaking guide made my tour of Knossis meaningful. The present palace, over-restored by early archæologists, was built in 1600 B.C. The previous one was destroyed by earthquake in 1700 B.C. Present-day pillars of cement that are wider at the top than at the bottom originally were constructed of Lebanese cedar. Frescos at the Temple are copies of the originals that are preserved in the museum at Herakleio. In the storerooms, enormous jars contained wine, olive oil, grain, and honey. When the palace was destroyed by earthquake, the olive oil caught fire, adding to the destruction. Charred evidence remains to this day.

A replica of the original throne is located in the throne room: the original is preserved in the Peace Palace at the Hague in Holland. Plumbing at the palace was quite advanced: toilets, a flushing system, and clay-lined pipes to carry away the waste water were separate from the fresh water system. There was also a method for the collection of rain water. Leaving the palace, we came upon the theatrical area with its raised box, believed to be the royal box.

Knossis minted most of the coins with the mythical Minotaur holding a stone in its hand on one side, as well as the head of Athena, the goddess who founded the dynasty of Knossis. The Labyrinth is depicted on the opposite side as is the double axe, the most sacred symbol of the Minoan religion, a decorative motif found everywhere at Knossis.

The owner of a breakfast shop and his daughter were helpful in planning my brief tour of Crete, an extremely mountainous island. They, of Baha'i faith, were interested in my impression of the world headquarters of the Baha'i in Haifa. Looking at the map with them, I decided to follow the coast from Herakleio to Rethymno, not knowing that we would encounter some of the highest mountains of Crete. My map indicated a campground near the sea at Rethymno. Had we taken the divided highway, we would have avoided the mountains, making travel much easier. It isn't that I had the desire to be a hero, it's that I wanted to be a law-abiding traveler for a change by not biking on a limited-access highway. At the campground in Rethymno, Leo, a moped owner, explained that bicycles and mopeds are permitted.

After a full morning's ride, we had gone only 26 km. Some of it was walking. Clear mountain air, spectacular scenery, and snow-capped mountains nearby made the hike worthwhile. Near the summit, a mountain view restaurant appeared. This welcome sight served an excellent Greek salad and orange drink. I fell into a deep sleep in a plastic chair immediately after lunch.

Our descent was long and gradual, in contrast to the steep climb on the opposite side of the mountain. At the 60-km mark, fatigue set in. A coffee shop had no food, but the packaged cookies and cold drink restored some of my energy. The campground at Rethymno was a welcome sight.

Outside the wall of the Citadel and museum at Rethymno, Roger and I became friends. He was lounging on the grass at the time I left a museum that permits no photography, no sketching, and has no slides for sale. The attendants act as if the visitors are intent on only one thing, stealing. Roger, an Englishman, visited Crete nine or ten times previously. We became acquainted as we walked the grounds of an abandoned fortress and Turkish mosque with a dome of huge proportions. Built of unplastered brick on the interior, I actually had a feeling of vertigo as if the dome at any moment might collapse. Swallows flew about the interior, entering and leaving through open windows. We then adjourned to a nearby tavern. Following supper, Roger and I exchanged addresses. We have since been in correspondence, expressing a desire to meet again.

At the campground, Thomas, a four-year-old, and I became pals. As semi-permanent residents, Thomas and his parents occupy a rather large tent equipped with electricity. They are especially friendly, sharing what little they have with others. Thomas and I rode our bikes around the grouds, he on his three-wheeler and I on the Globetrotter without its heavy load. Just for fun, Thomas and I had a pretend birthday party with pretend everything. I found a small gift in my pack so the pretend would have a little bit of reality. At the time I prepared to leave, everyone but Thomas turned out to say goodbye. Why did Thomas, my pal, not see me off? My theory is but a theory: Thomas has made friends with many campers only to find out this friendship is short-lived. Each of us in one way or another abandoned him, an event that in his young life he could not easily accept. Thomas, I miss you!

My return trip to Herakleio was challenging because of the wind, but at least I didn't have mountains to re-climb. Now that my mountain climbing experience was behind me, I was grateful for the memories. I felt that in a small way I had participated in the "Crete Experience."

Cornelia and her friend Thomas, on their rented motorcycle, shared a few moments with me at the side of the road before returning to the hostel where we first met. Cornelia, a citizen of Germany, had classes at the University the following day. A note from her awaited my return to the hostel: "Hello, you nature-hunting 'cowboy!' If you happen to be somewhere in Germany we would be happy to see you as our guest. Our addresses are_____. If you feel like telling us of your adventure or experiences, then just write to us, where you are in the world, and what you are doing. Good luck and fun, Cornelia and Thomas." I could live in Cambridge for ten years and not have this sort of unsolicited expression of friendship.

Back in Lions Square, I had time to say goodbye to my Baha'i friends. They advised Santorini, an island of great historical value as well as beauty.

At the port near the docking site of the Daliana, the Fortress at Herakleio became my final stop. The construction of the gate at the entrance made it impossible for me to bring the Globetrotter inside the grounds. With fingers crossed, I locked the bike, leaning it against a wall in an area highly visible to the public.

The view of the mountains I previously crossed, as well as the city of Herakleio from the ramparts, provided excellent composition for my photography. On the ground level several young boys were playfully riding their bikes toward the entrance. My past experience with the male gender, especially the teen-age variety, aroused my suspicion. I followed one of them to the gate, but not quickly enough to intercept the one who "pinched" my pump. Fortunately, I did seize one of his companions. Had his pal not dropped the pump, I planned to throw his friend's bike into the bay. I recovered my pump, released the young biker, and spared myself an explanation to the police. If I did what I contemplated, I probably would have had to compensate the boy for his loss. Goodbye Crete, hello Santorini!

Santorini

Chapter 16
SANTORINI

The crater lake at Santorini is the historical record of nature's past violence. This lake, a part of the Mediterranean, is overshadowed by a 300-meter high cliff and a 5-km roadway that snakes its way to the top, from which the main road leads to various parts of the island. The *Daliana* docked at a small pier near the entrance to the roadway. How was I to get the Globetrotter and myself to the top without total exhaustion?

While I was planning my strategy, an English gentleman approached, asking if I was at Sharm-el-Shaykh in the Sinai on my tandem the previous fall. He and his wife had seen me there while they were visiting Egypt.

For 2,000 drachma, or about ten dollars, I received a ride to a lovely inn with an attached restaurant not far from the port. A honeymoon couple, Roberto and Angelica-Marie from Italy, and I shared a table in the restaurant. The cloudless blue sky, the houses painted white, and the churches with their blue domes transform Santorini into a paradise. A lack of fresh water requires careful use of the facilities, yet at the same time causes little inconvenience.

The archæological excavations, Thera Akrotiri, are one of the major tourist attractions. A Minoan town of 30,000 people is in the process of being excavated under a fiberglass roof, giving workers and visitors an escape from the sun. Passengers from the original "Love Boat," the Princess, were touring the area at the same time as I; their English-speaking guide also became my unofficial guide,

The highly civilized Minoans lived in two- and three-story houses, with the ground floor reserved for their shops. A triangular Plaza was the center of the town's activity. Fabulous frescos as well as clay jars and a bed have been found in their entirety. The frescos, considered masterpieces, are presently in a state of preservation in the Athens Museum in Greece. My personal regret is that copies of the frescos have not been placed in Thera Akrotiri in the exact location where they were found, to demonstrate through visualization the accomplishments of these Minoans. This has been done at Knossis in Crete—why not here?

Thera Akrotiri was destroyed by both earthquake and volcanic eruption. The bed that's been found is only the mold of a bed. The original was incinerated by the surrounding volcanic ash that then became the mold for future casting. Archæologists poured plaster into the mold, reproducing the original shape and form of the bed. Flushing toilets and toilet seats have been found, in addition to a waste sewerage system and a separate fresh water delivery system. Spouts were used to collect rainwater. To this day, however, the written word on Santorini dating back to the Minoans has not been found. The volcanic explosion is dated at 1520 B.C.

Here is one of the theories concerning the destruction of Santorini and the disappearance of the Minoan civilization: the seafaring Minoan people had ample warning of the forthcoming disaster about to take their lives. Earthquakes and the smoldering of a volcano gave them every reason to plan their evacuation. With time on their side, they put their homes and businesses in proper order, expecting to return after nature's violence stopped. Even the jars were filled with grain in preparation for the return to "normalcy."

Being seafarers, the Santorini Minoans, with all their possessions, took to their sophisticated boats measuring as long as seventy feet. Their jewelry and sacred objects were easily transportable. From the sea they watched the eruption of the volcano with its inevitable tidal wave that not only took them to their watery grave but also covered the island of Crete as well. Their civilization ended forever.

A theory follows concerning the escape of the Hebrews from Egypt, led by Moses. It is speculated by some that this tidal wave occurred at the exact time that the Jews were escaping the bondage of the Pharaoh in Egypt. The division of the Red Sea, permitting the Jews' escape and drowning the Pharaoh and his army, may have been an act of nature rather than a deliberate decision of the God of the Hebrews.

Most of the ride to the city of Thira is a climb within view of the sea. A second port 300 meters below the city served as the port of call for the Princess. The cable car, in preference to a donkey ride or the donkey path, brought me to sea level. Passengers from the "Love Boat" were waiting to return to their floating hotel by small boat. It was a busy place. My return on foot to the summit was enjoyable except for the donkey droppings that litter the path. As I was returning to the Carlos Pension, two German cyclists called to me from a distance. We had met on the island of Rhodes but did not bike together at that time. Their photo taken of me on Santorini hopefully will be waiting for me when I arrive in Haifa in approximately two months.

My last day on Santorini took me to the northern part of the island to the small town of Oia, pronounced "Oheeah," where the barren cliffs along the shore attract a minimum of traffic. The road becomes a narrow two-lane path with a rough textured tarred surface. Natural formations of the land form innumerable small mesas upon which farming is done. On my left were sheer cliffs of red rock and volcanic black basalt. I stopped at regular intervals to enjoy the natural harbors in their untouched state. To my rear, Thira glistened in the sun.

Oia is a village with a square, bakery, mini-market, and a small restaurant. At the highest point a small Greek church, painted white with its blue roof, stands apart from the other structures. Motorcycles, motor scooters, and my Globetrotter attested to a certain amount of tourism.

Biking the 5-km, 300-meter descent to the port was difficult, especially with my heavy load. At one point I stopped to rest and enjoy the view. A tour bus coming up this tortuous road veered to his left in an attempt to negotiate the bend in the road. It then came to a stop. I was in the way. This bus driver reminded me of those in Israel who think they own the road, and perhaps the world. I tried to accommodate the driver as quickly as possible by mounting the bike and getting out of his way, but I wasn't quick enough for him. This irritable person began shouting epithets at me in Greek. By the time we passed each other, we were both shaking our fists.

Shortly thereafter, I was aboard the Da*liana* enroute to Piraeus, Greece.

Chapter 17
GREECE

The luxurious *Daliana* docked at the port of Piraeus, ten miles from Athens. With only a tiny map showing the location of the Athens hostel, I was again in unfamiliar territory. Piraeus is the main port of Greece as well as the site of "Never on Sunday." It's linked to Athens through an urban sprawl of factories and concrete apartment houses. To this uninitiated cyclo-tourist, the distance as well as the hills were more than expected, especially at such a late hour. Fortunately, most of the people I stopped to inquire concerning the best route into the city were fluent in English. By 11 PM, I located Omonia Square. Though warned about the pollution and intensity of traffic in Athens, I became excited. Friendly tourists at a campground in Italy tried to discourage me from visiting Athens in particular and Greece in general. They said, "If your time is limited, go to Turkey and avoid Greece. The air pollution in Athens in terrible."

A concerned couple on a motorcycle sensed my unfamiliarity with the area and offered to lead me from Omonia Square to the Athens hostel. I willingly accepted, arriving at midnight. I know this project would have been considerably more difficult without their assistance. I parked the Globetrotter in an area of a garage reserved for motorcycles and mopeds. The air and noise pollution from the small engines of these vehicles is the source of much of the problem.

"Do you have a bed on the first floor?" I asked the hostel attendant. The thought of carrying my gear to an upper level did not appeal, especially after my late arrival.

"You have biked all the way from Paris and are concerned about a few stairs. How come?" He didn't know that my 69-year-old knees did not like stairs. My assigned bed was located on the third floor, a strenuous walkup even for a person younger than myself. Two trips later I fell into bed.

My forewarning about the pollution proved to be an understatement. Fumes from auto emissions drifted into the hostel's open windows and the noise from motorcycles added to my discomfort to such an extent that I began to feel ill. Perhaps it was the contrast from the clean air of Rhodes, Crete, and Santorini, or maybe it was just my time to feel ill. I took refuge in an air-conditioned McDonald's, where a chocolate shake and Big Mac helped.

The purchase of a map of Athens plus a small guide book prepared me for my tour in spite of the "queasy" feeling in my gut.

In spite of the pollution, I spent the remainder of the day bicycle-touring Athens, a fantastic city. The view of the Acropolis from the center of the city is enough in itself to endear this very busy economic center of Greece. This is in spite of the attitude of the police. Finally, I found police more disagreeable than those in Israel. It didn't take long for me to learn that it's useless asking directions from them. Their reply, more often than not, is "Move on!"

The Temple of Olympian Zeus, begun in 174 B.C., located on the same level as the city, was my first historical site. By the year 125-130 A.D. construction was completed by Hadrian. He put a colossal statue of Zeus in the cella and a statue of himself of equal dimensions beside it. Sixteen of the original 104 columns are still standing. These columns are constructed of individual hollow sections, one placed upon the other until the completed column is in place, identical to those at the Greek temple in Agragento, Sicily. A Corinthian cap is then placed on the top. The sheer size of this temple makes it impressive. In spite of a continual feeling of fatigue and low-grade fever, I decided to visit the Acropolis.

From the center of Athens the climb to the Acropolis and the Parthenon appeared to be a challenge for the Globetrotter and me, but in actuality the gradual climb was not difficult. There stands the Parthenon, the most perfect and most magnificent ruin in the world, completed in 430 B.C. The literal meaning of Parthenon is "virgin's apartment."

In 1687 a bomb was thrown into the gunpowder magazines within the structure, rendering it a heap of ruins. Through the reconstruction program underway, every building block will eventually be put back in its original position. Unfortunately, the original statue of Athena was taken to Constantinople where it disappeared. Little wonder! The goddess was clad in a long dress of gold plate standing almost 12 meters high. Her hands and feet were ivory and the pupils of her eyes jewels. A Roman copy of Athena by Phidias is preserved in the National Archæological Museum.

Marty, a Californian, and I met outside the Parthenon following my conducted tour. She was resting on the steps prior to her luncheon date at the Agora and Roman Forum. A proctor for the State of California, Marty presides over the state board dental examinations. We had this in common. On her recommendation, I returned to the Tower of the Winds with the Acropolis in the background, making the scene perfect for picture taking. It was here that Socrates spent much of his time expounding his philosophy. In 49 A.D., Paul, intent on winning converts to Christianity, disputed and preached in the same area. I had difficulty visualizing this original center of classical Athens, the Agora, due to the condition of the ruins.

The National Archæological Museum, opened in 1874, is a treasure house of antiquity in spite of the pilferage by foreign archæologists. My first priority was the frescos found at Akrotiri, Thira (Santorini). In the second floor front room of the museum there is a collection of pottery found on the island of Thira. Beyond that room, the magnificence of the frescos is displayed.

These works of art are more varied and in a better state of preservation than those found on Crete. In addition to the lovely colors and harmony of design, they give an insight into the everyday life of the Minoans. On one of the frescos, two youths are boxing with only one hand gloved. Similar to the art of the Egyptians, the skill of perception was yet to be acquired. Though the bodies of the boxers are in profile, their faces are displayed "full view." A youth holding two strings of fish is another well-known Minoan masterpiece. Perhaps the most unusual fresco is one showing a flotilla of ships sailing from one coastal town to another. If the theory is correct concerning the retreat of the Minoans to their ships prior to the volcanic eruption on their island, these are the types of ships they employed. It is my understanding that the frescos will remain in Athens until a suitable museum is built on Thira.

After numerous tries, I finally made a telephone connection with Maggie and Ken Westwood, the English couple I met in a campground on the Adriatic in Italy. They received my letter from the Middle East and were looking forward to my visit in their new home in the mountains overlooking the Gulf of Corinth. Fortunately, the Westwoods were not traveling at that time. Maggie gave me directions to their villa in the mountains, but that did not get me out of Athens. I knew from her directions that I needed the Corinth Road once I exited the city toward the west. My compass as well as the map solved this problem nicely. Cycling was easy and downhill as we passed the port of Piraeus to the left. The ruins of the ancient city of Eleusis, built around the Sanctuary of Demeter, attracted my attention even though it was closed. I had the opportunity to rest for a few minutes in the shade and photograph the ruins prior to a gradual climb toward the mountains. On a level stretch of road, a car traveling in the opposite direction stopped. The driver obviously wanted to engage me in conversation. I discovered that the driver and his spouse are friends and neighbors of the Westwoods. Maggie and Ken asked them to watch for me and give me their telephone number. "You will soon encounter the mountains!" were their parting words.

The trucks and I shifted into our lowest gears when we hit the "wall." This was just about my "max," particularly after being ill. Two-thirds of the way to the summit, in sweltering heat, I unstrapped my fanny pack and leaned the Globetrotter against the side of the mountain. Using the pack as a pillow, I feel into a deep sleep for no less than fifty minutes. Upon awakening, the taverna at the summit became my escape from the intensity of the sun. I made a barely audible sound to the waiter, which he fortunately understood. The word was "Sprite." A few minutes later I recovered enough to start thinking about food. Ken Westwood was standing next to my table waiting for me to notice him. Knowing the severity of the mountains, he decided to come to the rescue with his station wagon. I was more than ready for this reunion.

Maggie, bubbly and gracious, made me feel at home immediately. She escorted me to the guest quarters, a separate building stocked with all the amenities I might want. The mountain air, free from Athens' noxious fumes, and the Westwoods' hospitality aided my recovery. We visited their friends and toured the mountains by car. When I discovered that my rear rim had fractured, I bussed back to Athens for a replacement. Ken picked me up at the bus stop on my return.

My "mission" prevented me from accepting the Westwoods' hospitality for a longer time. Turkey beckoned. Putting the Globetrotter in the wagon, Ken took me to the National Road following the coast north of Athens. The mountains were by this time reduced to gradual hills. I again felt fit and ready for additional adventure. Since that time the mailman has kept me in touch with this wonderful couple.

Entering the town of Livanantes, the shaft of my right pedal fractured, leaving me about three inches of remaining shaft to use as a pedal. We limped into a petrol station, a suitable place to consider the alternatives.

The driver of a van offered to drive me to a larger town nearby where he knew of a bicycle shop. I located a proper right pedal but with the wrong threads. The bike shop owner gave me a lift on his moped to the main road in the direction of the petrol station. I was then on my own. Auto-stopping became "mission impossible." Finally, in desperation, I approached a motorist, offering him payment in exchange for a ride back to my equipment. Perhaps they do not pick up hitchhikers in Greece. Now came the problem: I had the proper pedal but the wrong threads.

The steel threads of the pedal cut new threads into the alloy of the crank, creating a very tight fit that lasted for several months. Eventually when that pedal fell off outside Tel Aviv, the only solution was a new crank and new pedal. At least I was back on the road.

The port city of Volos was a bit of a misadventure. I was informed in Volos that I should take a ferry to the small island of Skiathos. At Skiathos a ferry would take me all the way north to Thessaloniki, the capital of Macedonia, a saving of many miles on my way to Turkey. In 1955 Volos was destroyed by earthquake but was rebuilt with sturdy earthquake-proof materials. The 2-1/2 hour ferry trip to the tiny island of Skiathos was well worth the ride even without a reason.

There are only two paved roads on Skiathos. My campground with an attached restaurant was at the end of the airport runway near the beach. Being early in the season, I was the only camper. Fortunately, the noise from the airplanes stops at dusk, leaving the isolated campground and beach my sole property. Except for a friendly English couple the following day, Terry and Maria from Worcestershire, I was alone. We walked the beach together and climbed the cliffs rising out of the sea. Departure time for the ferry to Thessaloniki was 1 PM.

It is not unusual for Greek ferries to go on strike. I was given the choice of waiting until the following Sunday or returning to Volos at my own expense. Although I liked Skiathos, I didn't want to be in the "isolation booth" for several days, especially with the possibility that the ferry would still be on strike. At the dock while waiting for the ferry, a cyclist and I became friendly. His money was stolen, leaving him with no funds to buy a return ticket to Volos. He appreciated my offer of assistance but did not accept. "Don't free-camp on the road toward Thessaloniki if you value your life," said my newest friend. "The Albanians crossing the border illegally into Greece have no money. They travel in bands and will rob and kill without any hesitation." He told me of his free-camping experience in which he could hear the voices of the Albanians, but fortunately they could not see him. This was the first time I actually feared humans.

In was 9 in the evening before I left Volos enroutc to the National Road, a strenuous climb, with no plans for my night's rest except that I knew not to free-camp. By the same token, I was in an isolated area with absolutely no hope of finding a hotel or campground. An iron ore smelter came into view on my right; the entire area was covered with red iron dust. A civilian sentry stood watch at the entrance while guard dogs patrolled the perimeter of the fenced-in property.

I asked permission to erect my tent inside the fence in addition to the use of their fresh-water hose. Number one was denied but number two was permitted. I erected my tent in the parking lot next to the fence. The workers' activity, the guard dogs, and the sentry gave me the peace of mind I needed. The only other choice was to bike through the night.

Following a restful sleep, I brushed the red dust off my tent. Using the cold-water hose for personal hygiene, I headed toward the National Road. It was 6 AM. With the wind at my back, cycling was easy as we headed toward the town of Larisa and a lunch stop. Larisa came and went without the much needed restaurant. Eventually I found a cafeteria to my liking, my only choice now that I was in farm country.

This particular day, the sun was intense, requiring frequent rest/drink stops. I tried to drink water whether I felt the need or not. At one point I remember experiencing the "bonk" with its resultant fatigue syndrome. Soon the tired feeling passed as we entered a gorge reminiscent of Franconia Notch in the White Mountains of New Hampshire. The entry in my photo log was so noted: the Franconia Notch of Greece.

Tour buses from nearby Athens and distant Czechoslovakia were visiting my Franconia Notch. Most of the people at the campground were of Czech origin. Grade deception was my only problem. Even though the grade appeared to be downhill, constant pedaling was required. Thessaloniki was now within 100 km of my campground, where the abundance of people, warm showers, and a mini-market made my night's stay enjoyable.

Ten kilometers north of the campground the next morning, having climbed a ferocious hill to the National Road, I instinctively reached back to verify the presence of my fanny pack. It wasn't there! I left it hanging on the door to the men's room with all my valuables inside. My passport, money, watch, and travelers checks were now in peril.

It is said that in Greece the people are so honest that a person could leave his wallet in the park at night and recover it untouched the next day. My experience may in some measure verify this statement. Returning to the wash house, I checked the contents of the pouch, strapped the belt around my waist, and headed back toward the National Road. This time, however, I found a gradual approach instead of the previous climb.

A 30-mph headwind persisted the entire day, requiring the lowest gear and a touring cyclist's mentality. Recollections from the book <u>Zen and the Art of Motorcycle Maintenance</u> helped pass the time, particularly after a sign announcing that for the next 70 km there would be no petrol or food. In addition to the wind and an empty stomach, the sun was punishing. A littered parking lot served as my impromptu lunch stop. I also stopped for refreshment at a cantina on wheels in the middle of absolutely nowhere. My throat was parched, and this was the last oasis before Thessaloniki.

Exhausted beyond description, I arrived at the city at 7 in the evening after 110 km of pedaling. I realized I was becoming faint and unstable on the bike. The most sensible action was immediate rest before even considering food or drink. A doorstep was my haven for as long as it was necessary to recover my strength and thought processes.

The Greek Youth Hostel, with excellent facilities, is centrally located in Thessaloniki. My room on the second floor was a slight improvement over the hostel in Athens. A warm shower and additional food helped ease some of the pain of the day's tortuous ride.

Thessaloniki, with a population of 406,500, is the second largest city in modern Greece. It was so named in 316 B.C. by a Macedonian general whose wife was a half-sister of Alexander the Great. In 1492, some 20,000 Jewish exiles from the Spanish Inquisition settled here, bringing their skills in trade and craftsmanship with them. By the 16th century, Jews constituted the major portion of Thessaloniki's population. Hitler and the Nazis changed all this. During World War II, 46,000 Jews were sent to their death at Auschwitz. Like so many territories today, Macedonia is looking forward to its independence.

A vexing problem to Greece is the formation of a new state in what previously was known as Yugoslavia. These people want their new country to be named Macedonia, generating a "call to arms" by the Greek Macedonians. I was aware of a northerly movement of tanks and motorized equipment during the time I was fighting the wind on the highway.

Alan Donnelly and I became friends at the restaurant across the street from the hostel. We talked for hours. He has plans to live in Thessaloniki with his daughter. In preparation for this move, she is learning Greek back in Liverpool, England. His son, with musical talent, though not Jewish, is studying at a Jewish school in the city. Alan gave me an insight into this city with Thessaloniki's own character, rather than it being a carbon copy of Athens.

Thessaloniki was destroyed by fire in the 1920s. It was rebuilt with wide streets, numerous parks, and a fairgrounds. The lovely promenade along the waterfront provides a lane reserved for bicyclists. Thessaloniki boasts a restaurant atop a tower in the park. The White Tower Museum, a very fine Byzantine museum, was once of dubious reputation. By order of the Sultan in 1826 many dissidents were massacred at the Bloody Tower, as it was called.

At one time Thessaloniki was second in importance to Constantinople, now known as Istanbul. It was a center for the minting of coins. The present port was built by Constantine the Great during the 4th century A.D. Romans, Goths, Slavs, Muslims, Franks, and Normans have either plundered or built, or both, on this strategic site at the head of the Thermaic Gulf.

Leaving Thessaloniki was not easy, especially with all signs written in Greek. A motorcycle couple from Milan, Italy, and I discussed the matter but we did not come to any firm conclusions. I decided to follow my compass as in the past when in doubt. This time I could have done better. A lot better!

I finally found a divided highway but without a nearby access road. Pushing the Globetrotter through the weeds and then a fence, I was finally on hard surface only to discover that we were heading south. At the first exit we reversed direction and headed east toward the town of Panorama in the mountains. The name Panorama should have given me a clue. Soon we were on the same level as a military radar station perched on top of the mountain overlooking Thessaloniki. For a moment I thought I was back in Israel with its mountaintop installations. At 2 PM, several hours after my departure from the city, I saw a sign that read Thessaloniki 15 km. In a linear direction I could have walked more quickly to the National Road. At Panorama this Sunday afternoon I decided to do what the citizens were doing: treat myself to an ice cream delight. Then came the descent.

The grade down the mountain was so severe that I felt I was endangering myself, especially with my heavy load. For the first 10 km I kept my left foot out of the toeclip just in case of a fall. My speed down the hill equalled my speed during the climb. Cars gave me as much latitude as required. Finally the road began to level off as I headed east with a tailwind. Making up time was now easy. In the late afternoon, signs began to appear indicating campgrounds nearby. The first available campground, though a bit primitive, was my choice.

The wooded mountains to the north and the beach to the west were almost too inviting, especially after my heroic "Panoramic" experience. I felt like staying on for a day or so to recover.

Until I arrived at Havala, there was little to write in my journal except "this was a day of biking." A fleet of flatbed trucks carrying military tanks passed me and then I passed them. Finally they passed me. These tanks were being transported to a site where they were converted to diesel. At an intersection, trucks were directed to the left and cars to the right, both going to Havala on the sea. Perhaps I should have taken the truck road where the hills were less steep. Diesel exhaust from trucks, however, is always a deterrent. The scenic route, though challenging, was worth the effort. The two roads converge within sight of the picturesque city of Havala, with its port the center of activity. Camping Irini, a large and comfortable camp on the water, was an excellent choice.

Jon Weber, a camp inspector, and I became acquainted, spending most of the evening in his caravan discussing Turkey. Being very knowledgeable of Turkey, Jon cautioned me about the mountains. "Between Alexandroupolis and Istanbul you will have to cross a chain of mountains," reported Jon. I began to wonder if my biking days were coming to an end, relying on bus transportation henceforth. Jon, being Dutch, was willing to talk about Turkey, in contrast to the Greek people. When I speak to Greek citizens, telling them of my plans to go to Turkey, they turn their backs and walk away. Jon and I talked until 1 o'clock in the morning.

The following day, except for a restaurant, I was traveling in farm country following the coastline. At times the road was dirt and at times hardtop. Stopping at a store in late afternoon, I replenished my breakfast supplies in preparation for the possiblity of free-camping in a safe area. At dusk an empty factory used for the storage of newly harvested grain was a good choice. George, the night watchman, agreed to my camping under cover of the building. With the dogs and George, I felt safe. Huge John Deere Harvesters drive into the yard where they empty their grain into sacks to be stored in the warehouse after their departure.

I looked for a campground with adequate facilities in Alexandroupolis. The city was only 48 km away. The terrain was variable, with some long climbs that did not require walking. Finally the sea was within view as we entered Alexandroupolis, with a campground within the city limits. The convenience of being in the city made restaurants and sightseeing easy.

Alexandroupolis, with a population of 34,000, is a modern busy city with ferry service to the island of Samothrace. Heavy military presence is immediately noticeable. In addition to being the capital of the prefecture, its proximity to Turkey justifies its existence. I would have taken the two-hour ferry ride to Samothrace where the Winged Victory, now permanently housed in the Louvre, was found, but no one had particularly good things to say about the island.

The previous day I met a 62-year-old cyclist from Sweden dressed in bathing trunks and no shirt to cover his enormous belly. With no toeclips, he did not look like your everyday touring cyclist. Every year he tours on his 10-speed bicycle.

At the campground, another 62-year youngster just came from Turkey on his bike. He spoke of danger from the Kurds as well as the fifteen tourists shot by the Kurds. The more I heard about this huge country, the more confused I became. "If your time is limited, go to Turkey instead of Greece." "Beware of the mountains in Turkey." "Watch out for the Kurds. They can be dangerous." I decided to bike to the border 40 km distant and, if possible, bike to Istanbul. From there perhaps this enigma would clarify itself.

From Alexandroupolis to the Turkish border, the cycling is relatively easy. The road divides the fields on either side. As signs begin to appear indicating the forthcoming border, I became more and more excited. Sjefud Vyver, the Dutch cyclist I met the previous day, arrived at the border at approximately the same time as I. We planned to meet again at a rest stop on the Turkish side.

Customs was uneventful. I changed $150 into Turkish lire and became an instant millionaire. It was now lunchtime. I enjoyed a sandwich and Pepsi at a cafeteria operated by the Turkish military for about $2.50. It was strange to be served by soldiers but apparently, that's the way it's done. At the Tourist Information I was given a map of Turkey and some excellent brochures printed in English. I then congratulated myself for having arrived this far on my journey, with anticipation of more to come.

Saint Sophia
Turkey

Chapter 18
TURKEY

Sjefud Vyver and I met as planned at the first fresh water stop inside the Turkish border. He was heading south and I east toward Istanbul. This 62-year young cyclist appeared happy and strong. He had bicycle toured in Turkey on several previous occasions.

A strong headwind as well as hills resembling the Appalachians of Pennsylvania made my progress slower than usual. In Pennsylvania the roads are straight and the hills endless, averaging one or two miles per hill. Just before the crest of each hill the pedaling miraculously becomes easier. The difference between Turkey and Pennsylvania is the condition of the road surface. A better word than pothole might be "porthole." This two-lane hard-surfaced highway has a gravel shoulder on either side. Tractors and farm machinery passed me on the right using the shoulder. At one point a group of Albanian children walking on the gravel escaped the angry wheels of a tractor by jumping to safety. In spite of these conditions, I felt gratified in being able to live this experience. The hills are miles long and the road straight as a string except in the mountains where switchbacks provide some variety.

Signs began to appear directing me to a campground on the Marmara, a body of water that extends beyond Istanbul to the east and the Aegean to the west. A dirt road dropped precipitously to the campground below, making my descent a harrowing experience. I convinced myself I would not be able to return to the main road the next morning without assistance. We coasted at a snail's pace. My left foot out of the toeclip, I was prepared for the worst. This was my first experience with Turkish hospitality: a father and son team insisted on helping me set up my tent. They then introduced me to the local dry red wine and shish-ka-bob. Their neighbor, the owner of a truck, offered to assist in the five kilometer climb up the hill in the morning.

At 7:30 the next morning the only person stirring was myself. Where was my friend with the truck? In reality, the climb was easier than expected. Istanbul was still more than 100 km to the east.

Following the relatively flat shore road, cycling was easy, but the Pennsylvania-like hills returned inland. At one point at the base of the longest climb, I stopped to rest, borrowing a chair at a tire repair station. Sleep came instantly! Feeling refreshed, I began to challenge the grade, holding my breath while diesel trucks blew exhaust in my face. Except for a water stop along the road, I did not feel the need to dismount. It is said that the water at campgrounds in Turkey may be contaminated, but out of a pipe at the side of the road it is pure. At no time did I find it otherwise.

Two interesting companions at my lunch stop, one French and the other Turkish, demonstrated once again the friendship of these people. Both work for a liquid gas company importing gas from Algeria. Raif Turegum, the Turk, was particularly concerned about my safety on the road, especially on the weekend when traffic is especially heavy. He asked me to send him a postcard from an interesting place. This was the identical request made by my little friend Sagiv, living in the Golan at Katzrin.

The closer I came to Istanbul, the more intense became the traffic and the higher the hills. Finally, truck traffic was so heavy that I opted for the auto route. In Turkey as in Mexico, diesel trucks blow their exhaust to the right, bathing bikers and pedestrians in a haze of smog. It reminded me of my Navy days aboard the LCT 1112 with her three diesel Gray Marine engines. The condition of the road added to my discomfort with the huge "portholes" and patched surface, making steering difficult. Constant vigilance was required.

Within the city limits of Istanbul-Edirene, the Londra Camping entrance demanded investigation even though I had decided to stay in a hotel in the center of the city as an added convenience. There, located on the main road into Istanbul, I discovered a beautiful campground with an excellent restaurant, a free kitchen for use by campers, and hot water showers. Twenty-four hour security was also included. My plans were immediately altered when I learned that transportation into the center of the city, a distance of 15 miles, is convenient and inexpensive. I still had thoughts of biking to the center of the city until my experimental ride on Route 100 East. A bicycle and the incredible mix of traffic on that road is nothing less than a death wish.

Istanbul traffic can be compared with the New Jersey Turnpike, with the added confusion of buses and mini-buses darting in and out to pick up passengers. To my dismay and a near disaster, the open rear door of a bus almost picked me off the road. Side vision compensated for the added width of the bus, but I had no concept of a door extending beyond that width. Last, but not least, my front tire went flat.

The flat tire was probably my salvation, forcing me to exit Route 100 to a safe haven along the side of the road. Two young men assisted me in changing the tire, and helped me carry the Globetrotter up the stairs to a pedestrian overpass to the opposite side of the highway where I headed back to Londra Camping. The experiment was over.

My evening was spent with a family of Australians camping next to me. I could not wait to meet the female belonging to the lingerie hanging on their line. I was not disappointed! She, a dainty and sexy nurse, could outcuss a longshoreman. In the morning this family, consisting of the father, son, and daughter Susan with the lingerie, were on their way to the airport and Paris, clothesline and all.

For 4,000 lire, a mini-bus delivered me to the transportation terminus named Topkopi Cannon Gate, not to be confused with Topkopi Palace, where for an additional 4,000 lire

a tram goes to downtown Istanbul. This was my second introduction to Turkey's transportation system, where the bus is the
major source of long-distance travel. Huge immaculately maintained buses worm their way without incident into designated
berths through crowds of people and animals. The bus driver
occupies a highly respected position in society, along with at
least one standing member of his crew responsible for the maintenance and internal cleanliness of the bus. Others are assigned
to washing the windows and/or the entire bus. For the most
part, these privately operated buses look as though they've just
come off the assembly line.

Merchandise and services, both indoors and on the
street, are offered by people of all ages. To an outsider, this
maze of people, animals, buses, and vendors may seem like a
zoo, but each person involved knows his or her position on the
team. Even the person with a container of water or beverage
on his back provides a valuable function serving the public. I
found the fake Izod socks especially interesting. Someone in
this system is sewing fake alligators onto socks so thin that a
fingernail will damage them. The other person is hawking them
as the genuine item.

For centuries, Constantinople, now Istanbul, was the
center of the civilized world. This metropolis of ten million
people is the business and cultural center of Turkey despite the
fact that Ankara is the capital. It is the first destination of tourists intent on learning about the culture of this complex nation.

The Blue Mosque built by Sultan Ahmet was a good
place to begin exploring Istanbul. The mosque gains its name
from the Iznik tiles that line the walls of this structure, built
between 1606 and 1616. We tourists, separated from the worshipers, entered through a side door where an attendant checked
our shoes. Robes are loaned to those inappropriately attired.

The following day, instead of taking the tramway, I
stayed on the bus taking me from Londra Camping to Topkopi,

thinking that I would again find the Blue Mosque. This is how I discovered the Bosporus and the Golden Horn. The Bosporus connects the Sea of Marmara to Asia by way of the Black Sea. Now ten kilometers from the Blue Mosque, I began asking questions about the return ride. While walking, a sign to a Turkish bath gave me an idea. Before leaving Turkey, I promised myself the hedonistic pleasure of a steam bath. The Hippodrome, the Obelisk taken from Karnak Temple in Egypt, and the magnificent cathedral of St. Sophia were now within walking distance.

In Greek, Hagia Sophia means the Church of the Divine Wisdom, built by Emperor Justinian and completed in 548 as an effort to restore the greatness of the Roman Empire. St. Peter is larger than Aya Sophia but it was built more than 1,000 years later. When Justinian entered the completed church, he is quoted as saying "Glory to God that I have been worthy of such a work. Oh Solomon! I have outdone you."

The cathedral was sacked when the Crusaders came through Turkey. Then when the Muslims conquered the city it was turned into a mosque. The mosaics representing human figures were plastered over. Now, however, since St. Sophia is a national historic site, the mosaics have been partially uncovered.

A special exhibit of Islamic art and porcelain was being shown at the lower level of St. Sophia by the artist N. Hur Avlupinar, a beautiful young woman. She enjoys the reputation of being the number one ceramist in all of Turkey. I had the good fortune of meeting and photographing this lovely and modest person. Born in 1966, N. Hur Avlupinar began exhibiting her work in 1984. Her costume was as decorative as her ceramics. I felt privileged to have been at the right place at the right time.

The following morning I was on my way by bus to Cappadocia, the region between Ankara and the Black Sea.

The Globetrotter and equipment were securely stored at Londra Camping. Cappadocia was once the center of the Hittite Empire, becoming a vast Roman province at a later date. Mentioned in the Bible, Cappadocia is today one of Turkey's most popular tourist areas. The moonscape of the town of Urgup and Goreme Valley were a wonderful experience. Rock-hewn churches, fairy chimneys created by erosion and wind, in which dwellings are hollowed out of rock, as well as huge underground cities of the Christians are but a part of Cappadocia's charm. Carpet making and selling is another attraction of the Goreme Valley that brings tourists from all over the world. The all-silk prayer rugs are particularly interesting. When tossed in a cartwheel fashion, the colors of the rug change from dark to light and back again. These handmade treasures were one-third the prices in Istanbul. They are so reasonable that in Istanbul the rug dealers doubted my word when I told them what I paid.

Bargaining is part of the Turkish culture. When I stated the top price I could afford for my two choices, the dealer added five dollars. He said: "This is not my price and it is not your price. In this way we have each arrived at a fair price." The deal was then closed. This included the cost of shipping to the US. I knew I had found a bargain.

The bus that brought me to Cappadocia was a like-new luxury bus with two attendants. Drinking water is provided upon request. At three in the morning we had a pit stop. Cafeteria-style food as well as souvenirs were offered at reasonable prices. Everyone kept his or her eye on the driver so that no one would be left behind. He was busy devouring a complete meal. During that time an attendant was busy washing the exterior of the bus. When we returned to our seats, the attendants provided warm dampened towels and a liquid skin refresher. At five after eight some of us took a taxi and then a mini-bus to Goreme where our Cappadocian adventure began.

The history of Cappadocia began with the eruption of

two volcanoes spreading ash called tufa over the region. The tufa hardened into soft porous stone. Over time, wind, water, and sand wore away portions of the tufa, carving it into the present unusual shapes that are unique to Cappadocia. Boulders caught in the porous stone protected the tufa from further erosion, the final result being a cone of tufa with a boulder perched on top. The interior portion was easily removed even with primitive tools, creating a dwelling space within. When the Mongols invaded the area, the inhabitants of Cappadocia went underground, building entire cities beneath the earth's surface. Then the Christians, newly arrived to the area, discovered they could create their churches by the same means, making them safe from the invaders by rolling stone wheel-doors across the entrance. The wheels resemble millstones with a hole created on one side of the door. The insertion of a wooden pole facilitates the opening and closing of the wheel-doors.

The underground cities were used only during the time of invasion from the enemy. As many as seven different levels were excavated, with an elaborate system of ventilation that brings fresh air to all levels. The animals were kept on the first level, with the areas for worship and communal meetings on the lowest level. There were no stairs to join one level to another. Instead, foot and hand crevices were dug out of the side of the walls. Cooking was done in a central kitchen where food for as many as 500 people was prepared at one time. The food was then taken to the individual apartments. Each apartment had its own toilet and sleeping quarters. Human and animal excretion were mixed together and used to fertilize the fields. An artificial mountain was then built over the entrance to the city to camouflage it. Cooking was done only at night, so the smoke created by the fires went undetected by the enemy.

Our guide explained that the lovely poplar groves in the valleys provide a specific need to the inhabitants starting at birth. Upon the birth of a child, a poplar grove is planted in his or her honor. When life's events begin to unford, such as the forthcoming marriage of that individual, some of the poplars

2 WHEELS, 2 YEARS, AND 3 CONTINENTS

are cut and sold to pay for the wedding. The last three trees are not cut until the death of the owner of the grove. These trees when cut are sold and reserved to pay for the funeral.

The Mongols, a mixture of Asiatic and Turkish people, invaded the area, desecrating much of the Christian art within the cave churches. The eyes of the Apostles, Christ Jesus, Mary, and John the Baptist were obliterated. Except for the eyes, the frescos were left undamaged. We were looking at frescos from the Old and New Testaments on opposite sides of the apse. Within the chapel, holes dug out of the tufa provided for pigeons laying eggs. Pigeons were sacred to the Christians.

A small town named Mustafapasa was an Ottoman Greek town before World War I. When repatriated, the property was assigned to the resident Turks. An old Greek house, now a hotel, is owned by Suleyman Ozturk; it was given to his father by the Turkish government. Suleyman was kind enough to pose for a photograph.

Across the street from the hotel, the preliminaries to a marriage were underway at the groom's home. Neither the bride or groom were present. The groom was receiving his ceremonial "shave." The wedding was to be held two days later, on Sunday. We were invited to join in the festivities.

We were soon dancing with family members and guests to the music of a two-piece combo of drum and clarinet. A beverage called *ayran*, a mixture of yogurt and water, satisfied our thirst. The hospitality of these people is typical of the Turks we met previously. Our tour ended at 7:30 watching the sun set over Sunset Valley.

My last day in Cappadocia was spent walking and biking. A rental mountain bike gave me the opportunity to do some touring on my own, while walking brought me to the Open Air Museum two kilometers from Goreme. Sixteen churches are located here in what is now a controlled historic site. Even though some of the churches were closed, this sun-baked area offers visitors the opportunity to climb on the rocks leading to the church entrances or staying on the level ground where other churches and their frescos are abundant. Since the interior of the churches are caves, the worshipers painted domes on the cave ceilings to give the appearance of the conventional dome. An actual dome ceiling was often carved in the rock before being painted. In one building a kitchen, larder, and refectory were carved from the tufa. The table, perhaps fifteen feet long, was of stone, with stone benches on either side. The depression in the refectory floor provided for grape pressing. A hole at the bottom of the depression and a channel carried the juice to a different location where it was processed into wine.

At 5 AM we were awakened by the bus attendant: "You are in Bursa." It was too early to do anything but sleep. I then thought of the perfect solution to this minor problem: go to a Turkish bath! A young French-speaking policeman directed me to a hotel referred to as a *caravanserai* with a Turkish bath. The modern-day hotel is the probable equivalent of the stopping place for caravans of yesteryear. I set off in that direction. A few minutes later a police car stopped alongside me. The French-speaking officer invited me into the car. Shortly thereafter we were at the entrance to the baths, renovated in 1522 by Sultan Suleiman the Magnificent on the site of the original baths built by Justinian. I feel certain that no baths at a caravanserai would compare with this one, in continuous operation since 1522.

After checking my belongings, except for soap and bath sponge, I wrapped myself in a large towel and entered the main arena with a large pool and separate bathing stations. Thermal water direct from the mountains provides the warmth and steam needed. Frigid mountain water is the source of the cold water. A huge glass dome centered over the pool admits natural light. There I met a 25-year-old Turk living near Goreme. An airplane mechanic, he was visiting his family in Bursa. We struck up an immediate conversation in English. He taught me the proper etiquette and procedure necessary for total enjoyment of the baths. Following a thorough washing, we entered the hot room heated solely by thermal mountain water. Three men were beating their bodies with switches made of pine boughs. We did likewise until the heat became so intense that it was necessary to retreat to a cooler climate. Why do people beat themselves with these branches? I used pine boughs in Montreal and oak branches in Leningrad, but did not know the significance except that circulation is improved when the blood is brought to the surface of the skin, aiding in cleansing the pores. The subliminal reason may be that the beating takes one's mind off the pain inflicted by the steam.

Following our retreat from the steam room, I refreshed myself with cool water before retiring to one of the relaxation rooms. A deep sleep was almost instantaneous.

Bursa, with a population of one million, was the first capital of the Ottoman Empire. Modern Turkish culture predating 200 B.C. began in this city. Thermal baths and the silk trade created interest in this 155 meter-high city. I felt relieved that the Globetrotter was safely parked in Istanbul where the terrain is flat.

A taxi took me to the Great Mosque of Bursa, Ulu Cami, with the dome of the mosque composed of twenty separate small domes and a sadirvan (ablutions fountain) in the center. Completion of the mosque occurred in 1396. I was in the center of the Old City, within walking distance of the silk and fruit markets. I unsuccessfully searched in the silk market for my Pension Arit roommate; Debbie's boyfriend is employed in one of the stores there. While looking for her, I had the opportunity to see silk in its many forms. There were bolts of silk cloth as well as the finished products for both sexes and for all occasions.

The raising of silkworms is a cottage industry in Bursa. Each April the villagers purchase the silkworms from their cooperatives and take them home to feed on mulberry leaves. After a month the worms spin their cocoons and are ready for a trip to the Silk Cocoon Caravanserai. There is a second harvest of the cocoons in September.

The nearby covered fruit market displays fresh produce in an artistic manner, creating one huge mosaic of color with perfect fruit and vegetables of every variety. This was obviously the growing season. I then headed toward the Green Mosque, dating to 1426, with twelve tombs dating from the 1400s to the 1500s. The beautiful Iznik tile work in the mosque makes it a must for the tourist.

Many of the other worthwhile sights in Bursa, are closed to the public on Mondays. Rather than stay over one more day, I decided to head back to Istanbul and Londra Camping, giving me 45 days to find my way back to Haifa. Since Bursa is known as the site of the origination of shish-ka-bob, I decided to experience the original before leaving. The meat is sliced from a rotisserie similar to shishlik and is served on toasted pita bread with tomatoes, yogurt, and hot peppers. It is called *Isakender Kebap*.

The end of the tram line in Istanbul is two stops beyond Sultan Ahmet. There the trains with their Olympic 2000 signs and a very busy port attract businesses and tourists. My intention was out of necessity. I needed more innertubes. It was also an interesting area to visit, within walking distances of places I knew. I could have covered much more distance in less time with the Globetrotter. Fortunately, one shop stocked Presta valve tubes. Now that I was again well stocked with replacement tubes, I decided to take a cruise on the Bosporus, starting at the nearby pier. It was enjoyable becoming a conventional tourist.

The cruise on the wide Bosporus was pleasureable but not exciting. Many expensive homes and hotels are situated along this shore, including the Palace Hotel offering only suites at $3,000 per night. We passed a public school that has graduated many of Turkey's leaders. Two of the sightseers on our craft were native-born Israelis living in Jerusalem. Dani Merovach, an accountant at the Moriah Hotel, asked me to contact him when I return to Israel.

Our boat docked at Rumelihisari, a castle built by Mehmet to control traffic on the Bosporus. We walked the grounds there and admired the natural setting that Istanbul enjoys. We then returned to our original mooring, boarded a mini-bus, and drove to Istanbul's covered market, the Egyptian Spice Market. The scent of spices permeated the air. By this time our group was rather cohesive, but this was short-lived. Following the tour of the Spice Market, the mini-bus dropped each of us off nearest our individual transportation needs.

A tour of Istanbul is not complete without a visit to Topkapi Palace in the Old City, next to Aya Sofya. The Palace is recognized as one of the world's great museums. For almost three centuries this was the residence of the Sultans. Mehmet built the first palace in 1453 and the last emperor of the Ottoman Empire to live here was Mahmut II (1808-39). After Mahmut the sultans preferred to live in European-style palaces.

In addition to my slides, the set I purchased add greatly to my collection. The opulence of the sultans and calefs is beyond belief. I wonder how the poor people got along during those times. I'm sure they did not sit on golden thrones or have solid gold candlesticks six feet high studded with jewels. By wandering about, I visited most of the Palace open to the public. The Bagdad Pavilion is perhaps my favorite, particularly due to its location overlooking the Bosporus and the Golden Horn. The interior dome and the subtle tile decorations are among the most beautiful Islamic art that I've seen in Turkey.

A display of carriages used by royalty occupies the Imperial Stables. The collection of Japanese and Chinese porcelains is enormous. "The Silk Road" Chinese porcelain collection numbers 12,000 pieces. Tea sets in solid silver, a silver bird cage, a model of a mosque, a pheasant, and a huge silver eagle are but a few examples of the silver. A silver vase 2-1/2 to 3 feet in height with silver wheat in the vase is extremely impressive. The European Glass collection includes Bohemian glass, Irish crystal, Russian drinking sets, and Venetian glass. Istanbul glassware and porcelain imitated European craftsmanship. The Sultans' costumes and embroideries include silk embroidered barber aprons, towels, and tablecloths ornately decorated. Nearby, 370 pieces are on display in the watch and clock collection. The clocks are of European and Turkish manufacture dating from the 18th to the 20th centuries.

Visitors are asked to respect the holiness of the Holy Relics, where items relating to Mohammed are preserved. Such items as a casket containing hairs from the Prophet, soil from His tomb, one of His teeth, and His sword represent some of the items.

My final exposure to Turkish culture in Istanbul was a visit to the Istanbul Archæological Museum, which received the 1992 award for excellence in Europe. The Alexander Sarcophagus is protected by plexiglas. It is decorated with fighting scenes on horseback and on foot. Figures are both clothed and nude. The killing of lions, fallen horses, and fallen men dominate the scenes. Alexander the Great (356-323 B.C.) died in Babylon at age 33. Known as a great military leader as well as a political figure, he was respected and revered by those he conquered as well as by the Greeks. An interesting sculpture exhibit of Roman emperors, judges, and athletes exemplify the realism and individual features of these people. I felt as though I was among the living!

A final comment on Istanbul: this city impressed me as being both European and Third World. Train service, except for the tramway, is poor, while bus service is superb. The presence of the buses definitely contributes to the pollution and congestion of the city. Even at Londra Camping, I could smell fumes from the road. The Turkish food is tasty and reasonably priced. Pork is absent in the ordinary restaurants. The food is spicy and bread is abundant. Summer days are warm and the nights cool. I was ready to move on.

The management at Londra gave me directions to Istanbul and the ferry, avoiding the main highway into the city. I pedaled along the water on an excellent road. Traffic was light in the early afternoon. Promenades, parks, and gardens made the ride a delight. Finding my ferry was quite easy. I purchased a ticket for Bandirma and headed into Istanbul for the last time. Departure time at 8 PM gave me exactly four hours before sailing in the direction of Gallipoli of World War I significance.

I then learned that *gulhane* is "zoo" in Turkish, and the word for "park" is *hayvanat*. Hayvanat Bahcesi was a good place to hang out near the *gulhane* until boarding time. I ordered a coke and began to do some serious reading.

Engin and I met for the first time on the way to the Bandirma pier. He is an industrial design student riding his mountain bike to his parents' summer residence in the shore resort town of Altinoluk. We were both headed for Bandirma. This blond, blue-eyed youth speaks perfect English. He resembles a European more than those living on or near the Mediterranean. Engin was not burdened with clothing or toilet articles; he had ridden long distances before and preferred to travel light. We became instant friends even though he was young enough to be my grandson. By coincidence, we sat next to his high school philosophy teacher on the ferry. She is an attractive 45-year-old woman traveling with her son. Engin quietly informed me that there is a father and husband back in Istanbul. The ferry docked at Bandirma at midnight. Engin and I discussed our plans for the night.

At his suggestion we decided to spend the night at the

Bandirma bus station. There we would be in a safe area with toilet facilities. A chair or two could serve as a bed until our early morning departure. Engin led the way. We, unfortunately, did not find any appealing places to "sack out," especially with the bright fluorescent lights overhead, nor did we know we were being observed by the local police.

A young officer asked us if we'd like to sleep in the police station, a small area within the bus depot. He assured us that our equipment as well as ourselves would be safe there. We could also turn out the lights. Engin explained to me privately that this invitation was extended to foreigners, not Turks.

I inflated my air mattress, put it on top of the ground cover, and unzipped my sleeping bag so Engin and I could share the bag as though it were a blanket. We then settled in for the night, or so we thought. The mosquitoes had no intentions of permitting us that luxury as they "dive bombed" to make their kill. Remembering my electric Raid device, I discovered that it would fit the electric wall outlets in Turkey as well as in Egypt where I bought it. Opening the foil-sealed package, I put a fresh tablet in the appliance, inserted the device into an outlet, and fell into a deep sleep.

Engin headed for Altinoluk to the south and I toward Bigma and Gallipoli to the east. At our breakfast stop, I accepted his invitation to visit him and his family in Altinoluk. The only problem was that I didn't know when that would be. In addition to Gallipoli, I wanted to see Troy at the approximate halfway point to Altinoluk.

Fortunately, the wind was at my back the next day, assisting in climbing the ever increasing hills that follow the Marmara. A truck driver at a restaurant/picnic area offered to take me and the Globetrotter to Canakkale, a distance of about 50 km. I tried to explain that wherever possible I prefer to pedal. He waved as we passed on the road.

At a rest stop at Lapseki, the owner of a coffee house helped me plan my next step. He recommended the ferry for Gallipoli. "From there you can bike to Cennet Camping, 20 km to the south, before dark," said Hussain, the coffee house owner. I took his advice. Cennet in Turkish means "paradise." The owners were friendly, but not effusively so. I met a German family there who invited me to have tea with them. We spent a pleasant evening discussing Gallipoli and its history.

Anzac Beach, at the eastern tip of the peninsula, was my next destination. Anzac stands for the Australian and New Zealand Army Corps, defeated by the Turks in World War I. In spite of the years that have passed, relatives from Australia and New Zealand still return to the graves.

Gallipoli National Park covers most of the peninsula and all the significant battle sites. Anzac Cove is about 3 km from the coast. where the ill-fated Allied landing was made on April 25, 1915. At the advice of Winston Churchill, an unsuccessful naval attempt was made to bring supplies through the Dardanelles to Russia. An estimated 33,000 Commonwealth troops,mainly Australians and New Zealanders, died in the nine-month land campaign following the sinking of the British fleet.

The modern, perhaps octagonal, Gallipoli Museum has a memorial sculpture dedicated to the fallen on both sides and relics of the battle. More than 500,000 Turkish soldiers fought here, with over 300,000 casualties. Some 86,000 Turks died, as did 43,000 British and Dominion troops. There was little point in visiting all the graves and monuments, with the exception of Anzac Cove. I had no personal involvement with the battle. Crosses and Stars of David were represented at one particular gravesite; these fallen soldiers were Australian.

Had I known, I might not have done a round-trip to Troy from my campsite at Canakkale. The wind, heat, and hills were beyond belief—one way would have been sufficient. Five kilometers east of the main road lay the ruins of ancient Troy.

I expected to see a living town in addition to the ruins, but there was none. A replica of the Trojan Horse welcomed me to a site where nine superimposed cities were built. This is the location, in Homer's Iliad, of the battle in the 13th century B.C., where the beautiful Helen, wife of Menelaus, was captured by Paris. Using my guide book, I tried to become interested in the history of ancient Troy, where the last layered city was built by Rome. The Romans finally abandoned Troy in favor of Constantinople as their eastern capital. I found it difficult to kindle an interest in what was now merely remnants of the ruins. The story of Helen of Troy is mythical, with a basis of truth. History has shown that the Trojan Wars lasted ten years and that there is evidence of an actual Trojan Horse.

The cobblestones of the town of Ezine forced me to dismount and walk the city street until it returned to the previous "corrugated" hardtop surface. Progress was slow. Around one in the afternoon two VW campers passed me, one bearing Canadian plates. Both VWs turned into a nearby restaurant. "In all likelihood the occupants know this to be a good restaurant, and if not, at least I'll have some company." I was anxious to meet English-speaking people. One young couple was New Zealanders touring Turkey on their own. They met the other couple, Canadians, at a previous campground and were now traveling with them. The husband, the former number two bicycle racing champion of New Zealand, quit racing because he didn't have the ability to become number one. "Have you considered bicycle touring?" I asked.

"If I cannot be number one, I do not want to bike!"

The Canadian couple was a totally different breed. John, an obese and disagreeable person, claims to be a psychologist. For unknown reasons, he took great joy in baiting me at every opportunity. His "less than charming" wife fit the same pattern. Unfortunately, I came in contact with this couple on three separate occasions, each one more unpleasant than the previous. It was after the third encounter that I decided that

John the Canadian was truly a "Turd on the Road."

The only reason I can think of for his confrontational attitude is that he was jealous of my ability to bicycle at my age, while he, much younger, could at most "waddle" in and out of his camper. During my entire journey, John the Canadian was my only disgusting and disagreeable human encounter. The New Zealanders shared my opinion. After the second meeting with the "Turd on the Road" they abandoned John.

The descent to the sea was breathtaking; it was my longest and steepest drop in elevation thus far. The Globetrotter's brakes began talking just prior to the odor of burning rubber. It was time to stop or suffer the consequences of a blowout. A panoramic view was an ideal place to take a break and give the rims a saliva test. They were too hot to touch. A group of French tourists on a bus at the "view" was immediately interested in me and my tandem. They were excited to learn I had started my tour in Paris and that I spoke limited French. I felt a bit like the Pied Piper.

There was no need to seek Engin's address once I arrived in Altinoluk; the Globetrotter did it for me. Engin had alerted all his young friends to watch for a tandem ridden by a solo rider, and if seen, they were to notify him immediately. It was great sport to hear my name shouted from a distance. Engin and I had an exciting reunion. I was introduced to his mother, brother, and friends. His father, a chef at one of the leading hotels in Istanbul, joins the family on weekends.

Two days later, I was rested and ready to head south toward Bergama, where my namesake, the Greek physician Galen, practiced holistic medicine. By this time I had met many family members and girlfriends of Engin and his brother Ugour. My gift to Ugour upon my return to the US was to be a copy of The ABCs of Sign Language, an instructive text for the deaf. "If you receive this letter and reply, I will send the book as promised." My letter was not returned, nor was it answered.

What my campground lacked in facilities, it more than made up for in friendship. An accordionist came into the dining area where I was writing my journal. "We are waiting for you," he said. This was my command performance. Following an impromptu talk, Turkish dancing began. Even though women were seated with their men, the men danced with each other to accordion music. On previous and future occasions, women were absent from the festivities. I learned later in the evening that the man playing the accordion and singing is a part-owner of the campground.

The following day the tailwind reversed itself. Geared all the way down, I had an air-conditioned ride to the city limits of Bergama. Caravan Camping, a very beautiful and upscale enterprise, cost a bit more but was well worth it. The price was 60,000 lire, or about US$5.50. There was only one problem: the "Turd on the Road" and his wife were also staying there. The campground was so pleasant that, except for the Canadian, I was not in a hurry to move on.

Modern Bergama, a city of 50,000, was originally the wealthy Greek city of Pergamum. Though a town has been in existence since Trojan times, Pergamum enjoyed its greatest period during the reign of Alexander the Great. It was then one of the richest small kingdoms in the Middle East. Tourism is but a portion of the reason for the activity in this all-Turkish city. It is a commercial center for the region, with stores of every description, including a well-stocked bicycle shop. I was again in rather desperate need of Presta valve tubes. I now felt confident to continue my journey, but not before a thorough visit to the antiquities of Pergamum.

The Acropolis, Archæological Museum, and Asclepion are the main attractions. Asclepion was an ancient medical center practicing homeopathic medicine from 131 to 210 A.D. The museum entrance is a treasure trove of Roman sculpture, so well executed that it can still be appreciated 2,000 years later. "Perhaps *this* period of history should have been called the

'Stone Age.'" It was interesting to notice that Greek writing often replaced Latin when engraved into the stone. A model of the Temple of Zeus within the museum is all that remains of the structure that was the dominant temple at Pergamum Acropolis. The original, sold by a Turkish Pasha for silver and gold, now resides in Berlin. There are now signs that state that no antiquity is permitted to leave Turkey. A one-year jail sentence is imposed on those who try. More about that later.

The native dress of Turkish women occupied a wall at the museum entrance. In another room, Turkish carpets woven in and around Bergama hang on the walls. Many of them are well worn, even threadbare in places. The especially worn ones are the most valuable. I would not have given any of them space in my home or office. The walls of a typical Turkish living room on display are lined with sofa-like couches. Last, but not least, a large mosaic is in a state of preservation. Medusa dominates its center. It was believed that a person would be turned to stone if he or she looked at Medusa or her sisters.

When I returned to Caravan Camping, Ayhan, the owner's son and a bike rider, presented me with a gift: a copy of the English edition of Pergamon by Vehbi Bayraktar. His gift was not only a valuable memento, it helped familiarize me with the Acropolis.

My last day at Bergama was spent at the Asclepion and the Acropolis. The most famous physicians of the day were Satyros and Calinos (Galen), practicing healing with music, drama, hot and cold baths, interpretation of dreams, and sunbathing.

The gradual climb to the Acropolis began with Bergama's cobblestone streets. A panoramic view of the river and valleys began to unfold. The Temple of Zeus would have been at the summit had it not been transported to Germany. Three trees that decorated the altar are still growing in their original location. Asclepion is built in a much more confined area than the Acropolis. The rebuilt theater was originally covered with white marble.

Despite the fact that I did not want to leave Caravan Camping, I left the next morning in the direction of Izmir. A strong northerly wind made pedaling easy in spite of the July heat. Izmir, a city of two million people, is not my choice for enjoyable cycling. It might have been possible to miss the city center, but my map did not agree with the posted signs. I elected to follow the signs. My compass was helpful once more, helping me follow a southerly course toward the city limits, where traffic began to thin. The campground Mo Camp 25 km south of Izmir was a perfect stopping point.

After finding my way in the dark to my campground, I met Robin and Audrey, a delightful English tandem couple. Robin is the headmaster and Audrey a secretary at the same school. Our tandems were the bonding agent that has carried our friendship beyond my return to Cambridge. In the summer of 1995, Robin and Audrey, with their tandem, spent three weeks cycling in New England.

Robin, Audrey, and I parked our bikes and boarded a bus for Pamukkale, which in Turkish means "cotton castle." This unique geologic phenomenon is a tourist attraction that we found worth the day's trip. The extremely high concentration of calcium-rich mineral water has left deposits on the rocks and cliffs that from a distance resemble snow. Fresh water warmed by the sun flows over the rock formations into small shallow pools where bathing becomes a hedonistic experience.

The following day, after biking to the port of Kusadasi, I again met Robin and Audrey at the entrance to Ephesus. They had both seen the city, but I had not. As I prepared to take a photo of my tandem friends, an elderly Turkish woman entered the scene. The photo shows Robin and Audrey waving goodbye with the lady doing likewise from the rear. The picture could not have been better if it was posed.

This lady was selling antique coins supposedly found during the excavation of Ephesus, at a price that was hard to resist. I did resist, for the moment. Later that morning her son offered those and other coins for sale. My grandson's birthday was coming soon, and as a young historian, I knew he would like these coins better than any other gift I might buy him. That afternoon I entered a jewelry store looking for a box to mail my valuable coins to Jason. "What do you need the box for?" asked the store owner.

"I would prefer not to disclose the nature of the articles I purchased." Finally, after a lot of coaxing, the shopkeeper knew my secret.

"Do you know there is a mandatory one-year jail term for persons who take antiquity out of Turkey? Don't worry, though, because the coins you bought are counterfeit. The people who sell them put them in the ground for a year to give them the appearance of authenticity." I showed him my purchase. When I went looking for the man who sold them to me, his mother's reply was "he has eaten the money." In other words, my money was spent. I began shopping for a birthday gift for Jason.

Ephesus was a great trading and religious city. Under the influence of the Ionians, Cybele became Artemis, the virgin goddess of the hunt and the moon. When the Romans conquered the area, Artemis became Diana and Ephesus became the Roman provincial capital. Its Temple of Diana was considered one of the Seven Wonders of the World. Being a very large port, ships and caravans came from long distances, making Ephesus one of the early Christian enclaves. Paul visited and preached here, and later wrote his epistles to the Ephesians.

My next stop was Priene, 40 km from my campsite. The climb to the ruins of Priene and its Acropolis was by foot, being too steep for the Globetrotter. The theater, in remarkably good condition, seated 5,000 people. Five stone seats with back rests are placed at the level of the stage, reserved for dignitaries. Holes drilled in the rock beside the chairs supported canopies to protect these VIPs from sun and rain during performances.

I left Priene for Miletos to the south, near the coast. At one time this city was on the coast, but silting moved the harbor farther away—now 15 km. The theater there, one of the strongest buildings of the Roman period, seated 15,000 spectators. The museum at Miletos was small and unremarkable, yet it did represent the ancient city. Had there been a campground in Miletos, I might have stayed, but instead went on to Didyma, the location of the spectacular Temple of Apollo.

The oracle at Didyma, pronounced "Didim" in Turkish, is as important as the oracle at Delphi. The existing temple was started in the late 300s A.D., replacing the original destroyed by the Persians in 494 B.C. An earthquake in the 15th century destroyed much of this site, but some of the most monumental columns imaginable are still standing. I promised myself to return to the temple before leaving for Bodrum on the Mediterranean. If my plan worked out, this second visit would be with my tandem friends Robin and Audrey.

One kilometer to the south is Altinkum Beach, a resort visited mostly by Turkish families. The campground was not easily found due to the massive crowds. I found a patch of grass for my tent, and following supper, settled into a beach chair to do some people-watching. "Ralph," called Audrey through the throng. She and Robin were looking for a restaurant when they spotted me. We had a joyous reunion. The fun then began as we, with tongue in cheek, formed the T.C.T., the Tandem Club of Turkey.

We came to the conclusion that we are probably the only tandem owners in the country, necessitating the formation of this organization with an open membership, should other tandem owners be located elsewhere. We three cited ourselves as its charter members. To give further validation to our Club, we selected "Three Little Fishies" as our anthem. For those who do not remember the songs of the 1940s, it goes something like this: *Three little fishies and the mama fishie too. Swim said the mama fishie, swim if you can, and they swam and they swam right over the dam. Boop boop didum dadum watum chu, boop boop didum dadum watum chu, and they swam and they swam right over the dam.* We merely substituted the word "Didyma" for "didum." The membership of the T.C.T. has now been increased by one-third: Rita Burt, of Medford, Massachusetts, and tandem stoker with charter member Ralph, is now a member with full rights and privileges. She was duly sworn in on Martha's Vineyard in the summer of 1995 by Robin, Audrey, and Ralph.

Our last evening in Altinkum, and one of the last in Turkey, was at the home of Yasar and Hurreyet Coskin. Yasar, an electronics teacher, and his wife, a domestic science teacher, invited us to dine with them and their two children. Other family members and friends were there to greet us. Most of these people speak English, making communication especially easy.

A ferry took us to the port city of Bodrum where the charter members of T.C.T. separated. Robin and Audrey bused back to Izmir and the airport. I continued by hydrofoil to the island of Rhodes and a revisit to Faliraki Camping and my friend the German shepherd. Since Greece and Turkey are not on friendly terms, Rhodes has become the intermediate common ground where passengers can go from one country to the other without too much inconvenience.

"The Birth of Venus"

Cyprus

Chapter 19
CYPRUS

Cyprus, an interlude before Haifa, was hot—too hot for mountain climbing on the Globetrotter. I was ready once again for some R&R and in the right place to do it. The travel agent near the Hotel Metropoli where I purchased my ticket for Haifa told me about his dental technician son-in-law when he learned I was a dentist. This led me to Andreas Paulides, D.D.S., a dentist with teaching experience at New York University. In exchange for three orthodontic consultations, Dr. Paulides recemented my bridge. It was my good fortune that his well-appointed office was closed for the day. He was there caring for the dental needs of his three daughters, who were as beautiful as his offices. It became obvious that Andreas was well-known and respected on the island. The previous day he was a guest on the presidential yacht, a 65-foot vessel.

An air-conditioned bus, appropriately named the "Heat Wave," picked me up in front of a seaside hotel. The tour to Paphos was more a joy ride than I expected. We drove past the British bases that are deeded to England by treaty, following the coast to the birthplace of the goddess of love, Aphrodite (Venus). The artist Sandro Botticelli painted "The Birth of Venus" on canvas in about 1480. The nude Venus, born of the sea and standing on an opened clam shell, is attended to by two wind gods on her left and a personification of Spring welcoming her ashore on the right. As hard as I stared at the rocks offshore, this celestial Venus did not reappear. According to Ficino, "She dwells purely in the sphere of the mind." "The Birth of Venus" resides in Florence, Italy.

We then drove to Paphos to tour the 300 B.C. to 300 A.D. Greco-Roman necropolis, the burial chambers carved from sandstone for the wealthy. It was almost too hot to become interested in antiquity. The burial chambers were designed like the homes of the living so the deceased would have all the creature comforts enjoyed while alive. Valuable art objects were buried with the dead, making the necropolis a bonanza for graverobbers. A castle nearby and open to the public as a museum was designed and built by the Venetians. This is the traditional site of the wedding of Richard the Lion Hearted, whose wife became Queen of England in 1191. The objects in the museum trace the development of Cyprus from the early Christian period through the Ottoman rule.

I stopped to say goodbye to the bike shop owner on the way to the port. What this man did not have in equipment he more than made up for in creativity. I was now ready for a two-week tour of a part of Israel that was new territory. I would then be ready to begin my volunteer work at The House of Grace in Haifa on September first.

A Canadian cyclist I met while on Rhodes waited in line with me for the ferry. While I was relaxing in Limassol, he biked to Nicosia, the capital of Greek Cyprus, and the highest mountain in the Troodos range. Slim and young, he had no difficulties on his mountain bike. The Globetrotter with its load would have been extremely difficult, if not impossible, to ride in the mountains.

Abed Shknini, my seatmate, and I became friends aboard the ferry. My assumption was that this dark-eyed handsome youth was an Israeli Jew. Abed and I talked about the things strangers talk about. He was attending pre-law school in Brussels, Belgium. The following semester he would be in law school. Abed was excited about coming home to his relatives, especially his twin brother. I talked about some of my experiences while traveling.

I remember telling Abed about my being lost in the Egyptian desert and being saved by two Canadian divers. Their last words to me before we parted were: "Just remember that you were saved by two Palestinians." Abed's remark came as a surprise: "Do you still remember?" It was then I knew that he is Palestinian. Isn't it strange the way things happen? I came into the Middle East with a certain built-in prejudice against Palestinians, and perhaps rightly so when the acts of terrorism of some of these people are considered. First, I was rescued by Palestinians. Shortly thereafter, I met Kamil Shehade, the director of The House of Grace, a humanitarian in his own right who is also Palestinian. Lastly, Abed Shknini, a Palestinian has invited me to visit him and his family in Dabburya Village, an all-Arab settlement in Israel. Was this preparation for my forthcoming volunteer position, or was I reading too much into these unrelated coincidences? If I was going to attribute to these events, I could also relate to the Katzrin campground in the Golan where Arabs, Jews, and Christians gathered in fellowship to try to resolve long-standing hatreds. Andrew Shishkoff at that campground reminded me that our chance meeting "was not a chance meeting." Thank goodness I have a level head and do not believe in this fate stuff—or do I?

Abed and I arrived in Haifa at 6 AM, got caught in the rush, and became separated.

ISRAEL
REVISITED

THE
IBEX

Chapter 20
ISRAEL REVISITED

G oing through customs at the port of Haifa could not have been easier. I compare these procedures to those when I boarded the ferry in Cyprus. The interrogation here was friendly yet very thorough. Once through the gate, I headed for the central bus station with the hope of seeing Abed, but his bus for Afula and Mount Tabor had left. I pedaled to The House of Grace and Kamil, the director. After a restful sleep, I began my tour of the part of Israel that a broken front fork had prevented. It was a relief to deposit some of my heavier gear with Kamil before my departure.

Safed, set high in the mountains of the Galilee, was my day's objective. With a tailwind, I had a false sense of security of what was to come. As we entered the mountains, a sign indicated that Safed lay 25 km ahead. An orchard of ripe peaches and Arab children selling ripe figs along the road took my mind off the heat and the elevation. At times I pedaled and at times I pushed. The going was tough!

The holy city of Safed appears picturesque and peaceful, with its maze of cobbled streets that are more suitable for walking than biking. From Jerusalem Street, the main street, I had an overview of this terraced city, with the valley below. This is the valley where the Davidka mortar was hauled by donkey to the upper level of Safed. It was fired during the 1948 War of Independence. The Davidka, now mounted permanently on top of a wall overlooking the valley, is given credit for liberating Safed from the Arabs. The Israelis spread a rumor throughout the Arab community that they had an atomic weapon, the Davidka. It is said that the damage done by this mortar when fired was minimal, but the detonation was thunderous. Shortly after being fired, rain miraculously began to fall. The enemy, fearing atomic fallout, evacuated the city, leaving their personal belongings behind.

Many of the wealthy Arabs, instead of using a bank, secreted their wealth inside the walls of their dwellings or shops. Reconstruction of buildings and walls have subsequently revealed hidden treasure of those who evacuated Safed. Our guide, Lloyd Carmel, told us of Arabs returning to Safed and asking for and receiving the return of their wealth from the Israeli government.

My intuition told me to linger in Safed long enough to sign on with a walking tour. I walked to the Old City from the hostel, visiting the artist colony in the Arab Quarter, and waited for our tour guide Lloyd Carmel. Lloyd, a schoolteacher of English heritage, is friendly and informative. A grandmother and her granddaughter from Connecticut were the only other people on this tour.

We learned that Safed is 800 meters above sea level. Having pedaled and pushed the Globetrotter, I could easily attest to its elevation. We were able to see the Lebanese border and Mount Meiron, Israel's tallest mountain, in the distance. Our main thrust of exploration was the Old City with 80-plus synagogues, some privately owned.

Rabbi Abuhav carred the Torah as he walked from Spain to Safed in 1492. This Torah is taken from the Ark three times a year and paraded by the congregation. Rumor has it that if taken out more than three times, the bearer will die. A skeptical rabbi is said to have had a heart attack and died when he tempted fate. On one of the permitted times, the Torah is paraded to and from Rabbi Abuhav's grave. The participants then celebrate with singing, dancing, and libation.

Lloyd pointed to the domed ceiling in the Abuhav synagogue with signs of the Kabbalah and the four central pillars that, according to Kabbalists, make up all of creation. The dome has ten windows, representing the Ten Commandments, and pictures of the twelve tribes of Israel. The candelabrum hanging over the central Ark is a memorial to Holocaust victims.

We and Lloyd had a first experience: we were invited by a rabbi into a privately owned synagogue. Quite by chance, the rabbi was opening the door at the time we were looking at the exterior, and graciously invited us inside.

The rabbi contrasted the architecture of the Jewish and Muslim Quarters in the Old City. In the former, cobblestone streets and buildings built close to one another form the ghetto. The Muslim Quarter, now the artists' colony, is spacious, airy, and typically Eastern in design. Those Arabs who evacuated Safed following the firing of the Davidka migrated to Syria. This event is commemorated as the Miracle of Safed. We four exchanged addresses before going our separate ways. Not unlike my young friend Sagiv in the Golan, Lloyd asked me to send him a postcard from an interesting place.

We left Safed on a rapid descent and then climbed a well graded road to an elevation of 950 meters. The excavations of ancient Hazor mentioned in Assyrian and Egyptian records became my goal for the night. Some of these records date to the 19th century B.C. when Hazor was the most important town in northern Canaan. Solomon made it one of his chariot towns in the late 10th century.

I was attracted to the spacious grounds of a hotel, guest house, museum, and hostel across the road from the excavations. Upon inquiry, I learned that a hotel room cost $75 per night. My single, air-conditioned room in the hostel cost $15 with room to store the Globetrotter. Supper and breakfast were included in the price.

As I arrived, a young American couple was walking toward their accommodations in the hotel. Sylvia and Bob Pear from Rockville, Maryland, and I met again later, creating a closer bond that ultimately resulted in my visiting at their home on my return trip to Cambridge.

Hazor Museum houses an exhibit of two pre-Israelite

temples, a scale model of ancient Hazor, and a selection of artifacts. Even if the museum had little to see, I would have been anxious to stay there merely to enjoy the air-conditioning. The desert heat was stifling across the road at the excavations. The Shrine of the Steles dates to the 13th and 14th centuries B.C., in which the center figure has raised hands to a crescent and a disc, symbol of the Moon God. Each of the steles is no more than 24 inches high. I finally left my air-conditioned surroundings and pedaled across the road to Tel Hazor.

The underground water supply is the most striking feature of these excavations. This well supported the occupants in case of a siege. The stairway deep into the earth did not result in water at this time, but the damp coolness was welcome. A four-room house was built at the top of the excavation in the 9th to 8th centuries B.C. It was fascinating to become a part of this early history as well as to be in an area presently under attack by Lebanon.

Qiryat Shemona was so named after the death of eight settlers in 1920; "Shemona" means eight in Hebrew. It is the largest town in the Upper Galilee, with a population of 21,000. The most prominent feature of the town is a children's playground. Three army tanks have been painted bright colors on the wide main street. Qiryat Shemona was especially useful to me for two reasons: the pizza restaurant was a welcome change from tent-side food, and a tire repair station restored my punctured tubes for future use. Now that I had four tubes, I felt confident I could return comfortably to Haifa. Tel Hai and the Courtyard off the Metulla Road were my next goal.

In 1920, Josef Trumpeldor, a Zionist hero, lost an arm while serving in the czar's army in Russia before emigrating to Palestine. With his self-styled Zion Mule Corps, he fought with the British in the disastrous Gallipoli campaign. Returning to Palestine, Trumpeldor established Tel Hai (Hill of Life) in 1917 as a shepherd's camp. He and seven other settlers were killed by Arabs three years later. His last words were "It is good to die for our country."

The rebuilt courtyard displays farm equipment and weapons the settlers used to defend themselves from attack. A wonderful multimedia film in the Memorial Room tells the story of Tel Hai. Rather than "hang out" until the hostel opened at 5 o'clock, I decided to head for the Lebanese border and the Good Fence at Metulla. This climb was formidable.

"Are you going to Metulla?" I asked the driver of a mini-van parked along the road. To this day I do not know if he drove me the entire distance out of friendship or if he was going there anyway. In any event, he took me the several kilometers up the mountain, dropping me off at the army post and checkpoint where friendly Christians from Lebanon come across the border for food and/or medical attention. My curiosity was satisfied following a visit with some of the Israeli soldiers. I was told about an ice rink built by Canadians but did not investigate it. There was no need to seek help down the mountain to unexpected camping at Kibbutz Ma'ayan.

Aaron and Dina Applebaum and their children invited me to visit when in Haifa. They originally lived in Pittsburgh, the home of my sister-in-law Harlene. Being approximately the same age, I was not surprised when I learned that Dina and Harlene were friends during their school years. I was anxious to write to Harlene so she could share my joy of meeting these folks from "home."

"From Dan to Beersheba" is the standard expression defining the northern and southern limits of the Promised Land in the Old Testament. I had seen Dan on the map many times and was now but a short distance from "reality." There are several reasons for visiting Dan: an extensive fish farm is located here, Tel Dan is an archæological site, and the Dan stream is one of the tributaries that contributes to the formation of the Jordan River.

A nature walk along the fast-moving Dan is atypical of the Israel that I know in the south. Lush foliage and huge trees reminded me of the Colorado Rockies. Some paths follow the water while others deviate, traversing the contours of the hills, and then return to the fast-moving stream. Small pools and waterfalls added to the pleasure of the walk.

Excavations at Tel Dan were underway in the intense sun. The outline of three- and four-room houses unearthed by archæologists gave us the opportunity to visualize in a limited way the culture of the early settlers.

Bob and Sylvia Pear were taking a break at a refreshment area. We tried to work out supper plans but it was not feasible. We exchanged addresses and photographed each other. They did not know at the time that I would be their houseguest the following May. Bob and Sylvia both recommended that I not miss Banyus Waterfall, just 2 km inside the Golan. I was not disappointed.

The rushing water of the falls and the deep ravines created by the water gives credence to the importance of this natural resource. Walks on nature trails along the stream are of one or more hours duration. A path leaves the stream, continuing up a hill that ends at the Banyus Kibbutz. My ice cream sandwich at the kibbutz market was perhaps the best I've ever eaten. It was certainly one of the most welcome. Feeling refreshed, I headed toward Mount Hermon.

A sign at an intersection indicated that Mount Hermon was 15 km distant. It didn't state that this distance was uphill, but I knew it was more than I cared to challenge, especially at that time of day. A round trip on the Globetrotter with no relief except at either end of the loop convinced me that I should resort to "auto stop." A Druze woman making leban bread at the intersection agreed to watch my possessions until 5 in the evening.

Ovit and Romen Katz, with their two children, stopped to give me a ride. They were the first travelers in the direction of the ski resort. For the next two hours I was adopted by the Katz family. We drove to the base camp well up on the mountain slope. From there the chair lift took us to the summit, where the temperature was easily ten degrees cooler. The Katz children enjoyed this experience, especially with a friendly stranger on board. From the summit we could see large artificial lakes being used as fish farms. My color slides of this area are sensational. Romen drove through two Druze villages on our return, giving me the opportunity to become acquainted with these people, who have their own religion and culture. At exactly 5 o'clock we returned to the Druze lady and the Globetrotter. She was getting ready to close her restaurant and return to her village by local bus. I could not have been more pleased or fortunate with my experience.

There was something about the restaurant food that disagreed violently with me. With the restaurant closed, I had no choice but to challenge the mountain in the direction of Katzrin regardless of my intestinal condition. The Druze village of Mas'ada, similar in name to Herod's summer palace, was a 27-km climb.

A house with a small garden with life-sized African animals painted in vivid colors was the most inviting. I knocked on the door. The owner, obviously a Druze, invited me in. His wife appeared almost immediately with a huge platter of food, leaving it on a table before she disappeared into the shadows. No words were spoken. I tried to explain that I was sick, that I needed a place to inflate my air mattress, and that I needed a bathroom. It might have been an insult to this family not to accept their generosity but I was helpless to do otherwise. A partially built cement structure next door became my bedroom. The family was leaving for the night and therefore unable to accommodate my needs. I was shown the unfinished building as an alternative.

Conditions were so bad, especially in the dark, that I choose not to describe them except to say that this was my worst sleep experience to date, especially with the frequent intestinal episodes. I was grateful for the dawn and my planned departure. Katzrin was only a day's ride. I stopped to rest whenever possible, the first time at an abandoned village along the side of the road, and the second at a market at Meiron Golan, the first kibbutz built in the Golan. Even though this kibbutz was off my planned route, I was grateful for its comfort.

Quite by chance, I chose a major military exercise as my day for biking in the Golan. Except for an enemy, this was all-out war. The road was temporarily closed to allow free use by the military. Tanks were maneuvering in the desert firing their cannons at a low angle into the nearby mountainside. There were no planes involved, nor was I instructed not to use the roads. Support vehicles and emergency medical teams were obviously in contact with the tank commanders as they sped up and down the highway.

Some of the cannon mounted on tanks were so large they were more appropriate for ships than mobile military machines. Detonation was deafening as they were fired at a low angle over my head. Four years in the military did not prepare me for this experience. This was the Middle East!

The road to Katzrin reopened and the Golan was again peaceful. I stopped at the SPINA Field School in Katzrin to inquire about the campground and was assured it was open. The Loyter home is a short distance from the Field School.

Jonathan Kembrey, a London attorney, and I struck up a friendship at the campground. This handsome and athletic young man was traveling for one month before resuming his practice. He previously visited Australia, New Guinea, and Nepal on a year's journey. It was good to listen to another person's travel experiences. A group of American rabbinical students soon began to filter into the campground. Around four separate fires, they sang to the accompaniment of a guitar, creating a very nostalgic sort of evening. Jonathan and I talked until midnight.

The gradual climb to the Golan became my gradual descent. I seldom needed brakes. Now on the level of the Kinneret, I decided to complete the loop I started on my previous visit. This became the shorter route to Tiberius, by way of the Jordan River, where vacationers paddle canoes or ride the inflated rubber tubes I had seen for the first time in the Galilee. Rather than climb the mountain to Camp Hittin where I previously camped, I decided to stay at the level of the Kinneret so my climb away from the water would be toward Mount Tabor and my friend Abed. A sign at the campground indicated there was no charge for bicycle campers.

The gale-like wind died down as evening approached, leaving conditions too hot for sleeping in a tent. The other campers and I slept under the stars until early morning. Awakened by flies, we retreated to our tents. By this time the wind was calm, leaving the area too hot to describe. Touching bare metal would blister the skin. By 9:30 in the morning I became so restless that I let my desire to see Mount Tabor and Abed overrule my better judgment. I challenged Route 767.

For the most part, I pushed my load rather than pedal until reaching the summit. Posted signs at the next mountain indicated a climb of 11 more kilometers, a challenge beyond my ability. I decided to wait at a bus stop, even if it meant camping nearby until morning. I had met my match! Within a half hour of making this decision, an EGED bus arrived. Village Tabor was the end of the line at the top of the mountain. Thank goodness!

Mohammed, a non-identical twin, and Abed walked from home to greet me. Even with his short hair, I readily recognized my young friend from the Cyprus-to-Haifa ferry. Their father, 90-year-old grandfather, and numerous children greeted

443

me in the garden. Three families with one car live in an immaculate three-story dwelling with an attached store. The store, near a large elementary school, provides income to the family by selling snack food, soft drinks, and falafel. The pace was leisurely because it was school vacation. We visited, took pictures, drank cold water, and enjoyed each other's company. I knew I was a special attraction in this small Arab community even though my hosts did not give me that feeling. Their genuine hospitality made me feel quite comfortable.

We were served rice with a special sauce in the formal dining room, a bean mixture of some sort, salad marinated with lemon and oil, pita bread, and an orange drink. Watermelon was served for dessert. I was just settling in for my nap when Abed asked "Did I wish to see Mount Tabor?" The family car had just returned and we were next in line for its use.

Neanderthal people came to Mount Tabor to make flint tools from 80,000 to 15,000 B.C. They were unable to settle here due to lack of water. It is also the traditional site of Jesus' transfiguration, where Jesus was seen by some of his disciples talking with the prophets Moses and Elijah. Two large churches, one Franciscan and one Greek, commemorate the event. To the three of us, the Jezreel Valley below, with multi-colored patchwork fields, was reason enough to climb the mountain.

We, along with the taxis, drove the snake-like road with difficulty to the summit. The landscape at the summit takes on the appearance of an aerial photograph. We saw a new village without vegetation. It provides housing for new arrivals from Ethiopia.

Abed and Mohammed then drove me back to their house where I prepared to leave. Their generosity and hospitality again overflowed: they wanted to give me the "store." Grandfather was praying at the mosque, so I was unable to express my appreciation to him. I was now one day away from Haifa and The House of Grace.

The Shehade family welcomed me to The House of Grace, my home for the next four months. I originally considered remaining a volunteer until the following May, at which time I planned to bike to the Ben Gurion Airport and fly home. Winter changed these plans.

To the surprise of some, I was given a private room in the main building instead of a bunk in the volunteers' quarters. Since I had no experience to base this on, I moved in. Then, at supper, things started to add up, especially when I was being waited upon instead of being the one who should do the "waiting upon." Arab culture was again at the forefront. Being a senior citizen, a grandfather if you will, I belong to a privileged class in which I was indulged upon for no reason other than my age. It became obvious why Kamil gave me a month's trial period. After a month his wife Agnes would probably be exhausted taking care of me in addition to all her other acts of generosity. Something had to change immediately. "If I'm not to be assigned work, it will be up to me to select the work that in my opinion will best suit The House of Grace and myself." Outdoor work was my choice.

The grounds outside the compound walls definitely needed attention. Stones, trash, and debris had accumulated as a facet of urban renewal. Buildings were torn down in preparation for construction of new high-rise structures, but for unknown reasons the plans were put on hold. Any equipment needed for this cleanup was available in the storage areas or in the back yard. A wheelbarrow, rake, shovel, and a pair of gloves became the tools of my profession for the next four months.

We work until 1 o'clock in the afternoon, when lunch is served. Rice is the mainstay at each of these meals. Meat is prepared with the rice on occasion, along with mid-eastern cuisine. Sweet dark coffee in small handle-less glazed cups is not only available at meals but also at break time. The average Arab male not only drinks many cups of coffee per day, but many do so while smoking. Cigarette smoking is not exclusive to men. Following lunch, volunteers, staff, and residents retire to their quarters for siesta. Since I had trained myself early in my career to nap at midday, siesta came easily.

I had the opportunity to study in the afternoon while the children were playing soccer and the staff returned to work. Intensive Hebrew, known as Ulpan, is offered at minimal cost to tourists. New immigrants receive this education gratis at a different location. We tourists attended Ulpan at the top of Mount Carmel in a building that was originally the home of the Rothschild family. It is now converted into a community center. Twice each week, members of my class and I worked with our teacher Tova. Most of us who did not live atop Mount Carmel rode Israel's only subway, the Carmelite, from one of its several stops to the summit. I'm pleased to say that members of my class represented a diverse group of people from different areas of the world. One of the more gentle members is a Catholic nun.

Most of our volunteers come from either Germany or Sweden. Matthias, a young German, lived on the West Bank for six or seven months. His opinion relative to the area of "occupied territory" differs from that of the average Israeli. Matthias talked about imprisonment without trial and the absence of rights of others with a degree of certainty that this form of treatment is common. As a German he assumed responsibility for the Holocaust, but has no forgiveness for Israel for the manner in which they "treat" people in the occupied area.

The English edition of the Jerusalem Post became my resource, along with television broadcasts in English. Learning a foreign language is one thing, reading the news in that language is another. I found the Post at the central library while living in Eilat.

Sunday, September 5, the headlines concerned an imminent peace accord with the P.L.O.: "On the 13th, the West

Bank and Gaza are to be turned over to the Palestinians even though Jordan has not been consulted." The editorial page was replete with accusations that the prime minister and his leftist government sold out to the opposition. "Because of secret negotiations, the people have not been given the opportunity to dissent." A Palestinian state at the doorstep of Tel Aviv and Jerusalem was a foregone conclusion. Those at The House of Grace, like most Israelis, follow the news as intently as they pursue the events of their personal lives, but they don't discuss politics during working hours. Kamil stresses repeatedly that religion and politics are personal matters that do not belong in the daily discourse at The House of Grace. Helping people during adversity or aiding students to study abroad are his everyday concern, as well as helping people pay their rent when they are unable to do so without assistance. In addition to the compound at 10 Palyam Street in Haifa, over 700 families in the Galilee and Upper Galilee are assisted in one way or another.

One day Agnes called me aside to tell me that a donation of clothing had just been brought in by a woman living in Cambridge, Massachusetts. She wrote the donor's name and home address on a piece of paper. The paper then went into my wallet without further thought. Some time later while touring Egypt for the second time, I experienced some sort of recall while pedaling along the Delta near Alexandria. "I know that lady!" I stopped the Globetrotter, removed the paper from my wallet, and would have spoken aloud if there was someone to hear me. My friend Edna Homa from Cambridge had come to The House of Grace to drop off some clothing.

I was planning my trip to Katzrin for the third time; the Loyters invited me to spend the Rosh Hashanah holiday with them. Information about the bus schedules advised me that I would transfer at Tiberius for a bus to the Golan, Katzrin being the last stop. I sensed that this would give me additional exposure to the controversial "occupied territory" of the Golan. In addition to buying new clothes for myself, I bought a house gift for Hinanit and a Michael Jackson album for my young friend Sagiv. Watching videos, Sagiv has learned to imitate his idol Michael Jackson. On my previous visit, he showed me his third-place award won at a school contest.

The eleventh anniversary of The House of Grace was a special occasion. Weeding and watering the various plants in the gardens became my contribution under Sami's tutelage. The magnificent marble flooring of the church took on a like-new appearance as residents did their utmost to prepare for the celebration. New icons were completed by a volunteer artist. The Greek Orthodox/Arab mass was conducted by the local archbishop with at least 150 people in attendance. Chanting, the burning of incense, singing, and readings continued for at least one and a half hours. Following the services, Kamil and Agnes were presented a special award from the local scouts representing approximately 80 families. Middle-eastern sweets, pastries, and beverage were then served. In a very short time I was exposed to and learned a great deal about these Arab Christian people, whose heritage goes back to the time of Jesus.

It is my choice not to discuss the residents of The House. Some are recovering drug addicts while others are homeless street people. Most are Arabic but some are Jewish. A distressed mother and her young son were also part of our family.

Kamil, Agnes, and their children have their own apartment, but they eat with the volunteers, residents, and guests. Hardly a day went by without visitors at the dinner table. Travelers singly or in groups come to visit for a day or a week. They have heard about The House and want to see it first-hand. The first question asked by their hosts Kamil and Agnes is "Have you eaten?" Some of the new faces come from the judicial system of Israel. Prisoners on furlough for the weekend register with the local police and then sleep at The House. To my knowledge, no funds come from the State even though The House of Grace has received Israel's highest humanitarian award. Fundraising in Europe by founder and director Kamil Shehade supplies the necessary funds. Most funds come from Sweden and Switzerland.

On one occasion we attended a court hearing, along with our criminologist. The hearing concerned one of our residents seeking freedom from the jurisdiction of the courts. If the judge looks favorably on the request, he has the authority to free the individual. Since there is no jury system in Israel, the final decision comes from one judge in minor to moderate cases, and three judges in crimes of a more serious nature. Until I learned more about the jury system in the United States, I was critical of this non-jury system. Now I'm not so sure which is better. Experienced jurists are probably more capable of rendering a fair decision then twelve untrained citizen jurors. There is, of course, one major question that has not been answered adequately to me: if I were an Israeli Arab, would I want to be judged by a panel of three Jewish judges? I might prefer being judged by a jury of my peers, especially if that jury was made up of both Arab and Jewish jurors.

Anna and Maria from Sweden were taking time out from their studies to become volunteers. Peter, a German student, was doing his externship in social work at The House. Because of the nature of his externship, he has a more intimate knowledge than I of the specific beneficiaries of assistance. Working out in the sun was my joy and selected responsibility. We four volunteers became fast friends in spite of the fact that I was old enough to be their grandfather.

Alice, a Holocaust victim, is one of our part-time volunteers. Prior to retirement Alice was an oral hygienist. She and her scientist husband Zeev live atop Mount Carmel in their beautifully landscaped home. She still has nightmares after these many years since she was picked off a pile of victims believed to have died of typhus in a Nazi concentration camp. The memories are as vivid to her today as when they were occurring.

Those doing community service at The House are assigned by the Israeli court system to work one-half day every day except Shabbat. They have been incarcerated and are now working their way back into society by doing this community service as part of their sentence. We serve the role of a traditional halfway house in this respect. These people do construction and repairs under the permanent staff's direction.

One of those incarcerated, whom we believe is innocent, became one of my very best friends. His wife and children visit him at the compound where he is confined to the perimeter of the building. I am pleased to say that at this time he is living with his family and is back at work doing strategic welding for the government, his previous employment. Not only do we correspond, but we have talked over the phone since my return home. The mother of their three children can now be a full-time mother as they try to put their lives back together. Their lawyer, a brilliant woman, believed in Francis and fought his battle in the courts with the success we knew she would have.

Alice and Zeev hosted us four volunteers at their home, giving us the opportunity to meet other Israelis socially. On the Globetrotter I had no difficulty meeting people, but as a volunteer I was viewed as a temporary resident who'd be returning home shortly. We found Alice and Zeev to be senstive, loving people who prefer a negotiated peace with their Arab neighbors.

There are now two women in my life named Tova. One teaches Hebrew at Ulpan atop Mount Carmel. The other teaches ceramics at The House of Grace. "Number two" was not only an accomplished ceramist but also an excellent teacher. Residents as well as staff meet twice a week learning the skills of molding clay, a craft dating back to the earliest of times. An unused garage was cleaned out and is used as a studio. Partially completed pieces are stored there until the next class. Those who wish to work on their own may do so.

Until this time, the weather was predictable—dry and hot. At Ulpan we tried to arrive early so the fan would be in our classroom instead of in another. Suddenly, the climate changed. Storm windows were hung at the first suggestion of the rainy season, even though rain was sporadic. The empty cisterns were now ready to be filled after months of predictable drought. My outside work began to be reduced due to the weather, much to my displeasure. Not only did I enjoy the outdoors, but with storm windows in place, cigarette smoking became my personal burden. Something I didn't like was happening physiologically: I began to enjoy the secondary tobacco smoke as though I were the smoker. Would this craving cause me to become a smoker again? It was indeed cause for alarm.

The damp cold was especially uncomfortable, both at Ulpan and The House. Thermal underwear and my new leather jacket purchased in Bodrum, Turkey, were welcome. We turned on the electric heaters at Ulpan. This sudden climatic change was expected by the Israelis—it occurs annually. My sleeping bag, used while traveling, became a necessity at night.

Now that most of the area surrounding the compound was cleared, there remained a rather large pile of broken roof tiles following the installation of a new roof. "Shall I move these tiles to the municipal dump?" I asked Kamil. He explained that he had a plan for them. "They are to be broken into small pieces and used for paths in the garden."

"How is this to be done?" I asked.

"When I come back from my European fund-raising tour, I'll find out and will tell you." I knew Kamil would be gone for several weeks and that my time at The House of Grace was growing short. My method chosen for this task required very little creativity: a heavy-duty mallet, a pair of gloves, a wheelbarrow, and a large flat stone surface.

The pile of crushed tiles gradually grew as my right

arm became stronger. This was my project and I was determined to see it through. The heart fashioned by Peter and I might not endure, but the tile walks will be there for years to come. I look forward to seeing them on my return visit, whenever that might be. Pleasing Kamil was another personal incentive. Finally the task was completed, ready for construction of the paths. My outside work was now finished, in time for a brief vacation with the Globetrotter. I would be testing my equipment for future traveling.

Akko and Rosh Hanikra on the Lebanese border were familiar stops. I wanted to leave Israel with fresh memories of these favorite places. Rain was, of course, a factor, but fortunately a minor one. My first stop was between Haifa and Akko at the home of my good friend whom we believed to be innocent of all charges against him. His wife and children greeted me as though I were family. I also planned to visit Jonathan, the owner of Moller Threads, but his daughter explained his absence. "Do you remember me?" I asked.

"How could we forget? You are the only bicyclist to have slept in our bomb shelter." She assured me she would relay my greetings to her brother Eitan and her father. My next and final goal on this short tour was the all-Arabic town of Ibillin, where Fr. Elias Chacour has successfully established a school, overcoming adversity that would have discouraged the average person. Fr. Chacour is far from average. His first assignment as a priest was Ibillin, then a small and insignificant Arab town with few redeeming features. I have read his books Blood Brothers and We Are the Land. Autographed copies can be purchased at the school. This is the location of the Prophet Elias High School where my German friend Klaus was a volunteer. Inasmuch as Kamil and Fr. Chacour are close friends, I felt compelled to visit Ibillin and the school prior to my departure from Israel.

The employees of Bezek, the electric company of Israel, gave me specific directions for finding Ibillin. Finally, after considerable difficulty, I was in the Arab villages. The last one is Ibillin. A youngster on his bike guided me the final two kilometers. He then turned around, without waiting for my "thank you." In the dark I saw the outline of the school and adjacent buildings at the very crest of a hill. This incredibly steep grade forced me to walk the Globetrotter the final few hundred yards.

Fr. Chacour arrived in time for the closing ceremonies before Christmas vacation. Without sleep, this tireless "educator" arrived from Ben Gurion Airport in time to address the student body. Christmas carols were being broadcast from strategically placed loudspeakers. One of the songs played was "Happy Birthday." Though the song was not intended for me, it reminded me of the most important day of my year.

My tour of the school and surrounding buildings verified the amazing accomplishments of Fr. Chacour. When he first arrived at Ibillin he slept in his car; there were no facilities available. On this day I was escorted through his new home, still under construction. His residence is but a part of a $10 million construction project that includes Prophet Elias College. The students explained to me that their school has received the highest commendation possible from the State of Israel. They are indeed proud, especially because this recognition was attained after practically impossible odds. Before my departure I had the pleasure of shaking hands with Abuna (Father) Chacour. The 1985-86 Yearbook entitled "Mosaics of Our Lives" and a child's white sneaker are my souvenirs of Ibillin and the school. This sneaker, once tied to the Globetrotter, is now a prized possession in my home.

At 6 PM that same day, Peter and I left The House of Grace by bus for Jerusalem. We four volunteers—Peter, Anna, Maria, and I—planned to spend Christmas Eve in Bethlehem and Christmas Day in the Old City of Jerusalem. The Swedish Christian Center near Jaffa Gate reserved a small apartment for us. My birthday party there came as a complete surprise.

One year ago Klaus celebrated my birthday with me. This year, with a cake baked and decorated by Maria, my 69th year ended in style. Happy Birthday balloons were hung in various places in the room. The candles were the kind that *can* be blown out.

Bethlehem and the Christmas festivities were the highlights of the day and evening. The weather, compared to the previous year, was unseasonably mild. We approached Manger Square in Bethlehem with a certain amount of apprehension, using 1992 as the benchmark for 1993. Nothing could have been more inappropriate. Israeli security was almost nonexistent, with the bulk of the spectators Palestinian instead of Israeli. The flag of the P.L.O. was hoisted to the roof of the post office. Except for the souvenir shop owners complaining of lower sales, the conduct of the people was no different than in 1992. From my point of view, the Fiji Islanders' performance stole the show for at least the second year in a row.

My last Hebrew lesson at Ulpan was held at the home of Lisbet, one of our classmates and a citizen of Denmark. This was a part of the holiday celebration of Hanukkah. Class members owning cars or vans drove the rest of us to the party. In the back seat of the van, a class member asked me a question: "My name is Connie. Do you travel on a big bike? Were you in Katzrin in the Golan some time ago when you met my husband Eitan (Andrew) and our son David at the campground?" This was the Eitan, now known as Andrew, who invited me to his home. Andrew and his family are members of the faith defining themselves as *Messianic* Jews. They have adopted the faith that Jesus is indeed the Messiah and believe in the message of the New Testament as Christians do.

"If you have the same belief systems as Christians, why don't you call yourselves Christians?"

"We believe in the gospel but not the church." Members of this splinter group, though unpopular with the classical practicing Jew in Israel, have a special interest in bringing peoples of different belief systems into common fellowship. Andrew was a rabbi in Baltimore and is now a businessman in Israel, spending much of his time in pursuit of peace with Moslems, Christians, and Jews.

I accepted an invitation from Connie and Andrew to visit them at the top of Mount Carmel. That visit with the Shishkoff family completed one of the many "loops" that I experienced on the road as well as in Cambridge following my return in 1994. They and I have since been in correspondence.

I knew I would be leaving The House of Grace after the first of the year, but had no specific plans at that time. While talking to Peter, I proposed an itinerary that was interesting but not practical. I had thoughts of returning to Egypt and pedaling to Alexandria on the Mediterranean. Alexandria and the Suez Canal are the only inhabitable portions of Egypt I hadn't seen. From there I thought of taking a ferry to Italy. I would then bike to Rome for my flight to Boston. Peter discouraged this plan. He had doubts that the ferry service operates during the winter. "Why not go below the Equator where our winter in Israel and Boston is summer there?"

I showed Peter my bus and flight tickets that evening at the supper table. In amazement at the influence he had on his volunteer friend Ralph, we began to go over the details that would take me back to Egypt before my flight to Johannesburg, South Africa, and ultimately bring me to Miami, Florida. This was the first time I considered traveling to the troubled and possibly dangerous country of South Africa. My reduced fare ticket stops at Johannesburg, a city of dubious reputation. I decided to inquire at the airport in Johannesburg relative to the safety of bicycle touring in that country. If this form of travel is not recommended, I will merely stay at the airport until a Miami-bound flight arrives with space for one passenger and one Globetrotter. Little did I realize then that I would be entering "a whole world in one country," nor did I know that I would meet some of the most congenial people, both black and white, on my tour. Turkey, South Africa, and Swaziland are without a doubt three countries with some of the friendliest people in the world. Kamil suggested that I wait until after the New Year's Eve celebration before leaving.

During the previous two weeks, I worked with the staff on the forthcoming House of Grace Yearbook. My knowledge of English grammar was helpful during the editing process of the publication. Another incentive to stay was an article Kamil asked me to write. In true Kamil Shehade style, he gave me freedom to express myself as I chose. He also asked Alice to make a similar contribution to the 1993 edition.

My article "A Life's Experience" began on page 8 and continued through page 10.

"Ralph, as long as you live you have a home at The House of Grace." These were the words of founder-director Kamil Shehade. Never have I enjoyed hearing the sound of my name as I did then.

Previous to my first visit to the city of Haifa, I pedaled through nine countries bordering the Mediterranean. My butane stove, tent, and sleeping bag as well as my books were my prized possessions. In preparation for this two-year journey I attended a refresher course in French, an introductory course in modern Hebrew, and a course in art history.

On my first visit to Haifa I pushed and pedaled up Mount Carmel to the very beautiful Baha'i Temple, the world headquarters of the Baha'i faith. A young woman kneeling in prayer and I were the only two visitors in the sanctuary at that time. We were also the only people in the gardens surrounding the Temple. Spontaneously we became friends. This young woman, a volunteer at The House of Grace, was so filled with enthusiasm that I asked to accompany her to her volunteer site where perhaps I could meet Kamil. Her name is Anne Marie.

I decided that my volunteer work in Israel should be located in a center of population so that I could work and also study Hebrew. Being a dental specialist in the United States, my thoughts naturally gravitated towards the field of dentistry. As a matter of fact, two separate facilities showed an interest in me. Then I discovered The House of Grace and the Shehade family: Kamil, Agnes, and their five vivacious children.

Kamil was in his office located near the entrance to this restored church/dwelling complex known throughout Israel as The House of Grace. Though busy, he found time to offer Anne Marie and me coffee. "Have you eaten?" asked Kamil. This I learned is one of the signs of the Shehade hospitality.

Following my third visit I knew I wanted to volunteer here in preference to a dental facility. Forty-two years of professional work was behind me; a life's experience, if accepted as a volunteer, lay ahead. Finally it was agreed that I would move into The House of Grace on September 1st, 1993. This gave me enough time to tour Rhodes, Crete, Greece, Turkey, and Cyprus by bicycle. I also had time to visit the Upper Galilee, the Golan, and Mount Tabor prior to my September 1st deadline. On this, my third visit, I asked Kamil a question that prompted an immediate response: "Do you know that I am Jewish?" His answer was succinct:

"Here your religion is of no concern except to yourself!" At The House of Grace we care for residents of many cultures. Both men and women of varying background find this loving environment when they arrive. Though the Shehade family has their own apartment, they cook and eat with us, as do the staff. The Shehade children are our children and the tasty Arab food is shared by all. It is here that new faces are constantly seen as we "break bread" with neighbors, strangers, and family.

Reading this brief account, you may ask yourself: "What sort of duties might a 68-year-old person of a professional background do at this halfway house?" I can truthfully say that I have shared my background and experience with those who have shown an interest or a need.

Within less than a month's time I will leave Haifa and The House of Grace as I continue my journey to Alexandria in Egypt, South Africa, and finally, to my home in Cambridge, Massachusetts. I leave with a sense of accomplishment as well as an increased knowledge of the complex multi-ethnic culture of the State of Israel.

House of Grace Closes Circle (pages 19-21)
Alice Raphael, Volunteer

In the closing days of World War II, the ill-famed German concentration camp Bergen-Belsen was liberated by the British army. As a Czechoslovak Jewess, I had been one of the camp inmates. I remember nothing of the actual liberation, as I was critically ill with typhus fever.

When I regained consciousness I found myself in the British military hospital which had been set up nearby. A Swiss nurse, member of a Red Cross team, visited me daily. Her name was Hanny Huber. Gradually she told me how she had rescued me from a pile of bodies. She had noticed that my limbs were still moving. I had the feeling that she was taking a special interest in me.

One day a group of survivor children was chosen by the Red Cross to go to Sweden for a period of convalescence. I refused to go. My father had instructed us to meet in our home town after the war. Hanny persuaded me to accept the offer and to search for my surviving relatives from Sweden.

458

I wrote to Hanny from Sweden and received a reply: ..."Foremost I should like to wish you a happy future and in particular that you may soon succeed in finding your family so that also you, dear Alice, may savor the joys of youth in all its aspects..."

Hanny and I lost touch. In time I found my surviving sister and brothers. The years passed. I married Zeev (a refugee from Nazi Germany) in England and we raised our family here in Israel.

Exploring downtown Haifa a few years ago, Zeev and I chanced to the Greek Catholic Church. Kamil asked us in and we became interested in his project. After the Gulf War I decided that I wanted to become involved and to contribute a modest share to The House of Grace. Agnes accepted me as a volunteer.

Recently, Zeev and I started to write our memories for our daughters and grandchildren. When I recalled the episode of Hanny Huber I thought that Agnes, being Swiss, might like to see the letter which I had carefully kept since August, 1945. Agnes turned over the envelope and exclaimed, "Ach, Haggenschwil!" It turned out that Agnes' father was born in that same small town. In short, within about two weeks I received the address of Hanny Huber, now Siegenthaler, in California. Since then I have had two letters from Hanny. My feelings about the renewed contact with this very dear person are difficult to describe. Like myself, she has enjoyed an interesting life, has traveled widely, lives with her husband in retirement, and has grandchildren.

The chain of coincidences which led me, the Jewess from distant Czechoslovakia, back to Hanny, now in California, via Haifa, the Greek Catholic House of Grace, and Agnes is incredible...

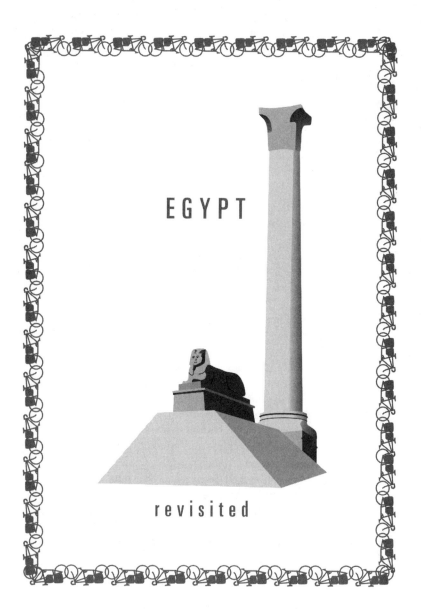

EGYPT

revisited

Chapter 21
EGYPT REVISITED

I was ready to leave despite the overcast sky on a cold and damp January 2. I looked over my shoulder, giving a final wave to my friends at The House of Grace. Francisco said it all: "We love you, Ralph." If my departure was not so emotionally charged, I would have returned to 10 Palyam Street at the first suggestion of rain. Under the circumstances, there was no choice. This was the rainy season!

I pedaled when weather permitted, and when there was no choice I took the bus. A storm center settled, surprising both Egyptians and Israelis and doing considerable damage to coastal roads and beaches. Treeless mountains were unable to hold back the wall of water that took everything in sight with it. The beautiful Negev desert, strewn with huge boulders, was no longer beautiful. The same was true of the Sinai beaches along the Red Sea. There was also loss of life.

On Friday, January 7, the Globetrotter and I headed for the Egyptian border and Nuweiba in the Sinai Peninsula. The Egyptian border police casually inspected my baggage, stamped my passport, and as far as I knew, until the first roadblock 10 km distant, I was legally permitted as a tourist in Egypt.

"How can I repay the Egyptian doctor now that I'm back at Taba? He cured my foot infection when others were unsuccessful. Is he still at the one-doctor hospital?" I decided to visit the hospital first to verify his presence before selecting a gift. Opposed as I am to cigarettes, this was the most appropriate gift. If he has moved on, I didn't want to be carrying a carton or more of Public Enemy Number One! The problem was solved—he was transferred.

Ten kilometers into the desert, the police at a roadblock informed me that my Egyptian visa was not properly stamped. Had it not been for the hills, I would have taken their advice and returned to Taba. The owner of a restaurant-motel graciously offered to take me both ways following my lunch at his establishment. He planned to drive to Taba for his noon prayers at the mosque.

While the owner was praying, I had ample time to correct the visa problem and wait for my return ride at a prearranged bus stop. Three tourists were waiting for the buses going toward Nuweiba, St. Catherines, Dahab, and Sharm-el-Shaykh. A young American and I exchanged information as we spent time waiting in the intense desert heat. Unfortunately, I didn't record the name and address of this cyclist from Brookline, Massachusetts, a former member of Charles River Wheelmen, my club. His final words, as he boarded the bus, were "Give my regards to Jamie King." Jamie is an active member and former president of CRW.

Once the Mediterranean came into view, I had no difficulty assessing the damage done by the flash floods. The tranquil beauty of the desert between the mountains and the sea was now transformed into an unsightly no-man's land. From Beersheba to Sharm-el-Shaykh, the floods wrought damage to the ecology that is probably uncorrectable except through time. Eons from now these boulders will probably be part of the "sandscape." This damage is too vast to be corrected by earth-moving equipment.

One year earlier, I made friends with Dr. Shish Ka Bob at Nuweiba. He welcomed me with an embrace and the words "hello, cousin." Back at the Nuweiba campground, a young Finnish couple, Jari and Satu, became friendly as we shared a table at Dr. Shish Ka Bob's. We were both acquainted with Esko, the first person I met in Israel. They were working on the Lebanese border building a school with Esko. My welding experience did not help Esko and his group as I originally planned. Instead, I spent my time profitably at The House of Grace.

I knew we had a mountain to climb out of Nuweiba toward Dahab, but this was an opportunity to once again see my friend Ya'akov, the manager of the cafeteria. This time, if invited to sleep over, I would accept. The large letters composing the word "cafeteria" came into view at the summit. A black Sudanese greeted me with "Welcome!"

"Where is Ya'akov?" I asked.

"Ya'akov came to Egypt with a three-month visa that he illegally extended for three years. He has been deported back to the United States." Part of the mystique disappeared when I learned that Ya'akov is in reality Larry Porter from Cleveland, not Ya'akov from Chicago.

A return to Mohammed Ali Bedouin Village at Dahab was my next goal. The next 60 km with a tailwind were welcome, especially through the mountains. Were I traveling north instead of south, the challenge might have been too much to handle without assistance.

Karen and Peter from New Zealand, now living with their three children on a kibbutz in Israel, shared a desert jeep with me on a four-hour tour of the Wadi Canaan. Karen helps prepare the meals at the kibbutz while Peter cares for the children. Even the jeep had difficulty with the soft sand of our off-road driving. The barren mountains, cloudless blue sky, and complete absence of vegetation creates an awe-inspiring experience. Our driver Salam stopped in the middle of nowhere at his home, a dwelling without doors or windows and sand floors. He does have electricity and an electric refrigerator. We were of the opinion from his posted ad at Mohammed Ali that we would be served a barbecue. In reality, Salam and his son baked pita bread for us on an open fire. Our barbecue consisted of pita bread and tea.

The effects of the previous storm in the Sinai were still visible, with pools of water in places one would not expect to see water. At one location a fresh water spring was erupting from the rocks. Although we didn't drink the water, it felt extremely soft. Desert vegetation in abundance at an oasis was a welcome surprise. A deserted Bedouin village nearby is inhabited only during the summer.

The Bedouin children ran across the road to greet me. With their characteristic brown teeth, each was vigorously chewing gum. "Do you want to ride a camel?" they asked.

"How much?"

"Seven pounds."

"No, thank you." The price was more than fair but I was waiting for my camel ride at Giza and the Pyramids. These animals were bedding down for the night and the women were herding the goats. As a result of the recent rain, the barren desert now provided ample food for the animals. I opted to continue until nightfall instead of camping with these hospitable people to get a hands-on experience of Bedouin life.

The Red Sea and Sharm-el-Shaykh soon came into view, the end of my day's journey.

Though I couldn't find the hostel on my first visit to Sharm, I was determined to do so this time, especially in daylight, despite a strong northerly headwind. By 5:30 in the afternoon I was registered. The workingman's supper at the hostel couldn't have been better. My roommate Andy, a Brit working on an Israeli moshav, had other ideas. We walked in to the native section of Sharm where I joined Andy for supper number two. We talked about Gaza, Ashdod, and Beersheba, all mentioned in the Bible. These wealthy cities were written about because they were on trade routes between Egypt and the Holy Land. Palestinian autonomy could return importance to Gaza with cooperation from Egypt and Israel.

My decision to take a bus to Suez City was based on logistics, not weather. The road along the Gulf of Suez alternately follows the coast and turns inland. My map indicated an absence of services and many miles of desert isolation. A strong wind coming from the north was another deciding factor. I realized once on the bus that biking would have been impossible because of the floods.

Our well used bus, driven by a small elderly Egyptian wearing the traditional male costume, chain-smoked cigarettes as he drove with incredible skill under the most challenging of conditions. The 5-hour trip to Suez City became a 10-hour ordeal. Where the road was washed out at one point, heavier trucks and buses created their own "Burma Road" on the mountain side of the flooding. I fully expected our bus to tip over on its side as we bounced from obstacle to obstacle on this lunar landscape until we finally returned to the mud surface of the previously washed out road. Finally this mud-covered bus arrived in a highly congested part of Suez City. Except for myself, the few tourists on board hired a taxi, Cairo their destination. I went in search of a hostel.

As usual, Egyptian hospitality is matched only by that in Turkey, South Africa, and Swaziland. "I will show you" is a common expression in Egypt. I rode slowly as another person escorted me to my accommodations. He accepted no payment for this courtesy.

My cost for the night, including a generous supply of mosquitoes, came to five Egyptian pounds. Parking my bike and gear in a rather large dormitory room, my only companion was Khaled Mohammed Aly, an accomplished athlete in boxing, soccer, and weightlifting. Wearing his medals and holding his certificates, Khaled sat on the edge of his bed posing for a photo. He insisted that I accept his cap as a gift. He drew the pyramids and the word "Egypt," and for unknown reasons, a Star of David on the cap.

The 80 km from Suez City to Isma'iliya was strictly a desert run, with a strong westerly wind which at times helped and at times hindered my progress. The entire road was lined on one or both sides with military installations. Compared to the Israeli military, the Egyptian equipment and installations are primitive. The Israeli tank is canvas-covered and maintained to perfection. In Egypt they are "just there."

Shortly thereafter I entered Isma'iliya, a lovely city with wide streets and waterfront hotels along the Suez Canal. The hostel, also on the water, compares favorably with an Egyptian four-star hotel. My private room and bath had an unlimited supply of hot water with a view of a sandy beach and the Canal for 18 Egyptian pounds, or about $6 American. Even though the cafeteria was closed, the director assured me I'd be well fed.

I was told that at Port Said on the Mediterranean, 80 km away, I could avoid strong headwinds by taking a ferry to Alexandria. This proved to be another case of information-misinformation. Since this was a bike ride, not a boat trip, I looked forward to the experience of pedaling.

Not once did I see the Suez Canal the next day. The railroad ran over an expanse of elevated sand to my right between me and the canal. Had I taken a right turn into El Qantar, I could have seen the water. The road was now a divided highway, part of which is a toll road. I rode free of charge.

One would never suspect that at one time this area was controlled by the British. Today it gives strictly a Third World appearance. Even Isma'iliya, appearing modern from a distance, is Third World. Potholes in the streets, donkeys with their carts, women carrying heavy loads on their heads, and bicycles with heavy burdens characterize the appearance of the community.

I easily found the hostel at Port Said, where I had a large dormitory room to myself. Rather than take the Globetrotter, I decided to spend the next day walking along the Mediterranean to the Suez Canal and then take a free ferry to Port Fu'ad located in Asia. My walk ended at the National Museum where a personable carriage driver enticed me into his cab. Instead of walking to Port Fu'ad, I saw the port from the carriage seat. Much of the French architecture is now Third World-French/Egyptian.

The National Museum was worthwhile, yet not exciting; I had seen much more at the Cairo Museum. A pair of sandals made of leather and reed were in excellent condition considering their age. Silver coins of Alexander the Great were interesting, as were the ceramic and alabaster vessels used for daily activities and funerals. I suppose my "fake" Alexander the Great coin purchased in Turkey is probably lead instead of silver.

Tanta, 90 km from Cairo and 110 km from Alexandria, is the largest city in the Delta. Its large commercial center supports three upscale hotels. I selected the Touristic Hotel at a cost of 20 pounds, or about $7 American. Room service delivered a chicken dinner so large I ate it in two installments.

Leaving Tanta in the morning, the sky remained overcast until noon. For a time I had a young cyclist as a companion, a man in his 20s. He was carrying a pair of scissors and a large load of steel wool. He offered to give me some of his product. We shook hands at an intersection and then separated. Soon another cyclist came along my right side. "Give me some money," he demanded.

"I have no money for you." He then reached behind me, pinched the fake Reebok jacket that I had removed earlier and stowed under the handles of my saddlebag, and sped away. He stopped once, still within earshot. At first I thought my voice would bring the return of the jacket that had seen better days but was still a comfort when needed, but he pedaled away with my property.

A small town not on my map became one of my favorite photo stops. A small mob gathered around me and the bike at a juice stand where sugar cane is squeezed by machine, yielding the sweet juice of the cane. This was the perfect time to photograph Moslems in their traditional costume, if permitted. I finally got my photo of Egyptian women carrying heavy loads on their heads. One gruff male wanted money for the privilege of being photographed. When I refused, he shoved his way through the crowd in anger. The photo I desperately wanted was one of the young woman selling the juice. She was a dentist's nightmare with her stainless steel front teeth. When I asked her for permission she gave me her broadest smile possible.

The book <u>Zen and the Art of Motorcycle Maintenance</u> reinforced what I already knew: investigate small problems before they become large ones. The rubbing of my tire against the frame demanded investigation. A spoke pulled out of the rear rim, distorting the wheel. The best I was able to do on the road was adjust the remaining spokes so the wheel spun freely. A replacement rear rim was now needed ASAP.

I asked a pedestrian in the city of Damahur the location of a hotel. In true Egyptian form, he walked me to one. It was full, but another pedestrian escorted me to hotel number two. Shortly thereafter my gear was carried to my room along with the Globetrotter. I then began to do definitive wheel truing so I could proceed to Alexandria where I'd probably find a bike shop with a replacement rim. A less appealing alternative would be a train to Cairo. I knew that once back in Israel I could find a replacement prior to my flight to Johannesburg.

Alexandria was only 65 km away and the wheel was holding up better than expected. This was a lovely day to be cycling, especially with an ideal winter climate. The sun was warm but not oppressive. This was my day for picture taking. Egyptian outdoor advertising, homes with straw sides and roofs, and women carrying heavy loads of fresh vegetables on their heads were all camera subjects. Carrots, beets, and turnips were being harvested and sold roadside. Pantomiming, I asked permission of these women to take their photo. When it was time to point the camera, they began to cry as they ran away. Perhaps they thought I was going to shoot them.

A BMW sedan pulled to the side of the road at the entrance to Alexandria. The driver got out and waited for me. "Do you remember me? I gave you directions outside of Tanta." Farther into the city I stopped to check my rear wheel. An adult cyclist came alongside, offering to render any assistance that might be needed. We then biked together to the entrance of the Egyptian Youth Hostel.

"May I show my appreciation by taking you to lunch with me?" I asked.

"Thank you, but I have eaten."

The warden of the hostel advised me not to offer my host money. "It will insult him," he remarked.

I was totally comfortable in my private room in the hostel. My air mattress remedied the not uncommon problem of a sagging bed. A small community of university students shared the bath facilities as well as a small kitchen with a two-burner stove. The rather large reading room became their study. A small balcony directly off my bedroom looked out on the Mediterranean.

Once moved into the hostel, a bike shop was the next consideration. A shop within walking distance stocked the necessary parts and had a mechanic with wheel-building skills. One problem still remained: the mechanic didn't have the specialized tool to remove the freewheel. This must always be done prior to wheel building so there is access for threading new spokes on the freewheel side. Unfortunately, I didn't have one, either! "How can you do your work if you don't have a freewheel remover?" I asked. The mechanic pointed to a sledge-hammer. My creativity was again tested.

An auto mechanic across the street from the hostel willingly loaned me his tools after I showed him my problem. I then began to experiment with different tools, hoping for an-other "bright idea." One socket of a set of socket wrenches looked promising. Using a large pipe wrench to grasp the in-verted socket, I easily removed the freewheel. The rest was up to the mechanic.

When I returned to the bike shop the owner advised me to have his work redone at my first opportunity. "The re-placement rim is made in India and is of poor quality." With his experience he knew this rim would not stand up under the heavy strain of the Globetrotter. At least I was now ready to challenge the desert road to Cairo, a distance of 223 km. If lucky, I might still have my night in the desert before returning to Israel.

One of the university students, Yassar, majoring in sociology, became quite friendly. During our conversation he and I decided to become pen pals even though it would be some time before I could reply to his letters. "You will have a pile of letters from me this high when you arrive home," said Yassar. He lives in Isma'iliya on the Suez Canal.

We decided to go out for dinner together with the un-derstanding that Yassar would be my guest. As a student and an Egyptian, I knew he had very little discretionary money. "Yassar, you pick the restaurant. I'm in your hands."

"We will go to Kentucky Fried Chicken," was his re-ply.

I had visions of an Egyptian or Middle Eastern meal with the waiters in native costume and the ambiance of a memorable restaurant. "Yassar, even though I asked you to pick the restaurant, I just cannot go to KFC." We settled for pizza.

Since that time Yassar has competed his studies and is entering the army for his compulsory military service. He and a young woman from Germany plan to be married in the near future. We still correspond even though we haven't seen each other for over a year and a half.

Following his victorious campaign in Egypt in 332 B.C., Alexander selected a fishing village on the Mediterranean as the site of his capital. He carefully designed this city with the concept of it becoming a naval base, a trading post, and the political-cultural center of his empire. In the last three centuries B.C. Alexandria attracted some of the finest scholars and artists of the time. Alexander the Great is buried in his city that today is known as the "jewel" of Egypt.

Mistakenly named, Pompey's Pillar is a 25-meter high pillar of pink granite, the remains of an Acropolis and the Temple of Serapis that is so tall it's impossible to visualize a structure with a roof of these proportions. A small sphinx is located nearby. The pillar has a circumference of 9 meters. Isabel Chan from Hong Kong and I toured the site together.

Isabel, a lovely young woman of 27, arrived at the site at the same time as I. She too was traveling alone. Our mutual interests brought us together then as now; we still correspond. Inasmuch as I remarked to Isabel that she is "adorable," her letters begin with "This is your adorable Chinese friend writing to you." I introduced Isabel to Egyptian macaroni on the way to the Catacombs of Kom el Shuqqafa, the largest Roman burial site in Egypt. This spicy dish is prepared and sold by street vendors. While eating, a group of children gathered around us. One child pointed to a bicycle shop nearby. When we went to investigate, the shop owner tried to sell me a pair of pedals for the rear of the tandem so Isabel could ride with me. How about the saddle?

The catacombs were discovered in 1900 when a donkey cart accidentally fell through the roof. These tombs are hewn out of sandstone to a depth of 100 feet and date to the first century A.D. Some statues have Egyptian bodies and Roman heads. Some 99 steps descend to the lowest level where the wealthy families buried their dead. At one family area carved out of the rock is "Preparation of the body of King Tutankamun." In another area there are family crypts that at one time were filled with the remains of family members.

It was late in the afternoon. I walked Isabel to the tramway. Before we politely hugged I gave her the address of The House of Grace with the suggestion that she visit Kamil and his family during her stay in Haifa. "I know my 'adorable' friend will be welcome."

As I was packing, my friend Yassar came to my room and asked for my photograph. Fortunately, I had one extra passport photo, now his. It will not surprise me if Yassar decides to visit the US on his honeymoon, now that he has an invitation.

The desert road near Alexandria appears more like the delta than the desert, with an abundance of heavy industry. For 20 kilometers, petrol, chemical, and food manufacturing dominates the scene. Industry ultimately thinned out and the desert came into being. A cool breeze and the threat of rain were the only problems. Rain became a reality later in the afternoon, forcing me to take cover at a Red Crescent station, the equivalent of our Red Cross. I was welcomed by the attendants and offered the use of a cot while I waited for the rain to abate. Cycling against the wind for several hours created perfect conditions for an hour's sleep.

My next stop was at an all-new city without hotels. The management of a combination restaurant and grocery offered their premises in French, saying that the next stop, the Sahara Inn, was 20 km farther. It was actually 40 km. At the 20 km mark, I stopped at a police station and hospital to inquire about the distance. Within moments I was sitting on the floor of the station sharing food provided by the police. From there I was escorted to the hospital and introduced to the doctor who offered me a room for the night. The police reminded the doctor that this is a hospital, not a motel. He backed off. "We will call for a car to take you to the Sahara Inn."

At my suggestion, I erected my tent between two ambulances and used the hospital's limited toilet facilities. My sleeping bag never felt better.

On the subject of facilities, the Egyptians have solved the problem of the high cost of toilet tissue. A small bent pipe inside the toilet bowl is attached to a water valve on the wall to the side of and behind the bowl. The water from the pipe serves as a douche for the user. When I first saw one of these devices the curved pipe appeared too close for comfort. I pushed it down into the bowl with my shoe.

With the Globetrotter safely parked in Giza, I was free to explore the area. Sami Tarfour, a desert guide, recognized me from one year ago. It was Sami who took my photo on his camel "Mickey Mouse." He was elated: I looked like dollar signs to him. "How much?" I asked.

"Nothing. All you have to do is pay the owner of this camel for the use. This is not Mickey Mouse."

"Where is Mickey Mouse?"

"Oh, he died." I knew this to be a scam but went along with it anyway. I had removed most of my money from my wallet in the hotel room, with the remainder reserved for a day of pleasure. Sami was the perfect person to assist me. I knew he'd leave when the wallet was empty.

We climbed a steep hill of sand on our camels, looking toward Cairo, where an old man brewed Egyptian tea for us using donkey dung as fuel. The scene was very authentic. From there we visited Sami's house and an adjacent perfume shop. The essence of the perfume is sold, as contrasted to the essence diluted in alcohol. As my supply of money rapidly began to diminish, Sami's interest also began to wane. This was an expensive camel ride but one that I longed for since my initial photograph with Mickey Mouse. The amount of money left was Sami's pay.

A display of Egyptian art at the Papyrus Institute in Giza is expensive yet impressive. Naturally, there's a vast difference in the quality of papyrus and fake papyrus art. At the bottom of the scale, banana leaf is used. The "Tree of Life" design was explained to me by a cordial salesperson/guide at the Institute. The lifespan of a person is depicted using birds as the symbol of the individual. All birds except the last one are looking to the east. The aged bird at the top is looking in the opposite direction toward his after-life.

At supper in a cafeteria-style restaurant I met Hopialy Ali, a desert guide, who invited me to join him and two others at their table. This newest acquaintance began aggressively to invite me to his home so he could give me a gift. He also wanted to read my fortune with his stones. Shortly thereafter his friends excused themselves, leaving me apprehensive and a bit threatened. What did Hopialy have in mind? Curiosity overruled my concern for personal safety. We went by taxi to a congested residential area of Giza, and climbed a short flight of steps leading into a bedroom with a female occupant in the bed. A large and rather obese woman was under the covers with several of her children. Other children were playing on the floor in front of a TV. Through a drape replacing what should have been a door I could see portions of a very small kitchen. This one-bedroom hovel was the dwelling of Hopialy's girlfriend who was in the bed.

Without being summoned, a young woman appeared from the kitchen area. "This is my girlfriend's sister," said Hopialy. "She likes you and would like to marry you." He then ordered food from an outside source. One of the children shortly thereafter brought in a large platter of kufta. At no time was I asked for money. My problem, of course, was getting out of this situation without insulting the young woman or bringing harm to myself. My explanation that I didn't wish to get married to this "lovely creature" must have been adequate. I left without further incident. Agreeing to go with a stranger to his home was obviously a very foolish thing to do.

Islamic Cairo is one of many sections of the city I hadn't seen. I mistakenly took the wrong bridge and arrived there quite by accident. Once across the bridge, I saw the Citadel and the Mohammed Ali mosque in the distance. It became obvious that this uniquely Egyptian area was worth exploring.

My short tour took me through typical Egyptian streets with an abundance of animals, people, donkey carts, food stalls, and dilapidated housing. Though the weather was cool with rain threatening, I was still biking dry potholed streets. During rain the potholes become invisible until discovered. I felt secure locking the Globetrotter next to the police guard at the Citadel entrance.

This spectacular fortress was the home of Egypt's rulers for about 700 years. It's located atop Midan Salah al Din as a combination of three mosques and four museums. Salah al Din began to build the Citadel in 1176 as a fortress against invasion by the Crusaders. It has been modified over the centuries with palaces and government buildings of subsequent rulers. Mohammed Ali, one of the last monarchs to reside here, leveled much of the Citadel as he built his own Alabaster Mosque and palace.

The Alabaster Mosque, built between 1830 and 1849, was open to visitors; it was not prayer time. Permission was given to photograph the interior, which has a delicately illuminated dome. The gilt tomb of its namesake is to the right of the main entry. The gingerbread clock in the center, which never worked, was given to Mohammed Ali by Louis-Philippe of France in exchange for a Pharaonic obelisk from the Temple of Luxor along the Nile. The obelisk still stands in the Place de la Concorde in Paris.

Outside the Mosque, four unescorted children speaking French as well as Arabic decided I was their friend and they were going to accompany me in my pursuit of culture. They ranged from 8 to 12 years of age. Why Nahla, Gaclene, Mahamd, and Thal adopted me I shall never know. I'm writing their names as they wrote them for me. The two boys, the youngest of the four, took my hand and refused to let go. Other visitors to the Citadel and the guards smiled as these children led the American from place to place. In the wax museum, a drawing of a camera with a cross through it indicates that photos aren't permitted. In spite of the sign and at my request I was given permission to photograph the children in the foreground of a wax figure. The police photographed me in a convict's pose in the prison cells with the children looking on. It then began to rain. Seeking shelter under an arch, the father of these four vivacious children suddenly arrived. The children vanished as quickly as they appeared; our party was over!

I end my tale of the Citadel with the name of a woman with extremely thick glasses, Safra Farid Ali. Safra decided that she and I should become pen pals, that she wanted to come to the US, and that she and I should be married. Her language was French, a tongue I hadn't used for over a year.

At ten AM, when traffic began to lessen, we headed for the Sixth of October Bridge on the way to Ramses Square that has a huge sculpture of Ramses in the center. This was my identical route one year earlier. While taking a photo of Ramses, a young Egyptian boy came toward me with tissues in his hand. His price for one packet of tissues was one pound. I indicated that I wanted three packes for a pound. He held up two. In the meantime another boy came over with the identical product. I bought three packets for one pound. Boy number one then began to beat up on boy number two, packets of tissues flying in all directions. Though there was a fence between us, I tried to intervene. They moved far enough away so they could settle their differences without a stranger's interference.

My compass was again helpful in locating the Palace and Old Cairo, a part of the city important to the early Christians. The Palace was closed to visitors. I used my map to locate the Coptic Museum along the Nile in the Old City. Originally called Babylon, the fortress was built about 900 years ago before the Fatamids founded Cairo. The Christian faith flourished here in the first century A.D. During the several centuries that Christianity dominated Egypt, this area was considered a holy place to Copts, Jews, and later Muslims. The Convent of St. George and the Coptic Museum cover a large area, typical of Egyptian city life. Dirt roads, small shops, barefoot people, and distressed housing predominates. The appearance of this housing goes back to Pharaonic times.

I returned to Roda Island on the way to my hotel. While pedaling, a young graduate student from the University of Cairo joined me on his bike as we crossed the El Gama Bridge to my pre-selected restaurant. He invited me to his home for a genuine Egyptian meal. I explained my concern about biking in the city at night. Being in a hospital in Cairo or worse instead of on a bus for Israel could spoil my day. My hot mixed grill for three pounds was the very best.

I was awakened the following morning at 4 in preparation for boarding a bus to Nazareth at 5:30. My reason for choosing the Arwa Hotel was two-fold: I received a discounted rate at the hotel with my bus ticket, and it was the first stop for the bus. Storage in the luggage compartment was facilitated with the front wheel of the Globetrotter removed. Except for myself, all passengers returning to Nazareth, Israel, were Palestinians. It became obvious that these people travel to Cairo to shop. The volume of their purchases left very little room for the Globetrotter. We had a tour of the city at sunrise to pick up passengers at various hotels. A ferry took us across the Suez Canal enroute to the border town of Rafiah.

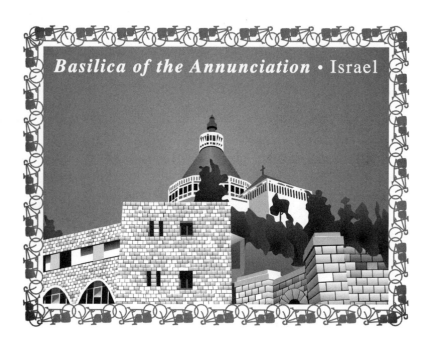
Basilica of the Annunciation • Israel

Chapter 22
A FINAL VISIT TO THE HOLY LAND

The Galilee Hotel in Nazareth, at $55 American per night, did not appeal, but the Hostel of the Sisters of Nazarene nearby did. Centrally located within sight of the Basilica of the Annunciation, this hostel could rival any for cleanliness and facilities. A fully-equipped kitchen and dining room are designed to accommodate many more people than I saw. A friendly atmosphere prevailed with the staff as well as the hostelers. In addition to a hospice and hostel, the Sisters operate a school for deaf and blind Arab children.

The Church of the Annunciation in Nazareth, resembling a lighthouse more than a basilica, was open to visitors. Mosaics of the Madonna from all over the world hang on the Church walls as well as in the courtyard. The Japanese Mary and Jesus have slanted eyes and are dressed in oriental motif. Mary's kimono is made of seed pearls. This modern church is built on the traditional site of the Annunciation. There are actually two churches in the complex, with the remains of the earlier structure retained within the new construction.

Though the date was February 3, I rode in comfort wearing shorts and a jersey. The gradual descent from the hills surrounding Nazareth to sea level was an invigorating experience. Haifa was my first stop. I spoke to Agnes at The House of Grace from the bike shop, asking permission to sleep in the volunteer quarters that night. She seemed excited to receive my unexpected call. By 6 PM the rear wheel was rebuilt and I was back with my friends, the residents, staff, volunteers, and Agnes. I learned that Kamil and Abuna Elias Chacour were in Washington, D.C., having breakfast with President Clinton. The purpose of their visit was to discuss the Christian presence in Israel and the occupied territories after the peace. Agnes was beside the phone patiently awaiting a call from her husband. Karen, the newest volunteer and my replacement from Switzerland, was likeable at first glance. Like myself, she's an assertive person. Most of my evening was spent visiting with Francisco, my special friend, and Youval Samsoun, our criminologist.

Youval, bearing a strong resemblance to Omar Sharif, willingly shares his views on Israel's judicial system compared to that of the US. At that time he was completing his master's degree in criminology. As one would suspect, Youval supports the Israeli system of justice by judges rather than by jury. A poem entitled "Then You Are Not Old" by Youval provides a glimpse into the personality of this interesting and handsome individual.

Then You Are Not Old

If you left your dreams behind
If hope is cold
If you no longer look ahead
If your ambition's fires are dead
Then you are old.

If from life you take the best
And if in life you keep the jest
If love you hold
No matter how the birthdays fly
Then you are not old.

A train was a possible alternative to biking in the rain to Tel Aviv and the Ben Gurion Airport. My ticket on South African Airways was rain or shine. To my disappointment, the train does not have a baggage car nor could I gain permission to take the Globetrotter on board. Like the proverbial rubber band, the Tel Aviv-Haifa highway beckoned.

Our goodbyes were brief; we had shown our feelings one month earlier. This time I was on my way for the last time, at least on this trip. I stopped to bid my friend Boaz goodbye at his bicycle shop.

Fortunately, the weather was ideal for cycling, with the wind in my favor. Dressed in bike shorts and a cycling jersey, I arrived without effort at Caesarea. Ellen, my young friend, was no longer employed at the souvenir shop and restaurant. The cafeteria-restaurant supplied the needed nourishment before heading toward Netanya, the home of my friends Faith and Asher.

Susie Halpern, my camping friend in France at the start of my trip, suggested that I call her aunt and uncle Rita and Joel in Herzlia, a Tel Aviv suburb. Recognizing my name, Rita said that she and her husband were looking forward to our meeting.

For an Israeli home, the Berg household and gardens are exceptionally spacious. When the house was first built, explained Joel, an orthodontist, he and Rita and their small family lived on the edge of the desert. Now they're situated in the center of Herzlia Patuach.

Having been exposed to the Arab point of view, it was interesting to again become acquainted with the Jewish perspective. Both Rita and Joel have lived with the pain and suffering on both sides. These gentle people are looking forward to a peaceful settlement of this age-old Jewish-Arab problem. I was anxious to write to Susie telling her of the hospitality I received from her relatives.

The threat of rain convinved me to pedal as quickly as possible to the airport. I could "hang out" in the terminal if necessary until my flight. I didn't want to board the plane in wet clothing nor did I realize the distance from downtown Tel Aviv to the airport. Once at Ben Gurion, "free camping" was always a viable alternative.

It sometimes takes time to assess all the possibilities before selecting the best solution. Once at the airport I decided to get a feel of the area, especially if I planned to free camp.

Considering security measures at this major international airport, I did not want to pick a site I might regret, especially on my last day in this country. The lack of hotel or motel facilities nearby necessitated a bit of creativity. Alan Lorber solved this problem for me.

I met Alan and his son Gideon outside of Netanya at the time I called Asher and Faith Krupnick; they were using one pay phone and I the other. Our brief conversation concerned my travels on the Globetrotter. We met again at the airport. Alan was awaiting the arrival of a colleague, a fellow graduate of MIT in Cambridge, my hometown. We met on the sidewalk outside the terminal.

"Do you know of a hotel or motel within biking distance of the airport?" I asked Alan. "I need accommodations close enough so that in case of rain I can reach the terminal without getting soaked."

"We live on a moshav nearby with plenty of room," said Alan. "Stay with us for the night. I'll give you directions so you can head there while I'm waiting for my colleague. Tell my wife Ellie that I have invited you, if you see her before I return home. We live almost within sight of the airport."

The next morning Ellie asked about my plans for the day, since my flight was not until late in the afternoon. She had the following suggestion: "Instead of turning to the right at the end of our road toward the airport, go to the left. Within a quarter of a mile you'll see a sign for Tel Gezer. Go to Kibbutz Gezer nearby. Perhaps they will adopt you for the day. Tel Gezer is enough to sustain your interest for at least a day." I thanked Ellie for her hospitality as well as the advice.

Brigit Rosenblat, the attendant at the kibbutz entrance, greeted me with a smile. "I know you from Haifa. You were in the same travel agency as I, near the Carmelite subway. You are flying to South Africa on the way to Boston. Welcome!"

Brigit had overheard my conversation with the travel agent. "Join us for lunch before you explore Tel Gezer."

Lisa, a kibbutznik, lives and works at the kibbutz with her husband Scott and their two children. Her home is originally Wilkes-Barre, Pennsylvania. Lisa attended Penn State University, the location of my first dental practice. During our conversation I learned that she and Scott had read my letter to the editor of the Jerusalem Post "Your Smoking Is Dangerous to My Health." Soon thereafter, Scott, the hardball and softball coach for the kibbutz, arrived for lunch. He and Lisa promised to send a copy of my letter to me in Cambridge.

Scott explained that Kibbutz Gezer is one of the few remaining kibbbutzim based on strict socialistic values. He invited me to meet him at their apartment at 4 PM for home-baked apple pie following my walking tour. Acceptance was easy! I learned from Scott that Tel Gezer and Tel Makor are one and the same. In the #1 best seller The Source, author James Michener, for his own convenience, moved Tel Gezer closer to Haifa, Akko, and Sefat, renaming it Tel Makor. I recently reread the book while at The House of Grace. On my last day in Israel some of the loose ends were coming together.

Except for one motorcycle and one car, I was in isolation for the afternoon, free to explore to my heart's content. Fortunately, I left the Globetrotter at the kibbutz. This was hiking and not biking territory. Brigit informed me that during the rainy season these roads are impassible even for four-wheel drive vehicles. I finally found what I was looking for: the well.

Much of Michener's story centers around this well. Barbed wire was probably placed around the well to discourage avid readers and curious tourists from being injured. It would have been tempting to climb into the tunnel that leads to the "source" of water hidden from view and from the enemy during attack. Now that my curiosity was completely satisfied, I returned to the kibbutz.

Before leaving for the airport, an hour's bike ride, Lisa, a nutritionist by profession, gave me an address in Kingston, Pennsylvania. She, Scott, and their children planned to visit her family in May, the scheduled time of my arrival in the Philadelphia area on my way to Cambridge. We talked about the possibility of meeting at that time.

Flight 269 left Ben Gurion Airport on schedule. The Globetrotter and I were on our way to Johannesburg, South Africa, an 11-hour flight.

The Source

Chapter 23
SOUTH AFRICA

Any concern for my personal safety disappeared at the Jan Smutts Airport, Johannesburg. Though I promised myself that I would inquire about biking conditions in this highly controversial country, my major concern was a safe route to the Pink House Backpackers Hostel in Yoeville, 25 km from the airport and close to Johannesburg. My newly purchased maps indicated a divided highway heading east, and little more.

Finding Yoeville was easy, but climbing the hills to get there was not. The hostel became a breath of fresh air. Located on a residential street in a "safe" area, there is no concern for walking the streets at night, as in Johannesburg. This well-equipped and clean hostel provides a complete kitchen, TV room, outdoor clothesline, and hot showers. One night's stay cost 20 Rand, or about US$6. The owners were as friendly as the guests. This was an excellent place to begin my two-month tour of South Africa and Swaziland.

Cape Town to the south and west has two drawbacks: it's over 1,400 km from Johannesburg, and there are about 400 km of desert—the Karoo—that are inhospitable for cycling. Kruger Park, on the other hand, a huge national game preserve to the north and west, is a more attainable goal, with population centers closely linked. I was beginning to appreciate the size of this large and diversely beautiful country.

I was impressed at the very outset with the friendly atmosphere in South Africa and the magnificent highway system, where potholes are non-existent. People of both races extend genuine friendship to strangers that can only be compared with my experience in Turkey. Both cases were pleasant surprises. I did, however, have a small problem asking directions from blacks. Their willingness to help often overpowered their ability to do so. This is just another example of the information/misinformation highway.

Marissa and Carl, owners of the Pink House Backpackers hostel, mapped out a scenic route to Kruger National Park that became the basis for my tour. They cautioned me to stay out of the townships and not to "free camp." Campgrounds and hostels abound in South Africa, making it unnecessary to take chances putting up a tent in non-protected areas.

Another route Carl recommended is the Garden Route along the Indian Ocean from Still Bay in the west to just beyond Plettenberg Bay in the east. Some of the most important tracts of indigenous forests are along or near this route. Giant yellowwood trees and flowers such as the proteas and gladiola grow profusely in this region. Blue gum and pine forests have been planted throughout the country and are cared for by the forest industry. The blue gum, or eucalyptus, imported from Australia, deplete the irrigation systems in the dry months due to their thirst.

Carl advised me to use trains as well as roads so "distances do not become a burden." As a senior citizen, I'm entitled to a 40 percent discount on the trains.

Pretoria is the administrative capital of South Africa, only 56 km from Jo'burg. I added considerable distance in an attempt to avoid one of the townships. Had I to do it over, I would have stayed on the road, minded my own business, and been perfectly safe. From this point, progress became challenging. Undulating hills and the summer heat took their toll. This was my first day of summer cycling since 1993 and I felt it (it was February, but summer in the southern hemisphere).

Pretoria is an uncompromising Boer city owing its existence and growth to independence and domination of the blacks. Its population is over one million, with approximately equal numbers of whites and blacks. There are embassies, a military base, and educational institutions. It's dominated during October and November by tens of thousands of flowering jacarandas. The city is named for Andries Pretorius, hero of the Battle of Blood River during the 1863-69 Boer Civil War. François, the owner of a bed-and-breakfast where I spent my arrival night in Pretoria, tried unsuccessfully to interest me in spending a day looking at the administrative buildings and statues. Except for Heroes Acre, the cemetery where Pretorius and Paul Kruger, president of the first South African Republic, are buried, and JK Strijdon Square, I did not feel I missed much. The square is an example of neo-Fascist architecture where the head of Prime Minister Strijdom, an originator of apartheid, is celebrated. Ironically, black street vendors have chosen the edge of the square as a place to sell their products.

We were soon heading east on Route N-4, recommended by Carl. Did he say this road was level? I dismounted on several hills. Threatening rain encouraged me to take an exit toward Bronkhorspruit for food and shelter. Storm number one struck while I was eating supper at a convenience store. The second prevented our progress beyond the town limits; I found shelter at a 24-hour petrol station. The management allowed me to put up my tent on a patch of grass near the toilet facilities. Moisture in the tent that night became a problem that haunted me for the rest of my African adventure. It was caused by deterioration of the tent material induced by age. Waterproofing such as Scotchgard was now a necessity.

By about 4 o'clock that Sunday afternoon we were at the Whitbank Recreational Resort, a municipal facility with a pool, lake, and recreational area. Arthur and Anet Harper became my friends for the evening. They also advised against "free camping." They used an expression,"don't flash cash," that I had heard and read before. It was obvious that more precaution is necessary in South Africa than in the other countries I visited. Security systems and barred windows of homes are another indication of potential crime. Signs list two, sometimes three, different security companies protecting a single residential property. I later discovered that homes are built with internal protection: areas such as bedrooms are isolated with locked steel doors to protect the owners while sleeping.

I stopped at a hotel in a suburb of Middletown to adjust the rear wheel spokes. A group of oriental tourists with cameras began to gather around me. One of them, a man about 65, invited me to have lunch with him and his friends at the hotel. He is a manufacturer of bicycle and moped tires from Thailand. This was my best meal to date in South Africa.

We continued on toward Belfast, a distance of 69 km. The rolling hills, farmland, and bright sun made the ride enjoyable. The following day we were in the mountains. The descent to an inn and the Krugerhof Museum was 9 km. Had the wind not been in my face, it would have been a sensational ride, through a tunnel and past a waterfall. This ride to Nelspruit became magnificent, following the railroad and streams through the valleys. The ultimate in mountain scenery, it reminded me of a tour through the Cascade Mountains of Oregon.

Holiday Resort became my campsite in Nelspruit. It did not take long to become acquainted with the ants and the monkeys. I heard a rustling while inside the tent. Looking out into the dark, I saw nothing, but in the morning I learned that the wild monkeys were having a party, leaping from branch to branch. They were living under ideal conditions, with food given to them by humans, creating a problem for campers and residents of the resort. Not only do the monkeys steal from the campers, they have learned to turn doorknobs. If doors are not kept locked, the occupants of the homes can expect to find a disaster area upon their return.

Another unique situation in South Africa is the hippo crossing. We have signs in the US indicating caution because of deer crossings. Imagine the consequences of hitting a hippo! The hippopotamus, a very belligerent animal, is responsible for more human deaths in South Africa than any other animal. Fortunately, the rhino does not enjoy the same reputation.

One camper at Holiday Resort, a white insurance salesman in the black townships, became friendly. He explained that blacks living on very little money are the people with the wealth. Not only do they buy expensive life insurance policies, they buy multiple policies, with the premiums taken out of their pay. Rather than selling these people life insurance, he tries to sell them annuities so they will have forced savings. His experience in the townships has been relatively uneventful and safe.

With a friendly farewell from the staff at Holiday Camping Resort, I was on my way to Kruger National Park, a tract larger than Israel. The town of Hazyview, 70 miles from Nelspruit, was my day's goal until I the first "stairway to the stars." There was just no way I was going to climb this mountain without help. The main road was closed, leaving the mountain pass as the only alternative. Placing my baggage next to the tandem, I put out my thumb in reverse direction, remembering that I was traveling on the opposite side of the road in South Africa. The first pickup truck driven by a white driver with a black companion stopped. In moments we had the bike and gear in the back of the truck. The companion climbed in with the bike, despite my objection. Chris, the driver, insisted that I join him up front. We practically flew to White River, a distance of 20 km, at a speed of 120 km per hour, climbing most of the way. After Chris and his companion helped me place my equipment back on the pavement, the black man returned to the front seat.

Hitching a ride at the base of the next mountain proved fruitless. Traffic thinned out to such an extent that the possibility of another pickup truck going in my direction was unlikely. Bored waiting, I reloaded the Globetrotter and found most of the mountains negotiable without too much difficulty. A long downhill brought us into a region dominated by banana plantations. Even though this fruit was in the developmental stage, roadside stands were selling first and second quality bananas.

I was the only guest at the campground just outside of Hazyview. This gave me the opportunity to become better acquainted with the owners. I was awakened the following morning at 5, departure time for a safari to Kruger Park was set for 5:30. Our closed vehicle, as required by the Park, transported an Israeli couple; an English youth born in Kenya; Joseph, a black employee of Kruger Park Backpackers; Terrance, the barman; myself; and Vickers, the driver. Terrance is what we call a "redneck." Overweight from too much beer and with a dislike for blacks, he carries a gun at all times except in the Park (all weapons must be surrendered at the registration desk for the duration of the safari). A hitch in the military may have given this man a creed to live by as far as weapons are concerned. To Terrance, all blacks are apes walking in an erect position. Guards riding in pairs on bicycles in the Park with high-powered rifles slung over their shoulders elicited the remark from Terrance, "Look at the baboons riding bicycles!"

Kruger National Park was a bit of a disappointment, as we drove on paved roads while the animals, for the most part, remained in their comfortable secluded habitat. Perhaps our "drive-by" was too low-key, creating a dreary atmosphere to what could have been exciting. Had the roads been unpaved and the terrain more mountainous, as occurred on a later safari, this tour would have been more enjoyable, though we did see 28 different animal and bird species over the course of the day.

Ofra and Haim, the young Israeli couple in our minibus, were fun to know. They, Simon, the English lad, and I reserved space on a night safari at a private game preserve. There, open Land Rovers are used instead of closed vehicles as at Kruger Park.

"Be back at three," I was told as I headed toward a crocodile farm, thinking the deadline was 3 AM instead of 3 PM. This privately-owned "croc" farm is about 7 km from Kruger Backpackers. It neither encourages or discourages visitors. There were no signs along the road indicating its presence. I found it by asking directions.

The crocodiles lay in an apparent stupor inside a circular cement wall behind a farmhouse. Green algae grows symbiotically on their backs, giving these reptiles a less than clean appearance. A sign on top of the wall about five feet high warns visitors not to reach over the wall. The moment I came to the wall, the crocs began to swim in my direction, crawling over one another in a violent effort to get to or at their potential victim. They may have thought I was bringing them food. I soon had a crawling, snarling, snapping audience that, fortunately, was separated by the wall. Testing their reaction time, I tossed some grass into the arena. I then knew that a hand or arm over the wall meant instant amputation.

A resident of the town of Sabie told me a supposedly true crocodile story: one Sunday morning a crocodile decided to get some old-time religion. He entered the open door of a church and slithered down the aisle toward the pastor, who was holding a plastic ruler in his hand. One "snap" and there was no ruler. On the advice of the minister, the organist played "Onward Christian Soldiers" as loudly and fervently as he could. With the church door still open, the crocodile turned around and went back to his digs.

Following this visit, I pedaled back to Kruger Park Backpackers. A pharmacist in Hazyview prepared my antimalarial medicine. The lotion, a part of this prevention package, is designed to discourage the mosquito from even thinking about an attack. Malaria is so serious in certain parts of South Africa that prevention is an absolute necessity. I took my first pills in the pharmacy.

Passing the crocodile farm on the Sabie road, we were entering uncharted waters in rather spectacular scenery. Sabie, a tourist center as well as a timber town, is the largest in the area. Pine and eucalyptus plantations have replaced the original forests that were cut down for the mining industry. A forestry museum in downtown Sabie explains in detail the past as well as the contemporary forestry industry. Bicycle touring around Sabie was interesting but not exciting. A companion would have helped me enjoy Horseshoe Falls and Bridal Veil Falls, both exquisite natural formations. The gentle spray of water flowing over the cliff at Bridal Veil produces a "filmy" appearance. When the wind dies down, the water returns to a vertical free-fall.

We stopped at a rather large general store owned and operated by a family of Indian descent on our return to Sabie. These people are referred to as "colored" in South Africa. The owner explained that he was closing his store, representing his life's savings, because theft had broken his morale. "The same people who have been breaking into my store at night come in during the day to buy cigarettes and candy."

"Why don't you protect yourself with an alarm system as others do?" I asked.

"It is too late. I cannot sell to people during the day who steal from me at night. I'm going back to the city." He was determined.

The distance from Sabie to Graskop to the north is 60 km, providing 30 km of climbing through the scenic areas of Mac Mac Falls, Pilgrims Rest (a restored mining village), God's Window, and finally Bourke's Pot Holes north of Graskop. I took a surface taxi, similar to the mini-buses in Turkey that have no regular schedule, to Bourke's Pot Holes, a natural formation of rocks and pools. I became the center of attention as the only non-black person in the surface taxi. These informed and well-spoken black people were anxious to visit. I respect them for their knowledge and culture; they spoke my language fluently, but I could not speak theirs.

The all-downhill ride from Graskop to Sabie was great fun, especially the stop at Mac Mac Falls. A steel cage, not a platform, is embedded into the face of the cliff. We were literally standing in space on the floor of the cage. In spite of the steel construction, I had that uneasy feeling of falling into the chasm.

A tourist in Scandinavia taught Dorothy and me a method of preventing this threatening feeling of vertigo. "Instead of leaning forward to look over the cliff or chasm, stand sideways so that you will be looking over your shoulder. This will eliminate the sense of falling."

Leaving Sabie, Long Tom Pass was one of the most difficult climbs to date. A communications tower is erected at the highest point in Sabie. Prior to descending the pass, I was looking down on that tower. This Saturday morning "hike" was 9 km long, with no possibility of a ride. Most of the climb was covered by walking, not biking.

We arrived after dark at Caravan Camping in Nelspruit. The monkeys with their small faces and long tails were at work once again swinging from tree to tree and chattering away to each other. At times their babies hang upside down clinging to the mother's stomach, and at other times they cruise along under their own power.

Speaking of mothers, the black African mother wraps a blanket around her waist, securing her baby to her body. The baby rides on her behind with the child's legs wrapped around the mother's waist. Carrying her baby in this manner leaves the mother's hands free to carry a load of wash or produce on her head and at the same time hold the hands of her older children. It is not unusual to see a female sibling carrying her younger brother or sister in like fashion. The father, of course, is totally unburdened.

The climb out of Nelspruit was especially difficult. Not only was the grade horrendous, but the chain began to overshift. In due course the road surface deteriorated into dirt and sand. We were obviously on the wrong road. Asking directions, I was told to return to Nelspruit if I hoped to find the national road N-4.

My memory of <u>Zen and the Art of Motorcycle Maintenance</u> and the author's approach to mechanical problems helped solve the annoyance of chain overshift. It required a step-by-step process of elimination. The solution: I tightened the loose derailleur; shifting was again crisp and accurate.

I was now enroute to Swaziland. The day was a hot and challenging one, especially having to return to Nelspruit in order to start over. I was now a short distance from the town of Melelane, where N-4 continues toward Mozambique and R-570 turns south toward the Swaziland border. South Africans advised me not to tour Mozambique unless I wanted a guarantee that my equipment would be stolen, or worse. A visa is also required. I decided not to press my luck. Forty-one more kilometers of heat and hills, with no planned rest stops in mind, would bring us to Swaziland.

I headed onto the less traveled road to Swaziland with a limited amount of food. One grade followed another as I began to feel the sun's effects. This was just one more exceptionally hot day of the summer months. A bakkie (pickup truck) passed me and then stopped along the edge of the road. Two black men got out and waited for me to come alongside. The driver took a badge out of his pocket, identifying himself as a constable. Both men were smiling. In short order the Globetrotter and I were in the back of the truck, heading for the border gate. The two men helped me unload at the border. We shook hands before they disappeared in the direction from which they had come. It was very obvious that they went out of their way to be friendly to a stranger in need. In their absence, I would have found myself in a wilderness situation that could have been hazardous.

My passport admitted me to Swazliland, one of my favorite countries.

Chapter 24
SWAZILAND

Information: Piggs Peak has caravan camping! We forged on toward the mountains in unbearable heat. At a shopping center (Swaziland-style), with the silhouette of the mountains in view, I decided to either get a ride to Piggs Peak, take a bus, or put up my tent near the petrol station and await the next day, hopefully, with cooler weather.

Misinformation: there is no caravan camping at Piggs Peak. The Highland Inn, a colonial-style complex of inn, bar, and gift shop, was my only alternative. When I explained to the hostess my penchant for camping, she suggested a grassy area to the side of the main building, with bathroom facilities within the inn—perfect for my needs.

I mistakenly enjoyed two Castle Light beers at the bar that did not mix well with the anti-malarial medicine I was taking once a week. This happened to be medicine day. I was kept awake all night with a 24-hour illness that included uncontrollable fever and chills the next day. In desperation, I crawled into my sleeping bag within the sun-drenched tent where the internal temperature was well over 100 degrees F. Two hours later the fever broke. Was I experiencing the symptoms of an induced malaria attack as a result of the medicine and/or the beer?

I decided to walk, not ride, into Piggs Peak, named for a man whose last name was Hogg. My Lonely Planet Travel Survival Kit reports that Piggs Peak is named for a prospector who found gold here in 1884. Perhaps his name was Hogg.

At a butcher shop I selected a piece of steak large enough for two people. When I asked for a fork and knife from the clerk, a problem arose. The Swazis do not use forks, they use their fingers. A broken piece of hacksaw blade serves as a knife. The clerk finally found what I requested. The braai, or barbecue coals next door were ready for the job ahead. This lunch was tasty!

Exhausted from my brief illness, I still planned to leave the next day for the capital, Mbabane. If biking became too difficult I would take a bus. Two campground companions, Mark Hooper and Christy Santos from Chico, California, had driven through the mountains from Mbabane to Piggs Peak. They strongly advised the bus.

For an additional two Rand, the Globetrotter was securely fastened on the roof rack of a Mercedes bus. The bus moaned and groaned through the mountains, barely up to this challenge. The terrain looked to be more negotiable from Mbabane to the border gate near Big Bend, a sugar cane growing area.

The National Parliament and National Museum in Mbabane were open to visitors. For a time I was the only visitor. My guided tour included the Parliament and a representative Swazi village outside the museum. The natives' huts have no windows and a very small and low doorway, keeping them cool in the summer and warm in winter. The Parliament building is a dignified structure with a full-sized preserved hippo and a female lion in glass cases. My guide explained that the government has a president and two chambers known as the House Assembly and the Senate. All members are appointed by the king, a polygamist.

One room of the museum is a memorial to King Sobhuza II, the most revered of Swazi kings. He is shown in full ceremonial dress as well as in top hat and tails. His son is the present king. Swazi kings are permitted to have only one son so that there is no contest to succession among brothers. If any of the king's many wives bears him a son, none are permitted any more children. I purchased a colorful string of warrior beads as a memento of this visit and now consider myself an unofficial Swazi warrior.

The thermal baths at Siphotaneni were recommended by Jimmy, the owner of a bar in Manzini, the industrial center of the country, where I camped one night. I did not know at that moment that Manzini, Siphotaneni, and Swaziland would take on great significance to me in the future. Ian McEwan; Mrs. D'Orsi, the wife of the Italian consul to Swaziland; Mangaliso Nhlapo; his mother Julia; and even Alessandra from Cap Martin near Monaco play a part in my Manzini adventure that continues to this day.

A small sign and arrow pointing the direction to the Italian consul stands at the crest of a steep climb out of Manzini. An idea made my visit to the consul irresistible: I would meet the consul and, with his consent, send a letter in his diplomatic pouch to my friend Alessandra Sartorio from Torino, Italy. We had met at Cap Martin.

A winding dirt road brought us to the consul's compound. He and his wife, unfortunately, weren't home, but a caretaker invited me in so I could write a note to the consul asking him to forward my short letter to Alessandra. As I was leaving, a downpour forced me to seek shelter at a pub I had visited previously in Manzini. After a delay of at least two and a half hours, a patron, Ian McEwen, offered me lodging in his home, warning me that I would not see any accommodations until Big Bend.

Ian and I decided to dine at Fontana di Trevi, an Italian coffee bar and trattoria owned by the Italian consul and his wife and managed by their nephew Mario. When we finally left at closing time, I told Mario that I had been trying to get in touch with his uncle or aunt. "My aunt is home. Would you like to talk to her?" At the end of our conversation I learned that Mrs. D'Orsi would not allow Mario to accept payment for our meal.

I was now trying out a new hill climbing technique. Watching bicycle racing on South African television, I became aware of a technique used by racers when climbing hills. They move their torso back so far that they are almost off the saddle. This puts their legs in a more horizontal position that applies additional power to the pedals.

My lunch stop in Siphotaneni was near the baths recommended by Peter, the former bar owner in Manzini. A layer of soap scum in the men's pool covered the surface of the more or less stagnant tepid water. One person interested in oral hygiene was using this water to brush his teeth. Was I going to immerse myself in water that probably has a bacterial count higher than Alewife Brook in Cambridge, which has not supported life for years?

I was awakened by a gentle voice speaking English. A handsome young black lad of 15, without shirt or shoes was standing before me. "My name is Mangaliso Nhlapo. I would like to be your pen pal."

"Mangaliso, if we are to be pen pals, do you have any money for a stamp?"

"I have no money."

"All right. I'll give you a small amount of money to buy your first stamp. Then, each time I reply I'll enclose a little money so you can buy another stamp. That way we can be pen pals and it will not cost you any money. But if you take this stamp money I'm giving you and buy a Coke, we will not be pen pals. You must write to me first, OK?"

I told Mangaliso during our brief conversation that I would like to send him something upon my return home. "A bicycle?" he asked.

"I will take a picture of you and your friends and will mail a copy to you when I return home." This was agreed. Mangaliso then requested a picture of just himself.

"Mangaliso, have you ever heard of Rotary Club International? They have a scholarship program whereby scholars come from other countries to study in the United States, and Americans study abroad. If you become enrolled in a college in Swaziland, I might be able to arrange for you to come to Boston one year as a Rotary scholar. I will not promise anything except to try." Now dry and rested, I decided to head for Big Bend. My head was swimming with ideas relating to Mangaliso, with little else to think about as I entered the sugar cane growing area of Big Bend. I was alone with my thoughts and the quiet sound of the bicycle chain. The big question of the moment: will Mangaliso buy a stamp or a Coke? I am pleased to say that he bought the stamp and that the photo of him is one of my favorites. We are pen pals forever!

More misinformation: Ian, did you say the road to Big Bend was downhill all the way? True, I did experience a drop in elevation, but I also had ample time to practice my new hill climbing technique. Leaving Big Bend the next morning, the sun was intense, the hills negotiable, and the scenery lovely.

After a night in the fly-infested Lavumisa Hotel at the border gate, my Swazi experience regrettably came to an end.

Chapter 25
SOUTH AFRICA REVISITED

Now that Swaziland was behind me, St. Lucia Park near the coast of the Indian Ocean became my next objective. At 98 km, it was more than a day's ride through mountains and wilderness. Except for the town or village of Mkuse, there appeared to be few amenities before St. Lucia. Game preserves and desolation are the characteristics of northeastern Natal. Mkuse, to the south, is not mentioned in my "Lonely Planet Guide."

I stocked up with a reasonable food supply and headed into new territory, unaware of the severity of the mountains I would be climbing on Route N-2. Dehydration, brought on by intense sun and hills, depleted my strength to about half its usual level. About two-thirds of the way up a very substantial mountain, a 4-wheel drive vehicle pulling a boat and trailer stopped at the top after passing me. Mike Barsdorf, the driver, asked me if I wanted a ride. We put the Globetrotter in the boat and headed for St. Lucia and Richards Bay. He drove me to Richards Bay Campground.

This municipal campground has two major problems: ants and theft. I was warned about both by friendly neighbors. Who would think about clean clothes being stolen! Though missing the next morning, I found my bike togs in a wash tub where the thief left them; he or she apparently is not a cyclist.

Some say that Richards Bay may be the next Hong Kong once the Chinese regain possession of their territory. The harbor and surrounding area are ideal for development. I learned about Eco Peeko Tours, owned and operated by Ron McDonell, at the harbor. He and I arranged to meet the following morning for a full day's safari in the game preserves. I told Ron about my disappointment with Kruger National Park. He assured me that our day together would be a rewarding experience. Ron, a retired TV cameraman of 62, was given early retirement so a black person could be trained and hired. At one time he accompanied Ian Smith, Rhodesia's prime minister, on a whirlwind tour of the United States. Eco Peeko Tours is now his post-professional employment. It was my good fortune to be the only client that day.

We drove to St. Lucia Park and boarded a riverboat for a two-hour ride on an estuary. It is here that we saw hippos, crocodiles, and fish eagles. A family of hippo was submerged, creating a huge dark shadow on the water's surface. Our pilot explained that this shadow represents dozens of hippos resting beneath the surface. With borrowed binoculars I watched a cow hippo nursing her calf. We drove after lunch to Hluhluwe (pronounced "shushluee") Game Reserve in search of the rhino. Even if we hadn't seen rhino, the drive through the reserve would have been a success. Impala, zebra, birds of various varieties, and a family of giraffe added to our visual enjoyment. By 8:30 PM, I was back at my campsite.

Mtunzini, 50 km south of Richards Bay, is not only the location of Xaxaza Caravan Park, owned by Noel and Merle Muller, it is the home and studio of Bruce McClunan, an artist and sculptor. Ron recommended both to me. A tailwind on Route N-2 brought me to the campground in less than four hours.

Xaxaza is probably the finest campground I've had the pleasure of visiting. Not only do Merle and Noel provide a complete market, their tropical vegetation and spacious grounds are outstanding. They also provide a free lending library. "If I can find this book on cycling," said Merle, "I'll bring it to the library." The title is The Wind In My Wheels by Josie Dew. Shortly thereafter, Merle brought the book to my tent.

The book concerns Josie, an English caterer by profession, who fell in love with the bicycle as a child, against the advice of her father who thought it not "feminine" enough for his daughter. The catering Josie does today is delivered on her three-wheeled human powered delivery bicycle. Her book relates the many adventures Josie has had while bicycle touring the world. Reading her book kept me at Xaxaza an extra day.

I was now in KwaZula/Natal, the heart of the land of the Zulus, where Shaka, the Zulu king, formed an army so powerful that he actually defeated the English. Shakaland, created as a set for the TV movie "Shaka Zulu," is located in the mountains near the town of Eshowe and became a "must" on my list of places to visit. Distance was the only problem. I felt I'd be unable to bike there and back to Xaxaza in one day without nighttime cycling. Merle found a solution to that problem.

She informed me that she had a ride for me with a neighbor to Eshowe at the top of a mountain. After a visit to the historical museum, I coasted to the Shakaland entrance at the bottom, a distance of 15 km. A rough dirt road then climbed tortuously to the entrance of the Zulu Village and entertainment center where tourists spend most of the afternoon visiting, eating, and being entertained.

The Zulu women were delightful to look at and photograph. They remain bare-breasted until marriage. Well-mannered older children gathered near their mothers, helping where necessary.

Native dancing, the medicine man, and the warrior are authentically represented at Shakaland. The chief occupies the largest hut. To his left a smaller hut is also reserved for him, where he can seek solace away from his seven or eight wives, each having her own hut. A small corral giving the appearance of an animal pen is the king's burial ground. In case the chief dies away from his kraal, his relatives take a branch from the kraal to the place of death where it picks up the deceased's spirit. They then return it to the burial site. As in Biblical times, the brother of the deceased inherits his brother's wives even though he may have his own.

We were entertained with authentic Zulu dancing to the beat of two drums. Wielding the wooden batons by male Zulus, the beat is loud and penetrating. Men, women, and children danced for us in their traditional costumes, with children imitating the gyrations of their parents.

I knew I needed a ride up the mountain if I had any expectation of reaching my campsite before dark. Biking in these mountains after sunset would have been dangerous, especially in South Africa where drivers have a heavy foot on the accelerator. By 4 PM, I returned to the main road leading to Eshowe with the hope of getting a ride to the top of the mountain. A white bakki driven by a woman in uniform passed at a high rate of speed. I stuck out my thumb as she passed. Shortly thereafter the same bakki approached from the opposite direction and stopped. "I had guilt feelings," said the conservation officer. "I will take you to Eshowe and then if I pass you on the road I will take you to Xaxaza." Once at the top of the mountain my problem was solved. I arrived at the campground just before dark.

Bruce McClunan, the sculptor, called for me at Xaxaza and brought me back later that evening. I visited his studio and home. His artistic bronze craftsmanship is magnificent; I immediately thought of him as the Remington of South Africa.

Though the sun was scorching, we headed south toward Durban, battling a headwind that forced me into my lower gears. I began looking for non-existent refreshment shacks or stores where I could replenish my rapidly diminishing water supply. Finding a shade tree, I decided to rest for a few minutes. A half hour later, after a second attempt at rising, I made it to the bike. A car traveling north stopped. It was Ron McDonell and his wife, who had been in Durban visiting their daughter. My first words were not "Hello" but "Have you water?" They, fortunately, always carry an emergency supply in the trunk of their car.

Ron and Jackie gave me no hope of finding food for the next 33 km. Perhaps they don't patronize black establishments. I came upon a petrol station and grocery within a few kilometers. A black patron there was generous with his advice, which turned out to be misinformation. It was not downhill with the wind at my back, as he described, but more of the same hills and headwinds so relentless I had difficulty keeping the Globetrotter on the road.

We left Route N-2 and followed alternate N-4 to the coast. The sky was now overcast and the headwinds diminished, making cycling much more comfortable. Ten kilometers before Durban, signs prohibiting bicycles began to appear, as did those stating that speed is controlled by photograph. I found myself at times staring into the lens of a camera. The local police were of no help in providing me with an alternate route into the city; I had no choice but to break the law.

Durban, like Johannesburg, does not enjoy a good reputation. Gangs of thieves, predominantly black, have gained the ignominy of mugging people of both races. Tourists have begun to patronize other areas in spite of the wonderful facilities and the beach. How was I to protect myself if accosted?

Remembering my days in the military and my association with the Marine Corps, where Marines wrap their belt and metal buckle around a closed fist, I decided to protect myself if necessary with my bike cable and lock. Holding the loop end of the cable, I could use the lock at the other end as a weapon, striking anyone who came into my path. Fortunately, this was not necessary. Durban was no more dangerous than the other parts of South Africa I visited.

Our first stop in Durban was the Transportation Center, a large and sophisticated facility with several bus companies. It resembles a modern airport terminal. Greyhound offered to take the bike in a box to Capetown; the others refused completely. I therefore opted for the train, with a 40 percent senior citizen discount. If I carry my luggage to my seat, the Globetrotter will go free.

A fellow cyclist escorted me to the Durban youth hostel. It offers complete facilities and safe bicycle storage and is within sight of the beach. Good inexpensive restaurants within walking distance gave me a break from cooking.

The Ark, a Christian shelter, is located on Brown Street near the docks. This large facility operates with a staff of 110. Alex, a volunteer of thirteen months, escorted me through the various buildings that house 700 distressed or homeless people. I was interested in comparing the Ark to The House of Grace. Both get all their funds from donations. In Alex's opinion, the Ark is the model for the *new* South Africa, being non-sectarian and non-racial. An outreach program provides for street people who prefer the streets to being housed. Residents have responsibilities such as spending fifty hours in Bible study and being free of drugs. Drugs are illegal at the Ark and in South Africa. Those who do not become "clean" or refuse the Bible study requirement are asked to leave. A separate section is set aside for full-blown alcoholics. Except for the blessing of food, religion is not emphasized at The House of Grace.

A school and youth center are provided for children of the residents. Those who have been at the Ark for twelve weeks are eligible for medical and dental care. Dental care is provided by dental school students in Durban.

When a person comes to the Ark, he or she is fed prior to any attempt at rehabilitation. In this regard, the Ark and The House of Grace have identical philosophies. I was invited to breakfast the following day. "Be there at 5:45 even though things do not begin to happen until 6:30," said Alex.

Breakfast was rather dismal until a group of children invited me to join them at their table. Our breakfast consisted of a glass of sweetened tea and a bowl of white gruel. Each resident brings his spoon and returns it to his room at the end of the meal. A spoon was finally found for me, but it would have made little difference. I was unable to swallow the gruel. When no one was looking I dumped it into the barrel.

Feeling hungry, I went to the nearest restaurant serving eggs, bacon, and coffee. I felt for the residents of the Ark! The big moment of my day was watching ostrich in the Karoo from the train enroute to Capetown. We arrived the next morning at 6:15.

I decided to pedal directly to Cape Point and the Cape of Good Hope, leaving my visit to Capetown for the return. I wanted, if possible, to travel the Atlantic coast on my outbound tour and the Indian Ocean on the return.

Except for the challenge of Chapmans Peak, the cycling was rather effortless on some of the best roads I have traveled anywhere except perhaps France. The scenery at first reminded me of the Italian Riviera, or perhaps the southern coast of Sicily, except for huge rock formations across the bay. Farther south a Cape Cod panorama began to take form with quarter mile-wide sandy beaches met by a vigorous surf.

At Caravan Camping at Kommetjie near the water, I shared a site with a group of young surfers. Janice Cocks, the mother of one of the boys in the group, offered to drive me to the supermarket. "When you come to Capetown, please call us," said Janice. "You will have supper and meet the rest of our family." This began a friendship that has continued through the mail.

Paul Smith, one of the high school-age boys, warned me not to go out at night in Capetown: "In the city there are pickpockets galore." Just what I needed!

I headed for the Cape of Good Hope in the morning. The first stop was a nature reserve, where I met Lovemore

Munombwi from Zimbabwe, the sculptor of the stone hippo that helps hold down my TV set at home. I also met a family of baboons playing at the side of the road. This was not my last meeting with the baboon population.

It's 13 km from the entrance of the nature reserve to Cape Point. This is where Atlantic and Indian Ocean waters commingle. Cape Point and the Rock of Gibraltar are two places I did not expect to see in my lifetime.

I found my night's stop at Muizenberg, having ridden 80 km for the day. My new hill climbing technique allowed me to arrive less fatigued than normal. Capetown was only 24 km to the north.

A number of cars stopped at a roadside rest to watch the baboons. Entire families of these animals were climbing the sheer surface of a cliff that looked impossible to a non-baboon. Others were sitting on the hoods of cars looking in at the driver and passengers as the humans returned the stares. One baboon yawned, showing his enormously long canine teeth. A young woman rolled down a car window just far enough to ask me if I was afraid, being unprotected from the baboons. My reply was that I was trying to get a photo of the animal on the hood of her car. A sign stated that "A fed baboon is a dead baboon." If fed, the animals become very aggressive and are then destroyed by park rangers.

Capetown finally came into view as I headed west, ever climbing. Rhodes Memorial and Preserve is located on Table Mountain. The Memorial is very large, with a sculpture of Cecil John Rhodes (1853-1902), a prime minister of the Cape Colony. He formed the British South African Company in 1889 that is presently Zambia and Zimbabwe (formerly Rhodesia).

Needing directions to a hostel at Camps Bay, I parked the Globetrotter near the entrance to the Lipshitz Motor Company in the Garden Section of Capetown. Noel Lipshitz, the owner, started to draw me a map, then stopped. "I will explain it to you later. Right now, I'm gooing to call my wife Shirley to let her know that you are coming to dinner at our house this evening." This is how a still-thriving friendship with the Lipshitz family began. For three days Noel, Shirley, and Noel's daughter went out of their way to be friendly. When Noel told me about a hostel nearby, I forgot about Camps Bay, especially when I learned that the name of the hostel is the *Globetrotter Backpackers.*

Anne, John, Isabelle, and I met at the Globetrotter. We toured the wine route together in a rented car. We unfortunately did not get to Stellenbosch, perhaps the best known winery because we spent so much time at the others. We returned to the hostel just in time for me to get ready for dinner with Janice Cocks and her family.

Anne, a hostel resident, and I drove into the mountains the next morning, hoping that the cable car to the top of Table Mountain was operating. Weather conditions at the summit are so unpredictable that it's difficult to know when safe conditions will prevail. The "tablecloth" of clouds occasionally vanishes completely, revealing this flat-topped mountain 1,000 meters above Capetown. The "tablecloth" was absent this day, and my color slide captured a spectacular view as a memory of this fascinating part of the world. The cable car was not running due to severe winds.

I spent the afternoon at a bike shop doing my own repairs. A new derailleur and rear tire put me back on the road in preparation for biking part of the Garden Route. My reservation to Miami on South African Airlines prevented me from touring the full length of this scenic drive.

I spent part of my last day in Capetown visiting the South African Museum with Janice Cocks and her mother. One traveling exhibit there concerned the Anne Frank story. It refreshed my memory of the book <u>The Diary of Anne Frank</u> and a previous visit by Dorothy and me to the Anne Frank House in Amsterdam. The other exhibit traced the history of white supremacy and apartheid in South Africa. I was quite amazed to see such a frank discussion of this sensitive subject. South Africa is obviously coming to terms with the injustices that have dominated much of the black population.

The overnight train to the town of George brought us to the highly acclaimed Garden Route. The scenery from George to Plattenberg Bay is not particularly spectacular except where a train trestle crosses a deep ravine. A coal-driven engine was pulling a trainload of passengers across the trestle at the moment I passed on the nearby highway. We both traveled at the same speed until the road began an endless climb while the train went through a tunnel.

I continued the next morning toward Port Elizabeth, the end of the Garden Route, 250 km away. Once over a mountain that I had to partially walk, the terrain began to level off. At a toll booth on Route N-2, the toll collector advised me to avoid the treadle and thus not have to pay the toll. The highway then became virtually flat even though there were high mountains to my left. I had breathtaking views of ravines hundreds of feet deep that the highway spanned.

A house came into view at the 100 km mark. I pulled into its driveway, looking for a place to camp. Alma, the owner, suggested a bed and breakfast 8 km over the mountain in the small town of Kareedouw, and offered to drive me there.

Our next stop on Route N-2 was Port Elizabeth, where I stopped at a hostel. There are no services in the 80 km between Port E. and Jeffrey's Bay.

My seatmate on the overnight train to Johannesburg was, unfortunately, a white racist South African. This redneck, from the moment he entered my compartment, focused on the inferiority of blacks. He predicted there would be a war, not an election. How wrong he was! Mandela won the election.

Johannesburg, fortunately, was not what I expected. Once off the train from Port Elizabeth, I experienced the best this beautiful city had to offer. I'm certain that had I been robbed or worse, I would have a different opinion. Carl and Marissa, owners of the Pink House Backpackers, suggested that I visit Gold Reef City, a distance of 25 km from Yoeville. An abandoned gold mine and amusement park comprise this amusement center. Free entertainment is booked as "The African Extravaganza," where black Africans do traditional dances in native costumes on stage. Unable to hold back my sense of rhythm; I climbed onto the stage at the end of the performance and did swing dancing with the women to the beat of the African drum. The photo of this event, taken by the chief, shows me wearing my "Slick Rock" bike cap.

The gold mine is the major attraction. We were lowered by elevator to the first mine level, 500 feet below the surface. The shaft terminates 3 kilometers below at a lake. All South African mines are linked underground for safety reasons. This mine, no longer active, could be reopened if the price of gold rises.

At the Pink House Backpackers, Larry and Wendy Carey from Cape Elizabeth, Maine, and I hired a car and guide to take us through Soweto, a large and overpopulated all-black township. I counted ten separate dwellings in one 20-by-20 foot area. These homes are made of corrugated steel or metal containers. Though congested, each house is clean and the yard immaculate. Vacant lots serve as trash dumps.

My ride to the airport was less than enjoyable. I was on an 8-lane high-speed highway of unknown legality for bicycles. Finally and with tremendous relief I arrived at Jan Smutts Airport. An attendant offered to watch my property while I refreshed myself in the bathroom. I made the mistake of not closing my bags, a usual practice. When I returned from the shower both attendant and bike shoes were missing. After reporting the incident to airport security, I hurried to the departure gate. Though I was a bit cramped on the C-47, the flight attendants and food could not have been better. With an 8-hour time difference, we arrived in Miami at 3:15 AM.

Chapter 26
BICYCLE USA

Pedaling to Homestead from Miami International Airport was uncomfortable without bike shoes; my stolen shoes were somewhere in Johannesburg. Homestead is the location of the Paul Dudley White Bicycle Club, sponsor of the "Winter Rendezvous" bike rally. I looked forward to seeing old friends there, but Hurricane Andrew spoiled this plan. If the club is still in existence, it's a closely held secret. The KOA campground, fortunately, had available tent sites.

I found cycling shoes on sale at a sporting goods store, which also returned my damaged tent to North Face; the company replaced it with a new one. There was one other piece of equipment I wanted: a safety flag. I had no intention of biking on US 1 without a flag's visible protection.

The standard bike flag with its long pole can be a problem when mounting and dismounting a single bike. This was not the case with the Globetrotter. I also wanted protection from vehicles passing too close on my left. The concept of the "I See You, not I.C.U." was born ("I.C.U." is an acronym for intensive care unit.). It's a flag system that can be flown vertically or horizontally., using a triangular-shaped pennant similar to those used to identify utility wires. I have since applied for a patent on this device.

I headed north through the string of ocean-front towns north of Miami. I tried to get special permission to camp in a public park in Boca Raton but was refused. John Prince Park west of Lake Worth served that purpose.

While having refreshments at a picnic table along the Intracoastal Waterway, I met Jim "Patches" Watson, QMS, USN Ret. We are both World War II Navy veterans and both interested in writing. Jim, one of the first Navy "Seals," recently completed his autobiography Point Man. He led a colorful life

521

as a career Chief Petty Officer and is now curator of the UDT Seal Museum in Fort Pierce. The museum's history of the Navy frogmen was especially worthwhile, now that I had met the curator. One of the pieces on display from the Vietnam era is a rebreathing device made by the Emerson Company in Cambridge. Bill Emerson, a patient of mine as a child, is now in charge, having succeeded his father as president.

By two the next afternoon, I was established at a campground near the Kennedy Space Center. These 70 km to Cape Canaveral were perhaps the easiest of my trip, but I missed the launch of the Space Shuttle by one day. I toured the Space Center the following day, where I watched two movies, "The Dream Is Alive" and "The Blue Planet" at the IMAX theater. Both films were quite an experience for someone who had seen only two movies in the previous two years. The highlight of "The Dream Is Alive" is being there at liftoff. Seeing the actual event might not be as vivid as the movie.

I became friendly with Jud Spitzer, a 24-year-old Navy career man. He had toured Europe and was a volunteer at Kibbutz Gezer near Tel Aviv, my favorite kibbutz. We spent time swapping stories concerning our travels.

Rather than follow the coast, I decided to go north and west to Orlando and Disney World. Pedaling along a divided highway, I saw two shirtless men pulling a shopping cart that was too heavy to push. Mike Faxon and Bill Maik had a sign on the cart "We will work for food." One of them had pulled the cart from his home in Raymond, Maine, seeking work, and the other joined him on the way. I offered them money. They refused my gift until I insisted. I then learned that Mike and Bill thought that I, too, was homeless. Instead of having my possessions in a shopping cart, they were strapped to an oversized bicycle. Was this why I was not harassed or molested or worse in the previous twelve countries?

I was welcomed at the International Hostel in Orlando. A sign at the reception desk suggests viewing a 30-minute promotional video about Disney World. The video had the opposite of its intended effect on me. For 23 months I was looking at the "real thing." At Disney World I would be looking at façades depicting real-world places. Even though I went out of my way to go to Orlando, going to Disney World was out of the question at that time.

With a tailwind, we continued back toward the coast, through Deland and Daytona Beach, where I enjoyed a motor tour around the banked track of the Daytona Speedway. In St. Augustine, the oldest city in the United States, Fort Castillo de San Marcos is the best example in the US of a Spanish colonial fortification, and for many years was Spain's northernmost outpost in the Western Hemisphere.

Route A1A along the coast is scenic but the wind is relentless. The natural sand dunes, low vegetation, and waterscapes are reminiscent of Cape Cod. A night's camping at Little Talbot State Park was interesting, with aggressive raccoons and "no-see-ums." Fortunately, my insect repellent from South Africa was an effective deterrent.

Once I crossed the border into Georgia, the wealth of Florida vanished. I chose the AYH hostel in Brunswick over the KOA. My down sleeping bag was barely sufficient to keep me warm on this early spring night. "Perhaps I should slow down and wait for warmer weather." The next morning, I had a different message: I wanted to be back in Cambridge two years to the day after I left. I made it to Savannah that day.

I followed Route 17 north to Charleston, South Carolina, ignoring the "no bicycles, no pedestrians, etc." signs on the immense bridge over the Savannah River. With a sigh of relief, I coasted down the far side of the bridge into another new state. Nearing the coast again, the maples and other deciduous trees were becoming dressed for the new season.

Charleston was badly damaged by Hurricane Hugo. Had there been a sightseeing bus, I would have taken it. Instead, I spent the rest of the day biking around the city. I fortunately found the narrow footpath over the massive Cooper River bridge, providing a superb view of the USS Yorktown and Fort Sumter.

We continued north on Route 17 through Georgetown and Myrtle Beach, from which I planned to head for Lynchburg, Virginia, the home of my son-in-law's parents. Rain was the only deterrent. And rain it did that afternoon and night. Just before the onset of the first storm, I found shelter in an open garage. I ignored the "no trespassing" sign and went in. The owner, a contractor and ex-motorcyclist, arrived in his pickup truck about 45 minutes later. He had no problem with my decision to seek shelter on his property, and even invited me into the house. I declined at the time, thinking the rain would end. He drove off. Two hours later, in the dark, with the rain still heavy, I reconsidered. The back door, fortunately, was unlocked and there was no dog. Eventually the contractor returned with his wife. They welcomed me into their run-down home that appeared to be recently occupied. They were still asleep when I left in the morning, leaving a note of appreciation with the washed cup and saucer from my morning coffee.

Quite by chance I encountered Bike Route #1. Local workmen explained that it connects with US Route 1 near Pinehurst. As a former golfer, I knew that Pinehurst has some of the finest courses in the country. At one time I looked forward to the day when I would play there. We followed Route 501, more or less, toward Virginia.

Arriving in Roxbury, North Carolina, well after dark, I began looking for a campsite. The lights of the Christian Faith Fellowship Church in the distance, with several cars in the parking area, was inviting. A meeting of the pastor, his wife, and members of the congregation had just ended. "Have you eaten? Are you thirsty?" they asked. I explained my need. One person knew the location of the cold water shutoff in the attic, and another turned on the lights to the parking lot. I assured them I was self-sufficient and expressed my gratitude.

Cycling through the Virginia countryside was picturesque but uneventful. Route 501 continued into Lynchburg. I appreciated the hospitality of Emlyn and Ruth Ann, my son-in-law's parents.

Following a late start, I headed in the direction of the Blue Ridge Parkway, following a road along the James River. My Parkway map indicated that the next restaurant was 30 miles to the north. It did not say that the 30 miles were uphill. Tired and footsore from many walked miles, I found the restaurant closed. Even the men's room was secured. Without water, free camping is not exactly ideal. I began to feel the chill of evening as the sun set. A nearby ranger invited me into his heated home, just in time. Hypothermia was beginning to take effect. He gave me food and drink and directed me to Montebello Camping and Fishing Resort at the base of the mountain.

Rather than be challenged further by the mountains, I decided to stay in the foothills and head for Charlottesville and eventually to Rockville, Maryland, the home of my friends Bob and Sylvia Pear; we met in the Upper Galilee in Israel. Despite some chancy weather, my trek north was progressing nicely.

Entering Culpeper, the rear tire blew with such force that both tire and tube self-destructed. I made the necessary repairs and biked into town for a spare tire and tube and inquired about a campsite. Rain was again threatening. After a wet night at Rolling Acres campground, where I set up my new tent under the pavilion. We then returned to Culpeper, seeking shelter for far longer than I wished at a convenience store. Finally, the nearest accommodations, a Super 8 motel, became my only choice.

Stacey Huntley held the door for me; she and her 11-year-old daughter were staying at the motel. Stacey was in the process of writing a book titled <u>She's Still Alive!</u> A jealous teenager stabbed and almost killed Stacey when she was a child. Later, she was threatened by a rapist. Other mishaps also occurred to her that she did not elucidate. I was interested to learn that while Stacey held the door for me and the Globetrotter, she too thought I was homeless.

Once on the Maryland side of the Potomac, I inquired about a campground. "Follow the Chesapeake and Ohio Canal towpath," advised a shopkeeper. "The towpath is restricted to hikers and bikers." This seemed like good advice until...

This towpath was no place for the Globetrotter, with an endless deep rutted surface. If there was a campground, it was so basic that I didn't recognize it as such. After many miles of unpleasant travel, I left the towpath at Edwards Ferry, a name, not an entity, spending the night next to Poole's General Store at Poolesville.

I called Sylvia Pear the next morning from Poole's, telling her I was within a day's biking of Rockville. Due to misinformation, I biked past my intersection and took a small side road to the right. I asked directions to Rockville from a man walking nearby. At the same time I noticed the home and professional sign of Dr. John Law, orthodontist. By coincidence, my friend John directed me to Rockville and the Pears' home.

I was determined to leave for Baltimore and the headquarters of L.A.B. in spite of the forecast of rain. Bob and Sylvia tried to convince me to stay another day, awaiting a more favorable forecast, but I, the perpetual optimist when it comes to the weather, decided to leave. I called L.A.B. and spoke to Donald Tighe, the editor of <u>Bicycle USA</u>, our magazine. He was expecting me. For the past 23 months, Donald had published my monthly reports in the magazine, and was anxious to meet the person behind the pen.

Thirty minutes later, I wished I had taken the Pears' advice. A McDonald's became my refuge for more hours than I want to remember. With a temporary pause in the rain, I reached Clarksville before the skies again opened up. A private home behind a convenience store would be my night's refuge if I could get permission. Rick, the owner, could not have been more helpful. He invited me inside in the morning for breakfast and a shower. "Call me on my 800 number when you get back to Cambridge," he said.

The L.A.B. office had two visitors that day: myself and Michael Ridgeway, a handsome and athletic tennis coach. He was completing a one-year trip around the perimeter of the United States representing the organization Dream Ride for AIDS, bringing the AIDS message to everyone with whom he came in contact. One of my favorite slides is of Michael pointing to a map with his route outlined in red. Coincidentally, Michael and my good friend Bill Hoffman, both of whom live in Lancaster, Pennsylvania, are the best of friends. I was looking forward to my visit with Bill in a day or so.

One of the features of L.A.B. is its Hospitality Homes directory, in which members open their homes to other bicycle touring members. All that's required is an advance phone call. This courtesy was extended to me by Dave and Susie Jones, living in Cockeysville, Maryland, a Baltimore suburb. Susie, L.A.B.'s Education Director at the time, drove me to League headquarters when she went to work. My extra bonus was their adorable 15-month-old daughter Carly. A magnificent 24-speed Santana tandem costing in excess of $5,000 in the Jones' basement was proof that I was staying with a cycling family.

Dave Jones routed me from Cockeysville to US 1. Conowingo Dam and the Susquehanna River soon came into view. I was now nearing familiar territory, having gone to college for a year and a half while in the Navy at Franklin and Marshall College in Lancaster. Then came the moment I was waiting for: a "Welcome to Pennsylvania" sign. I asked a paving engineer to take my photo documenting my arrival in my native state. Looking at the map, I saw a name that gave me an idea: Peach Bottom.

Peach Bottom is the location of a major nuclear power plant on the Susquehanna. It's also the home of a sweetheart during the time the Navy stationed me at F&M College. She was a freshman at Millersville State Teachers College (now Millersville University), a short distance from Lancaster. We had not seen or heard from one another for 50 years. "I am going to detour through Peach Bottom and try to find Anna Mae on my way to Lancaster!"

Following a car toward a barn, I waited for the driver and passengers to come toward me. I explained who I was looking for. They didn't know of the Weaver family, but they pointed down the road. "You can ask at the country store at the intersection in Little Britain." Finding an antiques store at the same intersection, I went in there first. After all, old things...old people. The owner, a Vermont resident, deferred to the country store. It is managed by Marc, a man in his 30s.

"I can help you," said Marc. "Anna Mae's sister, a nurse, is our babysitter. I know that Anna Mae lives in Quarryville. I'll give you the phone book. You can call her." I dialed the number and identified myself to the party at the other end. After three tries, I made a connection that spanned half a century.

Anna Mae, her husband Roland, a good sport if ever there was one, and I spent the evening in a Lancaster restaurant visiting and eating Lancaster County German cuisine. This was the first of two 50-year reunions; the next one occurred with two of my dental school classmates in Philadelphia.

Bill Hoffman and I were on the L.A.B. Board of Directors at the same time following my presidency of the organization. We have also biked together. Retired at an early age,

Bill is now free to work on bicycling affairs with the local club and the community and pursue his dream of writing and publishing. A good cycling host, Bill escorted me through the back roads and farmland to US 30, the direct route to Philadelphia. A brief but torrential rainstorm interrupted our progress. Seeking shelter in a garage that served as a horse stall for an Amish family that lived in the adjacent house, we were greeted by two young boys, Israel and Joseph. They were dressed in their all-black garments and wide-brimmed hats typical of the Plain People of Lancaster County. My request to photograph the boys was politely refused; their religion prohibits posing for pictures.

At first US 30, the Lincoln Highway, was not highly trafficked. Finally, I had to seek another route—Route 113 to Phoenixville and Valley Forge. I was now in familiar territory. An earlier phone call to my Temple Dental School classmates Mort and Walt led to another 50th anniversary celebration with them and their wives—we three graduated in 1950. Mort and Walter are still seeing patients and not contemplating retirement.

I had long wanted to visit the Metropolitan Museum of Fine Arts in New York City. This was the perfect opportunity, but not by bike. I parked the Globetrotter at my brother Larry's home in Bensalem and went by bus to New York City, a much more practical way than by trying to negotiate US 1 and the George Washington Bridge. My L.A.B. Hospitality Homes directory again proved worthy.

Elizabeth answered her phone, welcoming me to her apartment within sight of Central Park. Her touring bike that she had ridden across America with "Pedal for Power" was leaning against the wall. It was then that I decided to do this charity ride at my first opportunity. I knew immediately who the recipient of my fund-raising efforts would be: The House of Grace in Haifa. The pieces were coming together so nicely, creating a mosaic that would be fulfilled two years later.

My first full day in Gotham was a tour of Ellis Island and the Statue of Liberty. It was exciting to see the Immigration Center that welcomed my grandparents to the US.

Marvin Reisman was another reason for my visit to New York. Marvin was the only Chance Meeting in two years whom I recognized as a friend or acquaintance; we had met on the island of Rhodes. Unfortunately, illness kept him away from his Manhattan law office. I did, however, have the opportunity to visit with Mrs. Reisman by phone. The following morning, after saying goodbye to Elizabeth, I walked to the "Met" where my time was occupied until the scheduled bus ride back to Philadelphia.

Bill Hoffman had routed me from Philadelphia to Massachusetts. Brother Larry routed me from Bensalem to New Hope and the Delaware River. I was now on the last leg of my adventure. I followed the Delaware through Easton to Port Jervis and the Catskill Mountains, not far from where Marv Reisman and I met some 25 years earlier. We then crossed the Hudson River on the Kingston-Rhinecliff Bridge, heading for the Massachusetts border and Great Barrington.

Following a night of unauthorized camping at a wooded area owned by the New York State Department of Public Works, I stopped at the Martindale Chief Diner in Craryville for breakfast. Harvey Krentzman and his wife entered at the same time. In a very short time they learned that I was returning to Cambridge after two years of bicycling and I learned that Harvey is on the Board of Directors of the Norman Rockwell Museum.

Norman Rockwell, recreational bicyclist and world renowned illustrator, was an admirer of Dr. Paul Dudley White of Belmont, Massachusetts, a cardiologist, founder of the American Heart Assocation, and personal physician of President Eisenhower. Dr. White was also a cyclist. Rockwell had done a charcoal sketch from a photograph of Dr. White wearing saddle shoes with his necktie flying in the breeze riding his three-speed bicycle. The sketch was presented with his compliments to the Bicycle Institute of America.

At that time the L.A.W. was planning its national convention in Rockport, Massachusetts. B.I.A. was looking for an opportunity to donate the sketch for a worthy cause, and called me, as chairman of the event. Fifteen copies of the sketch were auctioned, with the proceeds going to the A.H.A. Dr. White personally signed each copy.

The day of the auction, a parade of antique and contemporary bicycles rode through Rockport with Dr. White at the head. Congressman Tip O'Neill, later Speaker of the House of Representatives, was the auctioneer. My personal copy is number 15, the last of the series. Our only regret is that due to illness, Normal Rockwell was unable to ride alongside his friend Dr. White.

I was anxious for obvious reasons to relate this story to Harvey Krentzman: does the Rockwell Foundation know about this sketch? Do they know the location of the original? He suggested that I visit the museum on my way to Cambridge. It's in Stockbridge, Massachusetts, not far away.

Linda Szekely, assistant curator, welcomed me into her office at the museum. Yes, she did know about the sketch but her information was limited. I felt that she was sincerely interested in my impromptu visit. A new and modern structure, the Rockwell Museum is the largest collection of original art by America's most beloved illustrator. My favorite illustration is the panoramic view of "Main Street, Stockbridge" that greeted me as I entered. Another might be the famous Saturday Evening Post cover illustration "The Runaway." I left the museum with the feeling that I wanted to return soon with someone with whom I could share the experience.

Some time after returning to Cambridge, a letter from Linda Szekely arrived, with a copy of a letter on CRW stationery. It was written in 1969 by Norman Satterthwaite, the club president, to Norman Rockwell: "With your consent, we should like you to become an honorary member of the Charles River Wheelmen." Strangely, we made Norman Rockwell and Maurice Chevalier honorary members but neglected a jewel in our own back yard, Dr. Paul Dudley White.

Route 20, the Boston Post Road, brought me from Stockbridge to Springfield and then to Marlborough. I could have continued on Route 20 all the way to Boston, but for personal reasons detoured to Milford.

Dorothy and I planned to do this trip together. At her gravesite I told her that I had returned safely.

At Ace Wheelworks in Somerville, with a bottle of Mont St. Michel champagne, Michael, Robert, customers, and staff of the store helped me celebrate the conclusion of this LIFE'S EXPERIENCE!

PEDAL FOR POWER

The League of American Bicyclists
Long-distance touring program
designed for fund-raising,
as well as personal enjoyment
of the participant.

Chapter 27
PEDAL FOR POWER

2 Wheels, 2 Years, and 3 Continents was the joy of my life. The journal of Allan Lowe that follows reflects the same intensity, when approximately 44 men and women challenged the roads and weather across America, riding from Los Angeles to Cape Henlopen, Delaware. This was "Pedal for Power," an annual event sponsored by the League of American Bicyclists. A more suitable name might have been "Pedal for Empowerment."

Each rider was encouraged to raise money for charitable purposes. My charity was The House of Grace. Membership in the Rotary Club of Cambridge made it possible to acquire a sizeable number of sponsors. Friends and members of other Rotary Clubs also contributed. In the end, I had 158 sponsors. Most of these pledges hovered around $33, or one cent per mile. I pledged to each contributor that "if I do not complete the ride, you don't have to pay." A total of $6,200 was sent to The House of Grace.

PFP lasted six weeks with a total of 56 riders ranging in age from 21 to 73. Most riders did the entire trip, but there was an option for people to do only a part if they didn't have time for the entire distance. Except for two cyclists, all who attempted the full continental crossing completed it.

We were blessed with seven paid and volunteer L.A.B. staff members and three support vehicles. A truck purchased by previous PFP participants carried our luggage, folding cots used at some of the motels, and a supply of bike parts. Two rented vans provided snacks and emergency aid during the day. One staff volunteer, Dick Neuman, rode the distance as "sweep" (the last rider who made sure nobody was left behind).

The following account is taken from Allan Lowe's journal.

Day Zero—Los Angeles, California

Our 3,200-mile, 13-state odyssey began as riders from all over the country collected in a motel near the Los Angeles airport. A sampling of the 40-plus cycling enthusiasts: Walter Shields will celebrate his 73rd birthday on Day 16. John Champagne, an alumnus from last year, is a retired airline pilot, undeterred by two bouts of cancer. Leonard and Susan Lodish from a Philadelphia suburb are the only tandem couple; he is a professor of marketing at the Wharton School of the University of Pennsylvania. Roo Makosky has completed two years of veterinary school at Viriginia Tech. Harry Vincent, a male nurse and recipient of a double kidney transplant, wears "desert" clothing to protect against further skin cancer; it makes him look like a member of the French Foreign Legion when he's seated on his recumbent.

Day 1 (Mother's Day)—Los Angeles to Riverside, California, 81 miles

We rode as a group from the Hacienda Hotel in El Segundo to Manhattan Beach for picture taking and the opening PFP ritual of dipping the rear wheel in the Pacific. The final ritual is dipping the front wheel in the Atlantic. Fortunately, it was Sunday, which minimized the traffic to some extent. However, at a left turn, after each of us signaled our intention and in spite of his "I See You, not I.C.U." safety flag, a motorist passing on the left almost took Ralph's arm off. A police car immediately stopped the offending motorist: justice was served!

After the first rest stop at mile 28, we broke up into small groups or rode alone, a pattern that continued for the rest of the trip. I rode today with three other 50-plus men.

Day 4—Blythe, California to Wickenburg, Arizona, 117 miles

A rule of the road: do not start before 7 AM due to the blinding sun from the east. We crossed the Colorado River into Arizona on I-10. Buzz and I finally overtook Lori Mendenhall, a 30-year-old physical trainer from Houston, and Jack Glaze, a retired airline pilot from Las Vegas, after a 10-mile climb. Lori can outride 85 percent of the men on the trip. A 20-mile-an-hour paceline led by Lori lasted for seven or eight miles until the others fatigued.

Front wheel oscillation resulted in a blowout for one rider. Before he knew what happened, Tracy, one of the volunteers, stopped. "We never change our own flats," said Tracy. That was the end of the oscillation.

Day 7—Cottonwood to Flagstaff, Arizona, 48 miles

We dropped a few hundred feet from the valley at Cottonwood, then started climbing toward Sedona. Red rock formations along the way were absolutely beautiful. Homes and business properties in Red Rock Canyon are designed in harmony with the environment. The ride through the canyon was spectacular on a two-lane highway with no shoulder. We were warned to ride defensively. "Motorists are so intent on looking at the scenery they might not see a bike in spite of its safety flag." We had our first full day of rest and relaxation at Flagstaff the following day. Some toured the Grand Canyon by bus while others did laundry and minor bike repairs.

Day 13—Albuquerque to Santa Fe, New Mexico, 72 miles

We got on old Route 66 and climbed out of Albuquerque. Then, after 17 miles, we started climbing the Turquoise Trail. Fortunately, there was a terrific tailwind pushing us up some long and steep grades. I recorded a top speed of 52.5 miles per hour on one tremendous downhill.

A tour with this many people could not exist without minor mishaps. Clipless pedals accounted for some of the accidents: at times a rider is unable to get out of his pedal in time to prevent a fall. Today, we had a crash of much greater proportions. Richard Kasakatis, a very strong rider from San Diego, was struck from behind by a young pick-up truck driver. While Richard was not injured as much as his bicycle, his collarbone was broken in three places and he was forced to drop out. On Day 15, Rebecca Peres, from Ruxton, Maryland, another experienced cyclist, was blown off her bike by the wind. She fortunately stopped rolling before striking a barbed wire fence.

Another source of potential accidents occurs during "drafting," when a group of cyclists ride very close together to reduce wind resistance. They take turns at the lead "breaking wind," so that everyone's strength is extended and the group travels faster than any rider could individually. Occasionally one rider's front wheel touches the rear wheel of the bike ahead of him, which immediately dumps him and usually brings others down, as they cannot steer quickly enough around the fallen rider. We escaped this kind of crash until the last day, when Trevor Brown, a financial adviser with Chrysler Corporation, was the victim. A native Australian, Trevor has lived in the US for 20 years. He rode the last ten miles to Henlopen Beach, Delaware, in the sag wagon with his left arm in a sling.

Day 16—Las Vegas to Tucumcari, New Mexico, 111 miles

After passing a few riders, I came upon Steve Levine and Eberhardt, the owner of a bicycle touring company in Germany, who joined us in Albuquerque. He added a great deal of congeniality as we pedaled together. We descended from a plateau of approximately 6,500 feet to a valley at about 5,000 feet in about four miles. The descent into Tucumcari was incredibly straight.

Walter Shields was third from last to arrive at our hotel. Everyone celebrated by singing "Happy Birthday." It's really remarkable that this septuagenarian celebrated his 73rd birthday by riding 111 miles.

Day 18—Dalhart, Texas to Guymon, Oklahoma, 74 miles

It was cold this morning, the first cloudy day so far. There are large ranches all around Dalhart where cattle are raised. When flying across the Great Plains one can see huge green circles in otherwise barren countryside. The circles are irrigated by rotary rigs connected to a central well. The rigs are from a quarter to half a mile long.

Day 20—Liberal to Dodge City, Kansas, 83 miles

There was a TV crew from the ABC affiliate in Garden City at our rest stop. I believe they took pictures of some of us along the road and interviewed our leader Curt and Lori Mendenhall. After leaving Minneola, I heard voices behind me. I was overtaken by Greg Shields, Lori, and Beth Ratcliff, also from Cambridge, Massachusetts. We rode into Dodge City averaging close to 25 miles an hour. Our hotel is located on Wyatt Earp Boulevard. Miss Kitty was not there to greet us, but the Boot Hill Museum provided some authenticity to the days of "Gunsmoke." The reproduction of the saloon, Boot Hill, and a shoot-out in front of the Museum provided entertainment for young and old.

Day 23—Salina to Manhattan, Kansas, via Abilene, 73 miles

Breakfast was served at a Lutheran church behind our motel. By 7 AM, we were on our way to Abilene, the home of President Dwight Eisenhower. We tasted one of Mamie's favorite cookie recipes at the visitors' center. Cinnamon buns and coffee at Jenny's authentic bakery and shop were also exceptionally tasty. The Eisenhower Center includes the original site of the President's home. We then walked up to an impressive statue of General Eisenhower in military attire before entering the Museum.

At mile 38.3, we celebrated the halfway mark of our trip with Coke and pizza. I had eaten a barbecue sandwich earlier, but indulged just the same.

Day 25—Topeka, Kansas to St. Joseph, Missouri, 84 miles

Breakfast was interrupted by lightning and lights out, the harbinger of a tornado. A flash flood watch was cancelled at 9:30 but the tornado watch continued until 11 AM. By coincidence, a group of us had gone to see the movie "Tornado" the previous night. Some decided not to ride while the rest of us donned raingear and headed east at 10 AM. My jacket did a good job of keeping me dry, but the Goretex socks did little good.

We observed a cylindrical, horizontal cloud parallel to the road. The cloud, called a "rolly," was only a few hundred feet above the ground. A rolly can be the prelude to a tornado.

Shortly after a rest stop, I was passed by a car which seemed to be only a foot or so away from my left arm. Ralph was 50 to 75 yards ahead of me. I was amazed to see the same car avoid Ralph by several feet. I was skeptical about Ralph's flag but now believe it has considerable merit.

Fortunately, fair weather returned until the last five miles before our night's stop. Strong winds and rain escorted a wet and tired group of cyclists across the Missouri River and into the state of Missouri.

That evening we were treated to a trolley tour of St. Joseph and the Pony Express Museum. The Pony Express method of delivering mail started in St. Joseph but lasted only 18 months before being superceded by the telegraph along the same route. The word "pony" is acutally a misnomer; ponies were too slow to do the job. We could go much faster on good roads on our bikes than the Pony Express.

Day 27—St. Joseph to Chillicothe, Missouri, 94 miles

The entire town of Maysville, population 1,500, turned out to greet us. I began a conversation with Carl I. Minor of Maysville, a spry 79-year-old. He is the Missouri state captain for the Wheelmen, an antique bicycle club. Carl's grandson rode his authentic (circa 1886) highwheeler for our entertainment. The women of the town provided a wonderful array of cookies, cakes, and beverages outside the town library and museum.

Day 31—Springfield to Champaign, Illinois, 90 miles

Good weather prevailed the entire day. I was amazed to see how sparsely populated central Illinois is, with farms and farmhouses widely spaced. The crops appear to be mainly corn and soybeans, with some cattle and pig farming. A cyclist's nose can become very sensitive to different odors. We rested the following day in Champaign, home of the University of Illinois.

Jack Williamson, a high school teacher from Missouri, joined us on his way to a National Education Association conference in Washington, D.C. He was interviewed by radio and TV stations each day relative to his progress. By coincidence, Jack was reading the new book <u>Over the Hills</u> by David Lamb. While Jack was biking from west to east, David Lamb had fought the wind from east to west.

Day 34—Crawfordsville to Indianapolis, Indiana, 63 miles

We arrived at the Speedway museum about 11 AM, spending over an hour looking at the extensive collection of antique automobiles and race cars. Our one lap around the speedway was scheduled for 1 PM, but was delayed a half hour due to late arrivals. One of the riders had six flats, preventing him and Dick Neuman, the sweep, from making this historic ride. We took the lap in single file around the well banked and smooth track behind a lead car provided by the Speedway.

Indianapolis is fortunate to have two tracks, one for car races and one for bicycle races, the Major Taylor Velodrome. Tracy Leiner, a staff volunteer, and Joe Messina, one of our riders celebrating his 50th birthday this year, challenged each other to a two-lap race. It was no contest even though Tracy coasted a portion of the race. The Lodish tandem team and others enjoyed the challenge of the steeply banked cement surface by riding at the top and then, in rapid descent, reaching ground level. All riding was put on hold once it began to rain, for obvious safety reasons.

We watched a 30-lap women's race on single-speed

track bikes that evening, where each lap except for the last represents a point. The last lap is worth two points. There is a winner for each lap and an overall winner in this type of race.

Day 36 (Father's Day)—Richmond, Indiana to Grove City, Ohio, 111 miles

We rode the Old National Pike, Route 40, due east toward Columbus, Ohio. Before leaving the motel, Tracy announced that John Champagne was hosting a picnic for us at the 84-mile mark. The price of admission was a *treasure* from the road or a limerick. Finding no treasure, Ralph presented an off-the-cuff limerick:

There was a man named Galen
Whose tired old knees were a-failin'.
To the pharmacy he went
For Tylenol he spent
And now his knees are not ailin'.

We all enjoyed the picnic. Thanks, John!

Day 40—Wheeling, West Virginia to Uniontown, Pennsylvania, 76 miles

Our morning started with a 3-mile climb out of Wheeling without the opportunity to warm up. This was followed by a series of hills along a twisting, winding road leading to the Pennsylvania border. After a series of steep up-and-down hills we arrived at a rest stop at the top of a hill. There were magnificent views of green grass, trees, and valleys. Some looked at this eastern scene with the same awe that we Easterners had looked at the rubic scenes in Arizona and New Mexico.

After crossing the muddy waters of the Monongahela River, there was a steep climb. The terrain then became much more rolling and the traffic increased as we rode into Uniontown.

I spent a considerable amount of time in late afternoon with Jack Williamson, going over a route for him to ride from Hagerstown, Maryland, to his in-laws in Gettysburg, Pennsylvania, and a route from Gettysburg to downtown Washington, site of the NEA convention.

Day 41—Uniontown, Pennsylvania to Cumberland, Maryland, 68 miles

The organizers of the tour did not realize that they routed us through an area of Uniontown controlled by a drug mob. These people began throwing rocks at the first riders through the area. Tracy Leiner took off after the 15-and 16-year-olds, threatening to retailiate. The arrival of the police calmed the situation, permitting the others to pedal by unharmed, Thanks, Tracy.

This day was billed as the most difficult of the trip. The first climb, lasting 3.2 miles, started about five miles from the motel. This could have been the topic of conversation for the day, but it was only the beginning. Back on US 40, the National Road, the hills had no end in our relentless attempt to follow the route laid out for us. The scenery was breathtaking.

After a downhill from Keyser Ridge at the Maryland border, there was an even longer climb to the top of Negro Mountain, an altitude in excess of 3,000 feet. Here we crossed the Eastern Divide, the point where water goes either to the Atlantic Ocean or the Mississippi River.

Day 44—Edgewood, Maryland to Dover, Delaware, 103 miles

After many ups and downs in Harford County, several cyclists and I began the long descent, which I knew to be to the Susquehanna River at Conowingo Dam. We were advised to claim the narrow lane on the bridge.

The Delaware state capitol, like the one in Maryland, does not resemble many of our US capitols. These two buildings predate the founding of the Republic and therefore do not mimic the Capitol in Washington, D.C.

After dinner that evening, each PFP members spoke about his or her group experience. My thoughts were more philosophical about the country as a whole. Most Americans, unfortunately, only see the sterile shopping centers where the automobile is king. Ralph, our septuagenarian and former president of L.A.W., urged our members to sign up for the League's Hospitality Homes program. It's a way for members to stay in the homes of other members while traveling. All that's needed is a phone call.

Day 45—Dover to Cape Henlopen, Delaware, 60 miles

This was a muggy morning with high expectations. We assembled at a rest stop about 10 miles from Cape Henlopen to ride as a group to the beach. All riders wore their PFP jerseys the League provided at the beginning of the trip.

Most riders removed their shoes at the beach and carried their bikes to the water's edge for the traditional "wheel dipping" in the Atlantic. Before leaving, we were hosted by a local bicycle club with a sumptuous lunch with sandwiches donated by Subway.

Some of the more experienced riders will look back on Pedal for Power as a wonderful experience traveling with a superb group of people. For those who did this sort of thing for the first time, it was a memorable and fantastic true-life experience. For those who collected sponsors, their added joy is the knowledge that they are helping those less fortunate than themselves.

In the words of Helen Keller, "Life is either a daring adventure or nothing!"

END NOTES

Akat Yucel. Istanbul. Keskin Color Kartipostalcilik, Ltd. Turkey, 1993.

Albright, W.F. The Archæology of Palestine. Pelican Books. Canada, 1954.

Allegro, John. The Dead Sea Scrolls: A Reappraisal. Penguin Books. London, 1990.

Anne Frank House. Boom Ruygrok. Amsterdam, 1992.

Askin, Mustafa. Troy (Ilion). Istanbul, Turkey, undated.

Baedeker. France. Prentice Hall Travel, English ed. Turin, Italy, reprinted 1994.

Baedeker. Sicily. Prentice Hall Travel, 1st English ed. Turin, Italy, 1933.

Baseman, Bob. Masada. Palphot, Ltd. Israel, undated.

Bayraktar, Vehbi. Pergamon. Net Turistik yayinlar Λ.S., 4th ed., 1989.

Becker, Peter. Hill of Destiny. Penguin Books. England, 1991.

Becker, Peter. Rule of Fear. Panther Books, Ltd. England, 1972.

Bonechi, Edoardo. A Day in Venice. Bonechi Editore. Florence, Italy, 1968.

Brosnahan, Tom. Turkey: Lonely Planet Travel Survival Kit, 4th ed. Lonely Planet Publications, Hawthorne, Australia, 1993.

Brown, Geoffrey. Visitor's Guide, Malta and Gozo. Moorland Publishing Co., Ltd., Ashbourne, England, 1995.

Buksbazen, Victor. The Feasts of Israel. Friends of Israel Gospel Ministry, Inc. USA, 1954.

Chacour, Elias, Fr. Blood Brothers. Fleming H. Revell Co. USA, 1984.

Chacour, Elias, Fr. We Belong to the Land. Harper Collins. New York, 1990.

Churchill, Randolph S. The Six Day War. William Heinemann, Ltd. England, 1967.

Colins, Larry, and Lapiere, Dominique. O Jerusalem!. 1972.

Crete. Michalis Toumbis Editions, SA. Athens, 1991.

Dayan, Yael. Envy the Frightened. Weidenfeld and Nicolson. Israel, 1961.

Dew, Josie. The Wind In My Wheels. Warner Books. London, 1994.

Donova, Robert J. Israel's Fight for Survival. New American Library, Inc. USA, 1967.

Elon, Amos. The Israelis, Founders and Sons. Sphere Books, Ltd. England, 1972.

Good News Bible. The Bible Society. Swindon, England, 1976.

Gouvoussis, C. Athens. Ancient-Byzantine-Modern City Museums. Athens, undated.

Hall, Rosemary. Greece: Lonely Planet Travel Survival Kit, 1st ed. Lonely Planet Publications, Hawthorne, Australia, 1994.

Hussey, Hazel A. Swaziland Jumbo Tourist Guide. R.O. Hussey & Co. Swaziland, 1994.

Janson, H.W., and Janson, Anthony F. A Basic History of Art. Prentice Hall, 4th ed. New York, 1992.

Khouri, Rami. Petra. Al Kutbal. Amman, Jordan, 1989.

Levieux, Eleanor and Michael. Cassell's Colloquial French. Macmillan Co. USA, 1977.

Magi, Giovanna. All Paris. Bonechi Publishers. Florence, Italy, 1975.

Magi, Giovanna. Paris. Bonechi Publishers. Florence, Italy, 1975.

Mansoor, Menahem. Contemporary Hebrew 1. Behrman House, Inc. USA, 1977.

Marcus, Jacob Rader, Ph.D., ed. American Jewish Archives. USA, Spring-Summer, 1991.

May, Herbert G. Oxford Bible Atlas. Oxford University Press. Oxford, England, 1990.

Meir, Golda. My Life. BPCC Hazell Books, Ltd., 10th printing. London, 1989.

Meydan, Hilmi. Guide to Miletos, Didyma, Priene. Alper Basimevi, undated.

Michener, James A. The Covenant. Fawcett Crest Books, 1st printing. USA, 1982.

Michener, James A. The Source. Fawcett Crest Books, 56th printing. USA, 1992.

Morton, Frederic. The Rothschilds. Fawcett Publications, Inc.

Murray, Jon. South Africa, Lesotho, and Swaziland: Lonely Planet Travel Survival Kit, 2nd ed. Lonely Planet Publications, Hawthorne, Australia, 1996.

Ozeren, Ocal. Ephesus. Keskin Color Kartpostalcillik, Ltd., 1993.

Papaioannou, Dr. Evangelos. The Monastery of St. Catherine. St. Catherine's Monastery, ed., undated.

Potek, Chaim. Wandering: Chaim Potek's History of the Jews. Ballantine Books. USA, 1992.

Rhodes, The Island of the Sun. Athens.

Rivka, Esther. A Survival Guide for Newcomers to Israel. Shock Absorption. Israel, 1992.

Rosenberg, Roy A., Rabbi. The Concise Guide to Judaism History, Practice, Faith. Penguin Group. New York, 1991.

Rosovsky, Nitza, and Ungerleider-Mayerson, Joy. The Museums of Israel. Harry N. Abrams, Inc.. New York, 1989.

Simonis, Damien, and Findlay, Hugh. Jordan and Syria: Lonely Planet Travel Survival Kit, 2nd ed. Lonely Planet Publications, Hawthorne, Australia, 1993.

Smith, Wilbur. When the Lion Feeds. Mandarin Paperbacks. England, 1991.

This Is Cyprus: Pictorial Guide and Souvenir. Triarchos Publishers. Nicosia, Cyprus, undated.

Tilbury, Neil. Israel: Lonely Planet Travel Survival Kit, 1st ed. Lonely Planet Publications, Hawthorne, Australia, 1989.

Tourist Guide Italy. Michelin Tyre PLC, England.

Tunay, Dr. Mehmet I. Cappadocia. Talat Matbassi. Istanbul, Turkey, 1991.

Vantress, Sally. Seeing Myself Seeing the World. SMSW Publishing. USA, 1990.

Venice, Queen of the Sea. Edizioni Storti. Venice, 1991.

Wayne, Scott. Egypt and the Sudan: Lonely Planet Travel Survival Kit, 2nd ed. Lonely Planet Publications, Hawthorne, Australia, 1990.

Weingarten, Murray. Life in a Kibbutz. Reconstruction Press. New York, 1955.

Wurmbrand, Sabina. The Pastor's Wife. Diane Books Publishing. California, 1985.

Yad-Mordechai Museum. Peli Printing Works, Ltd. Israel, undated.

GLOSSARY OF TERMS

Assegais—throwing spear used by Zulu warriors
Atélier (French)—workshop or studio
Boer (Afrikaans)—a Dutch colonist in South Africa
Boerwors (Afrikaans)—farm sausage in South Africa
Boetie (Afrikaans)—brother
Boulangerie (French)—bakery; baker's shop
Braaivleis; braai (Afrikaans)—barbecue
Bungee cord—slang term for elasticized cord with hooks at
    either end used for securing items
Bakkie (Afrikaans)—a pickup truck
Bakshish (Arabic)—term used when begging for money
Catalan; Catalonia; Cataluña (Spanish)—region and former
    republic of northeastern Spain
Charcuterie (French)—pork butcher's shop and delicatessen
Cidre (French)—cider
Cinelli (Italian)—a brand of hand-crafted bicycle made in
    Milan, Italy
Clipless pedals—a method of attaching bicycling shoes to the
    pedals without "toe clips"
Compeggio (Italian)—campground
Coptic Church—the Christian Church in Egypt adhering to the
    monophysite doctrine
Corderie (French)—factory manufacturing rope used in the
    Navy and shipping industry
Corniche—a boulevard bordering the Nile River
Dankie (Afrikaans)—thank you!
Dorp (Afrikaans)—small town
Druze (Druse)—sect in Syria, Lebanon, and Israel whose pri-
    marily Moslem religion contains some elements of Chris-
    tianity
Duomo—cathedral
Edomite—inhabitant of an ancient country of southwestern
    Asia, south of the Dead Sea; a descendant of Esau
EGED—the national bus transportation system in Israel
Epicerie (French)—grocery; a grocer's shop
Eretz Israel (Hebrew)—the land of Israel

Felucca—a narrow, swift sailing vessel propelled by lanteen sails

Forent (Hungarian)—Hungarian currency

Gamla (Hebrew); Gamal (Arabic)—camel

Globetrotter—brand name of a tandem bicycle having French components and sold in England

Goeie (Afrikaans)—Good morning!

Granny gear—slang term for a bicycle's very low gear designed for hill climbing

Hamzeem (Arabic)—the fifty hottest days of the year

Highwheeler (penny farthing)—the standard bicycle of the 1880s, having a large front wheel and small rear wheel

Ibex—any of several wild goats indigenous to the mountainous regions of Israel

Kabbalism, Cabalism (Hebrew)—Jewish mysticism; an occult theosophy of rabbinical origin based on an esoteric interpretation of the Hebrew Scriptures

Kfar (Hebrew)—village

Kibbutz, Kibbutzeem—a collective farm or settlement in Israel

Kinneret (Hebrew)—the Sea of Galilee

Knesset (Hebrew)—synagogue; the Israeli Parliament

Koran—sacred text of Islam, believed to contain the revelations made by Allah to Mohammed

Kufta (Arabic)—a form of prepared spicy beef made in the shape of a sausage

Malelukes—a member of a former military caste originally composed of slaves from Turkey that held the Egyptian throne from about 1250 to 1517 and remained powerful until 1811

Matzoh—unleavened bread eaten especially during Passover

Meneer (Afrikaans)—Mister

Menorah—ceremonial seven-branched candelabrum of the Jewish Temple symbolizing the seven days of Creation

Mevrou (Afrikaans)—Mrs.

Moshav (Hebrew)—privately owned Israeli farm

NIS—New Israeli shekel (currency)

Nubian Village—belonging to an ancient kingdom in the Nile
    River valley
Panini (Italian)—bread
Pannier (French)—shopping basket; storage bag attached to a
    bicycle and used to transport small items
Petra—ancient capital of Edom in southwestern Jordan, famous
    for its Hellenistic tombs carved in rock
Rondavel (Afrikaans)—round thatched hut in South Africa
Shoofly pie—Pennsylvania Dutch dessert consisting of layers
    of molasses and brown sugar mixed with flour and topped
    with a crumbly crust and whipped cream
Shwarma (Arabic), Giro (Greek), Shishlik (Turkey)—sandwich
    composed of pita bread, seasoned beef or lamb, and salad
Stoker—the rear rider on a tandem bicycle
Tapas (Spanish)—small portions of selected prepared foods
    on a single platter
Utlander (Afrikaans)—foreigner
Umfazi (Afrikaans)—female
Via Dolorosa—Jesus' route from Pilates' judgment hall to
    Golgotha
Wadi—a valley, gully, or riverbed in northern Africa and south-
    western Asia that remains dry except during the rainy sea-
    son
Wonderlik (Afrikaans)—wonderful!
Ya'akov (Hebrew)—Jacob; Jack
Yam (Hebrew)—sea
Yahudin—Jew
Zen—"quiet mind concentration;" a form of Buddhism intro-
    duced via China to Japan from India in the 12th century

ABOUT THE AUTHOR

This is the first and probably the last book that Ralph Galen will write, but it's a book that had to be written. Some write for the pleasure of others; Ralph wrote for his own. As bicycling in its many forms has been inexorably entwined in this dental professional's life, the author felt compelled to put some of his experiences on paper. The two years writing 2 Wheels, 2 Years, and 3 Continents were as enjoyable for him as the actual events. He hopes that others will also find it worthwhile reading.

There is nothing in this book that is earth-shaking or scholarly. It is merely the tale of a person's avocation started in mid-life and now extending far beyond his retirement.

The author has no illusions relative to his mortality, but bicycling has made the aging process an easier progression. From racing to touring at breakneck speed to casual touring following his nose and the front wheel of his tandem through thirteen countries and Egypt twice, Ralph now enjoys club riding with his Santana tandem and his special friend Rita.

A particular note of gratitude to Bill Hoffman and Spring Garden Publications. Without Bill's assistance, this volume still would have been written but might never have found its way into the form you're now reading.

Donald W. Tighe
Director of Communications
League of American Bicyclists

PLEASE CUT HERE

THE ULTIMATE IN BICYCLE SAFETY
A Complete Safety Flag System for Bicycle Riders of All Ages

▼ A combination **waist pack** and **safety flag system** is now available for bicycle riders of all ages that **Saves Lives** during daylight as well as at night.

▼ This patented bicycle **safety flag system** provides the convenience of a waist pack to carry wallet and watch/spare tube and tools for emergency road repairs.

▼ In the U.S.A. the highly visible **White** or **Orange flag** positions to the **left**; In Britain, Bermuda, South Africa and Japan to the **right**. For ease of dismounting the flag stows in the vertical position.

▼ Worn by Children and Adults with their **Snell®Approved Helmet** for maximum **safety, fun** and **fitness**.

▼ Brilliant night time reflection from the **3M® reflective strip** and the **LED** flashing lights provide a **safety zone** between vehicles and the biker.

▼ Sends a subliminal message to **motorist. "I NEED MY SPACE"**.

▼ **Customized flags** available for Bicycle Clubs and Bicycle Shops.

▼ **Endorsed by** Pres. Charles River Wheelman Bicycle Club and Chairman Cambridge Bicycle Committee, Cambridge, Massachusetts.

▼ Two sizes: **The Biker** and **The Biker Junior** with a unique **One Size Fits All** belt.

MADE IN THE U.S.A.
SATISFACTION OR YOUR MONEY BACK GUARANTEE.

FREE BROCHURE

ORDER NOW FOR SAFETY, FUN, AND FITNESS.

I See You (not I.C.U.)®
% Cycling Adventures
2210 Massachusetts Ave.
Cambridge, MA 02140
Tel: (617)497-8287
Fax: (617)497-8822

MADE IN USA
PATENT PENDING

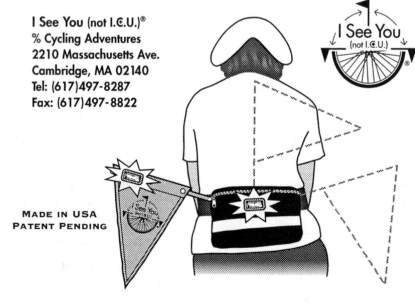